ROUTLEDGE LIBRARY EDITIONS:
URBAN STUDIES

I0128980

Volume 14

PUBLIC SERVICE PROVISION
AND URBAN DEVELOPMENT

PUBLIC SERVICE PROVISION AND URBAN DEVELOPMENT

Edited by
ANDREW KIRBY, PAUL KNOX AND
STEVEN PINCH

Routledge
Taylor & Francis Group

LONDON AND NEW YORK

First published in 1984 by Croom Helm Ltd.

This edition first published in 2018
by Routledge
2 Park Square, Milton Park, Abingdon, Oxon OX14 4RN

and by Routledge
711 Third Avenue, New York, NY 10017

Routledge is an imprint of the Taylor & Francis Group, an informa business

British Library Cataloguing in Publication Data
A catalogue record for this book is available from the British Library

ISBN: 978-1-138-89482-2 (Set)
ISBN: 978-1-315-09987-3 (Set) (ebk)
ISBN: 978-1-138-05035-8 (Volume 14) (hbk)
ISBN: 978-1-138-05040-2 (Volume 14) (pbk)
ISBN: 978-1-315-16877-7 (Volume 14) (ebk)

Publisher's Note
The publisher has gone to great lengths to ensure the quality of this reprint but points out that some imperfections in the original copies may be apparent.

Disclaimer
The publisher has made every effort to trace copyright holders and would welcome correspondence from those they have been unable to trace.

PREFACE TO THE REISSUE

Public Service Provision and Urban Development emerged in 1984 from an era of economic distress, urban riots, and—more significantly—the onset of a new politics. The nascent Reagan-Thatcher axis emphasized a remaking of the state and its welfare obligations, a loosening of regulatory controls, and a pushback against unions. It was also a period of a re-defined localism that emphasized 'urban social movements' and the emergence of a new identity politics organized, in place, around ethnicity, gender and sexuality (Castells, 1983).

Whether consciously or otherwise, the contributions to *Public Service Provision and Urban Development* were grappling with the big picture and especially the role of services like health care and education in providing opportunity and justice. One of the recurrent themes of the volume is the limitation of structuralist explanations. Then as now, it has been argued that Marxian theories of hegemony have problems in linking top-down ideological projects (formerly the postwar settlement that had seen the creation of welfare states, the ascendance of progressive city planning and the pursuit of social justice; now, neoliberalism and the ascendance of free-market principles) with the small scale everyday changes in attitudes and practices of ordinary people that can bring about social change (Barnett, 2005). The overwhelming political question posed by neoliberal perspectives is how do people submit to processes that are seen as against their own interests. Barnett sees recent restructuring as a response to populist 'liberal' tendencies such as changing consumer preferences, the decline in deference and a growing awareness of difference. Others have pointed out that in lieu of the hollowed-out social programmes of the postwar settlement there has emerged a discourse on the importance of resilience, in which the emphasis is on individual adaptability, self-reliance and responsible decisionmaking (Hudson, 2010). In the new orthodoxy, cities and local communities had to become responsible, resilient and entrepreneurial.

Looking back at this set of papers on the theme of public service provision delivered in June 1982, one cannot avoid being struck by the scale of changes that have taken place in this sphere in the last thirty years. Although it anticipated the growth of the 'New Right', *Public Service Provision and Urban Development* contains little or no mention of privatization, contracting out, de-municipalization or the panoply of other changes in the delivery of public service provision in recent years. In addition, there is scant attention to what are variously termed the "voluntary", "not-for-profit" or "third" sectors, together with the worldwide growth of social enterprises—firms that trade for a social purpose.

Public Service Provision and Urban Development was received as well as any collection of conference papers, with the usual observations about varied content. Despite the promotion of an agenda for future work, the postmodern turn (hailed by Jameson in the same year) served to limit interest in empirical work on 'mundane' things such as school catchments and access to health care, emphasizing instead the role of services in constructing the social world—a very different and in many ways more compelling set of issues. The attenuation of local autonomy under neoliberalism has shifted the research focus away from specifically urban contexts, as has the utterly changed meaning of 'access' in a world where many services are provided via digital rather than physical means. Nevertheless, the book still has much to offer the contemporary reader. In a world of sharpening inequality, the importance of public service provision is arguably more important than ever.

In this context a key lesson from *Public Service Provision and Urban Development* is the value of a multidisciplinary approach. With contributions from geographers, planners, political scientists and sociologists, the volume offered an unusually rich collection of viewpoints and demonstrated the merit of detailed empirical work integrating a plurality of perspectives. The contributors remind us that beneath the smokescreen of political rhetoric there remain a plethora of factors including urbanization imperatives, lobby groups, legal restrictions and vote-buying exigencies that affect outcomes in public policy. The volume's underlying theme of the tensions between policies to promote political legitimacy and those to promote economic efficiency are still evident in a world that has been transformed by neoliberalism and now seems likely to be driven increasingly by the populism that has been manifest in the election of Donald Trump as US President, the UK's vote to leave the EU (Brexit) and the rise of various right wing anti-immigrant movements in Europe.

References

Barnett, C. (2005) The consolations of 'neoliberalism'. *Geoforum* 36, 7–12.

Castells, M. (1983) *The City and the Grassroots: A Cross-Cultural Theory of Urban Social Movements*. Berkeley: University of California Press.

Hudson, R. (2010) 'Resilient regions in an uncertain world: wishful thinking or a practical reality?' *Cambridge Journal of Regions, Economy and Society*, 3, 11–25.

The Editors

AK   Arizona State University
PLK   Virginia Tech
SP   University of Southampton

Public Service Provision and Urban Development

Edited by
ANDREW KIRBY, PAUL KNOX and STEVEN PINCH

CROOM HELM
London & Canberra

ST. MARTIN'S PRESS
New York

© 1984. A. Kirby, P. Knox and S. Pinch
Croom Helm Ltd, Provident House, Burrell Row,
Beckenham, Kent BR3 1AT
Croom Helm Australia Pty Ltd, 28 Kembla St.,
Fyshwick, ACT 2609, Australia

British Library Cataloguing in Publication Data

Public service provision and urban
   development
   1. City planning – Congresses
   I. Kirby, A.   II. Knox, P.   III. Pinch, S.
307'.12   HT166
   ISBN 0-7099-1540-3

Library of Congress Cataloging in Publication Data
Main entry under title:

Public service provision and urban politics.

   Includes index.
   1. Municipal services–United States–Addresses, essays,
lectures. 2. Municipal services–Great Britain–Addresses,
essays, lectures. 3. Social choice–Addresses, essays,
lectures. I. Kirby, Andrew.   II. Knox, Paul L.
III. Pinch, Steven.
HD4431.P82 1984   363'.0941   83-40485
ISBN 0-312-65568-1

Printed and bound in Great Britain

CONTENTS

Acknowledgements

ACKNOWLEDGEMENTS

This book is based on the papers given at a symposium held in Falls Church, Virginia, in June 1982, together with a paper given by Ken Newton to the Annual Meeting of the Institute of British Geographers in Southampton, England, in January 1982. Both meetings were supported by the Social Science Research Council. Our first thanks, therefore, go to the Council and in particular to Professor Brian Robson, who provided useful advice and encouragement from the start of the project. Thanks are also due to the Institute of British Geographers, for in working together on the theme of public services and urban development we have enjoyed the support — both financial and institutional — afforded by our status as a Working Group of the Urban Study Group. We should also like to acknowledge the practical support provided by Virginia Polytechnic Institute and State University in facilitating the organisation of the symposium in Falls Church. The text was set by Paul Knox using the Monotype Lasercomp phototypesetter at Oxford University. Elizabeth Maclaran prepared the typescript and Carolyn Bain and Jimmy Ford helped to produce the final artwork for most of the illustrations. Finally, we wish to thank our contributors for the high quality of the papers presented in Falls Church and for their cooperation in meeting the demands of our publication timetable.

Andrew Kirby
Paul Knox
Steven Pinch

1

Changing Emphases in Public Services Research

Andrew Kirby, Paul Knox
and
Steven Pinch

Introduction

Despite the recent attractions of the Paris Left Bank, many British urban scholars still continue to have their gaze firmly fixed on North America. There are no doubt many complex historical, social and psychological reasons for this westward stance. At an obvious level it may partly be explained by the fact that North American cities seem more dynamic (and dangerous) than their British counterparts (the British riots of 1981 not withstanding). American cities represent the extremes of development in Western capitalist economies and as such are indicators of what might happen elsewhere. Thus, the sprawling 'Silicon Valley' near Palo Alto makes Britain's own concentrations of micro-chip industries in 'sunrise strip' (from Reading to Bristol) and 'Silicon Glen' (from Stirling to Dundee) seem small by comparison. Similarly, the scale of attack upon the public sector in California following Proposition 13 makes even Thatcherite policies seem (so far) relatively moderate. Another reason may be the fact that we have more knowledge of North American cities than any other urban centres on earth. When researchers were primarily concerned with patterns of residential segregation in cities, the early lead given by the human ecologists meant that our knowledge was dominated by the case of Chicago. After the Second World War the vast literature produced by American political scientists (whatever its theoretical limitations) provided considerable insights into machine politics and reformed local government systems of the major cities. Today, when political processes of resource allocation are a major focus, the pace of North American research is such that we still know more about patterns of service delivery in Detroit, Oakland or San

Antonio than in an average British city (Jones *et al.*, 1980; Levy *et al.*, 1974; Lineberry, 1977).

It is this imbalance in empirical research which may account for the fact that, with a few exceptions, North American scholars seem to pay less attention to developments in Britain than British researchers pay to developments in the United States. Certainly in recent years, when the study of public policy has been a major preoccupation, there would seem to have been a growing insularity of outlook in North America which contrasts markedly with the rapid exchange of ideas prevalent during the 'quantitative revolution' in urban studies. This may partly be explained by the very differing governmental and institutional frameworks which exist in the two countries. There is of course a much greater degree of local government fragmentation in the United States and the differing roles of local politicians, the judiciary and central government often make comparisons difficult. The United States is also different from Northern Europe by virtue of the lack of any unified working class movement as represented in local politics. The rift may also be explained by the fact that, despite the efforts of Harvey, Castells, Walker, the Fainsteins, Dear and many others in North America, British researchers have, since about 1975, appeared to display a much greater preoccupation with understanding the structuralist approaches of Althusser, Poulantzas, Lefebvre, Lojkine and other neo-Marxists while, in contrast, many recent North American books and papers in the realm of urban studies continue to be dominated by liberal political science, welfare economics and systems-type urban geography.

It was against this background that the authors organised an Anglo-American conference on the theme of Public Provision and Urban Development, the proceedings of which are presented in this volume. The focus is upon what are often termed 'local public goods', 'urban services' or 'collective-consumption'. Many previous conferences and readers have examined diverse aspects of these phenomena and we therefore deliberately avoided concentration upon the well-worn questions such as What is 'efficiency' in service provisions?; How do we measure service 'quality'?; and What is meant by service 'outputs'? Important though these questions remain, the basic problem facing researchers today is the wide variety of theoretical perspectives available. The crucial issue addressed by the conference was, therefore, how to achieve satisfactory explanations for patterns of public sector provision and their effects upon urban development.

In our view the apparent divergence between European and North American research, noted above, is highly undesirable and we sought in the confernce to achieve a genuine two-way exchange of ideas and evidence. Fortunately, the early years of the 1980s have displayed rapid intellectual changes which are breaking down many of the barriers between established approaches on both sides of the Atlantic. In general terms three major types of explanatory framework may be recognised: the public choice approach, the neo-Weberian approach and the neo-Marxist approach. Developments in the seventies might be characterised by initial fierce skirmishes, as structuralists made critiques of positivist approaches, and then by a form of 'trench warfare' as various factions regrouped and attempted to consolidate the ground lost and made. At the risk of stretching the analogy too far, it may be suggested that there is now a much greater willingness in certain quarters to engage in a somewhat more peaceful and constructive dialogue (see Duncan and Goodwin, 1982 and Saunders, 1982). This is not to argue that the fundamental differences between these approaches have been eliminated; indeed they are as deep as ever. Nevertheless, as the papers in this volume make clear, the battle lines are shifting rapidly. There is a growing theoretical pluralism in urban studies such that conventional labels such as 'Marxist', 'positivist', 'idealist' and 'empiricist' have begun to lose much of their value.

In organising these papers we have sought to depart from convention in two ways. First, we have deliberately avoided grouping the papers into smaller sections. A glance at many of the edited volumes currently available will soon show the increasingly arbitrary nature of many such groupings. In our own case many different classifications would have been possible (American versus British, empirical and theoretical, public choice versus neo-Weberian and so on) but these would not have done justice to the complexity of the interrelationships between these papers. Second, we have avoided introducing the papers with a simple summary. The professionalism of our contributors is such that the contents of the chapters can easily be obtained by reading their introductions. Instead, we seek here to outline some of the themes which link the papers.

The Role of Public Choice Theory

One of the most puzzling issues for many British students is how to account for the continuing dominance in North America of the set of ideas which can be collectively labelled public choice theory. The question arises because the ideas, which range from the economists' theory of pure public goods through to the pluralist notions of political science, have been subject to such a barrage of criticism in recent years. A detailed knowledge of American political culture, democratic institutions and local government structure is of course necessary to resolve the issue. There are many features of the American system which contrast sharply with the British system and which have encouraged the public choice analysts: the stronger business ethos and drive for efficiency in municipal affairs, the extraordinary degree of municipal fragmentation, the widespread devolution of powers, the separation of the legislature and executive, the highly visible nature of local political issues and the frequently overt role played by local politicians and pressure groups. The role of public choice theory seems rather more questionable in the centralised and somewhat 'closed' British system in which local conflict is often less visible and in which pressure groups may be more easily incorporated into the local political system. Nevertheless, it is clear that most criticisms of public choice theory, on both sides of the Atlantic, stem from considerations of very early work in this tradition. Furthermore, although there are fundamental differences, it is all too easy to characterise the British and American systems in a stereotyped manner. The old notion that the American system is open and democratic while the British is closed and autonomous has been undermined by studies such as those of Jones (1980) and Lineberry (1977) which have exposed the power of professionalised bureaucracies in American cities. Certainly there is also a continued interest in the application of Tieboutian ideas in Britain (Davies, 1982). In the light of all these considerations we sought to obtain some recent reformulations of public choice theory upon which more informed judgements could be passed.

Archer has been one of the major advocates of public choice theory in political geography (Archer, 1981) and in his paper he develops one of the major themes of the approach — the vote maximising behaviour of politicians (Chapter 3). In particular, he seeks to examine if presidential electoral considerations affect the geographical distribution of federal expenditures. Politicians seeking re-election not only have to time their vote-buying policies carefully but also need to be mindful of their political impact throughout various parts of the nation. Archer's paper emphasises the complexity of translating speculative comments into firm testable hypotheses and further stresses the need for continued rigorous quantitative analysis in the field of policy analysis. The results are complex but suggest a decline in the strength of the links between federal spending and presidential political considerations over time. Given the sharp geographical divisions in major party political support in Britain, Archer's paper suggests many hypotheses for further evaluation.

Shelley (Chapter 4) provides an excellent review of recent goegraphical applications of public choice theory. The amount of new literature produced since other comparatively recent reviews of the field (Archer, 1981; Reynolds, 1981) serves to emphasise the continuing dynamism of this type of analysis. A relatively new development has been the growth of constitutional choice analysis. Here the focus is not only upon justice in terms of distributive outcomes but also in terms of procedural justice and the ways in which decisions are made. Shelley's paper makes it clear that public choice analysts have become aware of many of the criticisms directed against their approach. Thus, the assumption of methodological individualism, in which persons are free to make rational decisions, ignores the social, economic and political antecedents which constrain individuals' attempts to maximise utility. However, Shelley maintains that public choice approaches can interact with historically-oriented approaches to provide insights often overlooked by large scale 'deterministic' approaches.

The fragmentation of local government in the United States is well represented by the system of school districts. The growing pressures of falling school rolls, suburbanisation and fiscal retrenchment have led to controversial decisions regarding which local schools should be closed. Reynolds (Chapter 5) describes some of these conflicts and suggests that a constitutional choice approach is an appropriate methodology for identifying. alternative institutions of school decision-making. From the social choice perspective the fiscal retrenchment problem in education raises three issues: first, the potential budget reduction alternatives must be identified and their locational impacts assessed; second, the distributive impact of the budget adjustments must be assessed, and third, a particular choice amongst all the available options must be made and justified. Generally only the third issue is considered in debate. Reynolds then outlines an experimental constitutional choice approach designed to attain an evaluation of a method of procedural justice followed by agreement on a group objective function.

Empirical applications of the method, although still preliminary in character, produced some fascinating results. In five of the eleven experiments groups were successful in resolving conflicts over school closures by reaching procedurally based agreements calling for changes in school districts' decision-making structures and procedures. Surprisingly, such agreements were most common where there was an initial high degree of polarisation of views. Preliminary analysis of group discussions indicated that participants were so inflamed by the threat of having their own schools proposed for closure that they were liable to agree to any solution that rationalised closure of fewer schools or no schools at all. This approach does nothing to redress some of the fundamental underlying factors which precipitate conflict, and it does not specify how alternative courses of action can be implemented; but it does broaden the debate by helping to identify alternative social choice institutions.

The political complexities of school closures are further developed by Honey and Sorenson (Chapter 6). They focus upon what procedures are currently used in determining which schools should be closed, what criteria are used in the decision-making process, and upon which sections of society the school closures fall most heavily? They reveal the ways in which seemingly objective technical standards can have a regressive impact upon the poorest neighbourhoods when translated onto the physical fabric and political structure of older declining cities.

Massam's paper (Chapter 7) serves to illustrate in a broader context the difficulties involved in evaluating the impact of public goods and services. He is essentially concerned with the costs and benefits emanating from a set of fixed point facilities such as hospitals, schools, fire stations and refuse tips. The identification of these effects is clearly of immense potential benefit to the constitutional choice approach. As Massam's paper makes clear however, although the pace of research has recently quickened in this field, there is still a considerable difference between the complexity of public policy problems and our abilities to model them formally. Significantly, there is now an emphasis not only upon the most sophisticated solution which can find *the* optimal location (which is often not politically feasible anyway) but upon relatively simple, quick and inexpensive methods which can reduce the range of options available.

Many of the remaining papers are highly critical of public choice theory, the pure theory of public goods and pluralist notions of social organisation (see Smith, Chapter 9; Cox, Chapter 12; Jones, Chapter 14; Piven and Friedland, Chapter 15). However, Burnett's comparison of neighbourhood participation and political demand-making in British and North American cities makes clear the enormous degree of pressure group activity in the latter which provides the continual spur for the focus upon demands from 'below' (Chapter 13). It is also clear from his paper that the pattern and structure of political demands and their degree of success depends upon the interaction of an enormously complex set of factors. Furthermore, pressure group activity is by no means insignificant in the British local government system — the major differences from North America are those of 'style' and character rather than content. Whatever the merits of public choice theory, these pressures clearly require much more detailed analysis in future research.

The Role of Professions and Organisations

Compared with public choice theory, the so-called managerialist approach, with its neo-Weberian emphasis upon the independent power of bureaucracies, has had a much greater impact in Britain than in North America. This may in part reflect the very strong Weberian tradition in British sociology which has recently been reflected in the urban sphere (Pahl, 1977; Saunders, 1981). It is also tempting to suggest that the strength of the managerialist approach in Britain reflects the greater autonomy and number of professinals in British local government compared with their American counterparts. However, a closer inspection would tend to undermine this view. The work of Lineberry (1977), Jones (1980), Nivola (1979), and Mladenka (1980) has highlighted the ways in which the fragmentation of powers in North America can enhance the relative autonomy of public agencies. The city-manager system also tends to restrict the potential of elected representatives to participate in decision-making, as does the proliferation of special district agencies.

It is therefore not surprising that the power of public bureaucracies is a strong theme running through many of the papers, both British and American. It is clear that this emphasis is very different from the early managerialist approaches in which 'social gatekeepers' were seen as largely independent allocators of scarce resources. There is now a much broader emphasis upon a range of institutions, organisations and professionals, and an effort to place these in the context of wider economic, social and political constraints.

This approach is demonstrated in the paper by Knox, Bohland and Shumsky (Chapter 8) in which the emergence of the medical profession is placed in the context of changing city structures in America in the late nineteenth and early twentieth centuries. The rise of professional medical care is conventionally ascribed to changes in science and technology. However, their analysis indicates that, although this was undoubtedly important, many other factors, including the growing demand for medical care, the consequent growth of non-orthodox therapeutics, the increase of para-medical personnel, and the intervention of paternalistic capital, are also essential for a full understanding.

The strength of bureaucracies in contemporary American cities is emphasised by Jones (Chapter 14). He stresses that it is not sufficient to examine only the formal policy decisions of politicians. By modifying and not infrequently replacing formal policy decisions, administrators not only alter the character of the policy-making process, but also subtly alter the manner in which the state influences the broader political economy. Furthermore, there is evidence that many local services are provided in a political vacuum in which service distribution is the unintended by-product of the organisation's decision rules. Even in politically active environments, such as the classic case of Chicago, the decentralised character of the urban political machines enables ward organisations to make separate demands upon service organisations.

Smith's paper (Chapter 9) illustrates the power of organisations to create or define social problems. It is suggested that public concerns about social problems are essentially created at the agency or governmental level and then legitimated by public acceptance and recognition of the problem. It has been argued that the Marijuana Tax of 1937 was the result of an intense campaign by the Bureau of Narcotics rather than a response to moral outrage amongst the general public who seem to have been generally indifferent at the time. The agency was facing a reduction in its budget and decided to demonstrate its social usefulness in the face of what they portrayed as a deadly problem. More recently, the attempt by the National Institute of Alcohol Abuse and Alcoholism to focus upon the problems of teenage drinking has been interpreted as an attempt to increase the relatively low budget of the agency and resist the threat of incorporation into some more general substance-abuse agency.

Neo-Marxist Theories, Historical Perspectives and Human Agency

One of the most striking revelations of these papers is the extent to which neo-Marxist theories of the capitalist state and urban development are now widely recognised (even if not accepted) within the realm of American policy studies. There is now much greater attention paid to the work of writers such as Castells and O'Connor than could have been detected even a few years past. A common theme underlying much of this work (both Marxist and non-Marxist) is the growing dissatisfaction with the ahistorical character of many structuralist theories and their functionalist-like frameworks. Amongst many Marxist writers there is thus a renewed emphasis upon the historical evolution of class relations and their representation in the various forms of the local state.

Cox (Chapter 12) provides a good illustration of this in the context of what he terms 'turf politics' — the comparatively recent (i.e. post 1945) proliferation of locally-based conflicts within defined geographical boundaries. Cox argues that such conflicts cannot be understood in terms of conventional concepts such as externalities, 'quality of life' indices or 'consumption cleavages'. Essential for the emergence of turf politics is the commodification of the neighbourhood which enables people to identify their local area as a 'thing' from which others can be excluded. This, he argues, can in turn only be understood by historical analysis of the capitalist mode of production and its separation from the place of reproduction. This separation and the growth of 'turf politics' is seen as enabling the resolution of numerous contradictions within the sphere of production which initially were overcome by mutual aid amongst the working class, the labour movement, the rise of the welfare state and the growth of the women's movement. This mutual aid and the close personal relations associated with the extended family are seen as a response to the chronic material uncertainty which existed in traditional working class areas of the major cities. However, the growth of the welfare state and the rise of the womens' movement are seen as enabling the removal of informal types of mutual aid and enabling the privatising impulses of the nuclear family to be given full rein in the suburbs.

Within a Marxist framework it is necessary to probe beneath the level of phenomenal forms to apprehend the reality of class relations within a capitalist mode of production. At the root of most controversies between Marxist and other perspectives lie conflicts between this method of historical materialism and other approaches. Smith's paper (Chapter 9) makes it clear that in the field of health care, positivist approaches are dominant. As such there is a mechanistic focus upon the individual and a neglect of broader social, environmental and political implications of disease aetiology. Smith is highly critical of pluralist explanations of alcoholism and drug abuse and instead seeks to locate public provision to cope with these 'problems' firmly within the nexus of the capitalist mode of production. He argues that individuals in a capitalist society may encounter or experience social problems either as a result of numerous direct contradictions in the capitalist mode of production or as the result of disturbances in the system of class rule. An example of the former is the requirement of capitalism for a healthy workforce but the tendency of the capitalist system to make many unfit to offer their services in the labour market. In the latter case many initiatives designed to serve class-based interests may rebound and serve only to promote further disturbances to the system. Policies designed to cope with alcoholism are based almost exclusively upon individual 'medical engineering' solutions and as such suit the needs of numerous agencies created to cope with these problems and the wider social and economic structure of society.

Smith's paper makes it clear that the way in which a problem is identified and treated by a society depends upon the complex interaction of many factors. Much depends upon the degree of public legitimation of officially designated problems, the behaviour of governmental organisations designed to cope with these problems, together with political initiatives. Recognition of such complexities has fostered the dissatisfaction with many earlier theories of the capitalist state, and this is expressed in many of the papers. In particular, there is a rejection of the tendency to reduce all developments to the inexorable logic of the capitalist mode of production — whether this is the need for private profitability or political legitimacy. Institutions, policies and local government structures have to evolve in the context of a capitalist system but, as comparisons between Britain and America reveal, there is enormous scope for variation in forms. Thus, theories which focus solely upon the requirements of the capitalist mode of production may ignore political struggle and local conflict.

This theme is developed by Piven and Friedland (Chapter 15) in their consideration of the origins of fiscal crises in American cities. They welcome, as do most of the authors in this volume, the broadening of the debate to a societal level. However, they reject the tendency of neo-Marxist theories to assert the effects of public policies on the basis of *a priori* categories rather than to subject these effects to empirical scrutiny. Furthermore, they argue that structuralist theories tend to explain causes in terms of effects with a form of 'circular functionalism'. Some of their comments echo those made in Britain by Giddens (1981) who has stressed the inadequacy of Marxist thinking in accounting for 'human agency'.

Piven and Friedland argue that the principal failure of public choice, bureaucratic and structuralist theories is that they all highlight particular elements to the exclusion of others. In relation to the fiscal crises of American cities they ignore the relationships between these elements which are largely structured by specific institutional arrangements which have evolved over many years. These arrangements did not emerge through the unfolding of some inevitable historical process but were developed through the efforts of particular classes and groups to enhance their power in relation to the state, and also by a reciprocal effort of the state to exert its power and advantage over these groups. They argue that policies promoting profitability or political legitimacy arise from political conflict, and that by thus specifying the causes of public policy and separating them from their consequences, their approach escapes the circular reasoning mentioned previously.

The interaction between various 'levels' of explanation is also a theme developed by Jones (Chapter 14). These levels he terms 'micro-politics', 'political ecology' and 'political economy'. He also notes that at the level of political ecology public outputs are influenced by the interaction between government agencies and their complex environments — the clients, other bureaucracies and politicians. The crucial issue is, of course, how to specify and analyse the complex causal connections between these levels. Jones develops these links in the context of building code enforcement. His study in Chicago highlights the exclusion of tenants groups and neighbourhood organisations from the policy-making process but emphasises the power of public officials. Rigorous code enforcement often antagonises private sector interests and especially architects and builders. His analysis suggests that, although economic imperatives exert a strong influence upon the local policy system, the relationship is not rigidly deterministic.

The ideas of Piven, Friedland and Jones are part of a set of approaches attempting to integrate various perspectives (although this is of course bitterly resisted in certain quarters). Saunders (1979), for example, has argued that the applicability of theories depends upon the type of service which is under consideration. Thus, pluralist bargaining-type explanations may be more relevant in the context of 'social expenses' at the local level whereas corporatist ideas may be more applicable to 'social investment' at the national level. Johnston (1980) has suggested that the value of theories depends upon the time-scale under investigation. Structuralist theories may be most suitable in unravelling general patterns over many years whereas other theories may explain short-run political manoeuvres and policy shifts. Yet another suggestion is made in the conclusion of Pinch's paper (Chapter 11) which is that in services such as those for the under-fives the importance of the myriad agents at work depends upon the spatial scale. Thus, local bargaining by pressure groups is most relevant in the context of isolated facilities within local authorities. The role of politicians and public bureaucracies becomes much more important when comparing local governments one with another. However, Pinch stresses the inadequacy of structuralist explanations at the macro-level in the context of pre-school services. Not only is it extremely difficult to relate capitalism with the need for any particular level of pre- school provision but it remains to be demonstrated that capitalism could not survive without the present system of domestic labour and childrearing. Conspicuously absent from many existing neo-Marxist theories is understanding of the role of women in society, and it is thus in the realm of feminist theories that the position of pre-school services can be better understood. However, many would assert that society can only be fully understood in terms of both capitalist and patriarchal strutures. The crucial and difficult issue is how to conceptualise the role of women in a way that is not either completely autonomous from, or determined by, the economic relations of the capitalist mode of production.

The Role of Space

Developments in urban studies in the 1970s at times saw two disciplines apparently moving in opposite directions. Ironically, just as geographers were reacting against the spatial fetishism of the 1970s and playing down the importance of simple geographical explanations, so a number of political scientists were recognising the importance of issues such as metropolitan fragmentation upon local politics. Thus Newton (1978) argued that 'the proliferation of politically autonomous suburbs during the first half of this century may have played as important a part in social and political life in the US as the growth of the joint stock company has played in the development of its economic life'.

The role of space in the analysis of society is still enormously controversial (contrast Saunders, 1982, with Kirby, 1983) and ironically is still played down by many geographers. Some would argue that spatial forms are socially produced and cannot be seen as independent from society, whereas others argue space will always constitute an independent constraint whatever the mode of production. Nevertheless, the papers in this volume indicate a remarkable degree of convergence of thought amongst both political scientists and geographers. There is now a widespread recognition of the importance of placing geographical factors into their broader social, political and economic context but this is coupled to a recognition of the powerful influence spatial factors can play in shaping these broader phenomena.

Not only has Newton been at the forefront of attempts to compare British and American local governments but he has also been one of the leaders in recognising the importance of locational factors in political science. His paper (Chapter 2) addresses the seemingly intractable issue of explaining inter-authority variations in local government expenditures in England and Wales. He notes that conventional regression-based approaches using a battery of political, economic and demographic variables have been extraordinarily unsuccessful. Not only are the results often statistically insignificant but it is often difficult to relate those results which do emerge to the main types of theory available — whether pluralist, neo-Weberian or neo-Marxist. Inevitably there is an element of *ad hoc* explanation in many of these studies. However, Newton's ostensibly simplistic approach of ranking variations in expenditures does make some startling revelations. As in the case of certain fixed-point facilities within cities (Knox, 1978), it seems that what can be termed 'ecological', locational or geographical factors frequently hold the key to explaining the extremes of variations in expenditures. This does not imply, as assumed in many earlier 'outputs' studies, that there is some automatic transmission of environmental inputs into policies. Local pressures from the environment have to be perceived and acted upon by local politicians and bureaucrats; but the results do suggest that the environment produces certain pressures which can force a response. Thus, urban authorities spend more on parks than do smaller centres surrounded by extensive green belts. Larger centres also spend more on refuse (garbage) since they have to transport the collections further to refuse sites. Cities which suffered most from bombing in the Second World War have larger planning expenditures — no doubt a legacy of the large planning teams initially recruited to rebuild these centres. The position of an authority in the urban hierarchy also appears to have an important effect upon other factors such as police and libraries. Political and demographic factors are important in those services which are restricted to certain subsections of the population such as public housing, social services and education. Nevertheless, Newton's results show that many factors do not work in a unidimensional way across all authorities. Rather, there is a complex interaction between many of these factors in particular circumstances. The results have important implications for future studies of services and would seem to confirm the view that nothing is so important for formal modellers as some previous knowledge of the system they are about to model.

All three of the locational themes noted above are relevant to the work on school closures. Not only does the fragmentation of school districts result in enormous fiscal disparities between areas but the location of schools *within* these districts affects the degree of access to the facilities. Finally, since schools are generally regarded as a valuable community asset, the closure of a school is generally regarded as equal to the imposition of some noxious facility within the area. When these factors are combined with the enormous significance attached to education in North America in enabling social mobility, it is not difficult to appreciate why school closure has aroused such ferocious controversy.

Pinch (Chapter 11) also considers various locational factors in the case of British pre-school services. Here the influence of externalities is relatively unimportant; a nursery school is unlikely to be a major determinant of residential location as is good-quality primary and secondary education. Nevertheless, there are enormous variations in levels of local authority provision of pre-school facilities and, given the relative immobility of mothers with young children, the location of pre-school facilities within authorities has an important effect upon access to the facilities. His analysis suggests that in Britain jurisdictional partitioning is associated with greater disparities between local authorities rather than within their boundaries.

The relationship between locationally-based explanations and aggregate social theories is discused explicitly by Kirby (Chapter 10) in relation to health care in both Britain and the United States. At present there is clearly a wide gulf between the positivist-oriented studies of disease and health care in particular localities, and the neo-Marxist studies of the relationships between the structure of health care and the overall organisation of society. Much of the structure is determined at the national level through bargaining between the state and various interested parties — doctors, trade unions and drug companies. It is for this reason that the system is essentially insulated, both in Britain and North America, from many local pressures. Nevertheless, the consequences of the system are manifest at the local level. The important and difficult task for future research is to link local studies to the crucial issues raised by the aggregate approaches.

Knox, Bohland and Shumsky's approach (Chapter 8) shows how this can be accomplished in a historical context. They reveal a complex interaction between the evolving structure of health care in terms of doctors, nurses and various quacks, technological change such as the introduction of automobiles, telephones and medical technology, and the distribution of health care facilities such as hospitals, dispensaries and surgeries in the rapidly evolving American cities.

Looking Ahead

Among the various potential permutations of these topics, empirical approaches and theoretical orientations there are several which, we feel, merit particular attention. One outstanding issue not directly addressed in this volume, for example, is the description and explanation of the ways in which the 'New Right' has gained power and sought to redirect urban development and alter the material and moral frameworks of city life through public expenditure cuts, the encouragement of voluntarism, and the growth of 'authoritarian centralism' (Elliott and McCrone, 1982). There are also certain broad issues which require attention. The distinction between public and private provision requires articulation, and it follows that our theoretical understanding of the role of the state must be further developed. This, in turn, requires further study of the *evolution* of service distributions. At the very least they represent a palimpsest of various geographical distributions, each relating to rather different circumstances and constraints (McLafferty, 1983). Equally, this research must synthesise the rather disparate foci that presently exist: namely upon decision-makers, clients/consumers, and political issues. The realities of present service provision are the outcome of many long struggles which have spilled over from the sphere of consumption into workplace and back again, while the form of the (local) state has itself been influenced, in part, by these changes.

We must also be prepared to evaluate intermediate explanations — like externality 'theory' — and attempt to relate these where possible to wider issues. It is clear that, in some contexts, public services are sought by residents in order to increase the exchange value of property; in other circumstances we are witnessing far less tangible attempts to change or maintain particular styles and qualities of life, which produce broad political alliances. This, of course, feeds back into the possibilities of exploiting particular theoretical perspectives, while the emphasis on the quality of life reintroduces the importance of service outcomes: i.e. the true value of the social wage in capitalist society. For many groups, welfare inputs are of central financial importance and, where these are being eroded, serious social problems are predicted (Knox and Kirby, 1984).

Finally, we would emphasise once again the value of cross-cultural comparisons within advanced societies. As we have pointed out, this has happened to some degree in Western Europe, but less so between Western Europe and North America. Among the themes which seem to lend themselves most readily to comparative research are the consequences of efforts to 'privatise' the urban service economy, the political role that municipal employees play in establishing service strategies, the effects of the evolving sociology of the various professions involved in the administration and delivery of urban services, and the role of different agencies in the 'commodification' of neighbourhoods.

References

Archer, C.J. (1981) 'Public choice paradigms in political geography', in A.D. Burnett, and P.J. Taylor, (eds.), *Political Studies from Spatial Perspectives,* John Wiley and Sons, Chichester

Davies, H. (1982) 'Fiscal Migration and the London Boroughs', *Urban Studies,* **19,** 143-154

Duncan, S.S., and M. Goodwin (1982) 'The local state: functionalism, autonomy and class relations in Cockburne and Saunders', *Political Geography Quarterly,* **1,** 77-96

Elliott, B. and D. McCrone (1982) *The City: Patterns of Domination and Conflict,* Macmillan, London

Giddens, A. (1981) *A Contemporary Critique of Historical Materialism,* Macmillan, London

Johnston, R.J. (1980) 'On the nature of explanation in human geography', *Transactions, Institute of British Geographers,* (New Series) **5,** 402-412

Jones, B.D., with S. Greenberg, and J. Drew (1980) *Service Delivery in the City,* Longman, New York

Kirby, A.M. (1983) 'On society without space: a critique of Saunders' non-spatial urban sociology', *Society and Space: Environment and Planning,***D**

Knox, P.L. (1978) 'The intra-urban ecology of primary medical care: patterns of accessibilty and their policy implications, *Environment and Planning,* **A 10,** 415-35

Knox, P.L. and A.M. Kirby (1984) 'Public Provision and the Quality of Life' in A.M. Kirby and J.R. Short (eds.) *Britain Now: A Contemporary Human Geography,* Macmillan, London

Levy, F.S., A.J. Meltsner, and A. Wildavsky (1974) *Urban Outcomes: Schools, Streets and Libraries,* University of California Press, Berkeley

Lineberry, R.L. (1977) *Equality and Urban Policy,* Sage Publications, Beverley Hills

McLafferty, S. (1983) 'Reply to Kirby's comment on "Urban Structure and Geographical Access to Public Services" ', *Annals, Association of American Geographers,* **73,** forthcoming

Mladenka, K. (1980) 'The urban bureaucracy and Chicago Political Machine: who gets what and the limits to political control', *American Political Science Review,* **74,** 991-998

Newton, K. (1978) 'Conflict avoidance and conflict supression: the case of urban politics in the United States', in K.R. Cox, (ed.), *Urbanization and Conflict in Market Societies,* Methuen, London

Nivola, P. (1979) *The Urban Service Problem,* Lexington, Massachusetts

Pahl, R.E. (1977) 'Managers, technical experts and the state', in M. Harloe, (ed.), *Captive Cities*, John Wiley, Chichester

Reynolds, D.R. (1981) 'The geography of social choice', in A.D. Burnett and P.J. Taylor, (eds.), *Political Studies from Spatial Perspectives*, John Wiley and Sons, Chichester

Saunders, P. (1979) *Urban Politics*, Hutchinson, London

Saunders, P. (1981) *Social Theory and the Urban Question*, Hutchinson, London

Saunders, P. (1982) 'Urban politics: a rejoinder to Hooper and Duncan/Goodwin', *Political Geography Quarterly*,**1**,181-187

2

Public Services in Cities and Counties

K. Newton

Introduction

Conventional attempts to explain the variations in public expenditure on the part of local authorities in the Western world have not proved particularly successful. By and large, the research has major problems; first, it lacks theoretical coherence and, second, it has not resulted in particularly good empirical results. On the first problem, an excellent overview and summary of the literature has concluded that 'Rather than a comparative theory of performance, we seem to be laying the foundations for another monument to "adhockery" ' (Fried, 1976, p.320). And in what is one of the best studies of local spending carried out in Britain and elsewhere, Danziger writes: 'The broadest criticism of the approach has argued persuasively that it lacks any theory of linkages which explicates the relationships between policy outputs and characteristics of the environment' (Danziger, 1978, p.83).

Lack of theory to explain interesting results would be a severe failing but, unfortunately, interesting results are few and far between. Danziger concludes that his own work provides 'a weak and generally unsatisfactory explanation for the variation in county borough resource allocation ... the demographic approach has minimal explanatory power for most allocation measures' (Danziger, 1978). By the demographic approach Danziger means that method (used in most studies) which tries to explain variations in local services and expenditures by establishing a statistical fit between them and a bank of social, economic, and political variables describing the characteristics of the units of government under study. Danziger's poor results were repeated in our own work. Although it is unnecessary to go into any detail, various statistical techniques and approaches were used, in the way of correlation and regression analysis, analysis of variance, and various forms of hierarchical cluster analysis, but all delivered very little in the way of statistically and substantively significant results.

Consequently, it was decided to go back to the simplest of string-and-sealing-wax methods which entailed nothing more complicated than ranking authorities from the highest to the lowest *per capita* spenders on their full range of main services, and inspecting the resulting league tables in the hope that they would tell us something of general interest. By and large the method produced results, which, though simple and crude, are more interesting and powerful than anything the complex computer programmes produced. The work reported here deals with all the top tier of the local government system of England and Wales, which includes urban (county boroughs) and more rural (counties) authorities. The financial years 1960/1 and 1972/3 were chosen for study in order to (i) reduce the possibility of trying to generalise from an odd or unusual year, and (ii) examine stability or changes over time. This chapter will examine each service in turn, and then suggest some generalisations at the end.

Parks

Although parks consume a small proportion of the local authority budget, they are as good a place as any to start because this item has firmly resisted satisfactory analysis in the past. The hypothesis that wealthier authorities spend more on parks, in the absence of the most pressing demands for other services, is barely supported by the British evidence, but nothing else of any significance materialises in regression analysis, and most of the variance (85-95 per cent) is unexplained.

When authorities are ranked from the highest to the lowest, however, two explanations for high expenditure jump out of the league tables. At the top of the table in 1960/61 come a group of seaside resorts (for a list of city types see the Appendix). The reasons for high parks expenditure in these cases scarcely needs comment — the economic success of a resort partly depends upon beautiful and extensive public parks. At the same time, there is another, but completely different group of cities, which also spend heavily on parks. These are the capitals of large urban agglomerations, which, because they are surrounded by large urban areas, have great need of their parks. In contrast, the smaller county towns which have rural surroundings spend little, since they are surrounded by open space and natural parkland.

Systematic evidence for these relationships is presented in Table 2.1, which shows how much more than average the seaside resorts spend on parks. Evidence is produced for two years (the first and last financial years of the analysis) in order to show consistency over time. The table also shows how little the county towns spend, but how much is spent by the middle class suburbs. The second part of the table demonstrates the differences between urban and rural authorities. The 83 county boroughs were divided into four groups, as follows:

1. *Conurbation authorities* — those which are at least 75 per cent surrounded by other authorities with a population density of at least five people per acre.
2. *Semi-urban authorities* — those which are mainly (75 per cent) surrounded by other authorities with a population density of more than three but less than five people per acre.
3. *Semi-rural authorities* — those which are mainly (75 per cent) surrounded by other authorities with a population density of less than three but more than one person per acre.
4. *Rural authorities* — those which are mainly (75 per cent) surrounded by authorities with a population density of less than one person per acre.

As the figures show there is a fairly strong relationship between high spending and an urban or semi-urban environment. If the seaside resorts are removed from the rural category, the relationship is stronger.

Table 2.1: *Per Capita* Parks Expenditure (£) by Type of Authority, County Boroughs, 1960/1 and 1972/3

Type of Authority	1960/1	(n)	1972/3	(n)
Conurbation	0.956	(17)	1.881	(14)
Semi-Urban	0.834	(18)	1.882	(18)
Semi-Rural	0.826	(22)	1.838	(23)
Rural	0.797	(26)	1.699	(28)
Seaside Resorts	1.167	(8)	2.240	(9)
County Towns	0.661	(12)	1.510	(12)
Suburbs	1.135	(2)	1.615	(2)
County Borough Mean	0.846	(83)	1.795	(83)

The relationship holds irrespective of the social class of local authority populations. Table 2.2 illustrates the point by comparing working class and middle class authorities embedded in urban areas with those in rural areas. Urban authorities, both middle and working class, spend relatively heavily on parks, compared with rural ones.

Two general points emerge from these findings. First, when looking for factors which might explain expenditure variations it is not enough to deal only with the characteristic of resident populations. Most demographic studies collect detailed, census-type data about such things as population size and change, age, density, housing conditions, wealth, voting turnout, etc., and little or nothing else. Table 1 shows that factors which are not simply aggregates of individual characteristics can be much more important — in this case, the economic function of the city (the seaside resorts), and the nature of the city's physical environment (in the case of conurbation and rural places). The demographic approach generally makes the implicit assumption that most expenditure variation can be explained in terms of aggregated individual data. Many other attempts to explain variations of local service provision and spending, such as the 'consumer-voter' approach of the American economist, Charles M. Tiebout, also make explicit assumptions about rational, economic, individualism. Consequently, the Tiebout hypothesis has virtually no explanatory power, and the demographic approach has much less than it might.

Second, it is clear that different kinds of cities can spend similar amounts on a given service but for different reasons, and vice versa. This greatly complicates the picture and renders useless complicated cluster and factor analysis programmes. It is not enough to be multivariate; analysis must be multivariate *and* multidimensional. For example, the seaside resorts are similar to

Table 2.2:   *Per capita* Parks Expenditure, by Social Class and Urban/Rural dichotomies, County Boroughs, 1960/61

	Urban		Rural	
Middle Class	Croydon	1.555	Ipswich	0.502
	Wallasey	1.059	York	0.556
Working Class	Salford	1.201	Burton	0.505
	Oldham	1.003	Barrow	0.605

the county towns in that both are wealthy, conservative, residential and commercial, and small to medium sized. But the seaside resorts spend a lot and the county towns spend little on parks. In contrast, the seaside resorts have little socially, economically, or politically in common with the conurbation capitals, but both have a high parks expenditure. Thus when the computer searches for significant correlations, or for common dimensions on which to base its cluster, it finds little to go on — there are at least two sets of significant correlations to be sorted out, and at least two dimensions requiring discrimination. The sorting out and the discrimination must be done before feeding figures into machines. Analysis may start with simple figures in order to elaborate powerful theory, but it cannot start with nothing but a powerful computer and elaborate statistics.

Having investigated parks expenditure in some detail, and drawn out the general implications of the results, we can proceed with the analysis of other services at a greater pace.

Sewage

Sewage expenditure is another which resists satisfactory analysis in conventional demographic studies. It correlates weakly with only a few social and economic variables, and no political ones, and regression explains no more than twenty per cent of its variance. However, a casual inspection of the county league table of high and low spenders shows that a crucial factor is the geographical location of the authority: very simply, those on the coast spend less than inland authorities. Of the 25 at the bottom of the table in 1972/3, 17 were coastal cities; and of the 25 at the top, 21 were

Table 2.3: *Per Capita* Sewage Expenditure (£), by Coastal and Inland Cities, County Boroughs, 1960/61 and 1972/73

Type of Authority	1960/61	(n)	1972/3	(n)
Inland	0.971	(57)	3.183	(56)
Coastal	0.619	(26)	2.247	(27)
Seaside Resorts	0.667	(8)	2.523	(9)
Others	0.597	(18)	2.109	(18)
County Borough Average	0.801	(83)	2.878	(83)

inland. There seems also to be a regional variation in that in 1960/1 and 1972/3, all six Tyneside authorities were among the nine lowest.

Among the coastal cities, the seaside resorts are notable for their relatively high spending — whereas the coastal cities had a *per capita* average of £2.247, the seaside resorts averaged £2.523. No doubt the seaside resorts spend in order to keep their sea and beaches free of pollution. The overall figures for all coastal and inland county boroughs are shown in Table 2.3.

Refuse

Refuse is yet another service cost which has weak associations with population characteristics; only population size is significantly (but barely so) correlated with *per capita* spending, and less than 20 per cent of the variance is explained by our whole bank of social, economic and political variables. Common sense and a little knowledge suggest that, like parks expenditure, refuse costs may be determined to a greater extent by the physical setting of a city, than by its population characteristics. That is, authorities which are in the middle of large conurbations are likely to have to transport refuse long distance to rubbish tips, or else invest in expensive capital equipment for burning or crushing rubbish. Conversely, the costs of rural and free-standing authorities are likely to be lower. Transport costs are a high proportion of refuse expenditure.

The validity of this explanation may be judged by the figures in Table 2.4 which show that urban authorities do, indeed, spend more than rural and free-standing ones. At the very top of the league table in 1960/1 came Birmingham Manchester, Leeds, and Liverpool, all of which are surrounded by miles of continuously built up area; at the bottom were Bristol, Reading, Wakefield, Newport, Dewsbury, West Hartlepool, Gloucester, and Plymouth, all of which are free-standing cities, or on the periphery of conurbations. It is notable that some of the seaside resorts are also high spenders, presumably because they go to special trouble to attract tourists by being clean and hygienic, and emptying the dustbins of their many hotels, restaurants, and guest houses as frequently as possible.

These figures suggest that it is not population size and diseconomies of scale which cause high refuse expenditure, but rather the scale of urban society in England and Wales which

Table 2.4: *Per Capita* Refuse Expenditures (£), by Urban and Rural Authorities, County Boroughs 1960/61 and 1972/73

Type of Authority	1960/1	(n)	1972/3	(n)
Conurbation	0.810	(17)	2.909	(14)
Semi-urban	0.843	(18)	2.740	(18)
Semi-rural	0.759	(22)	2.324	(23)
Rural	0.730	(26)	2.270	(28)
County Borough Average	0.779	(83)	2.495	(83)

Note: Authorities are classified in the same way as in Table 2.1

causes the high spending of authorities which are embedded at the centres of the largest urban areas. It is notable, for example, that Bristol was at the very bottom of the table in 1960/1, for although a large city of almost half a million people, it also had the advantage of being relatively free-standing. Like Bristol, Leicester, Nottingham, and Stoke-on-Trent also spent relatively little on this service. Conversely relatively small, urban authorities such as St Helens, Barnsley, Stockport, Wigan, and Halifax were high spenders.

Housing

Housing is the first divisible service discussed so far, and it is also the first which is well explained by the demographic approach. By a divisible service is meant one which is provided for a specific and identifiable set of individuals, families or social groups (such as children, old people, or those in poor housing) in contrast to indivisible services, or public goods, such as parks, police, fire, libraries and roads, which are available (in theory) to all members of the community. The size of the rate fund contribution to the housing revenue account of county boroughs correlates strongly with a wide range of social, economic, and political variables. In stepwise regression analysis, six of these retained their statistical significance, namely:

Variable	*Beta*
Years Labour Control	0.441***
Overcrowding	0.418***
Absence of hot water	0.248**
% local authority housing	-0.148**
Standardised male mortality rate	0.209**
% school-aged population	-0.212**

***   significant at 0.001 level
**   significant at 0.01 level

Together these variables explain 70.2 per cent of the variance in 1960/1. A slightly different combination of variables is included in the regression for 1972/3, but basically the results are similar, in that they show that housing expenditure is basically a function of Labour control in authorities with poor housing, a poor population, and a relatively small school aged population.

The 'league table' approach adds little to this, except to illustrate with examples. At the top appears a series of the poorest, industrial county boroughs — Bootle, Gateshead, Warrington, West Ham, Wakefield, Sunderland, Wolverhampton, and South Shields are in the top ten. At the bottom of the table are the more affluent and predominantly residential and commercial cities — Blackpool, Southport, Bournemouth, Southend, Croyden, Hastings, Eastbourne, Bath, Oxford, and Ipswich. In 1960/1, seven of the eight seaside resorts are in the bottom ten. In other words, housing expenditure is not much of a surprise. The most important single factor determining its level is a political variable — years of Labour control — but this acts in conjunction with variables which act as indicators of poverty (male mortality being the strongest), and of poor housing (overcrowding and lack of amenities).

Libraries, Museums, and Art Galleries

In the majority of authorities, expenditure on libraries is included with museums and art galleries, but for the sake of brevity all three will be called library expenditure. As with other indivisible services, library spending has resisted explanation, although it does correlate with statistical (but not much substantial) significance with wealth and class measures which explain about a third of the variance. A ranking of county boroughs, however, shows that the biggest and most important conurbation capitals have rather high figures. Liverpool is right at the top of the table. At the other extreme, many of the smaller, industrial satellites which exist in the shadow of the major capitals, spend the least on libraries. In between, but with higher than average figures come the secondary capitals, and below them with lower than average figures are the third tier cities, such as Southampton, Bradford, Plymouth, Portsmouth, Wolverhampton, and Derby.

This raises the distinct possibility that library expenditure is closely connected not with the size or nature of the resident population of a city, but with the size and nature of the population for which that city is a regional capital. Fortunately, Carruthers (1967) has ranked and grouped cities in England and Wales (excluding London) according to their importance as service centres, and the average library expenditure for each group in the hierarchy shows clearly enough that spending does decline as the importance of the city as a service centre declined (Table 2.5).

Table 2.5: *Per Capita* Library Expenditure (£), by Importance of Service Centres, County Boroughs, 1960/1 and 1972/3

City Rank[a]	Examples	1960/1	1973/3	(n)
Group 2B	Manchester	0.667	2.424	(5)
Group 2C	Cardiff	0.590	1.703	(4)
Groups 3A/3a	Bradford	0.530	1.777	(31)
Groups 3B/3b	Halifax	0.472	1.493	(27)
Groups 3C/3c	Burton	0.421	1.427	(7)
County Borough mean		0.503	1.672	(74)[b]

Notes:
a. The ranking is that of I. Carruthers, 'Major shopping centres in England and Wales', *Regional Studies* (1967): 65-81.
b. The total number of observations is 74 because Carruthers does not classify all county boroughs and because, for comparative reasons, the analysis is limited to boroughs which existed in both 1960/1 and 1972/3.

This approach does not lend itself to the counties, but a league table of high and low spenders reveals that the former consists mainly of the wealthier, larger, and rather more urban authorities, while the latter includes mainly poorer, smaller, more remote, and rural counties. Four of the top ten are home counties (Essex, Surrey, Bucks, and Kent) which are not only large, but also wealthy, and fairly urban. Seven of the top ten are fairly large and densely populated by county standards (the four home counties plus Nottinghamshire, Durham, and Lancashire). The average population of the top ten is slightly more than a million, compared with that of the bottom ten which is 400,000. The low spenders also include some of the smallest and most sparsely populated counties (Isle of Ely, Lincolnshire Holland and Kesteven, Anglesey, Pembrokeshire, and Caernarvon).

It may be that diseconomies of scale help to explain the relationship between population size and high spending, but correlation and regression analysis does not support this interpretation. Rather, the common thread linking library expenditure in counties and county boroughs seems to be not the population size or density of the spending authority,but the number of people within regular using distance of libraries, which is in turn a function of absolute numbers and density. Among the county boroughs, the capitals of the largest conurbations spend the most, and among the counties it is the largest and most urbanised authorities. In short, spending seems to be a function of the total number of people who are within reasonable travelling distance of the libraries. The spatial element has rarely been considered in previous studies of local government outputs.

Town and Country Planning

Planning expenditure constitutes a small part of local authority budgets (less than half a per cent) and, of course, a good deal can be done without spending much money. This cannot explain the low and thinly scattered array of correlations with the population characteristics of county boroughs, however, because the counties show a considerably stronger array of figures, with the highest spending in the relatively small, affluent, and high-turnout counties. Nevertheless, little of the county variance is explained by these factors (15 per cent) and even less of the county borough variance. It is also notable that there is a greater variation in planning expenditure than any other service. In 1960/1 the highest *per capita* figure was £0.001.

Yet the league tables show up something of interest, for it is clear that cities which suffered from heavy bombing during the war are grouped at the top. In fact, of the twelve county boroughs listed as having had major air attacks and at least 150 tons of high explosives dropped on them, ten are in the top twenty in 1960/1 for planning expenditure — these being East and West Ham, Birmingham, Plymouth, Bristol, Coventry, Portsmouth, Southampton, Hull and Sheffield. (O'Brien 1955). If one adds to these the cities of Exeter, Great Yarmouth, Hastings, Southend, Eastbourne, and Birkenhead, because they were also attacked by air at least fifty times and suffered great damage, then there are few county boroughs among the twenty highest spenders which did not suffer from extensive wartime damage. The position is not drastically changed by 1972/3, when Portsmouth, Newcastle, Manchester, Exeter, Coventry, Plymouth, Hull, Birkenhead, Sheffield, and Birmingham are all in the top twenty. It seems that cities which had to set to work planning and rebuilding on a large scale in 1945 were still spending relatively heavily on planning 25 years later. By comparison places such as Chester, Carlisle, Blackpool, Solihull, Southport, and Bournemouth, which received no more than the odd stray bomb, spend well below the national average.

This is not the whole story, because some heavy spenders, such as Bath, St Helens, Warley, Leicester, Worcester, and Norwich, did not have much bomb damage, while two cities which suffered moderately (Cardiff and Nottingham) are almost at the bottom of the league table. Another part of the story seems to involve many of the smallest, poorest, and most industrial cities, many of which fill the bottom places — Sunderland, Oldham, Walsall, Wakefield, Barrow, Blackburn, Dewsbury, Rochdale, Preston, and South Shields, for example. These sorts of cities make up by far the greatest part of the bottom 25, and conversely, few of them appear among the top 25 — St Helens, Warley, and Stockport excepted.

Besides the heavily bombed cities, a group of historic county towns also spend relatively heavily on planning Once again, not all historic, county towns spend a lot (Chester and Ipswich, for example), but the majority are on or above the average.

Turning from county towns to the counties themselves, it is clear that war destruction does not account for their planning expenditure. Few of the counties which were the targets for flying bombs and rockets are notable for high spending; on the contrary, the counties which took the brunt of the action more usually appear at the bottom of the table (Sussex West, Berkshire, East Suffolk, Essex, and Kent) (O'Brien, 1955). Nor is there much evidence that the poorer and more industrial counties spend the least; on the contrary, some of the wealthiest counties do so (Kent, Buckingham, Berkshire, Essex, Hunts and Peterborough, and Kent) (Newton and Garcia, 1977). There is a regional bias in the table in that a high proportion of the top ten spenders in 1972/3 are Welsh counties. Beyond this, however, little sense can be made of the league table, and planning expenditure among the counties remains much of a mystery.

Police

A study of police expenditure is complicated by the amalgamation of many counties and county boroughs to form a smaller number of police districts. Nevertheless, police expenditure responds reasonably well to the correlation and regression analysis of the demographic approach since it is associated with a range of population characteristics including size, density, and commercial property. Nonetheless, the regressions explain less than a half of the variance in *per capita* police spending in the boroughs, and less than a third in the counties.

The league tables reveal that the conurbation capitals spend the most, followed by slightly less important urban centres. Bottom of the list comes a group of small, industrial cities which are overshadowed by the more important urban capitals. It looks as if police expenditure may be strongly influenced by the importance of a city as a regional or metropolitan centre.

Cutting across this trend, however, are the seaside resorts which, though not centres of great importance, spend relatively heavily on police services. Six of the eight seaside resorts are among the top sixteen spenders, presumably because their pubs, clubs, casinos, and dance halls require fairly intense police attention, and also because a visible police presence in seaside resorts creates the sense of safety and security which is good for business.

If seaside resorts are removed — as special cases — from the list of county boroughs, and if the remainder are grouped, as they were in Table 2.5, according to the Carruthers urban hierarchy, it can be seen that police spending is associated with the importance of a city as a service centre. Table 2.6 shows that the most important provincial capitals have the highest figures, and that these gradually decline as one goes down the hierarchy, although the curve turns up

Table 2.6: *Per Capita* Police Expenditure (£), by Importance of
Service Centre, County Boroughs, 1960/1 and 1972/3

City Rank	Examples	1960/1	1972/3	(n)
Group 2B	Manchester	3.12	10.856	(5)
Group 2C	Cardiff	2.34	8.102	(4)
Groups 3A/3a	Gloucester	2.103	7.493	(27)
Groups 3B/3b	Rochdale	2.148	7.016	(24)
Groups 3C/3c	Merthyr Tydfil	2.198	7.920	(6)
County Borough Average		2.271	7.715	(66)

Note: The total number of observations is 66, because the seaside resorts have not
been included, because Carruthers does not classify all county boroughs, and
because for comparative reasons, the analysis is limited to authorities which
existed in both 1960/1 and 1972/3.

again at the very bottom. Nevertheless, police and library spending
appear to follow the same general pattern.

It is more difficult to discern trends or patterns among the
counties, partly, no doubt, because quite a large proportion of the
smaller ones are amalgamated into larger police authorities,
together with the county boroughs within them. The Welsh
authorities appear among the high spenders, with nine of the
counties making up the four Welsh authorities in 1972/3 being at
the top of the list, and only two at the bottom. There is also some
evidence that population sparsity makes a difference. Among the
English counties in the top twenty spenders, 16.4 per cent of
geographical area is classified as urban, compared with 10.8 per
cent among the bottom twenty. The top group have a density of
1.25 per acre, compared with 1.08 at the bottom. Yet these
differences are so small, and there are so many exceptions to the
generalisation that sparsely populated rural counties spend
relatively little, that it cannot take us far as an explanation.

Fire

Fire and police services are often grouped together, and yet
correlation analysis suggests they have rather little in common.
Neither is strongly related to the characteristics of local authority
populations, and neither is at all satisfactorily explained by the
regression analysis of demographic studies. Also police and fire

expenditure, so far as they correlate with anything, are not correlated with the same set of social, economic, and political variables. The picture is further obscured by the existence of joint fire authorities, especially among the smaller counties.

Fire service expenditure is influenced by Home Office standards of fire cover, which are based on four categories of fire risk (CIPFA, 1978).

Class A.   Includes concentrations of factories in towns, shopping and business centres in large cities and towns, docks and shipbuilding yards in congested areas.

Class B.   Model factory estates, shopping and business centres in smaller cities and towns, old timbered property in medium sized towns, and large seaside holiday resorts.

Class C.   Built up areas not falling in Class A or B.

Class D.   All other areas.

Given these risk categories one would expect higher spending authorities to have large industrial and commercial areas, and ports and shipyards. The league table for fire expenditure shows this to be the case, in general. Ten ports are in the top 25, and only four are in the bottom 25. Of the remaining 15 high spenders, most are small industrial county boroughs — Bootle, Dewsbury, Wakefield, Halifax, Bury, St Helens, Burton, Rotherham, Barrow, and Barnsley. In addition, the seaside resorts have higher-than-average expenditure, and five are in the top 25. The fact that they spend relatively heavily, although they are only Class B risk, indicates that they may finance a specially good service. Front-page pictures of blazing hotels are not good for the holiday business.

It is difficult to categorise the low spenders, since these cover a fairly wide range of cities, including some of the small industrial authorities, some ports, and some seaside resorts. Consequently a distribution of high and low risk fire areas is only part of the explanation.

The counties show a distinct but different pattern. In the first place, nine of the ten Welsh fire authorities appear in the top 20, and with an average *per capita* expenditure of £2.026, they are well above the county average. In the second place, of the remaining eleven non-Welsh authorities in the top 20, seven have above-average densities of more than one person per acre (their average is 1.38). Compared with this, 14 of the bottom 20 have below average densities (their average is 0.49 persons per acre). Low density counties not only have less risk of fire starting and spreading, but it

Table 2.7: *Per Capita* Fire Expenditures (£), by Fire Risk[a] and Population Density, among English County Boroughs with Highest and Lowest Expenditures, 1972/3

	High Density	Low Density
High Risk	1.643 (8)	1.385 (2)
Low Risk	1.597 (3)	1.387 (9)

Note:
a. The classification is approximate since fire risk figures in 1972/3 are estimated from those available for 1977/8.

is also more difficult and more expensive to provide them with more than a fairly minimal cover. Sparsely populated counties tend to have a fairly high proportion of part-time and volunteer firemen. For example, in 1972/3, the most sparsely populated county (Westmorland) employed whole to part-time staff in the ratio of 1:6, but the most densely populated (Lancashire), had a ratio of 1.6:1. It should be noted that most of the high spending Welsh counties have a low density, so that density, as such, will not show up as a significant demographic correlation.

The Home Office's fire risk categories are only loosely related to expenditure among the counties. Of the eleven high spending English counties, seven have Category A risk areas. Of the 20 low spenders, nine have no high risk areas, but five do. Although the determination of fire risk categories is partly dependent upon population density, the league tables suggest that a combination of high risk and high densities is likely to result in high expenditure, and vice versa. This is confirmed by the figures in Table 2.7, although the expenditure of the low risk, low density counties is marginally high.

Highways

The demographic approach explains with a modest degree of success the *per capita* highways expenditures of the county boroughs, but the league tables suggest ways of improving upon this. The metropolitan capitals are notably heavy spenders, as are the seaside resorts. Presumably the major capitals spend heavily because of their particularly high traffic densities, whereas the seaside resorts do so partly because of their heavy summer traffic, but also because they provide wide and well maintained roads to attract tourists and minimise traffic congestion. Casual observation of seaside resorts suggests that they often have exceptionally good roads.

Cities spending the least on highways include many of the smaller, industrial boroughs of the major conurbations - and also free-standing industrial boroughs. The suspicion that the small industrial cities spend relatively little is strengthened by the fact that the smaller residential and commercial cities spend an average or above average amount. A simple relationship between an industrial tax base and low highways expenditure, however, is disturbed by the seaside resorts, at one extreme, and by the major capitals at the other.

The demographic approach works rather better in the counties, where spending is highest in the small, more rural, and more sparsely populated authorities. In fact, one indicator or another of these variables, plus a high voting turnout, explains 80 per cent of the variance in both 1960/1 and 1972/3. The league tables confirm this pattern, with Westmorland, Cumberland, Hereford, and Devon consistently at the top, and West Yorkshire, Nottinghamshire, Staffordshire, Lancashire, and Surrey usually at the bottom. The tables also show a strong regional effect, with nine of the thirteen Welsh counties in the top thirteen spenders in both years. The Welsh placing reflects the sparsely populated, rural nature of the counties, it is true, but over and above this, their virtual monopoly of the top ten places suggests a special regional factor at work.

Public Health

Like planning, public health accounts for only a small proportion of total local expenditure (little more than 2 per cent),and like planning it is firmly resistant to the attempts of conventional output studies to pin down the causes of variation, particularly in the county boroughs. An examination of the high and low spenders reveals some regularities, although they are faint and indistinct. The seaside resorts stand out, once again, for their high spending, no doubt in order to maintain a high service quality. The two wealthy suburban authorities of Wallasey and Croydon also spend heavily. The ports are also notable for having an average of £0.60 in 1960/1 compared with a county boroughs average of £0.44. At the other extreme, some of the industrial satellites spend the least. Of the 25 low spenders, 14 are cities of the industrial periphery. What confuses the picture, however, is the fact that the highest spenders also include these sorts of cities and it is not clear what distinguishes one group from the other. What is clear, however, is that public health spending is consistently associated with Labour strength, or an absence of Conservative strength, these being among the few significant variables which appear in the regression equations.

Politics does not seem to matter as far as public health spending in the counties is concerned where the smaller, more rural, and/or poorer seem to spend the most. Cornwall, Norfolk, Suffolk, and Lincolnshire all appear in the top 15, as do seven of the thirteen Welsh counties. Only three of the Welsh counties are among the lowest 20. The latter consist largely, but not exclusively, of the wealthier and/or more urban counties such as Cheshire, Oxfordshire, Kent, Essex, Sussex, and Surrey. There are quite a few exceptions to the general pattern, however, and a good deal of the variation remains to be explained in other ways.

Personal Health Services

One would expect personal health costs to be higher in the poorer, more urban, and more industrial authorities, and so it is in both the counties and the county boroughs, although the association is not strong. By comparison, the more affluent and commercial/residential cities such as the seaside resorts and the county towns, make up the majority of the bottom 20. The association between poverty and high spending is not strong, however, because boroughs like Tynemouth, Bootle, Walsall, St Helens, Barrow, and Dudley also appear in the bottom 20. As with public health, it is not clear what distinguishes them from similar but high spending boroughs.

Among the counties, high spending is associated with the proportion of small self-employed workers, uncontested local elections, a large school-aged population, and a large percentage of Labour seats on the council, and while these are statistically strong (explaining 54 per cent and 71 per cent of the variance in local health and health services in 1960/1 and 1972/3), they make no great theoretical sense. Why should a large proportion of uncontested seats, and of small, self-employed workers be associated with personal health expenditure, and why should the relationship with school age population be negative in the boroughs but positive in the counties?

The league table explains some of these mysteries. Once again, the Welsh counties stand out, with eight of them appearing in the top 15 (they fill the first four places in 1960/1) and only one in the bottom 20. Many of the remaining high spenders are the more urbanised or industrial counties, such as Lancashire, Nottinghamshire, Essex, Durham, West Yorkshire, and Staffordshire. In contrast, a clear majority of low spenders are the most rural of the English counties (Suffolk, Rutland, Devon, East and North Yorkshire, Shropshire, and Lincolnshire). The exceptional high spending of the rural and sparsely populated Welsh counties obscures the tendency for their English equivalents to spend rather little.

Education

The results of an analysis of education expenditure depends on whether one takes *per capita* or per pupil figures. So far, expenditures have been analysed on a *per capita* basis, either because they are community-wide services (e.g. parks or libraries), or because there are no appropriate figures for the target population (e.g. those in need of public housing). But, in the case of education, the school age population is known, and the more interesting figure is what is spent on each pupil, rather than what is spent on education *per capita* of total population. It is worth noting that the greater the proportion of pupils in an authority, the higher its *per capita* education expenditure, but the lower its per pupil spending.

Per pupil expenditures are also less well explained by the regression equation of the demographic approach than are *per capita figures*, although the results are better for the counties, where between 65 per cent and 80 per cent of the variance is explained. Generally speaking the authorities with a large commercial tax base, and a small proportion of school aged children, spend more on each pupil, particularly if they have a large proportion of

Table 2.8: Correlations Between *Per Capita* and Per Pupil Education Expenditure, and the Percentage of the Population of School Age, Counties and County Boroughs, 1960/1 and 1972/3

		County Boroughs	County Councils
Education *Per Capita*	1960/1	0.69***	0.29*
	1972/3	0.74***	0.20
Education Per Pupil	1960/1	-0.40***	-0.32*
	1972/3	-0.50***	-0.40*
(N)	1960/1	(77)	(61)
	1972/3	(76)	(56)

*** Significant at 0.001
* Significant at 0.05

Labour councillors. The latter is a strongly significant variable in both the county and the county borough regressions. Translated into the terms of actual cities, this means that the seaside resorts and the county towns, which are wealthy and have relatively few school children, have the highest spending figures, followed closely by a group of relatively wealthy and larger cities such as Derby, Leicester, Croydon, Coventry, Nottingham, Portsmouth, Southampton, and Reading. The large industrial and commercial tax base of these places, plus a relatively small school aged population, combined with a strong Labour presence, seems to result in relatively high spending. At the bottom of the table come the major capitals and their industrial satellites. The latter are both relatively poor and have a large proportion of children, which means that the *per capita* spending is high, but per pupil spending much lower.

Among the counties the Welsh authorities stand out, once again, at the very top. In this case, eleven of the thirteen were in the top 20 in 1972/3, and none in the bottom 20. Education costs are notoriously high in sparsely populated counties, and the Welsh figures may be due in part to this, but on the other hand, Glamorgan and Monmouth with relatively high densities (1.62 and 1.05 per acre) are also high spending, while some English counties with a low density spend rather little (Devon, Suffolk, Cornwall, and Dorset, for example). Besides, if the Welsh counties are excluded, the high spending authorities have a higher population density (0.95 per acre) than the low spending (0.84). A combination of a relatively large industrial and commercial tax base, a relatively small working class and school age population, but a significant Labour presence, seems to contribute to the high spending of some English authorities.

Children's Welfare, and Social Services

The regression equations of the demographic approach have a mixed success with spending on welfare and on children per child, but rather little when the two are amalgamated to form social services. This is to be expected since different types of city spend heavily on the two services, and this cancels out any simple, linear relationships. Taking the children per child figures first, the nigh spenders are the major urban capitals and the industrial satellites. At the other extreme the low spenders are primarily the more affluent seaside resorts and county towns. This pattern is partly reversed for welfare spending, where the high spenders are the more affluent commercial and residential towns and a fairly large number of the smallest and poorest industrial boroughs among the low spenders on welfare (Smethwick, Bury, and St Helens, for example).

However, something of value emerges from the league tables for they show two fairly strong tendencies which contribute to an explanation:

1. Children's spending is generally highest in the smallest and poorest industrial boroughs, which often have a large proportion of children and bad housing and social conditions.
2. Welfare spending is high in some of the industrial boroughs with high children's spending (Oldham, Bradford, Huddersfield, West Ham, Sunderland), but it is generally even higher in the small but affluent commercial and residential boroughs — particularly the seaside resorts and some of the county towns. Whereas poverty and a relatively large old population explain the former, the sheer weight of retired people, though many of them are well off, explains the latter.

The county figures are also mixed. Once again the Welsh counties stand out for their exceptionally high spending on welfare in the early years, and on social services in the later years. They do not spend heavily on children, but, on the other hand, it is possible that some of their spending appears under the education columns, for in some authorities the education department is financially responsible for some children's welfare activities. This may also explain the seemingly low children's spending of some of the county boroughs. Be that as it may, the Welsh authorities clearly spend heavily on welfare and social services, as they do on many other services. In addition, some of the south coast retirement counties spend a lot on welfare (East and West Sussex, and Dorset, but not Hampshire) and social services, as do some of the poorer counties such as Cornwall, Lancashire, Lincolnshire, and Durham. What these counties have in common is either a large proportion of old people or low personal incomes.

Lastly, politics matter to a significant degree for the social services. In both the county and the county borough regressions, the percentage of Labour members of the council is significantly associated with high social services spending, and a political variable of one kind or another is included in three of the four regressions for children's and welfare spending. While it is the low turnout, Labour authorities which spend most on children, it is the high turnout and more affluent authorities which spend most on welfare.

Total Expenditure

Total spending is, of course, heavily determined by the major spending services, which are education, housing, highways, police, and social services, and authorities spending more than the average on most or all of these are likely to emerge at the top of the league table for total expenditure. These are likely to be authorities which combine a relatively heavy need for local services (a large working class and school aged population, poor housing and social conditions, and a large hinterland population making demands upon libraries, police, fire, and highways), a relatively good tax base of commercial and industrial property, and a disposition to tax and spend relatively heavily (a large Labour group on the council). The great majority of top spenders in 1972/3 fit this profile: four are major conurbation capitals, and 15 are the smaller, industrial boroughs.

At the other extreme are the predominantly commercial and residential cities which are Conservative controlled, and which have relatively little demand for or inclination to spend on many services. These include six of the seaside resorts, both of the middle class suburbs, and an assortment of county towns and commercial centres. The pattern is not perfect, by any means, however, for the low spenders also include some small, industrial boroughs, just as some of the league leaders include the county towns of Exeter, Lincoln, Norwich, and Oxford.

Because the Welsh counties are so regularly league leaders on a wide range of services, it is no surprise that they also emerge at the top of the table for total expenditure. In fact, twelve of the thirteen are in the top 20 (Flint alone has a low figure, and it is in the bottom 20 in 1972/3), and the Welsh average of £102 compares with the English average of £80 — 27.5 per cent higher. The top six counties are Welsh.

Of the English counties in the top 20, most are rural but relatively wealthy (Buckinghamshire, Hertfordshire, Gloucestershire, Herefordshire), while many of those at the bottom of the table are urban and/or relatively industrial, but relatively wealthy — Essex, Surrey, West Yorkshire, Lancashire, Nottingham, Derbyshire, and Kent. There are enough exceptions to this general tendency, however, to suggest that further analysis is necessary, and it may well be that the exceptional nature of the Welsh figures has obscured general trends and tendencies among the English counties.

Conclusions

This paper has worked its way through a great mass of data, and although only a small fraction of the statistical material has been presented, there are still far too many trees obscuring the wood. It is possible to draw out some generalisations, however, and these will serve as a basis for more systematic analysis in future research. The most important of these are as follows:

1. Some service expenditure such as police, libraries, and possibly highways, appear to be related to the position which a city has in the urban hierarchy of the country as a whole; high order or central place cities, tending to spend relatively heavily on some services, and vice versa.
2. Other services such as parks, public health, highways, police and fire seem to be associated with city types, that is with the

main economic role a city plays in the national system of cities. Ports stand out in one or two services, but mainly it is seaside resorts, county towns, industrial satellites, the major conurbation capitals which appear to have their own special spending patterns.

3. What might be termed geographical, spatial, or locational variables are also important influences on some service spending levels. Coastal cities generally spend little on sewage, unless they are seaside resorts, whereas cities which are embedded in large urban agglomerations spend heavily on parks and refuse, for example.

4. Regional variations also appear, most notably in the case of the Welsh counties which regularly appear at the top of the league tables for total, education, social services, police, highways, public health, local health, and fire, but not libraries or planning. Although the high spending of some Welsh counties may well be strongly affected by their characteristics of poverty, population sparsity, and strong Labour voting, there seems to be a strong regional effect operating on top of these, and which causes the Welsh counties to stand out head and shoulders above other counties of the same kind.

5. Historical factors also play a part in the case of planning expenditure which is high in the cities which were bombed heavily during the war. The effect of wartime damage was still clearly noticeable in 1972/3.

6. The evidence reinforces the view that politics matter, not generally as the major determinant of public policy, but often as a major determinant on some of the most expensive local services. It is difficult to disentangle the effects of social, economic, and political variables, but even allowing for the effects of such factors as class, poor social conditions, or the size of the local tax base, it is clear that political considerations, particularly the presence of a large Labour group, or the absence of a large Conservative group, is associated with high spending on some services and in total.

7. By and large the indivisible services (parks, police, fire, refuse, highways, libraries) are best explained by what may be termed 'holistic' variables which describe the type of city, its rank in the national urban hierarchy, and its relationship to nearby urban and rural areas. Divisible services (education, social services, personal health, and housing) are best explained by the

demographic approach which concentrates on the aggregate social and economic characteristics of local authority populations.

While these seven points will help towards a more complete and satisfactory explanation of local outputs, they are still far from satisfactory, in the sense that the league tables reveal many exceptions to the general rule, or fail to suggest any general rule in the first place. The seven points indicate ways in which some major gaps in our understanding may be filled, but some gaps will inevitably remain.

Notes

1. In 1972/3 there were 44 police authorities in England and Wales, and although a large majority covered one or more counties and/or county boroughs, this makes the statistical analysis much less precise, but still enables a rough and ready analysis to be carried out.

2. It is important to note that the wealth of a city's resident population may not be a good indicator of the wealth of the local authority. This is because the size of the local authority tax base is primarily dependent upon offices, shops and industrial, rather than domestic property, as the following correlations show.

Pearsonian Correlations between Rateable Value Per Capita and the Proportion of Total Rateable Value made up by Domestic, Industrial, and Commercial Property, Counties and County Boroughs, 1972/3

	Counties	*County Boroughs*
Domestic	0.30*	0.10
Industrial	0.33**	-0.21*
Offices	0.48***	0.36***
(N)	(56)	(76)

***   significant at 0.001 level
**   significant at 0.01 level
*   significant at 0.05 level

Therefore it is important to distinguish between the wealth of an authority's resident population, and the wealth of the authority itself. It is perfectly possible for an authority with quite severe social problems to have a relatively good tax base, and this is generally the case in the largest cities, although generally the wealthiest urban authorities are those which combine a wealthy resident population with a large commercial tax base, particularly among the commercial cities, the seaside resorts, and some of the county towns.

3. Per pupil and per capita education expenditures are reasonably strongly correlated in the counties (0.78 and 0.67 in 1960/1 and 1972/3), but not in the county boroughs, where the figures are 0.35 and 0.18.

It is widely suggested that population sparsity is a major cause of high education spending among the counties (cf. IMTA, *Local Expenditure and Exchequer Grants*, pp. 116-124), and it is certainly true that the Welsh authorities are both sparsely populated (0.40 people per acre) and high spending. But the fact that many sparsely populated English counties do not spend heavily, and that the population density of the top spending English counties is higher than that of the lowest, suggest that the sparsity factor may be really a Welsh factor. Indeed, the disproportionate weight given to the high Welsh expenditure figures for most services may well distort the overall picture.

Appendix

City Types

Metropolitan Capitals. Manchester, Birmingham, Liverpool, Newcastle, Leeds.

Secondary Capitals. Bolton, Bradford, Coventry, Huddersfield, Salford, Wolverhampton.

Large, free-standing cities. Hull, Leicester, Nottingham, Southampton, Sheffield, Stoke, Teeside.

Small, free-standing industrial cities. Barrow-in-Furness, Burnley, Burton, Darlington, Derby, Doncaster, Grimsby, Luton, Merthyr Tydfil, Newport, Northampton, Preston, Rochdale, Rotherham, St Helens, Swansea, Wakefield, Warrington.

Industrial satellites. Barnsley, Birkenhead, Blackburn, Bootle, Bury, Dewsbury, Dudley, East Ham, Gateshead, Halifax, Hartlepool, Oldham, Smethwick, South Shields, Stockport, Sunderland, Tynemouth, Walsall, West Bromwich, West Ham, Warrington, Wigan.

Suburbs. Croydon, Solihull, Wallasey.

Seaside Resorts. Bournemouth, Brighton, Eastbourne, Hastings, Southend, Southport, Blackpool, Great Yarmouth, Torbay.

County Towns. Canterbury, Chester, Exeter, Gloucester, Ipswich, Lincoln, Norwich, Oxford, Worcester, York.

Administrative Centres. Bath, Bristol, Cardiff, Carlisle, Plymouth, Portsmouth, Reading.

References

CIPFA (1978) *Fire Services Annual Statistics*, London

Danziger, J.N. (1978) *Making Budgets*, Sage, Beverly Hills

Fried, R.C. (1976) 'Comparative urban performance' in F.I. Greenstein and N.W. Polsby (eds.) *The Handbook of Political Science*, Addison-Wesley, Reading, Mass., 305-381

Newton, K. and J. Garcia (1977) 'Rateable values, personal incomes and taxable capacity', *Public Administration*, **55**, 33-42

O'Brien, T.H. (1955) *Civil Defence*, HMSO, London

3

The Spatial Allocation of Federal Outlays and Presidential Politics: A Vote-Buying Linkage?

J. Clark Archer

Introduction

In the 1980 Presidential contest the two major party candidates had ostensibly equal campaign resources. Each received almost $30 million in federal funds, about half of which was spent on television advertising (Moore, 1981, p. xiv). However, Reagan's candidacy was reinforced by Republican-oriented Political Action Committees, or PACs. Direct PAC support of a Presidential contender is disallowed in a general election campaign, although supposedly multicandidate PACs often seem to target their efforts. Furthermore, such restrictions do not apply during primaries. As early as 1978, Citizens for the Republic had spent $1.9 million. 'Most of this money was used for fund raising and for the travel expenses of the Citizens' principal speaker, Ronald Reagan' (Wayne, 1980, p.43). On the incumbent's side, it is plausible that an even greater, indeed a massively greater, resource pool was drawn upon.

In December, 1980, more than two score individuals 'who had played major decision making roles in the various Presidential campaigns gathered at Harvard University to explore how the whole campaign worked' (Moore, 1981, p. ix). In summarising the published transcript of this meeting, the editor remarked that 'the role of federal largess doled out by the incumbent, especially during the primaries, was barely touched upon' (Moore, 1981, p. x). Since conference participants were campaign workers, this may have been an accidental omission. Nevertheless, other reports made relevant assertions. A *Time* article, for instance, noted announcements of $150 million in new mass transit funds, and $300 million in agricultural aid by Carter during the campaign and commented of the incumbent President that he 'acted a bit like Santa Claus distributing gifts' (Warner, 1980, p. l4). Some political reporters, it would seem, subscribe to a view that the federal treasury is occasionally allocated as though it were a repository for election campaign contributions.

Although the popular press appears inclined to stress ethical matters in relation to possible politically-motivated manipulation of the flow of federal funds, there are broader pragmatic questions to be raised as well for with expansion of its protective, productive, regulative and redistributive activities in the last quarter century, the federal government has emerged as the single largest influence upon the American economy. Not surprisingly, geographical variations in patterns of federal taxing and spending impact geographical patterns of economic growth and decline across the nation Richardson, 1974). Yet students of regional economic patterns have tended to ignore, or to treat as exogenous, the geography of federal spending; similarly, students of elections have tended to ignore the budgetary process. Most available research tying electoral concerns to budgetary matters has focused upon the Congress (Archer, 1980; Arnold, 1979; Ippolito, 1981; Johnston, 1980; Kinder and Kiewiet, 1979; Mayhew, 1974; Ray, 1980; Ritt, 1976). Questions, therefore, remain about whether a President acting a 'bit like Santa Claus' is merely a journalistic exaggeration or an apt description of an important influence upon the geographical distribution of federal spending. Put simply, do Presidential electoral considerations influence the spatial pattern of federal outlays; if so, under what circumstances and to what degree?

The next section examines research dealing with economic conditions and national voting patterns. The third section focuses upon literature involving politicians' efforts to manipulate the national economy over time. Also in the third section the few studies which have looked at possible election-motivated manipulation of the geography of spending are reviewed. The fourth section conceptualises models formulated to test for Presidential vote-buying in the geography of federal spending. Such a test is the focus of section five. This test leads to the conclusion that geographical patterns of federal outlay are not immune to electoral concerns, though the degree of sensitivity varies from time to time and context to context.

Economic Conditions and Electoral Outcomes

One type of evidence regarding economic conditions and electoral outcomes can be found in the statements of Presidential candidates and their advisors. For example, Nixon accounted for his narrow loss to Kennedy in 1960 in these terms (Nixon, 1962, p. 309; cited in Tufte, 1978, p.6):

> The bottom of the 1960 dip did come in October and the economy started to move up in November — after it was too late to affect the election returns. In October, usually a month of rising unemployment, the jobless rolls increased by 452,000. All the speeches, television broadcasts, and precinct work in the world could not counteract that one hard fact.

In late 1980, Patrick Caddell, one of Carter's chief strategists, observed that 'The economy had gotten quite bad in the spring, particularly the inflation rate, and we had paid an enormous price for that' (Moore, 1981, p. 188). Republican strategists called the economy 'the single issue before the campaign, during the campaign, and today' (Moore, 1981, p. 209). According to the chairman of the Republican National Committee, Bill Brock, (Moore, 1981, pp. 253- 254):

> There was one strategic decision that was of enormous consequence and more important than any other single decision made, and that was the decision to stay within the parameters of the economic issue ... We took the frustration of 12, 14, 18 per cent inflation, interest rates, unemployment, and offered the positive alternative.

Despite such perceptions among participants, whether the electorate behaves as though matters of economics are paramount appears to remain a somewhat open question. Nevertheless, a great deal of positivisitic social science theory is based upon the premise that people seek to 'maximise their personal benefit or advantage when engaging in political acts' (Pennock, 1979, p. 170). Illustratively Downs's classic work on *An Economic Theory of Democracy* (1957, pp. 7-8) depicted the average voter as proceeding to the polling place with 'one eye on the gains to be had, the other eye on costs, a delicate ability to balance them, and a strong desire to follow wherever rationality leads him.'

The seminal empirical study of voting in response to economic conditions was Kramer's 1971 analysis of national support for candidates for the US House of Representatives between 1896 and 1964. His assumption was that 'To some extent, at least, an individual's vote in a national election represents a choice or judgment between alternative governing "teams" ' (Kramer, 1971, p.133). The governing 'team' in each election was judged to be that of the party occupying the White House. Kramer's basic hypotheses were that increases in real income would advantage Congressional candidates belonging to the President's party but rises in prices or unemployment would hurt them at the polls. Using time-series regression, he found that 'economic fluctuations can account for something like half the variance of the Congressional vote, over the period considered' (Kramer, 1971, p. 141). He cautioned, however, that while income and price levels were related to Congressional voting in the predicted manner, coefficients for unemployment were of the wrong sign (positive) and had standard errors too large to allow them to be significant. Since the income and unemployment measures were highly correlated ($r = -0.77$), apparent problems with multi-collinearity make it hard to view his findings regarding unemployment as conclusive. Kramer also examined cross-temporal covariations between economic and Presidential election series, but with evidently ambiguous results given his merely passing reference to the subject.

A later study of Congressional voting using similar techniques, but with different model specifications, found that while regression coefficients for the level of unemployment were small and insignificant, those for changes in unemployment were significantly negative as hypothesised (Lepper, 1974, p. 74). Coefficients for consumer price index changes were also significant, pointing toward 'voters' aversion to increases in unemployment and to changes (in either direction) in prices' and leading to the conclusion that 'information regarding public preferences over unemployment-price- change targets is embedded in voting statistics' (Lepper, 1974, pp. 74 and 67).

Available evidence appears to make a response linkage running from national economic conditions to national voting series at least plausible and perhaps even probable (Bloom and Price, 1975; Meltzer and Velrath, 1975; Monroe, 1979). More closely related to the subject of the present research, however, is the question of whether policy makers who owe their incumbency to past actions of the electorate are motivated toward and capable of endeavouring to influence economic trends at national or regional scales. Once again both anecdotal quotations and quantitative social science research findings may be brought to bear on the matter.

Politicians' Behaviour and Economic Conditions

'Gearing up for the 1972 campaign,' according to one source (Tufte, 1978, p. 136),

> staff members of the office of Management and Budget ... developed statistical models and ran multiple regressions assessing the influence of economic conditions on the outcomes of Presidential elections. The OMB studies concluded that between-election increases in real net national product per capita had a strong impact on the electoral support won by the Presidential candidate of the incumbent party. These findings were then reported to George Schultz and John Erlichman ... Finally, the economic policies of 1971-1972 led to a fresh test and reconfirmation of the proposition that good economic times benefit incumbents.

In his work on *Political Control of the Economy* Tufte argued that recent American Presidents have sought to manipulate the level and timing of national economic trends since they 'desire re-election and they believe that a booming pre-election economy will help to achieve it' (Tufte, 1978, p. 5). The book represents a popularisation and test of the conviction that in the post-Keynesian era politically-motivated economic fluctuations have become an important component of the short-run swings characteristic of private market economies. Examining a graph of yearly changes in real disposable income *per capita* in the United States for 1946 to 1976, he found that, excepting the Eisenhower era, 'real income growth accelerated in eight of eleven election years (73 per cent) compared to only two of ten years (20 per cent) without elections' (Tufte, 1978, p. 15). Tufte's time-series, it should be noted, included both Presidential and Congressional election years.

Investigations of whether employment, inflation, gross national product and other macroeconomic series follow 'political business cycles' extend back at least as far as 1946 (Paldam, 1981, pp. 295-296). Much of the modern literature on the subject, however, expands upon a study by Nordhaus (1975) of unemployment patterns in nine countries from 1947 to 1972. In Nordhaus's assessment, policy makers face a Phillips curve trade-off between unemployment and inflation with the result that (Nordhaus, 1975, p. 184):

> The typical cycle will run as follows: immediately after an election the victor will raise unemployment to some relatively high level in order to combat inflation. As elections approach, the unemployment rate will be lowered until, on election eve, the unemployment rate will be lowered to the purely myopic rate.

By the phrase 'myopic rate', Nordhaus implies a short-run unemployment level which will inevitably stimulate a return to inflationary price increases in the long-run.

A more recent follow-up investigation of economic trends from 1948 to 1975 among seventeen OECD countries found congruence between economic shifts and election timing to be virtually universal; contrary to the Nordhaus thesis, however (Paldam, 1981, p. 298):

> The strongest effect found in the real series is that real growth is highest in the second government year ... The second year is the first year where the new (or newly re-elected) government can really influence events — it is thus here we should observe the lowest growth and highest unemployment according to all arguments advanced under the maximization hypothesis. The second year expansion is easy to explain: it is very likely to be the result of the new government trying to redeem its *election-promises*.

Specifically with respect to the United States, other researchers have found significant shifts in levels of national economic activity coincident with changes in administration (e.g. Davis, Dempster, and Wildavsky, 1974) as well as in the partisan balance of the Congress (e.g. Bozeman, 1977). There is evidence that the two major parties place different emphasis upon the basic Phillips-curve trade-off posited by election-cycle theorists: relative to a 'steady state' economy, recent two-term Democratic administrations have been associated with 1.2 per cent lower unemployment and recent two-term Republican administrations with a 1.2 per cent higher unemployment for a net 2.4 per cent difference between them (Hibbs, 1977). This difference is consistent with their popular ideological stances.

One point neglected by political business cycle theorists is that American Presidential elections are federal rather than national in nature. It is possible for a candidate to win the national popular vote and lose the Electoral College vote (Archer and Taylor, 1981). This happened in 1826, 1876 and 1888, and perhaps again in 1960. The significance of the federal character of Presidential elections for various vote-buying formulations is not hard to reason out. Indeed, Tufte (1978, p. 4) seemed on the verge of doing so when observing that 'incumbents may seek to determine the *location* and the *timing* of economic benefits in promoting the fortunes of their party and friends'. Unfortunately, he did not follow up on this observation. While geographical targeting of fiscal impacts would seem to be as electorally-significant as temporal targeting, there has been little empirical research in this area. Most has involved legislative elites. In Reid's (1980, p. 37) words:

> Only a few studies, and these recent ones, have dealt with the causes of federal fund distribution. For the most part these studies have sought causal explanations within Congressional process. This research has rested on several common assumptions about power within Congress: that it tends to be exercised by policy subsystems which are centred in committees and subcommittees; that party leadership and seniority are important sources of power; and that Congressmen who are in a position to do so will use their power to derive constituency benefits from federal spending.

Despite the novelty of the issue, several recent reviews have been presented by political scientists (Arnold, 1979; Rundquist, 1980) and geographers (Johnston, 1979, 1980; Bennett, 1980). A common, though not universal, finding is that those variables often presumed to be salient, particularly seniority and committee position, seem but weakly related to geographical variations in governmental outlays. For example, after one of the most thorough investigations to date, Johnston (1980, p. 82) concluded that 'there is no unequivocal evidence that members of the various Congressional Committees and Sub-Committees are able to bias the allocation of federal funds towards their home states'. Similarly, Ray's (1980, p. 22) analysis of annual per cent changes by state in federal outlays for five federal departments, one independent agency and one branch of the Executive office of the President between 1969 and 1976 in relation to a variety of Congressional influence variables, yielded R^2s below 0.10 in six cases and below 0.20 in the remaining instance. In his words (Ray, 1980, p. 28): 'It appears that institutional position on the Hill makes little difference in determining the geographical distribution of federal spending. The powerful, on the average, get neither more or less than less well-placed legislators'.

It is plausible that Presidential influence simply outweighs Congressional influence upon the geographical allocation of federal funds. As Fisher recently noted in his examination of Presidential Spending Power (1975, p. 3):

Billions of dollars are impounded, transferred, reprogramed, or shifted one way or another by the President and his assistants. Billions more are used in confidential and covert ways, without the knowledge of Congress and the Public. In many cases the decisive commitment to spend funds is made not by Congress but by executive officials.

This pattern may have been even more pronounced prior to the current era. For example, when the Emergency Relief Appropriation Act of 1935 was debated in Congress, Senator Arthur Vandenberg suggested a substitute bill consisting of two brief sections (Fisher, 1975, pp. 62-63): 'Section 1. Congress hereby appropriates $4,880,000 to the President of the United States to use as he pleases. Section 2. Anybody who does not like it is fined $1,000'. Although Senator Vandenberg's substitute bill failed to receive Congressional authorisation, there is evidence that President Roosevelt's power over the geographical allocation of federal spending was substantial during the New Deal. A recent regression analysis attempting to 'predict' the state-by-state distribution of *per capita* aggregate spending between 1933 and 1940 from 'needs' variables such as the number of cases on general relief accounted for less than 20 per cent of the statistical variance; in contrast, a political model involving electoral votes, the variability of election results over the years 1896 to 1932, and the closeness of the Presidential vote in 1932 explained almost 80 per cent of the variation in *per capita* federal outlays among states (Wright, 1974, p. 33).

Studies of relationships between geographical spending patterns and Presidential electoral considerations for more recent times have produced less spectacular results. Johnston (1977a), for example, looked at selected departmental and grant-in-aid outlays for the early 1970s to find that whether Nixon had won a state in 1968 or a state's Electoral College marginality (defined as the proportion of all Electoral College votes held by a state divided by the vote difference between Humphrey and Nixon) had little explanatory power regarding the geography of federal spending. However, another study by the same author focusing on outlays during the Great Society period of the mid-1960s indicated that 'Total expenditure is very clearly related positively with a state's marginality in the Electoral College' (Johnston, 1977b, p. 323). Yet other research by Johnston (1979, p. 120) suggests that Nixon was able to direct 1970-1972 Defence Department spending towards states which he had won in 1968.

Conceptualising the Analysis

'In this entire area of budget execution', according to Fisher (1975, p. 3), 'our knowledge is sketchy and primitive'. However, as the foregoing literature review demonstrates, there is no paucity of suggestive ideas. For example, it is widely held in Congress and the nation 'that the President has achieved dominance in budgetary decision making' (Ippolito, 1978, p. 48). Normally, the President sets the agenda on spending matters through the executive Office of Management and Budget (Wildavsky, 1974). The Congressional role is then one of 'advise and consent'. Since the annual budget is essentially a political document, it is also a widely held view

> that an incumbent administration while operating within political and economic constraints and limited only by the usual uncertainties in successful economic policy, may manipulate the short-run course of the national economy in order to improve its party's standing in upcoming elections and repay political debts' (Tufte, 1978, pp.3-4).

As previously mentioned, most geographers and regional economists have treated geographical variations in government spending as exogenously determined while most political scientists and economists interested in the politics of spending at the national level have shown rather meagre concern for geographical variations within the country. Thus, although the political business cycle literature has expanded considerably in the last decade, it scarcely acknowledges that regional variations underlie national macroeconomic trends as well as national election series. Campaign strategists and political geographers, therefore, may be aware of something which business cycle theorists choose to ignore: a popular vote in Vermont is not equivalent to a popular vote in California in the contest for the Presidency. Consequently, efforts to manipulate the short-run course of the economy for electoral gain are as apt to be aimed at geographical as at temporal targets. Put tersely, 'Presidents should direct money to states which support them and to others which could easily be won' (Johnston, 1979, p. 119).

This study looks to federal spending and Presidential election data selected from the 1968 to 1980 period for evidence regarding this premise which essentially says that the causal link of concern is from electoral considerations as independent variables to spending allocations as dependent variables. The basic hypothesis is that White House incumbents will direct federal outlays toward states which have traditionally supported their party as a reward to the faithful and as a bribe for them to remain so, toward states which have been electorally competitive as an enducement to gain their allegiance, and away from bastions of the opposition where the costs of vote-buying may be too high. Such targeting is likely, given Tufte's evidence for the US political business cycle just prior to an election. However, such targeting may be more politically feasible, given Paldam's evidence on the political business cycles of various countries, in the wake of a national contest in which a newly-elected President enters office in an atmosphere of victory and with claim to a popular mandate.

This basic hypothesis can be operationalised via linear regression models positing federal outlays by state as a function of the average proportion of a state's popular vote for the President's party in the last election and the coefficient of variation of the Presidential party's popular vote share during the past five elections. Including both the average level of support for the President's party and the coefficient of variation in support for the President's party in a single equation would be unwise; the latter involves the former in its computation and the impact would be vexing multicollinearity. These formulations involve two close, but alternative variations on the same basic premise: (a) spending will be allocated in response to prior average support for the President's party; and (b) spending will be allocated in response to the President's performance in the last election, but with an eye to electoral variability over the past as well.

Two other sources of causal influence viewed as germane are: (1) a state's importance in the Electoral College tally and (2) a state's regional setting. The most populous states have several times the potential Electoral College pay-off of the smallest states. In 1980, for example, California boasted 45 electoral votes while Wyoming held but three. Analytically, a marginal popular vote bought in California is worth more than a marginal popular vote bought in Wyoming (Brams, 1978). Research demonstrates that this is recognised in actual campaign strategies (Wayne, 1980; Archer, 1982). The analysis, therefore, includes the percentage of the total electoral vote held by each state as an independent variable (see also Johnston, 1980).

Regional setting is deemed relevant for two reasons. First, there is strong evidence that regional cleavages are an important characteristic of American Presidential politics. Campaign strategists often seem to couch their electoral priorities in terms of regions rather than in terms of individual states (Archer and Taylor, 1981; Wayne, 1980). Second, regional divisions correspond with differences in the spatial division of labour, thus the meaning of 'political benefit' is not independent of location. For analytical purposes, the country was divided into three regions: the Northeast or traditional American Manufacturing Belt, the West beyond the 100° meridian, and the South below the Mason-Dixon Line. Previous study has shown this partition to correspond with a long-standing political sectionalisation of the United States (Archer and Taylor, 1981) which is still evident (Archer, 1982). Binary dummy variables are used to specify Southern or Western regional settings. A dummy variable for the Northeast is not included in order to avoid multicollinearity.

It needs to be kept in mind that some of the independent variables (Table 3.1) pertain to Democratic Presidential candidates when a Democrat occupies the White House and to Republic

Table 3.1: Variables Included in the Analysis

Independent Variables:

$\bar{V}$ = average % of the popular vote for the party of the incumbent in the previous five Presidential elections

V = % of the popular vote for the incumbent President's party in the preceding Presidential election

CV = coefficient of variation of the % of the popular vote for the incumbent President's party in the five preceding Presidential elections

EV = % of national electoral vote held by a state

S = 1 if a Southern state, 0 otherwise

W = 1 if a Western state, 0 otherwise

Dependent Variables:

$F\$$ = federal outlays in the form of either:

$\%FY1 - FY2$ = % change (positive or negative) in federal outlays allocated to a state from one fiscal year to the next

$PCFY$ = per capita federal outlays allocated to a state during a fiscal year

---

Presidential candidates when a Republican occupies the White House. Since total popular votes, including those cast for minor party candidates, were used to compute election proportions for each campaign, Republican and Democratic values are not exact complements. The independent variables are regarded as measures of the attractiveness of states as targets for vote-buying activity by the Presidentially incumbent party. The posited models do not, therefore, seek to account for all geographical variation in federal spending, but only for that variation which arises as result of re-election motivated expenditure targeting.

In all, the geographical expenditure patterns of six departments and the federal government as a whole are treated as dependent outcomes. Payments of interest on the national debt are excluded. Except for this, no effort was made to differentiate 'controllable' from 'uncontrollable' expenditures. At any moment this distinction may be meaningful since the latter are mandated by existing law (e.g. Social Security) or ongoing contractual obligation (e.g. Defence procurement contracts). In the long run, however, the distinction becomes a gradation since contracts expire and statutes are subject to amendment or repeal (Gist, 1977). While some studies of political influence have looked at 'controllable' expenditures only (Ray, 1980), others have found that 'uncontrollable' expenditures are equally responsive to apparent political considerations (Johnston, 1978b). If, as Tufte (1978, p. 57) argues, 'incumbents prefer increases in transfer payments, not only because they more surely improve voters' economic well- being at the right time, but also because many types of transfer payments go to particular organised interests', then grants and transfers ordinarily classed as uncontrollable will be as much the focus of political manipulation as expenditures ordinarily classed as controllable.

The six departments whose outlays are investigated were chosen because of their variation in size, function, clientele group, associated bureaucracy and public visibility. Together, their outlays comprised an almost constant three-quarters of the federal budget during the period of study (Table 3.2). In Fiscal Year (FY) 1969 the proportion was 73.8 per cent while in Fiscal Year 1980 it was 74.9 per cent. However, the six departments experienced quite different success in maintaining their budgetary bases. Those representing a higher proportion of total federal outlays, excluding interest on the national debt, in 1980 than in 1969 were: Health, Education and Welfare (HEW), or Health and Human Services combined with Education after FY 1978, reflecting expansion in income security programmes; Labor, reflecting expansion in job training; and Treasury, reflecting the initiation of Revenue Sharing in the early 1970s. Those representing a lower fraction of the federal budget in 1980 than in 1969 were: Defense, reflecting the conclusion of the Vietnam conflict; Agriculture, reflecting retrenchment in commodity support levels; and Housing and Urban Development (HUD), reflecting a shift from categorical grant programmes towards Revenue Sharing during Nixon's tenure.

Expenditures by state are available from the Community Service Administration's annual *Federal Outlays in Summary* for all fiscal years between 1967 and 1980 (Community Services Administration, various years). However, this analysis focused upon outlays in Fiscal Years bracketing the Presidential elections of 1972, 1976 and 1980 to allow examination of shifts in patterns between the first and second, and the third and fourth years of executive incumbency (Table 3.1).

It is often overlooked that federal Fiscal Years do not correspond with calendar years. Further complicating matters, the Congressional Budget and Impoundment Control Act of 1974 caused the federal Fiscal Year to shift from a July 1 to June 30

Table 3.2: *Per Capita* Federal Outlays and Proportion of Federal Budget, Selected Departments, Fiscal Years 1969, 1973, 1977 and 1980 (Current Dollars)

	Fiscal Year							
	1969		1973		1977		1980	
Department	$	%	$	%	$	%	$	%
Agriculture	68.07	7.4	77.42	6.7	91.94	5.0	123.44	5.3
Defense	312.72	33.9	311.98	26.8	421.94	23.1	561.2	24.0
HEW[a]	231.67	25.1	400.35	34.4	682.73	37.3	910.59	39.0
HUD	52.41	5.7	12.30	1.1	19.50	1.1	35.33	1.5
Labor	9.82	1.1	21.30	1.8	63.96	3.5	67.15	2.9
Treasury[b]	5.68	0.6	42.43	3.6	54.92	3.0	51.12	2.3
Included Departments	680.37	73.8	865.78	74.4	1334.99	73.0	1748.92	74.9
Total[b]	922.25	100.0	1162.85	100.0	1828.36	100.0	2334.11	100.0

Notes:

a. Department of Health and Human Services combined with Department of Education after FY 1978

b. Interest on national debt excluded

interval to an October 1 to September 3 interval so that spending values before and after the Transition Quarter of FY 1976 to FY 1977 are not strictly comparable. The elections of 1972 and 1977 occurred during FY 1973 and FY 1977 so that state-to-state variations in *per capita* outlays for these years are examined (PCFY). Data for FY 1981, when the 1980 election was held, were not available when the analysis was undertaken; FY 1980 figures are used instead. Per cent changes in outlays by state from FY 1969 to FY 1970, FY 1973 to FY 1974, and FY 1977 to FY 1978 are examined in order to ascertain whether spending shifts right at the start of an administration reward electoral support. Per cent changes in outlays by state from FY 1972 to FY 1973, FY 1976 to FY 1977, and FY 1979 to FY 1980 are also examined in order to capture electorally motivated shifts just prior to an election (%FY1-FY2). The former pattern was posited by Tufte while the latter was observed by Paldam at national levels of analysis.

Consideration was given to nonlinear functions which might capture an increasing and then decreasing relationship between voting and spending. Realistically, however, contrasting Presidential landslides of 1964 and 1972 suggest that entirely safe states are empirically rare. And, research on Congressional links to spending imply that real politicians infrequently behave as though they place strong credence in the theory of minimum winning coalitions (Rundquist, 1980). For these reasons, and to keep the analysis as simple as possible, linear models are employed.

Results of the Analysis

One hundred and twenty-six multiple regression analyses were conducted for different time periods and different sets of independent variables. These break down into separate analyses for each of the six departments and total federal outlays, for two independent variable combinations and for second and fourth year spending changes and fourth year *per capita* spending levels by state. The two models used are (see Table 3.1 for definitions):

$$F\$ = B_1 \hat{V} + B_2 EV + B_3 S + B_4 W + e \qquad (1)$$
and
$$F\$ = B_1 V + B_2 CV + B_4 S + B_5 W + e \qquad (2)$$

The dependent variable, F$, is a spending variate, either per cent change in outlays from one to the next fiscal year, or *per capita* outlays in a given year. The error term, e, is presumed to capture variance owing to non-political sources such as local 'needs'. The models do not require an intercept since regression coefficients were transformed to standardised form. Standardised partial regression coefficients, or Beta-Weights, permit direct comparisons between independent variables in terms of their relative importance in accounting for the statistical variation of the dependent variable. Thus a standarised coefficient of 0.5 means a one-half standard deviation change in the dependent variable for each standard deviation change in an independent variable. Since the dependent variables change in magnitude over time, in part owing to changes in price levels, and because the independent variables are measured on a variety of scales, ordinary partial regression coefficients would be less easily interpretable.

Numerical results are presented in Table 3.3. Each section (I to VIII) of the table corresponds to one of the departments chosen for examination or to total outlays at various times. The first six columns of each table contain standardised regression coefficients; the last shows the R^2 or total variance explained by an equation. To avoid cluttering the tables, cells corresponding to variables omitted from a particular equation are left blank. Coefficients which are 'significantly different' from zero at 0.05 are in bold type and those at 0.10 are italicised to draw attention. Although these standards, and particularly the latter, are less stringent than is conventional, the equations are based upon the entire population of the fifty American states. Coefficients, therefore, can be viewed as parametric values for this level of areal aggregation (Johnston, 1978a).

The analysis deals both with static, *per capita*, variations at the time of an election and dynamic, per cent change variations just after and just before an election. Regarding the latter, if the aim were to account for a large proportion of year-to-year variations in changes of federal spending by state, it would not be possible to regard the effort as very successful. On average, the 84 equations pertaining to annual percentage changes in federal outlays by state explain only 13.7 per cent of the total variance. (A value of about 17.5 per cent would correspond to a 0.10 significance level.) The average R^2 of 0.132 for the second year increment equations is slightly below that of 0.142 for the fourth year increment equations.

Table 3.3: Standardised Partial Regression Analysis (Independent Variable = B)

Dependent Variable	$\bar{V}$	V	CV	EV	S	W	R^2
			I. TOTAL FEDERAL SPENDING (excluding interest)				
A. Second Year Increment							
%69-70	0.081			-0.182	0.226	**0.343**	0.175
%69-70		0.009	0.027	-0.177	0.208	0.348	0.170
%73-74	-0.230			-0.049	0.141	-0.246	0.187
%73-74		-0.117	0.267	-0.057	0.153	-0.245	0.203
%77-78	-0.225			-0.078	0.034	0.056	0.078
%77-78		-0.067	0.269	-0.041	0.025	0.114	0.092
B. Fourth Year Increment							
%72-73	0.030			0.048	-0.201	-0.806	0.040
%72-73		0.079	0.023	0.052	-0.171	-0.109	0.041
%76-77	**0.470**			-0.024	-0.187	0.160	**0.367**
%76-77		-0.061	**0.622**	-0.165	0.035	0.195	**0.492**
%79-80	-0.030			0.095	-0.101	-0.274	0.079
%79-80		0.176	0.294	0.137	-0.329	-0.187	0.140
C. Fourth Year Per Capita							
PC73	**-0.443**			-0.059	-0.076	**0.634**	**0.530**
PC73		**0.390**	**0.615**	0.039	0.191	**0.452**	**0.579**
PC77	**-0.387**			-0.062	0.049	**0.612**	**0.412**
PC77		-0.253	**0.358**	-0.025	0.137	**0.611**	**0.407**
PC80	0.282			-0.089	0.185	**0.471**	**0.184**
PC80		-0.043	0.089	-0.038	-0.042	0.382	0.142

II. DEPARTMENT OF AGRICULTURE OUTLAYS

A. Second Year Increment

-0.143			-0.018	-0.006	*0.317*	0.106
	-0.254	-0.062	-0.029	-0.090	**0.385**	0.111
-0.413			-0.202	-0.065	-0.207	**0.242**
	-0.299	**0.332**	-0.177	0.065	-0.210	*0.214*
-0.317			-0.001	*-0.351*	0.054	0.152
	-0.187	0.150	-0.026	-0.188	0.097	0.126

Rows: %69-70, %69-70, %73-74, %73-74, %77-78, %77-78

B. Fourth Year Increment

-0.045			**0.423**	0.101	-0.186	**0.296**
	-0.187	-0.093	**0.407**	0.027	-0.129	**0.306**
0.162			-0.117	-0.089	**0.334**	**0.239**
	-0.096	-0.150	-0.167	0.024	**0.365**	**0.239**
-0.076			-0.005	-0.034	-0.272	0.063
	0.182	0.154	0.006	-0.143	-0.159	0.089

Rows: %72-73, %72-73, %76-77, %76-77, %79-80, %79-80

C. Fourth Year Per Capita

0.302			-0.116	0.210	**0.394**	**0.272**
	0.115	-0.128	-0.135	0.196	**0.392**	**0.226**
0.142			-0.160	0.102	**0.463**	**0.303**
	-0.175	-0.167	-0.226	0.279	**0.501**	**0.325**
-0.185			-0.190	-0.017	**0.418**	**0.336**
	0.103	-0.085	*-0.237*	0.125	**0.548**	**0.326**

Rows: PC73, PC73, PC77, PC77, PC80, PC80

III. DEPARTMENT OF DEFENSE OUTLAYS

A. Second Year Increment

0.046			-0.117	0.167	*0.287*	0.125
	-0.041	0.018	-0.113	0.109	*0.374*	0.108
-0.074			-0.130	0.078	-0.092	0.038
	-0.073	0.209	-0.102	0.072	-0.071	0.072
-0.343			-0.029	-0.204	-0.152	0.075
	-0.388	0.220	-0.008	-0.005	-0.191	0.119

Rows: %69-70, %69-70, %73-74, %73-74, %77-78, %77-78

	$\bar{V}$	V	CV	EV	S	W	R^2
B. Fourth Year Increment							
%72-73	0.012			-0.140	-0.062	0.066	0.038
%72-73		0.118	0.010	-0.138	-0.008	0.029	0.44
576-77	0.111			0.172	-0.030	-0.115	0.054
%76-77		-0.117	**-0.328**	0.089	0.152	-0.113	0.143
%79-80	0.071			0.015	0.041	-0.260	0.090
%79-80		0.141	-0.007	0.015	-0.045	-0.225	0.098
C. Fourth Year Per Capita							
PC73	**-0.623**			0.017	0.001	**0.515**	**0.516**
PC73		**0.475**	**0.820**	0.148	**0.343**	**0.283**	**0.575**
PC77	**-0.446**			0.009	0.177	**0.446**	**0.283**
PC77		-0.060	0.485	0.103	0.085	0.418	**0.297**
PC80	0.296			-0.043	0.274	0.326	0.086
PC80		-0.139	0.080	0.012	0.075	0.133	0.049
IV. DEPARTMENT OF HEALTH, EDUCATION AND WELFARE[a]							
A. Second Year Increment							
%69-70	0.026			0.102	**0.420**	0.165	0.144
%69-70		**-0.627**	-0.288	0.053	0.126	*0.373*	**0.265**
%73-74	0.006			-0.130	-0.100	-0.283	0.063
%73-74		-0.022	0.117	-0.113	-0.118	-0.263	0.075
%77-78	-0.069			-0.083	0.204	0.255	0.106
%77-78		-0.089	-0.034	-0.092	0.299	0.244	0.108
B. Fourth Year Increment							
%72-73	0.149			-0.122	0.004	0.219	0.113
%72-73		0.125	-0.070	-0.132	0.031	0.196	0.114
%76-77	**0.405**			0.255	0.203	0.013	**0.233**
%76-77		0.296	**-0.366**	0.224	0.085	0.010	**0.230**
%79-80	-0.121			0.068	0.066	0.326	0.149
%79-80		-0.223	-0.069	-0.084	0.259	0.276	0.169

C. Fourth Year Per Capita

	V̄	V	CV	EV	S	W	R²
PC73	0.111	0.013		0.047	**-0.318**	-0.099	0.117
PC73			-0.053	0.039	*-0.337*	-0.091	0.109
PC77	-0.026	-0.232		0.228	**-0.334**	**-0.530**	**0.363**
PC77			-0.006	0.188	-0.160	**-0.501**	**0.388**
PC80	0.195	**0.383**		0.134	*-0.289*	*-0.559*	**0.469**
PC80			0.018	0.160	**-0.547**	**-0.464**	**0.525**

V. DEPARTMENT OF HOUSING AND URBAN DEVELOPMENT

A. Second Year Increment

	V̄	V	CV	EV	S	W	R²
%69-70	-0.065	-0.150		-0.208	-0.031	*-0.318*	0.111
%69-70			0.039	-0.203	-0.090	-0.278	0.126
%73-74	0.007	0.174		-0.029	0.198	0.164	0.042
%73-74			-0.013	-0.001	0.073	0.137	0.056
%77-78	0.202	0.185		**0.394**	-0.056	-0.157	**0.305**
%77-78			-0.111	**0.388**	-0.172	-0.154	**0.307**

B. Fourth Year Increment

	V̄	V	CV	EV	S	W	R²
%72-73	0.027	-0.043		-0.022	0.001	0.039	0.113
%72-73			-0.067	-0.069	-0.072	0.110	0.026
%76-77	**-0.469**	0.065		-0.057	0.069	0.231	**0.225**
%76-77			**0.543**	0.001	-0.132	0.186	**0.273**
%79-80	*-0.321*	-0.271		0.186	0.014	0.131	0.135
%79-80			-0.033	0.157	0.323	0.143	0.113

C. Fourth Year Per Capita

	V̄	V	CV	EV	S	W	R²
PC73	-0.034	-0.130		-0.057	-0.117	0.005	0.017
PC73			-0.029	-0.062	-0.169	0.043	0.022
PC77	**-0.419**	*-0.369*		-0.081	0.120	-0.054	**0.216**
PC77			*0.254*	-0.081	0.324	-0.057	0.167
PC80	0.196	*0.300*		*0.241*	-0.016	-0.276	*0.295*
PC80			0.025	*0.260*	-0.297	-0.250	**0.302**

VI. DEPARTMENT OF LABOR OUTLAYS

	$\bar{V}$	V	CV	EV	S	W	R^2
A. Second Year Increment							
%69-70	-0.065			-0.208	-0.031	-0.318	0.111
%69-70		-0.150	0.039	-0.203	-0.090	-0.278	0.126
%73-74	0.157			-0.020	**0.489**	0.179	**0.221**
%73-74		0.308	-0.081	0.012	0.282	0.156	**0.248**
%77-78	0.016			-0.033	-0.363	-0.169	0.114
%77-78		-0.162	0.040	-0.016	-0.349	-0.253	0.129
B. Fourth Year Increment							
%72-73	-0.134			-0.222	0.089	0.038	0.080
%72-73		0.281	0.156	-0.196	0.250	-0.069	0.088
%76-77	0.001			0.043	0.093	-0.053	0.019
%76-77		-0.144	-0.075	0.006	0.222	-0.040	0.034
%79-80	*-0.318*			*0.167*	*-0.237*	**-0.420**	*0.173*
%79-80		-0.229	0.290	0.196	-0.149	**-0.398**	*0.191*
C. Fourth Year Per Capita							
PC73	**-0.538**			-0.099	**-0.384**	**-0.329**	**0.484**
PC73		0.054	**0.474**	-0.025	-0.248	0.247	**0.418**
PC77	**-0.550**			-0.045	-0.073	**0.406**	**0.390**
PC77		**-0.492**	**0.439**	-0.028	0.171	**0.416**	**0.376**
PC80	0.097			0.038	-0.167	0.003	0.055
PC80		*-0.037*	*0.324*	*0.110*	**-0.430**	-0.064	0.109

VII. DEPARTMENT OF TREASURY OUTLAYS

	$\bar{V}$	V	CV	EV	S	W	R^2
A. Second Year Increment							
%69-70	-0.051			0.063	0.117	0.221	0.039
%69-70		0.025	-0.052	0.054	0.142	0.209	0.041
%73-74	-0.159			0.146	0.097	0.229	0.063
%73-74		0.119	0.161	0.202	-0.036	0.196	0.069
%77-78	0.136			-0.050	0.306	0.050	0.061
%77-78		**0.511**	0.223	-0.019	-0.089	0.225	*0.212*

B. Fourth Year Increment

%72-73	0.111	-0.264	-0.068	*-0.274*	**0.329**	-0.041	*0.174*
%72-73				*-0.285*	0.177	0.056	*0.188*
%76-77	-0.103	0.122	0.024	0.010	-0.187	-0.162	0.051
%76-77				0.040	-0.283	-0.200	0.049
%79-80	0.098	0.034	-0.148	-0.043	0.037	0.304	0.086
%79-80				-0.061	0.060	0.281	0.094

C. Fourth Year Per Capita

PC73	-0.072	-0.264	0.023	0.044	-0.100	0.122	0.031
PC73				0.046	-0.211	0.199	0.070
PC77	**-0.465**	-0.259	**0.486**	*0.216*	-0.225	0.025	**0.306**
PC77				**0.278**	-0.169	0.024	**0.330**
PC80	0.273	-0.015	0.016	0.092	-0.012	0.238	0.119
PC80				0.144	-0.252	0.111	0.081

Notes:
a. Combined Health and Human Services with Education after 1978

Italicised figures are significant at 0.10
Bold figures are significant at 0.05

Small as these averages are, they seem larger than might have been expected. The best predictor of federal spending in a state during one fiscal year is federal spending in that state during the previous fiscal year. Regressions of departmental outlays by state as a function of previous year departmental outlays by state generally yield R^2s of 0.90 or above and time-lagged auto-regressive coefficients are usually close to what would be expected from total annual budget shifts (Archer, 1979; Johnston, 1980). Hence after recognising the overwhelming influence of incremental change, there would seem, *a priori*, little systematic variance left to be accounted for. In addition, Ray's (1980) recent investigation of per cent changes in the 'controllable' federal recepts of Congressional districts between 1968 and 1976 for five departments (DOA, DOD, HEW, HUD, and Interior) and three agencies (Executive Office of the President, OEO and VA) as a function of a battery of Congressional influence and 'needs' variables yielded R^2s averaging 4 per cent. In the present case, not only is the average R^2 more than three times greater, but nearly one-third of the individual equations are statistically significant at 0.10 or above. None of Ray's equations seem to have been significant even at that level.

Why the difference? Among the possibilities are the following. First, the current analysis treats changes cross-sectionally and biannually while Ray pooled all cases into one grand 435 by 8 year or 3480 observation analysis. To the extent that expenditure changes are compensatory over time, this would have washed out explicable variance in the previous analysis. Second, Ray's battery of explanatory variables did not allow for regional cleavages. Of the 45 instances in which an independent variable is significant at 0.10 or above in a per cent change equation in the present analysis, it is a regional dummy in 20. This implies that year-to-year spending changes often impact states classed by regional setting in systematic rather than random fashion. Since Presidential election campaign organisations often address the electorate as a regionalised entity (Archer and Taylor, 1981; Archer, 1982; Wayne, 1980), federal expenditure targeting for electoral gain is also apt to be regional in strategy as well. Third, except for a variable on Congressional agreement with Presidential programme posture, Ray's measures of political influence pertained to the House of Representatives rather than to the White House, with its presumed discretionary influence following formal appropriations procedures.

Although the relationships between spending changes and the

independent variables assembled for this research are not very strong in an absolute sense, they warrant closer inspection. Looking first at changes in Department of Agriculture outlays, these are more often linked to the chosen independent variables than are changes in any of the other departmental outlays on a state-by-state basis. Furthermore, fourth year spending shifts show significant R^2s in all four of the Republican fourth year increment equations, though for apparently different reasons. Also, the 1973-1974 equations show a move away from Republican voting states toward more competitive states. Each of these patterns is significant. During the second Nixon administration an effort was made to reduce the expense of agricultural programmes. Much to the chagrin of agrarian areas which had given Nixon overwhelming support, Department of Agriculture outlays were cut back by 21 per cent just after the 1972 election. One wonders whether this would have occurred in the absence of the Twenty-Second Constitutional Amendment limiting Presidents to two elective terms in office. The fourth year, 1976-1977, westward shift in agricultural outlays can thus be interpreted as an effort by Ford, Nixon's unelected successor, to mollify agrarian displeasure in anticipation of the upcoming 1976 election. Here we see strong evidence for an electoral cycle in the geographical spending pattern. None of the Carter term equations, however, maintain this appearance.

That none of the increment equations is significant in the case of the Department of Defense comes as a bit of a surprise given the amount of attention generally levelled at this sector of the budget. However, several *per capita* Defense equations are significant as will be noted below. A possible reason for the geographically unpatterned character of per cent changes in Defense Department outlays is that much Defense spending represents relatively long-term commitments. As Ray (1980, p.6) relevantly noted, 'it would be unreasonable to expect that, overnight, the Charleston Polaris submarine base would become the New Orleans submarine base'. The result is that Defense outlays are strongly incremental in geographical pattern and there is little systematic variance in the pattern of changes to explain (Archer, 1979, p. 10).

Only one of the HEW second year equations is significant as a whole (1969-1970), and with the wrong sign (-) on the voting variable. However, shifts toward the West and South can be noted for this period so that the Nixon administration's tilt in these directions is, nonetheless, discernible. Despite Tufte's emphasis on manipulation of Social Security benefits leading up to the 1972 election (Tufte, 1978, pp. 29-36), Nixon fourth year increment equations are not significant. But both of those associated with Ford's re-election bid (1976-1977) are; in this instance, a state's prior history of Republican support is associated with a greater than average rate of increase in HEW outlays.

Changes in HUD outlays present an interesting case. The 1976-1977 equations show a shft toward more competitive states late in the Ford administration: a standard deviation increase in election variability corresponds with an increase in HUD outlays more than a half standard deviation above the norm. Then, early in Carter's administration the analysis shows a shift toward larger states (1977-1978). The overall volatility of the HUD budget, however, is somewhat disguised by this analysis. Total HUD outlays dropped by 81 per cent from 1969 to 1970, squirted upward by 66 per cent from 1971 to 1972, dropped by 56 per cent from 1972 to 1974, leapt upward by 118 per cent from 1974 to 1975, and then moved up by more than 50 per cent between 1976 and 1977, and between 1978 and 1979. At the national scale, this pattern is consistent with a strong election cycle and offers evidence that a department's base is not always secure in the face of variable political winds. Against this background, positive signs associating 1973-1974 state-by-state shifts with Republican voting, although too small to be statistically significant, gain interpretive relevance: by implication the more Democratic states did worse than the more Republican states in that era's HUD retrenchment so that there is also suggestive, though not conclusive, evidence for a geographical election cycle here too.

Department of Labor outlays, while not as volatile as HUD's, also show considerable overall movement, with, for example, an 80 per cent sprint in 1974-1975 and a 20 per cent drop in 1977-1978. Again, despite an overall 14 per cent drop from 1973 to 1974, the signs for Republican voting in the corresponding second year increment equations while insignificant are also positive. Labor fourth year increment equations are significant only for 1979-1980, mainly capturing a systematic shift away from the West where Carter was expecting to do poorly (Archer, 1982).

Although Treasury outlays, excluding interest, took a huge 372 per cent jump in 1972-1973, at the time the Revenue Sharing Program was introduced, this department's biannual changes seem to have been mainly incremental, providing little geographical variance to explain. Hence, most of the per cent change equations for this department's outlays account for less than 10 per cent of the variance.

Examining per cent change equations for total federal outlays (minus interest) it can be noted that nearly half of them are statistically significant; indeed, the R^2s reach as high as 49.2 per cent. However, there are some surprises. From fiscal years 1976 to 1977 total outlays increased by over 19 per cent, more than between any other pair of years under investigation. A large chunk of this increase was directed toward historically more Republican states, in preparation for the 1976 election. Competitive states did significantly less well, though multicollinearity problems with V and CV make it impossible to say which of these was the stronger pattern. Explaining exactly why the total increment equations are so strong for 1976-1977 and so weak in the other cases is problematic, but this pattern is also seen in results for individual departments. Eight of the 1976-1977 increment equations are significant while the same is true of only four of the 1972-1973 and two of the 1979-1980 equations.

Turning to the analysis of election variations in *per capita* outlays among states, several issues stand out. For one, the strength of relationships with the independent variables is generally considered higher than is the case for per cent changes in outlays. On the average, 27.6 per cent of interstate variance is accounted for by the included independent variables which depict the attractiveness of states as targets for Presidential vote-buying in terms of their prior election returns and regional settings. Perhaps the most consistently powerful relationship involves the regional partition of the country employed in the analysis. *per capita* spending is shown to be significantly higher in the West by each of the fourth year total federal spending equations. However, there was an erosion of this pattern from 1972 to 1980 suggesting interregional convergence, a trend noted elsewhere in the literature (Haveman, Pierce and Stanfield, 1977). By a different interpretation the Carter administration had few faithful to reward west of the $100°$ meridian. Western *per capita* outlays are also significantly higher for the Departments of Agriculture and Defense, with the difference increasing for the former and decreasing for the latter over time. In contrast, outlays are significantly lower in the South and West for HEW. Interregional variations are considerably less pronounced for the other departments.

In most instances, a state's electoral vote is not tied to its *per capita* federal spending level. None of the electoral vote coefficients are significant for total spending; this is also true of Defense and Labor outlays. There are a couple of significant electoral vote coefficients for the Department of Agriculture; not surprisingly these are negative in view of the rural orientation of this department's progress. However, the most meaningful electoral vote coefficients are probably those found in the HUD equations. For 1973 and 1977 these coefficients are mildly negative, but rather strongly positive for 1980. This may reflect Carter's national urban policy and the success of the Northeast-Midwest Congressional Caucus in altering some of HUD's assistance formulae late in the 1970s. This interpretation is also consistent with the significantly positive sign associated with the 1976 Democratic vote in one of the 1980 equations.

Perhaps the most interesting finding regarding the *per capita* spending equations is that the strength of associations between spending variations and popular voting patterns seem to have diminished, though some of the investigated departments reverse this overall trend. At the end of Nixon's first term and at the time of the Ford-Carter election, total federal spending favoured more electorally competitive states. This, in addition to the regional variations, made total *per capita* equations for 1973 and 1977 highly significant. Perhaps because Republicans have been a national minority, Republican administrations seek to secure election support from states with more volatile electoral histories. In 1980 when a Democrat was the Presidential incumbent, however, none of the election measures, including competitiveness, is found to be significant in the total expenditure equations.

Conclusions

The statistical analysis suggests that the power of a Presidential inicumbent to target federal spending in a manner designed to enhance his, or his party's election prospects diminished at the end of the 1970s. One plausible cause was reassertion of Congressional influence over the budget signalled by the 1974 Congressional Budget and Impoundment Control Act, several of whose provisions did not become effective until after the 1976 election. Among other things, this Act created the Congressional Budget Office and was intended to make Congress 'a more effective partner in Government'. Congressmen viewed the Act as 'one of the most monumental reassertions of Congressional prerogatives' and 'the most significant reform of the 20th century' (Ippolito, 1981, p. 22). Whether these aspirations were in fact achieved is still being debated. In the words of one recent asssessment (Huddleston, 1980, pp.85-86):

> ... there is insufficient evidence to conclude that the 1974 Congressional Budget Reform has fundamentally changed the appropriations process ... Basic pre-reform appropriations patterns have been carried over into the post-reform period. Presidential budget requests appear still to provide the major cues for Congressional action.

Still, according to the present analysis, something did change: what were strong relationships between *per capita* federal spending by state and Presidential election variates during the earlier part of the period of study vanished by the 1980 Presidential election. This disappearance occurred for total federal spending exclusive of interest, for Department of Defence outlays which strongly favoured electorally competitive states in FY 1973 and FY 1977 but not in FY 1980, as well as, though to a lesser extent, the Department of Labor and Department of Treasury outlays. Exceptions to the trend are found for HEW outlays, though its expenditure pattern is more notable for expanding interregional than expanding voting-linked variance, and for HUD.

While Nixon and, to a surprisingly greater degree, Ford apparently had the political clout to enhance their re-election prospects by exerting influence over the geographical allocation of federal dollars, Carter, who won in 1976 on an essentially anti-Washington platform and who found his popular, Congressional, and bureaucratic support ebbing away, was apparently unable to repeat the performances of his predecessors. This is not to say that Carter failed to try. As we noted previously, several of those who followed Carter's incumbent campaign saw Santa Claus-like quality in his proposals to assist residents of the Love Canal area in New York and in his executive order to turn over federal land to the city of Chicago, whose Mayor Byrne supported Kennedy during the primary season.

Without more cross-temporal analysis, perhaps at a finer scale of expenditure categorisation, it is not possible to draw firm conclusions about the ability of a President to geographically target federal spending to enhance his or his party's election prospects. Still, in light of the geographically incremental character of changes in federal outlays from year to year it is surprising that any statistically significant trends at all are discernible in the empirical record. Furthermore, while Congressional influence and Presidential influence variates were not directly compared in this research, there is enough to suggest that the latter deserve more attention than they have received in the literature. In addition, inter-regional spending variations should not be overlooked in future research since the current study yields evidence of political manipulation at this geographical scale. Put simply, regional setting seems important in the geography of federal spending as it is in the geography of voting. Finally, if the results of other investigations of the spatial patterns of federal spending at the time of the New Deal (Wright, 1974; Reading 1973), and during the New Frontier (Johnston, 1977b) are assembled with those presented here for the elections of 1972, 1976 and 1980, there seems to be an emergent trend: the more recent the date, the looser the link between the geography of Presidential politics and the geography of federal spending. Whether this trend will continue and whether we should look to personality-based or to institution-based explanations deserve further inquiry. Since the loosest associations found were those leading up to the contest of 1980, an academic re-examination of patterns after the 1984 election may prove most enlightening; provided, of course, that academic funding isn't all gone by then.

References

Archer, J. (1979) 'Incrementalism and Federal Outlays Among States', *Geographical Perspectives*, **44**, 5-14

Archer, J. (1980) 'Congressional-incumbent Reelection Success and Federal-outlays Distribution: A Test of the Electoral-Connection Hypothesis', *Environment and Planning A*, **12**, 263-277

Archer, J. (1982) 'Some Geographical Aspects of the American Presidential Election of 1980', *Political Geography Quarterly*, **1**, 123-135

Archer, J.and P. Taylor (1981) *Section and Party: A Political Geography of American Presidential Elections*, Wiley, Chichester

Arnold, R. (1979) *Congress and the Bureaucracy: A Theory of Influence*, Yale University Press, New Haven

Bennett, R.J. (1980) *The Geography of Public Finance, Methuen, London*

Bloom, H. S., and H. D. Price (1975) 'Voter Response to Short Run Economic Conditions: An Assymetric Effect of Prosperity and Recession', *American Political Science Review*, **69**, 1240-1254

Bozeman, B. (1977) 'The Effect of Economic and Partisan Change on Federal Appropriations', *Western Political Quarterly*, **30**, 112-124

Brams, S.J. (1978) *The Presidential Election Game*, Yale University Press, New Haven

Community Services Administration (1968 to 1981) *Federal Outlays in Summary*, US Government Printing Office, Washington, DC

Davis, O., M.A.H. Dempster, and A. Wildavsky (1974) 'Towards a Predictive Theory of Government Expenditure: US Domestic Appropriations', *British Journal of Political Science*, **4, 419-452**

Downs, A.(1957) *An Economic Theory of Democracy*, Harper and Row, New York

Fisher, L. (1975) *Presidential Spending Power*, Princeton University Press, Princeton, New Jersey

Gist, J.R. (1977) ' "Increment" and "Base" in the Congressional Appropriations Process', *American Journal of Political Science*, **21**, 341-352

Haveman, J., N.R. Pierce, and R.L. Stanfield (1977) 'A Year Later the Frostbelt Strikes Back', *National Journal*, **9**, 25, 1028-1037

Hibbs, D.A.(1977) 'Political Parties and Macroeconomic Policy', *American Political Science Review*, **71**, 1467-1487

Huddleston, M.W. (1980) 'Assessing the Congressional Budget Reform: The Impact on Appropriations', *Policy Studies Journal*, **9**, 81-86

Ippolito, D.S. (1978) *The Budget and National Politics*, Freeman, San Francisco

Ippolito, D.S. (1981) *Congressional Spending*, Cornell University Press, Ithaca, New York

Johnston, R.J. (1977a) 'Environment, Elections and Expenditure: Analysis of Where Governments Spend', *Regional Studies*, **11**, 383-394

Johnston, R.J. (1977b) 'The Geography of Federal Allocations in the United States: Preliminary Tests of Some Hypotheses for Political Geography', *Geoforum*, **8**, 319-326

Johnston, R.J. (1978a) *Multivariate Statistical Analysis in Geography*, Longman, London

Johnston, R.J. (1978b) 'Political Spending in the United States: Analysis of Political Influences on the Allocation of Federal Money to Local Environments', *Environment and Planning A*, **10**, 691-704

Johnston, R.J. (1979) *Political Electoral and Spatial Systems*, Oxford University Press, Oxford

Johnston, R. J. (1980) *The Geography of Federal Spending in the United States of America*, Wiley, Chichester

Kinder, D.R., and D.R. Kiewiet (1979) 'Economic Discontent and Political Behavior: The Role of Personal Grievances and Collective Economic Judgments in Congressional Voting', *American Journal of Political Science*, **23**, 495-527

Kramer, G.H. (1971) 'Short-Term Fluctuations in US Voting Behavior', *American Political Science Review*, **65**, 131-143

Lepper, S. (1974) 'Voting Behavior and Aggregate Policy Targets', *Public Choice*, **18**, 67-82

Mayhew,D.R.(1974) *Congress: The Electoral Connection*, Yale University Press, New Haven

Meltzer, A.H., and M. Vellrath (1975) 'The Effects of Economic Policies on Votes for the Presidency: Some Evidence from Recent Elections', *Journal of Law and Economics*, **18**, 781-798

Monroe, K.R. (1979) 'Econometric Analysis of Electoral Behavior: A Critical

Review', *Political Behavior*, **1**, 137-173

Moore, J.ed. (1981) *The Campaign for President: 1980 in Retrospect*, Ballinger, Cambridge, Massachusetts

Nixon, R. (1962) *Six Crises, Doubleday*, Garden City, New York

Nordhaus, W.D. (1975) 'The Political Business Cycle', *Review of Economic Studies*, **42**, 169-190

Paldam, M. (1981) 'An Essay on the Rationality of Economic Policy: The Test-case of Electoral Cycle', *Public Choice*, **37**, 287-305

Pennock, J.R. (1979) *Democratic Political Theory*, Princeton University Press, Princeton

Ray, B.A. (1980) 'Congressional Promotion of District Interests: Does Power on the Hill Really Make a Difference', in B.S. Rundquist,(ed.), *Political Benefits*, Lexington Books, Lexington, Massachusetts, 1-36

Reading, D.C. (1973) 'New Deal Activity and the States, 1933-1939', *Journal of Economic History*, **33**, 792-810

Reid, J. N. (1980) 'Politics, Program Administration, and the Distribution of Grants-in-Aid: A Theory and a Test', in B.S. Rundquist, (ed.), *Political Benefits*, Lexington Books, Lexington, Massachusetts, 37-60

Richardson, H.R. (1974) 'Empirical Aspects of Regional Growth in the United States', *Annals of Regional Science*, **8**, 8-23

Ritt, L. G. (1976) 'Committee Position, Seniority, and the Distribution of Government Expenditures', *Public Policy*, **24**, 463-489

Rundquist, B.S. (1980) 'On the Theory of the Political Benefits in American Public Programs', in B.S. Rundquist, (ed.), *Political Benefits*, Lexington Books, Lexington, Massachusetts, 227-254

Tufte, E.R. (1978) *Political Control of the Economy*, Princeton University Press, Princeton, New Jersey

Warner, E. (1980) 'The Jackpot States: Eight States will Decide an Election that Carter Now Leads', *Time*, **116**, 15, 12-16, 23

Wayne,S.J. (1980) *The Road to the White House*, St Martin's, New York

Wildavsky, A. (1974) *The Politics of the Budgetary Process*, 2nd ed., Little, Brown, Boston

Wright, G. (1974) 'The Political Economy of New Deal Spending: An Econometric Analysis', *Review of Economics and Statistics*, **51**, 30-38

4

The Public Choice Perspective in Contemporary Political Geography

Fred M. Shelley

Introduction

The analysis of conflicts is central to political geography. Political geographers have studied many conflict resolution processes — wars, insurrections, social movements, and legislative, executive, and judicial activities. In contemporary societies, social choice institutions are of particular importance to the management and resolution of conflicts. Social choice institutions are legitimated procedures through which individual and group preferences are aggregated into decisions affecting an entire collectivity. These institutions take many forms and can be found at all spatial scales. They include world-wide organisations such as the United Nations and the International Court of Justice; national, state, and local governments; and organisations such as neighbourhood tenants' unions, suburban homeowners' associations, and farmers' cooperatives.

Continued emphasis on locational conflicts and institutions has led political geographers to analyse them from a variety of theoretical and methodological perspectives. The public choice approach, which focuses on rational behaviour in non-market decision contexts, is one such perspective. The public choice approach examines the implications of rational economic behaviour for the design, implementation, and operation of social choice institutions. The purpose of this paper is to describe and evaluate the application of the public choice perspective in contemporary political geography. A brief review of the public choice literature is followed by a more detailed survey of its recent applications to problems of interest in contemporary political geography. Finally, the validity and applicability of the approach to political geography is evaluated.

Public Choice Theory and Social Choice Institutions

Public choice theory has developed in response to recognition that public sector decision processes are not directly analogous to private market behaviour. In the private sector, individual utilities are enhanced following voluntary exchange. However, public sector conflicts are seldom resolved through voluntary exchange; conflict-specific external effects preclude unanimous utility enhancement through decentralised exchange processes. Public choice theory examines the performance of various social choice institutions intended to resolve conflicts that cannot be settled through mutually beneficial exchange.

The economics of public goods has contributed to the development of public choice theory. Economic theory has indicated the failure of decentralised market economies to provide public goods adequately (Head, 1974). Public goods are defined by their consumption characteristics of jointness and non-exclusion; individuals cannot be excluded from public goods once they have been provided (Samuelson, 1954, 1955). The logic of collective action (Olson, 1965) provides a rationale for market failure. Individuals confronted with decisions concerning the extent to which they will contribute to the provision of public goods will recognise that their consumption cannot be affected by the extent of their individual contributions. Aware that their contributions do not affect individual consumption, rational persons will withhold their contributions to the provision of public goods. Instead, each attempts to become a 'free rider', consuming public goods provided through the contributions of others. However, when all members of a collectivity withhold their contributions simultaneously, public good provision cannot be effected at levels consistent with demands. The optimal provision of public goods is consequently impossible; collective activity is needed in order that public goods be provided adequately. Recognising market failure and the external effects associated with decentralised markets, public choice theorists have investigated the properties of various institutions intended to ensure the provision of public goods.

Many different social choice procedures have been investigated from the public choice perspective. Voting processes are among the most important institutions. The analysis of majority voting and its properties was spurred by Arrow's (1951) recognition that equilibrium outcomes of majority voting processes could not be expected under general conditions. Arrow's work initiated a related body of literature, known as social choice theory, which is concerned with the analysis of optimal procedures for aggregating individual preferences into social welfare functions (this literature is reviewed by Plott (1976) and Sen (1977)). Public choice theory, in contrast, is more concerned with the analysis of *actual* social choice institutions.

Public choice analysis of majority voting has emphasised the conditions necessary for the achievement of equilibrium outcomes. As Archer (1981) has pointed out, Hotelling's (1929) analysis of the locational impacts of competitive economic behaviour has been recognised as a major initial conribution to public choice theory as well as to location theory. Hotelling's work led to recognition that equilibrium could be achieved when individual voter preferences are single-peaked. That voter whose preferences are at the median of a unidimensional distribution of preferences would determine the outcome of a majority vote (Black, 1948). This led to the analysis of two-party competition in representative democracies, emphasising the efforts of competing political parties to maximise voter support (Downs, 1957). The 'spatial' analysis of voting has extended this analysis to more complex situations (Davis *et al.*, 1970; Hinich *et al.*, 1973; McKelvey, 1975).

The effects of various modifications to majority voting procedures have also been subjected to systematic analysis. For example, the outcomes of majority decision procedures can be influenced by the agenda specifying the order in which proposals are voted on (Plott and Levine, 1978; McKelvey, 1981). In addition, when voters cast ballots on several unrelated issues over which preference intensities vary, logrolling or vote trading may occur (Wilson, 1969; Tullock, 1970; Haefele, 1971). Analysis of vote trading has indicated that excessive vote trading can result in excessive public expenditure levels in a manner analogous to the free-rider problem (Riker and Brams, 1973; Koehler, 1975). The effects of the behaviour of budget-maximising bureaucrats on public expenditure levels has been investigated by Niskanen (1971), and public choice analysis has been used to account for recent bureaucratic expansion in advanced economies (Fiorina and Noll, 1978; Kristensen, 1980).

Frequently, public choice analysis has involved searching for equilibrium conditions underlying legislative processes. Several studies have demonstrated that determinate equilibria in models of legislative processes occur only under restrictive and seldom-observed conditions. Consequently, public choice theory has placed emphasis on the analysis of sufficiency conditions for equilibrium in different institutions, especially in the light of empirical evidence showing that existing institutions demonstrate long-run stability (Tullock, 1981; Koford, 1982).

This brief survey of public choice represents a small selection of the topics analysed. Detailed and comprehensive reviews of this literature are provided by Mueller (1976; 1979). Many issues of concern can be addressed and investigated from a public choice perspective. The next section is concerned with the geographic dimensions of public choice theory; it includes discussion of current research relating the public choice approach to political-geographic analysis.

Public Choice Analysis In A Geographic Context

In a recent review, Archer (1981) called attention to the potential for political geography of the public choice approach. As Archer indicated, the fundamental concepts of public choice theory have well-defined geographic dimensions. In this section, recent geographical research concerned with public choice is reviewed; particular attention is paid to research undertaken since the publication of Archer's paper.

Geographical applications of public choice perspectives have developed along several lines of inquiry: public good provision in a spatial context, specific institutional procedures, constitutional decisions, and individual responses to institutional procedures. Spatial considerations affect the defining consumption character-istics of public goods. As defined in economic theory, pure public goods are characterised by jointness and non-exclusion. In practice, these defining characteristics are influenced by distance and location. For example, fire protection and emergency medical services, intended as equally available throughout a region, become less effective with increased distance. The effects of distance decay and jurisdictional boundaries on the optimality conditions for the provision of public goods have been investigated by Smolensky *et al.* (1970), Borukhov (1972), Lea (1978, 1982), Harford (1979), Honey and Strathman (1979), and Portugali (1980). Analyses of public good provision in geographic contexts have been integrated with welfare economics (Bigman and ReVelle, 1978, 1979; Lea, 1979) and with land-rent models (Fisch, 1977; Thrall and Casetti, 1978; Brueckner, 1979; Thrall, 1979).

The geographic dimensions of vote trading have been investigated in an empirical study by Archer and Reynolds (1976). Honey and Erickson (1979) based their analysis of fiscal disparities amplification in suburban areas on a model predicting that utility-maximising jurisdictions compete for revenue-generating land uses, with the intent of increasing tax bases and improving public service provision. The distribution of government spending has been investigated with reference to relationships among spending patterns, vote distributions, and the behaviour of politicians and bureaucrats. Empirical evidence has been used to illustrate these patterns and their relationships to locational perceptions of vote-maximising politicians and budget-maximising bureaucrats (Archer, 1980; Johnston, 1979, 1980; Cowart, 1981).

Voting procedures themselves have been subjected to recent geographical analysis. Locational differences among alternatives affect the possibility of an equilibrium outcome. When voters preferring to minimise individual distances to a salutary public facility must determine its location by majority vote, disequilibrium frequently results (Rushton *et al.*, 1981; Hansen and Thisse, 1981; Wendell and McKelvey, 1981). Recent analysis has been directed to formalising the conditions under which these intransitivities occur (Shelley and Goodchild, 1983).

Political geographers have paid particular attention to the processes of electoral organisation, in which space is divided into constituencies for the purpose of electing representatives to legislatures. Redistricting has long been of interest to political geographers (Taylor and Johnston, 1979). Redistricting has been conceptualised as a choice among all possible districting solutions (Taylor and Gudgin, 1976a). Supposedly non-partisan attempts to constrain the selection of redistricting patterns by eliminating malapportionment and gerrymandering are not necessarily successful in reducing electoral bias. This so-called myth of non-partisan cartography has been demonstrated in England (Taylor and Gudgin, 1976b; Johnston, 1982), Canada (Norcliffe, 1977), New Zealand (Johnston, 1976), and Australia (Johnston and Hughes, 1978). Separation of electoral bias into components indicates that locational considerations often affect the extent to which electoral bias is evident; for example, districting processes tend to be biased against the interests of parties whose strength is concentrated in large cities (Gudgin and Taylor, 1980, 1981).

Recently, the analysis of electoral bias has been complemented by the measurement of voting power. Game-theoretic indices of voting power determine the probability that particular individuals can influence social choice outcomes. These game-theoretic indices have been applied to comparing the relative power of the states in the Electoral College (Banzhaf, 1968; Blair, 1979), legislators in weighted voting systems (Banzhaf, 1965; Grofman and Scarrow, 1981), and delegates to the European Parliament (Johnston, 1977a, 1977b; Taylor and Johnston, 1978). Power indices indicate those areas in which utility-maximising politicians should concentrate their efforts in order to maintain legislative power. For example, game-theoretic analyses of the Electoral College have demonstrated that voters in the larger states have more power than do those in the smaller states. It is no accident that the most recent Presidential elections have been decided in the larger states (Archer, 1982). Political leaders have therefore devoted disproportionate efforts to the larger states.

Both the myth of non-partisan cartography and the spatial analysis of voting power are subject to interpretation from the public choice perspective. Even when constrained by regulations intended to eliminate electoral biases, politicians intent on maximising support for preferred legislative proposals can design districts in order to take advantage of geographic differentials in voting power (Musgrove, 1977). By viewing districting as a problem in constrained optimisation, politicians can design districts maximising their re-election potential.

Public choice perspectives have also been applied to the prediction of locational conflict outcomes. Its conflict-oriented perspective renders public choice analysis appropriate for the prediction of the outcomes of conflicts concerning land use, public service provision, urban development, environmental management, and other issues. Locational conflict analysis has been based on case studies involving the location of highways, hospitals, airports, schools, and other controversial facilities (Wolpert *et al.*, 1972). By focusing on the behaviour of utility maximisers attempting to undertake social choices, the public choice perspective has contributed to the development of theory enabling the prediction of conflict outcomes. Voting processes leading to the location of public facilities that generate both positive and negative external effects have been analysed (Mumphrey and Wolpert, 1973).

Several distinct locational conflict types can be distinguished on the basis of the generalised distributions of resources, external effects, and threat conditions. The interaction of these factors affects conflict resolution in many ways. Disparities in initial resources affect conflict resolution; those individuals or groups with greater access to existing power structures are more likely to achieve favourable resolutions. These resource disparities help to explain the disproportionate concentration of noxious facilities in lower-income areas. Locational conflicts can also be distinguished on the basis of external effect patterns. Accordingly, conflicts concerning the location of salutary public facilities such as hospitals and parks are conceptually distinct from conflicts concerning the location of noxious facilities, because the decision tasks facing the social choice institution are distinct in each case. Finally, the threat condition, or expected outcome should social choices not be made, affects the outcome. Actual locational conflicts are frequently affected by these threat conditions. Redistricting in many states, for example, is undertaken by courts when political leaders cannot agree on a solution (Morrill, 1973, 1976).

Despite conflict-specific differences in benefits, costs, resource differentials, and external effects, several conflict models can be isolated, analysed, and compared. In some cases, failure to resolve the conflict results in utility declines accruing to all interested parties. The N-person prisoners' dilemma, typified by the tragedy of the commons (Hardin, 1968), represents a situation in which individual rationality leads to long-run collective disutility. Social problems including pollution (Dawes *et al.*, 1974), fisheries management (Acheson, 1975), and energy conservation (Stern, 1981) have been conceptualised in terms of the N-person prisoners' dilemma. Furthermore, the free-rider problem characteristic of public good provision is also conceptually isomorphic with the dilemma (Hardin, 1971). Theoretical and empirical research has indicated the importance of social choice institutions in the resolution of the prisoners' dilemma; by agreeing on a set of institutional procedures to make social choices, the negative effects of the dilemma can be mitigated (Dawes, 1980; Edney, 1980; Orbell and Wilson, 1978a).

In other conflicts, the expected distribution of costs and benefits is such that a few areas suffer disproportionate costs while the majority of the population benefits. Noxious-facility conflicts, such as those regarding school closing, hazardous waste disposal, and controversial facility siting, illustrate this possibility. In other cases, the level of expected costs and benefits varies through space. Stream pollution conflicts typify this case: downstream communities are more likely to suffer negative externalities than are their upstream counterparts; therefore, the downstream communities would more likely advocate legislated controls on pollution. Still other locational conflicts can be modeled as zero-sum games. For example, conflicts over electoral districting exhibit this structure; electoral bias favouring one party is offset by bias against its opponent.

The conflicts described above illustrate that the effects of particular institutional structures on conflict resolution will vary from one conflict to another. That institutional structure best suited to the resolution of the prisoners' dilemma, for example, should differ from that most successful in resolving conflicts concerning noxious facility location. Constitutional choice analysis extends the public choice approach to attempting prediction of the principles selected in order to resolve different types of conflicts. Developed within the context of public choice theory, constitutional choice analysis can provide a common denominator for institutional evaluation. However, its application to locational conflict resolution requires substantial modification of the assumptions adopted by political scientists and economists.

Economic theories of constitutional choice were originally developed under assumptions that parties to constitutional decisions were characterised by complete uncertainty concerning future preferences, utilities, and prospects. Under such an assumption, Buchanan and Tullock (1962) investigated the choice of a decision rule, or that percentage of the voting public whose approval must be secured for the passage of legislation. In their view, rational persons would only agree to minimise the costs of collective choice under uncertainty. Buchanan and Tullock argued that these costs comprise two components: the decisionmaking costs associated with achieving a collective decision, and the external costs imposed upon those not agreeing with the eventual decision. Majority rule was shown to minimise the sum of these cost components; these results have been extended and generalised by Barton (1973), Barnett (1981), Kiesling (1968), Kafoglis and Cebula (1981), and Koford (1982b). Meanwhile, Rae (1969) argued that majority rule maximises the possibility that any individual's preferences will be consistent with the group's decision; Taylor (1969) demonstrated this mathematically while Badger (1972), Curtis (1972), Schofield (1972), and Straffin (1977) extended the analysis. Rawls' (1971) theory of distributive justice, which suggests that rational persons would agree upon distributional principles constraining social choice procedures, can also be regarded as a theory of constitutional choice under uncertainty.

Recent analysis has modified the assumption of complete uncertainty characteristic of constitutional choice analysis. Models such as those of Buchanan and Tullock and Rae are based on an assumption that parties to constitutional decisions are completely ignorant of individual circumstances. However, actual decisions concerning the establishment and modification of social choice institutions are not undertaken under complete uncertainty. Parties to actual constitutional choices are expected to use any available information concerning their individual circumstances in order to influence the constitutional decision process favourably. Each participant would prefer that institution which enables individual utility enhancement; whenever possible, each will use available information in arguing for rules enabling them to enhance their utilities. The application of constitutional choice analysis to realistic locational conflicts must therefore be undertaken under conditions of *partial* uncertainty. Parties to actual constitutional decisions remain unaware of future events that might affect social choices, but they remain mindful of current resources and future prospects.

The difficulties associated with the rational selection and implementation of constitutions have also been recognised. The assignment of expected utility values to prospective constitutions is all but impossible (Reynolds, 1981; Grafstein, 1981); it has therefore been suggested that *procedural* fairness should dominate constitutional choice (Reynolds, 1981; Reynolds and Shelley, 1981). In contrast to more frequently analysed conceptions of distributive justice, analyses of procedural justice focus solely on the methods by which decisions are undertaken. Only those procedures perceived as unbiased by all interested parties should command unanimous constitutional agreement.

The accurate prediction of constitutional choice is problematic and may be dependent on conflict-specific factors. Orbell and Wilson (1978a, 1978b) have compared the success of various decision procedures — majority rule, dictatorship, other decision rules, and 'uncoordinated individualism' — in overcoming the N-person prisoners' dilemma. They concluded that majority rule and other, expanded decision rules can achieve resolution of the dilemma only under certain payoff conditions. In a later analysis Orbell and Wilson (1979) considered the success of various constitutional decision procedures in overcoming the dilemma created when each of several communities could engage in stream pollution, passing the negative externalities along to downstream neighbours. Again, the likelihood that any institution can successfully resolve the problem is dependent on context-specific factors; different institutions are more successful in resolving various combinations of spacing, pollution incentives, and pollution rights.

Geographical analyses of constitutional choice processes have recognised differences in locational conflicts in attempting to predict constitutional decisions. For example, Shelley (1982a) has investigated the application of constitutional choice analysis to electoral district boundary delineation. Here, procedural fairness demands that electoral bias be reduced as much as possible. However, the reduction of electoral bias is conceptually equivalent to equalising the level of bias suffered by each party. When the elimination of bias is impossible as a result of locational factors, party leaders should be expected to agree on a bipartisan system of redistricting that most effectively promotes the long-run equalisation of electoral bias.

Current research is being devoted to the comparative analysis of constitutional choice in varied locational conflict situations. The problem of urban school retrenchment, in which educational officials must determine how to cope with the problem of revenue reductions coupled with projected enrollment declined (Reynolds, 1982) is conceptually distinct from that involving the management of groundwater supplies in the American Great Plains (Shelley, 1982b). The former conflict typifies the noxious facility conflict case: a decision to reduce district-wide expenditures by closing one or more schools impacts disproportionately upon the immediate vicinity of the school(s) selected for closure. In contrast, the groundwater management case is a typical N-person prisoners' dilemma. Utility-maximising farmers draw water for irrigation from commonly held supplies in order to maximise crop yields. By refusing to limit their extraction to levels consistent with recharge rates, the collective welfare is imperiled. The comparative analysis of constitutional choice is intended to determine how the effectiveness of institutionalised procedures for social choice will vary between these conflict situations. It is expected that procedural fairness should dominate the constitutional choice process in both cases, although the content of those procedures regarded as fair should vary.

The constitutional choice approach described above focuses upon the design and operation of large-scale institutional structures. Individuals and collective responses to institutional operations and decisions are also of interest in public choice theory. For example, Tiebout's (1956) model suggests that decentralised market mechanisms can provide local public goods adequately under assumptions concerning community structures and individual decisions. In Tiebout's model, equilibrium is achieved if mobile consumers choose to relocate in communities whose public good outputs correspond with individual demands. Each factor signals preferences for public goods through migration; this supposedly overcomes the free-rider problem. Jurisdictional fragmentation has therefore been viewed as a stimulus to market-type competition among local governments; this improves the responsiveness of local governments to individual demands (Bish and Ostrom, 1976). However, spatial analysis of Tiebout processes has indicated that equilibrium can only be achieved under highly restrictive and unrealistic conditions (Buchanan and Goetz, 1972; Wheaton, 1975; Westhoff, 1977). Furthermore, individual relocation decisions are seldom made on the basis of public good demands alone; moreover, production relationships affecting the provision of services in local jurisdictions are often ignored in applications of the Tiebout model (Clark, 1981; Cox and Nartowicz, 1980).

Analysis of the Tiebout process illustrates that social choice does not occur in closed systems. The Tiebout process is an 'exit' option, in contrast with the 'voice' option of active participation in social choice institutions (Hirschman, 1970). The extent to which this 'voice' is affected by institutional structure remains at issue. Public choice analysis can contribute to the resolution of this problem by isolating the extent to which individual inputs in social choice processes are effective in determining collective decisions.

Evaluating The Public Choice Approach In Political Geography

Public choice theory in political geography is rich in potential predictive value. However, an uncritical acceptance of the public choice approach is perilous; careful scrutiny of its implications is necessary if it is to provide new insights into political-geographic processes. A critical discussion of the limitations and constraints on the public choice approach must be initiated. The limitations described below should indicate some of the shortcomings inherent in applied public choice analysis.

Any theory whose predictions are based on the systematic analysis of rational behaviour must take into account the limitations associated with that perspective. Political-economic models of public choice are based on assumptions of individual utility maximisation. While rational decisions and their implications can be predicted easily in simple decision contexts, they are much more difficult to predict in more complex, yet more realistic situations. Limited information, uncertainty concerning future events, changing preferences, and other considerations prevent even intendedly rational persons from utility maximisation. Application of rationality postulates to complex social choices often generates tradeoffs between accuracy and complexity. Attempts to compare the relative effectiveness of different institutions illustrate the dependence of theoretical predictions on specific situational factors. Indeed, the practice of constitutional choice in conflict management is seldom represented as a single decision, as typified by the United States Constitutional Convention of 1787. Rather, many social choice institutions have arisen less formally over long periods of time; these include a variety of strategies for coping with the tragedy of the commons in many forms (Acheson, 1975; Anderson and Hill, 1978; Palsson, 1982).

Within the utility maximisation framework, public choice is based on assumptions of methodological individualism and voluntary exchange. Individual preferences are critical to the outcome of public choice processes. Persons are viewed as entirely free to make rational decisions on the basis of these preferences. However, realistic preferences are constrained by social, economic, and cultural antecedents. Furthermore, individual and collective preferences for social choice procedures are influenced by previous experiences. For example, majority rule is widely institutionalised in Western societies. It is likely that persons would prefer this procedure to alternatives even if rational arguments supporting the superiority of alternatives were presented.

In practice, individual attempts to maximise utility are subject to social, economic, and political constraints. Recognition of the difficulties associated with voluntary exchange processes in the public sector — the very cornerstone of public choice theory — demands recognition that individual utility maximisation is necessarily constrained by social and economic forces beyond individual control. Generally, individuals or groups who, for whatever reason, are initially endowed with more resources will be those whose choices are less constrained. Such individuals are in better position to take advantage of resource differentials in order to maximise their utilities.

The interdependence of economic and political systems must be recognised. Attempts to understand the development of actual institutions requre an historical perspective lacking in public choice theory (Taylor, 1982). Although the public choice perspective can describe relationships between preferences, institutions, and conflict outcomes, it cannot account for antecedent conditions. It is in this way that public choice analyses can interact with more historically oriented approaches to political-geographic analysis. Public choice approaches contribute meaningful insights into social choice processes often overlooked in large-scale, deterministic perspectives; interaction between public choice perspectives and alternative approaches would be useful in the meaningful development of political geography.

In applying public choice perspectives to locational conflicts, distinctions between allocation and distribution must be given careful attention. Public choice theories are often presented as value-free explanations. In practice, public choice theorists have emphasised questions of allocative efficiency at the expense of distributional considerations. Emphasis on allocational issues may not be surprising, for these represent technical problems while distribution involves more fundamental ethical, philosophical, and political considerations (Papageorgiou, 1977). Yet there is danger in regarding the allocation-oriented results of public choice analyses in normative terms. Emphasis on allocative efficiency without reference to distributional and procedural questions implies a tacit acceptance of existing distributional inequalities and injustices, and, consequently, of the social and economic forces responsible for the production of these inequalities (Dear and Clark, 1978). Attempts to develop public policy on the basis of literal interpretations of abstract public choice theory must be resisted. However, a focus on the effects institutional structures on social choice renders public choice theory useful in comparing the effectiveness of different institutions. Yet implementation of implicit improvements demands consideration of ethical issues beyond the scope of public choice theory.

When its inherent limitations are recognised and understood, the public choice approach is valuable to the understanding of locational conflict resolution processes. The application of utility maximisation postulates to non-market decision contexts has great potential for understanding collective decision mechanics. Public choce analysis should not be viewed as a comprehensive theory of conflict resolution; its results must be applied with careful sensitivity to ethical values and distributional goals. The value of public choice theory is its ability to predict conflict outcomes. This can aid in the reform of existing social choice institutions in order to eliminate procedural biases.

Geographically relevant knowledge of social choice processes remains limited. The effects of locational and spatial considerations on social choice must be studied in greater detail, emphasising empirical corroboration of theoretical predictions. It is clear that locational differences affect social choice significantly; these effects should be isolated, analysed, and tested empirically. It is hoped that public choice perspectives can provide useful insights into social choice. When integrated with context-specific knowledge of conflict development and the understanding of ethical concerns, public choice should continue to serve as a useful methodological approach by which political geographers can develop insights into locational conflict analysis.

Acknowledgements

The helpful comments of David R. Reynolds, J. Clark Archer, Costas Lagos, Mickey Lauria, and Edward J. Malecki on earlier drafts of this paper are gratefully acknowledged.

References

Acheson, J.M. (1975) 'The Lobster Fiefs: Economic and Ecological Effects of Territoriality in the Maine Lobster Industry', *Human Ecology*, **3**, 183-207

Anderson, T.L., and P.J. Hill (1977) 'From Free Grass to Fences: Transforming the Commons of the American West', in G. Hardin and J. Baden (eds.), *Managing the Commons*, W. H. Freeman, San Francisco, 200-216

Archer, J.C. (1980) 'Congressional Incumbent Re-Election Success and Federal Outlays Distribution: A Test of the Electoral Connection Hypothesis', *Environment and Planning*, **12A**, 263-278

Archer, J.C. (1981) 'Public Choice Paradigms in Political Geography', in A. Burnett and P.J. Taylor (eds.), *Political Studies from Spatial Perspectives*, John Wiley, London

Archer, J.C. (1982) 'Some Geographical Aspects of the American Presidential Election of 1980', *Political Geography Quarterly*, **1**, 123-135

Archer, J.C., and D.R. Reynolds (1976) 'Locational Logrolling and Citizen Support of Municipal Bond Proposals: The Example of St. Louis', *Public Choice*, **27**, 22-40

Arrow, K.J. (1951) *Social Choice and Individual Values*, John Wiley, New York

Badger, W.W. (1951) 'Political Individualism, Positional Preferences, and Optimal Decision-Rules', in R. G. Niemi and H.F. Weisberg (eds.) *Probability Models of Collective Decision Making*, Charles E. Merrill, Columbus, Ohio, 34-59

Banzhaf, J.F.III(1965) 'Weighted Voting Doesn't Work: A Mathematical Analysis', *Rutgers Law Review*, **19**, 317-343

Banzhaf, J.F.III (1968) 'One Man, 3.312 Votes: A Mathematical Analysis of the Electoral College', *Villanova Law Review*, **13**, 304-332

Barnett, R.R. (1981) 'Frequent Voter Recontracting: On Constitutional Choice and Minority Group Power', *Public Finance Quarterly*, **9**, 309-319

Barton, D.M. (1973) 'Constitutional Choice and Simple Majority Rule: Comment', *Journal of Political Economy*, **81**, 471-479

Bigman, D., and C. ReVelle (1978) 'The Theory of Welfare Considerations in Public Facility Location Problems', *Geographical Analysis*, **10**, 229-240

Bigman, D., and C. ReVelle (1979) 'An Operational Approach to Welfare Considerations in Applied Public Facility Location Models', *Environment and Planning*, **11A**,83-95

Bish, R.L., and V. Ostrom (1976) 'Understanding Urban Government: Metropolitan Reform Reconsidered', in H. Hochman (ed.) *The Urban Economy*, W.W. Norton, New York

Black, D. (1948) 'On the Rationale of Group Decision Making', *Journal of Political Economy*, **56**, 23-34

Blair, D.H. (1979) 'Electoral College Reform and the Distribution of Voting Power', *Public Choice*, **34**, 201-215

Borukhov, E. (1972) 'Optimal Service Areas for Provision and Financing of Local Public Goods', *Public Finance*, **27**, 267-281

Brueckner, J.K. (1979) 'Spatial Majority Voting Equilibria and the Provision of Public Goods', *Journal of Urban Economics*, **6**, 338-351

Buchanan, J.M., and C.J. Goetz (1972) 'Efficiency Limits of Fiscal Mobility: An Assessment of the Tiebout Model', **Journal of Public Economics, 1**, 25-43

Buchanan, J.M., and G. Tullock (1962) *The Calculus of Consent*, University of Michigan Press, Ann Arbor

Clark, G.L. (1981) 'Democracy and the Capitalist State: Toward a Critique of the Tiebout Hypothesis', in A. Burnett and P. Taylor (eds.) *Political Studies from*

Spatial Perspectives, John Wiley, London

Cowart, S.C. (1981) 'Representation of High Demand Constituencies in Review Committees: A Research Note', *Public Choice*, **37**, 337-342

Cox, K.R., and F.Z. Nartowicz (1980) 'Jurisdictional Fragmentation in the American Metropolis: Alternative Perspectives', *International Journal of Urban and Regional Research*, **4**, 196-209

Curtis, R.B. (1972) 'Decision-Rules and Collective Values in Constitutional Choice', in R.G. Niemi and H.F. Weisberg (eds.) *Probability Models of Collective Decision Making*, Charles E. Merrill, Columbus

Davis, O., M.J. Hinich and P.C. Ordeshook (1970) 'An Expository Development of a Mathematical Model of the Electoral Process', *American Political Science Review*, **64**, 426-448

Dawes, R.M. (1980) 'Social Dilemmas', *Annual Review of Psychology*, **31**, 169-193

Dawes, R.M., J. Delay, and W. Chaplin (1974) 'The Decision to Pollute', *Environment and Planning*, **6A**, 3-10

Dear, M., and G.Clark (1978) 'The State and Geographic Process: A Critical Review', *Environment and Planning*, **10A**,173-183

Downs, A. (1957) *An Economic Theory of Democracy*, Harper and Row, London

Edney, J.J. (1980) 'The Commons Problem: Alternative Perspectives', *American Psychologist*, **35**, 131-150

Fiorina, M.P., and R.G. Noll (1978) 'Voters, Bureaucrats, and Legislators: A Rational Choice Perspective on the Growth of Bureaucracy', *Journal of Public Economics*, **9**, 239-254

Fisch, O. (1977) 'Spatial Equilibrium with Local Public Goods', *Regional Science and Urban Economics*, **7**, 197-216

Grafstein, R.(1981) 'The Problem of Choosing Your Alternatives: A Revision of the Public Choice Theory of Constitutions', *Social Science Quarterly*, **62**, 199-212

Grofman, B., and H. Scarrow (1981) 'Weighted Voting in New York', *Legislative Studies Quarterly*, **6**, 287-304

Gudgin, G., and P.J. Taylor (1980) 'The Decomposition of Electoral Bias in a Plurality Election', *British Journal of Political Science*, **10**, 515-521

Gudgin, G., and P.J. Taylor (1981) 'The Myth of Non-Partisan Cartography: Clarifications', *Urban Studies*, **18**, 219-222

Haefele, E.T. (1971) 'A Utility Theory of Representative Government', *American Economic Review*, **61**, 350-367

Hansen, P., and J.F. Thisse (1981) 'Outcomes of Voting and Planning: Condorcet, Weber, and Rawls Locations', *Journal of Public Economics*, **16**, 1-15

Hardin, G. (1968) 'The Tragedy of the Commons', *Science*, **162**, 1243-1248

Hardin, R. (1971) 'Collective Action as an Agreeable N-Prisoner's Dilemma', *Behavioral Science*, **16**, 472-481

Harford, J. (1979) 'The Spatial Analysis of Local Public Goods: A Note', *Public Finance Quarterly*, **7**, 122-128

Head, J.G. (1974) *Public Goods and Public Welfare*, Duke University Press, Durham, North Carolina

Hinich, M.J., J.O. Ledyard, and P.C. Ordeshook (1973) 'A Theory of Electoral Equilibrium: A Spatial Analysis Based on the Theory of Games', *Journal of Politics*, **35**, 154-193

Hirschman, A.O. (1970) *Exit, Voice, and Loyalty: Responses to Decline in Firms, Organizations, and States*, Harvard University Press, Cambridge

Honey, R., and R. Erickson (1979) 'Fiscal Disparities and Land Use', The University of Iowa, Institute of Urban and Regional Research, *Technical Report*, **115**

Honey, R., and J. Strathman (1978) 'Jurisdictional Consequences of Optimizing Public Goods', *Annals of Regional Science*, **13**, 32-40

Hotelling, H. (1929) 'Stability in Competition', *Economic Journal*, **39**, 41-57

Johnston, R.J. (1976) 'Spatial Structure, Plurality Systems, and Electoral Bias', *Canadian Geographer*, **20**, 310-328

Johnston, R.J. (1977a) 'National Sovereignty and National Power in European Institutions', *Environment and Planning*, **9A**, 569-577

Johnston, R.J. (1977b) 'National Power in the European Parliament as Modified by the Party System', *Environment and Planning*, **9A**, 1055-1066

Johnston, R.J. (1979) 'Congressional Committees and Department Spending: The Political Influence on the Geography of Federal Expenditure in the United States', *Transactions, Institute of British Geographers*, **4**, 373-384

Johnston, R.J. (1980) *The Geography of Federal Spending in The United States*, Wiley, Chichester

Johnston, R.J. (1982) 'Redistricting by Independent Commissions: A Perspective from Britain', *Annals, Association of American Geographers*, **72**, 457-470

Johnston, R.J., and C.A. Hughes (1978) 'Constituency Delimitation and the Unintentional Gerrymander in Brisbane', *Australian Geographical Studies*, **16**, 99-110

Kafoglis, M.Z., and R.J. Cebuals (1981) 'The Buchanan-Tullock Model: Some Extensions', *Public Choice*, **36**, 179-186

Kiesling, H.J. (1968) 'Potential Costs of Alternative Decision-Making Rules', *Public Choice*, **4**, 49-58

Koehler, D.H. (1975) 'Vote Trading and the Voting Paradox: A Proof of Logical Equivalence', *American Political Science Review*, **59**, 954-960

Koford, K. (1982a) 'An Optimistic View of the Possibility of Rational Legislative Decisionmaking', *Public Choice*, **38**, 3-19

Koford, K. (1982b) 'Optimal Voting Rules Under Uncertainty', *Public Choice*, **38**, 149-165

Kirstensen, O.P. (1980) 'The Logic of Political-Bureaucratic Decision-Making as a Cause of Governmental Growth: Or Why Expansion of Public Programs is a Private Good and their Restriction is a Public Good', *European Journal of Political Research*, **8**, 249-264

Lea, A.C. (1978) 'Interjurisdictional Spillovers and Efficient Public Good Provision', unpublished paper presented to the 74th Annual Meeting, Association of American Geographers, New Orleans, Louisiana

Lea, A.C. (1979) 'Welfare Theory, Public Goods, and Public Facility Location', *Geographical Analysis*, **11**, 217-239

Lea, A.C. (1982) 'Optimal Jurisdiction Size for Impure Public Goods with Spillovers', unpublished paper presented to the 78th Annual Meeting, Association of American Geographers, San Antonio, Texas

McKelvey,R.D. (1975) 'Policy Related Voting and Electoral Equilibrium', *Econometrica*, **43**, 815-843

McKelvey, R.D. (1981) 'A Theory of Optimal Agenda Design', *Management Science*, **27**, 303-321

Morrill, R.L. (1973) 'Ideal and Reality in Reapportionment', *Annals, Association of American Geographers*, **63**, 463-477

Morrill, R.L. (1976) 'Reapportionment Revisited', *Annals, Association of American Geographers*, **66**, 548-556

Mueller, D.C. (1976) 'Public Choice: A Survey', *Journal of Economic Literature*, **14**, 395-433

Mueller, D.C. (1979) *Public Choice*, New York, Cambridge University Press

Musgrove, P. (1977) *The General Theory of Gerrymandering*, Sage Publications, Beverly Hills and London

Mumphrey, A.J., and J. Wolpert (1973) 'Equity Considerations and Concessions in the Siting of Public Facilities', *Economic Geography*, **44**, 109-121

Niskanen, W. (1971) *Bureaucracy and Representative Government*, Aldine-Atherton,

Chicago

Norcliffe, G.B. (1977) 'Discretionary Aspects of Scientific Districting', *Area*, 9, 240-246

Olson, M., Jr. (1965) *The Logic of Collective Action*, Harvard University Press, Cambridge

Orbell, J.M., and L.A. Wilson II (1978a) 'Institutional Solutions to the N-Prisoners' Dilemma', *American Political Science Review*, 78, 411-420

Orbell, J.M., and L.A. Wilson II (1978b) 'The Uses of Extended Majorities', *American Political Science Review*, 72, 1366-1368

Orbell, J.M., and L.A. Wilson II (1979) 'The Governance of Rivers ', *Western Political Quarterly*, 32, 256-264

Palsson, G. (1982) 'Territoriality Among Icelandic Fishermen', *Acta Sociologica*, 25, 5-13

Papageorgiou, G.J. (1977) 'Fundamental Problems of Theoretical Planning', *Environment and Planning*, 9A, 1329-1356

Plott, C.R. (1976) 'Axiomatic Social Choice Theory: An Overview and Interpretation', *American Journal of Political Science*, 20, 511-576

Plott, C.R., and M.E. Levine (1978) 'A Model of Agenda Influence on Committee Decisions', *American Economic Review*, 68, 146-160

Portugali, J. (1980) 'Distribution, Allocation, Social Structure, and Spatial Form: Elements of Planning Theory', *Progress in Planning*, 14, 227-310

Rae, D.W. (1969) 'Decision Rules and Individual Values in Constitutional Choice', *American Political Science Review*, 63, 40-56

Rawls, J. (1971) *A Theory of Justice*, Harvard University Press, Cambridge

Reynolds, D.R. (1981) 'The Geography of Social Choice', in A. Burnett and P.J. Taylor (eds.) *Political Studies from Spatial Perspectives*, John Wiley, London, 91-109

Reynolds, D.R. (1982) 'School Budget Retrenchment and Locational Conflict: Crisis in Local Democracy?', University of Iowa, Institute of Urban and Regional Research, *Working Paper 52*

Reynolds, D.R., and F.M. Shelley (1981) 'Modelling the Choice of Constitutional Constraints on the Provision of Public Goods', The University of Iowa, Institute of Urban and Regional Research, *Technical Report 132*

Riker, W.H., and S.J. Brams (1973) 'The Paradox of Vote Trading', *American Political Science Review*, 67, 1235-1247

Rushton, G., S.L. McLafferty, and A. Ghosh (1981) 'Equilibrium Locations for Public Services: Individual Preferences and Social Choice', *Geographical Analysis*, 13, 196-202

Samuelson, P.A. (1954) 'The Pure Theory of Public Expenditure', *Review of Economics and Statistics*, 36, 387-389

Samuelson, P.A. (1955) 'Diagrammatic Exposition of a Pure Theory of Public Expenditure', *Review of Economics and Statistics*, 37, 350-356

Schofield, N. (1972) 'Ethical Decision Rules for Uncertain Voters', *British Journal of Political Science*, 2, 193-207

Sen, A. (1977) 'Social Choice Theory: A Re-Examination', *Econometrica*, 45, 53-89

Shelley, F.M. (1982a) 'A Constitutional Choice Approach to Electoral District Boundary Delineation', *Political Geography Quarterly*, 1, 341-350

Shelley, F.M. (1982b) 'A Constitutional Choice Approach to Groundwater Supply Management', The University of Iowa, Institute of Urban and Regional Research, *Working Paper 53*

Shelley, F.M., and M.F. Goodchild (1983) 'Majority Voting and the Location of Salutary Public Facilities', *Geographical Analysis*, 15, forthcoming Smolensky, E., R. Burton, and N. Tideman (1970) 'The Efficient Provision of a Local Non-Private Good', *Geographical Analysis*, 2, 330-342

Shelley

93

Stern, P.C. (1981) 'Psychological Research and Energy Policy', *American Psychologist*, **36**, 329-342

Straffin, P.D., Jr. (1977) 'Majority Rule and General Decision Rules', *Theory and Decision*, **8**, 351-360

Taylor, M. (1969) 'Proof of a Theorem on Majority Rule', *Behavioral Science*, **14**, 228-231

Taylor, P.J. (1982) 'A Materialist Framework for Political Geography', *Transactions, Institute of British Geographers*, **7**, 15-34

Taylor, P.J., and G. Gudgin (1976a) 'The Statistical Basis of Decisionmaking in Electoral Districting', *Environment and Planning*, **8A**, 43-58

Taylor, P.J., and G. Gudgin (1976b) 'The Myth of Non-Partisan Cartography: A Study of Electoral Biases in the English Boundary Commission's Redistribution for 1955-1970', *Urban Studies*, **13**, 13-25

Taylor, P.J., and R.J. Johnston (1978) 'Population Distributions and Political Power in the European Parliament', *Political Studies*, **2**, 61-68

Taylor, P.J., and R.J. Johnston (1979) *The Geography of Elections*, Holmes and Meier, New York

Thrall, G.I. (1979) 'Public Goods and the Derivation of Land Value Assessment Schedules with a Spatial Equilibrium Setting', *Geographical Analysis*, **11**, 23-35

Thrall, G.I., and E. Casetti (1978) 'Local Public Goods and Spatial Equilibrium in an Ideal Urban Centre', *Canadian Geographer*, **11**, 319-333

Tiebout,C.M. (1956) 'A Pure Theory of Local Government Expenditures', *Journal of Political Economy*, **64**, 416-424

Tullock, G. (1970) 'A Simple Algebraic Logrolling Model', *American Economic Review*, **60**, 419-426

Tullock, G. (1981) 'Why So Much Stability?', *Public Choice*, **37**, 189-202

Wendell, R.E., and R.D. McKelvey (1981) 'New Perspectives in Competitive Location Theory', *European Journal of Operational Research*, **6**, 174-182

Westhoff, F. (1977) 'Existence of Equilibria in Economies with a Local Public Good', *Journal of Economic Theory*, **14**, 84-112

Wheaton, W.C. (1975) 'Consumer Mobility and Community Tax Bases: The Financing of Local Public Goods', *Journal of Public Economics*, **4**, 377-384

Wilson, R. (1969) 'An Axiomatic Model of Logrolling', *American Economic Review*, **59**, 331-341

Wolpert, J., A. Mumphrey, and J. Seley (1972) *Metropolitan Neighborhoods: Participation and Conflict over Change*, Association of American Geographers, Commission on College Geography, Resource Paper **16**, Washington D.C.

5

School Budget Retrenchment and Locational Conflict:
Crisis in Local Democracy?

David R. Reynolds

Introduction

The 1950s and 1960s were decades of unprecedented expansion in
the scale of public education in the United States. From 1950 to
1970, elementary school enrollment grew from 22 million to 37
million while secondary school enrollment doubled from 6.5 million
to nearly 15 million (National Center for Education Statistics,
1975). Such expansion was facilitated in part by the increases in the
aggregate demand for public education stemming from the baby
boom of the 1940s and 1950s and by the generally ample fiscal
resources made available through the expansion of the US
economy (Abramowitz and Rosenfeld, 1978). Guiding this
expansion was an ideology suggesting that large, well-designed
facilities, specialised programmes of instruction and the
introduction of new educational technologies de-emphasizing the
role of parental involvement in the educational process contributed
to social progress. School boards and administrators implemented
expansion without any particular attention to long-range planning
and with increasingly tenuous and bureaucratic avenues of
community involvement in school decisionmaking processes
(Bishop, 1979).

By the early 1970s, however, demographic and economic
conditions had changed. Enrollment in US public schools peaked in
1971-72 and has been declining ever since (Trotter, 1976). Decline
has been particularly dramatic in central city districts, where, on
average, enrollments are projected to have dclined by more than 25
per cent of their peak levels by 1985 (Bins and Tounsel, 1978).
Almost invariably, declining enrollments have been accompanied

by reductions in the resources available to school districts. As general economic conditions worsened through the 1970s, questions about educational quality, the proper role of schools in the community, and the representativeness of school government were raised with increasing frequency and acrimony (Berman and McLaughlin, 1978; Paulsmayer, 1977). To many, local democracy as it impacts on educationally-relevant policy indeed appears to be in or on the verge of crisis.

The purpose of this chapter is threefold: first, to identify the more salient patterns of social conflict accompanying the responses of existing institutions to enrollment decline and fiscal retrenchment; second, to suggest that a constitutional choice approach is an appropriate methodology for identifying alternative institutions of school decisionmaking; and, third, to outline a research project designed to simulate the collective choices of such institutions under varying conditions of conflict.

Patterns of Fiscal Retrenchment and Social Conflict

The typical chronology of retrenchment followed by school officials in urban districts has been, first, to reduce budget allocations for expendable supplies; second, to reduce other general operating and maintenance expenditures; third, to reduce teaching and support staff in elective courses not mandated by state law; and, finally, to begin the process of closing schools (typically, closing elementary schools first, followed by junior high schools as a 'last resort'). In deciding on which schools to close, the most frequently cited criteria include enrollment decline *vis-à-vis* capacity; size, age, and condition of facilities; the number of additional students who would require busing; the degree to which facilities could be used for other public or educational purposes; the complexity of programmes housed in school facilities; the effect of closure on the level of socioeconomic segregation; the effects of closure on maintaining stable neighbourhoods; and difficulties of reassigning teaching staffs.

In many areas, school officials have come to view school closures as the only option remaining that does not place their concept of educational quality in jeopardy. Hence, the closing of schools has become the institutionalised response to decline. However, when closures are proposed, conflict often reaches explosive levels, resulting in community upheaval, school board member resignations, and the firing of school district superintendents (Boyd, 1979). Severe conflict has been avoided only in small, homogeneous, and wealthy districts (Hosler and Weldy, 1977) or in those rare cases when alternative uses for closed schools are perceived by impacted residents to counterbalance the loss of a school (Anderson, 1978). Only recently have researchers begun to realise that the failure of urban school officials to adequately and acceptably resolve the conflicts associated with retrenchment may be due to their unpreparedness or unwillingness to recognise that the key to successful reform lies with political and procedural change (Cohen, 1978).

The responses of school boards and administrators to decline have resulted in specific conflict patterns that have shifted as the crises deepened. Concomitant with, but not necessarily caused by, the onset of retrenchment was the growing dissatisfaction of many parents and community leaders with the more readily observed outcomes of public education — declining test scores, high dropout rates, functional illiteracy among central city high school graduates, etc.. The appearance of these and other problems caused members of the lay public to question seriously the effectiveness of the educational programmes and innovations promulgated by school officials and professional educators who had possessed a virtual *carte blanche* in the definition and delivery of education ever since the school reform movement early this century. In the late 1960s and early 1970s, dissatisfaction led to demands from the lower socioeconomic classes and ethnics for increased citizen participation and/or community control in the governance of education. Quite transparently, such demands were a call for the 'repoliticisation' of school governance — the substitution of the political ethos of interest-group bargaining for the norms of technical, 'value-free', professional competence (Davies and Zerchykov, 1981). The relatively unfocused conflict produced possessed all or most of the trappings of class conflict but tended to be politicised and responded to in racial or ethnic terms. Responses included the creation of citizen advisory groups, the establishment of bilingual and multicultural education programmes, and the like, but excluded any fundamental reform in governance. Decisionmaking remained firmly within the control of those committed to a technocratic ideal of educational quality.

As retrenchment moved to the faculty-reduction stage, the

teacher unionisation movement received the sense of collective immediacy it has been lacking previously. State after state passed collective bargaining legislation which led to the establishment of relatively uniform tenure and fringe benefit policies in school districts (Erickson, 1975). Since on average 60 to 65 per cent of a school district's budget consists of teacher salaries (Wilken and Callahan, 1978), tenure and fringe benefit policies rendered budgetary savings even more difficult to achieve and served to enhance the expediency of school closures.

Given the criteria employed by school officials in selecting specific schools for closure, it is not surprising that the locational incidence of closure in large urban districts duplicates that described in almost all studies dealing with the siting of noxious facilities: a preponderance of closures in neighbourhoods without sufficient political and economic clout to deflect them elsewhere. However, in districts without large concentrations of low income and/or minority group residents or those with particularly precipitous enrollment declines, schools have also been closed in decidedly middle-class neighbourhoods, albeit with considerable acrimony. It was only when school closures became institutionalised as the response to enrollment decline that conflict escalated to open opposition to school board decisions and increasingly to a questioning of the conventional wisdom surrounding existing procedures and structures of school policy decisionmaking (Valencia, 1980).

In general, there appear to be three broad patterns of conflict surrounding school closure. First, the response of parents in minority and low-income (working class) neighbourhoods has been to view the closure of a school as a devastating blow to the integrity of a neighbourhood as a social unit and as even further eroding parental involvement in education (Valencia, 1980). As a result, the pattern of conflict that has emerged is quite clearly class-based and one less easily managed through policy palliatives. Since school closures have primarily affected low-income neighbourhoods, parents in such areas are usually opposed in principle to school closure as a suitable retrenchment option.

When school officials propose the closure of a school in a stable middle class 'neighbourhood', a second pattern of conflict is produced. Here the conflict is far more clearly locational. Middle-class parents who are fearful of losing a 'neighbourhood' school typically have no history of accumulated grievances predicated on the outcome of past school district policies.[1] As a result, they tend not to be opposed to school closure in principle but only to the closure of their 'neighbourhood' schools. Nevertheless, given the evidence that the 'savings' realised through closure can be minimal (Keough, 1978), and hence unjustifiable on purely economic grounds, even middle-class parents have begun to question the appropriateness of depoliticised structures of educational decision-making.

The third pattern of conflict pits the taxpayer without school children against school and other local government officials. From 1968 to 1975, the percentage of eligible voters nationwide with school-age children dropped from 28 to 23 per cent (Timar and Guthrie, 1980). This trend is expected to continue for at least another 20 years. This fact of demography in a period of economic decline has made it increasingly difficult for school districts to muster sufficient popular support for school tax increases. At the same time, it has led many taxpayers to demand a reallocation of tax money to public services other than traditional local education, services that better suit their perceived needs (services for the elderly, adult education, increased police protection, public transportation, etc.). Given the majority status of such citizens, school officials have not remained insensitive to these demands. The typical response, however, is to close schools and attempt to convert the closed facility to 'preferred' community uses. However, a depoliticised structure of decisionmaking is ill-suited for identifying what such 'preferred' uses might be. As a result, school retrenchment conflicts become so broad based and so multi-issued as to immobilise existing institutions of school governance and to seriously undermine their legitimacy.

School Retrenchment and Social Choice

From a locational perspective, the social choice problem caused by fiscal retrenchment is three-fold. First, potential budget reduction alternatives must be identified and their locationfal impacts assessed. Some alternatives can be viewed as having a generalised impact across a school district, while others can have decidedly localised impacts. Second, if alternatives with localised impacts are to be considered, it is necessary to justify why a locationally and hence socially identifiable subset of the population in the district must be singled out to bear the brunt of budgetary reductions. This is clearly a question of distributive justice.[2] Third, a particular choice among the alternatives must be made and justified. From the general description of urban school retrenchment responses above, it is clear that only the third issue has been widely politicised in rationalising the actual choices of school officials. In almost all cases, the options considered have been treated as nonpolemic givens. To be sure, questions of distributive justice have been raised by some parents, but given the pervasiveness of the technocratic conception of progressive education shared by professional educators and those serving on school boards, specific retrenchment policies continue to be justified on administrative or technical grounds rather than on distributional grounds. Whether this approach can be maintained into a future likely to be characterised by continued enrollment decline remains very much in doubt.

In short, it is our contention that the recent history of educational retrenchment has produced a social dynamic that demands the reform of local education governance — reform that should be procedural, structural, and, hence, fundamental. What is lacking in both the literature and in practice is a method of identifying the more specific directions such fundamental reform should take. Although by no means the only approach that can be taken, one that seems to hold particular promise in societies imbued with liberal conceptions of democracy is an experimental constitutional approach.

The Constitutional Choice Perspective

Constitutional choice analysis attempts to predict the selection of principles constraining social choice institutions. In general, a constitution is construed to be a form of social contract negotiated by rational individuals who, although in conflict over the specific aims of social choice, nonetheless anticipate that their welfare will be enhanced over the long run if they agree to abide by rules employed to allocate material values and resolve conflicts. Methodological individualism is assumed and each party to constitutional choice is viewed as acting independently and voluntarily under conditions of relative ignorance of the specific future public policy preferences of potential group members.

Following from these assumptions is the normative conclusion that any constitutional agreement must be consensual and implicitly ratified unanimously by all those whose future behaviour is to be constrained. To be efficacious, a constitutional agreement is expected to constrain clearly defined social choice institutions over a indefinite time horizon. Other details of the constitutional choice perspective are described and reviewed elsewhere (Reynolds, 1981; Shelley, this volume).

In most constitutional choice analyses, it is argued that specific constraints will be selected so as to optimise generalised objective functions. For example, Rawls (1971) argues that rational individuals, if conceptually placed behind a 'veil of ignorance', will choose to allocate social and economic inequalities in such a way that the benefits of the worst-off members of society are maximised. In a similar vein, Buchanan and Tullock (1962) based their analysis on the assumption that rational decisionmakers would agree to minimise the costs of social interdependence. However, uncertainty concerning individual evaluations of the costs of social interdependence precludes the accurate estimation of the expected utilities associated with a large number of prospective constitutional agreements (Reynolds, 1981; Grafstein, 1981). The result is that while individual utility enhancement may be a necessary condition for constitutional agreement it is by no means a sufficient condition. It is argued elsewhere (Reynolds and Shelley, 1981a) that under conditions of conflict the evaluation of constitutional provisions in any social choice institution should be dominated by considerations of procedural justice;[3] only those provisions that are considered procedurally fair will be viable alternatives. To be considered as fair, a proposed constitution should contain no identifiable biases in the manner in which the policy preferences of particular individuals, groups, or regions are treated in the rendering of social choices.

Under the assumptions outlined, the constitutional choice process should consist of two lexicographically ordered steps: (1) evaluation of the procedural justice of prospective constitutions, followed by (2) agreement on a group objective function (Reynolds and Shelley, 1981b). In general, it is expected that the group objective function will involve the minimisation of the generalised costs of collective activity and/or the maximisation of its benefits, subject to context-specific distributional constraints. This two-step model of choice has been tested successfully in experimental research involving an abstract collective choice problem (Shelley, 1981), but remains untested in the context of social choice conflicts characterising urban reality.

The successful application of a constitutional choice perspective to the identification of alternative systems of school governance — the focus of the remainder of this chapter — requires that the parties to prevailing school conflicts recognise (1)that conflicts are likely to be a persistent feature of school politics, (2) that existing systems of governance are inadequate to deal with existing and likely future realities, and (3) that the grounds upon which many school conflicts are founded are all legitimate and, hence, require political resolution rather than technical solution. If our interpretation of conflict surrounding school budget retrenchment is accurate, it would appear that these conditions would be met in many, if not most, urban school districts in the United States.

The process of constitutional choice, if it were to occur, would surely be sensitive to the general patterns of costs and benefits expected by participants in the absence of institutional change. For example, parents from lower income and/or minority neighbourhoods can be expected to be particularly concerned that the procedures and structures characterising school governance ensure the identification of a set of policy alternatives not limited to the closure of schools. General expectations of the behaviour of other urban actors should likewise flow reasonably directly from what we described earlier as typical patterns of conflict surrounding school budget retrenchment. What is not known, however, is to what, if anything, such diverse conflict participants would agree if they were actually placed in a constitutional or quasi-constitutional choice context in which they must either agree or all be 'worse-off'. It is toward answering this question that the simulation of constitutional choice appears particularly well suited.

Simulation of Constitutional Choices in a School Budget Retrenchment Context

The remainder of this chapter describes an experimental design recently developed by the author for simulating constitutional decisionmaking in an urban school district confronted with the prospect of continuing budgetary retrenchment. Some preliminary results from employing the design to identify possible resolutions of an actual retrenchment conflict in Cedar Rapids, Iowa, are also presented. The research reported on here is part of a larger comparative study of applied consitutional choice being conducted in conjunction with Fred M. Shelley of the University of Oklahoma.

Quite obviously, what has here been referred to as constitutional choice occurs infrequently, if ever, in reality, and that which is constitutional *in effect* is typically incremental and usually confused with administrative an technical decisionmaking. Therefore, the most feasible way to investigate genuinely constitutional decisionmaking and its sensitivity to contextual and historical factors is through some form of simulation. The simulation of collective choices through experimental designs with human subjects has been found to be a highly effective means of examining the logical consistency and potential empirical validity of public choice models in a wide variety of contexts (Smith, 1976; Plott, 1979). Permitting the manipulation of selected variables under carefully controlled conditions, small-group experimentation enables the identification of potentially relevant factors influencing collective decisions.

Study Context: School Closings in Cedar Rapids

Subjects in the project were all residents of the Cedar Rapids, Iowa, school district. Cedar Rapids is the second largest school district in Iowa, with a 1981-82 enrollment of approximately 18,500. Over the past decade the district has increasingly become embroiled in controversy over how to cope with precipitous enrollment decline and the consequent loss of state revenues. Enrollments have declined 26 per cent since their peak in 1970-71. The first several years of decline were welcomed as a relief to overcrowding, but by 1976 enrollment decline had become widely perceived as a problem. The issues, as defined by administrators and school board members were two: excess classroom space and the need to cut expenditures. The basic solutions proposed and implemented were gradually to peg teacher reductions to district-wide enrollment declines and to close elementary schools, primarily, but not exclusively, in neighbourhoods with the greater actual and projected enrollment declines.

By 1982-83 the number of regular classroom teachers had been reduced approximately 22 per cent and ten elementary schools had been closed and another was slated for closure in 1984. To offset declining enrollments in the district's three high schools, the school board narrowly voted to shift from three-year to four-year high schools, and to avoid multiple closures of the district's six three-year junior highs had voted to convert five of these to three-year middle schools (consisting of grades six through eight). The fifth junior high — the district's smallest and the one whose attendance area had the district's lowest median income — was to be slated for closure in 1984. By the spring of 1982 after the school board had narrowly voted to close the junior high and after it had become apparent that a four-year high school and a three-year middle school system really was to become a reality, conflicts between a loose coalition of parents groups and neighbourhood organisations and school decisionmakers reached unprecedented levels of intensity and acrimony. Both the City Council and the county Board of Supervisors passed resolutions urging the school district not to close the junior high school. During summer 1982, the district's superintendent resigned and, in the September school board elections, the three candidates elected had all indicated opposition to school closures. In most respects, the situation in Cedar Rapids was ideally suited as a study area for constitutional choice experiments appropriate for testing our basic hypotheses.

Experimental Design

The first and by far most difficult task in designing the experiments was to ensure that it was possible to bring the essential features of the real conflicts confronting the school district into a laboratory-like setting. In this regard, much of summer 1982 was spent trying to ferret out what policies had been implemented with regard to budget retrenchment and why. This involved open-ended interviews with school administrators, members of advisory committees and members of opposition groups and the assemblage of all publicly-accessible data on enrollment trends and district policies, including the proceedings of public hearings. What became clear rather quickly was that conflict in Cedar Rapids had escalated to such an extent that it was no longer a relatively simple case of locational conflict in which there was community agreement on the necessity of school closures but disagreement on which schools to close. The school administration and board tended to conceive of the conflict in these terms but sizable numbers of the lay public did not. Indeed, opponents to school closing and district reorganisation had been successful in focusing public debate on the fact that possible alternatives to school closures and faculty reductions had been ignored in the district's decisionmaking. Neighbourhood schools are strongly supported in Cedar Rapids and citizens appeared loath to abandon them except as a last resort.

Conditions of conflict in Cedar Rapids forced a change in the nature of the project from one of analysing the selection of a constitution to constrain the process of school closings to the broader one of attempting to simulate ways in which the conflict surrounding budgetary retrenchment in general might be resolved. In this way, the project became a much more basic test of a constitutional choice approach to conflict resolution.

The experiments were to entail bringing together small groups of persons (between seven and nine) who were known to be in conflict with one another over ways of achieving school district budget reductions and attempting to simulate both the conflict and its resolution. The resources available constrained the design to six basic experiments, each with only two replications. Half were to be conducted under conditions of high conflict wherein the district was confronted with a large expected enrollment decline, and half under lower conflict conditions wherein the district was confronted with a smaller expected enrollment decline.

Two other factors were also to be varied systematically across the experiments. The second factor was the degree of conflict polarisation. Its two levels were (a) *high polarisation* wherein the group was sharply polarised into two subgroups — one strongly in favour of school closures as the favoured budget-reducing alternative and one strongly opposed to school closures; and (b) *low polarisation* wherein there were three subgroups in the experiments — strong pro-closers, conditional pro-closers, and anti-closers. The third factor, the threat condition, was the expected policy result if the groups failed to reach agreement. It was to be simulated by a specific set of budgetary cuts across the district (including school closures) rigged so as to be objectionable to subjects in an experiment. The two levels of this factor differed in that in half of the high conflict experiments the expected policy result identified the specific schools to be closed and in the other half it merely specified the number of schools to be closed. The schools identified were rigged to be the schools nearest the subjects participating in the experiment.

Before subjects could be selected, it was essential that a considerable amount of information pertaining to the budget reduction policy preferences of potential subjects be obtained. Thus, a detailed questionnaire eliciting information on individual budget-cutting priorities and viewpoints on the appropriate role of school closures *vis-à-vis* other responses to enrollment decline was developed. It also contained questions designed to assess individual conceptions of the fairness of alternative ways for the school district to reach decisions on school closings.

To form a subject pool, a list of school and community activists thought most likely to be knowledgeable of past and present school closing controversies in the district was developed. This was developed from the lists of persons attending school board meetings concerning school closures in 1981 and 1982, from the memberships of declining enrollment study groups in the district, and from the members of three of the more influential community organisations in the city — the Rotary Club, the Jaycees, and the Junior League. From this master list, we randomly selected households and, after an initial telephone contact, mailed questionnaires to 425 persons in October and November 1982. A random sample of fifty teachers was also included in the survey. The intent was to include one teacher in each experiment so as to increase the likelihood that groups would not lose sight of the possible educational consequences of their decisions.

Three hundred and thirty-three questionnaires were returned (a response rate of 70 per cent). Of these, 76 per cent indicated a willingness to participate further in the project. These exceptionally high response rates were a clear indication that school closings and district organisation had produced rather intense feelings throughout the district. Not surprisingly, those preferring other forms of major budgetary reductions to school closures outnumbered the pro-closers by more than two to one. Seventy-five per cent thought there should be much more public input in reaching decisions about school closures and almost every respondent could identify at least one change in the present system of decisionmaking that he/she thought would result in greater 'fairness'.

The Experimental Procedures

After four rounds of pretesting versions of the experimental design, a set of procedures was identified that appeared to strike an appropriate balance between the specific conditions of conflict in Cedar Rapids and the general theoretical conditions necessary for a test of our expectations regarding the efficacy of procedurally-based constitutional choice. Subjects were recruited from among the 253 persons responding to the questionnaire who had indicated an interest in participating in the experiments. Nine persons with school closing policy preferences appropriate for simulating the two levels of polarisation in the project were asked to be subjects in each of the twelve experiments. (In practice, the number of subjects who participated varied from five to nine.) Each experiment was restricted to a two-hour time limit and was facilitated by a graduate assistant especially trained for the task. Each experiment was tape-recorded. Subjects were paid $10. All experiments were conducted in Cedar Rapids during February and March of 1983. An experiment was considered valid if the subjects who actually participated met the stipulated preference polarisation conditions of the experiment in question. Only one of the twelve experiments was invalidated on these grounds.

Each experiment consisted of three general phases. In the first phase the facilitator explained the purpose of the project and the general nature of the task the group would confront. He/she then engaged the group in a structured discussion designed in part to sensitise subjects to their individual differences regarding expectations of future conflicts in the district, perceptions of how decisions over conflictual issues are actually made in the district and assessments of how appropriate existing decisionmaking procedures are for resolving anticipated conflicts. Next, subjects were presented with information on the district's present budget and deployment of personnel and asked to indicate where they would cut the budget, if a budget reduction of a certain magnitude had to be realised because of some specified decline in enrollment. This first phase took 30 to 45 minutes and served, in a preliminary way, to indicate to the group areas in which they were in agreement or conflict. By design, the subjects were in conflict over school closings.

In the second phase, the group was presented with a scenario specifying (1) the expected enrollment decline over the next five years, (2) the expected loss in state revenues, and (3) the expected policy response of the school board. This response, the 'threat condition', was a simple extrapolation of the district's past policies and hence freighted heavily toward saving monies by reducing the number of teachers and by closing additional elementary and junior high schools. Two general scenarios were utilised — one entailing an enrollment decline of 1,000 students (over the next five years) with a $2.3 million revenue loss; and one entailing an enrollment decline of 2,000 students with a $4.6 million revenue loss. Each of these scenarios was credible given the district's own enrollment projections. The scenarios also differed on whether or not the schools slated for closure were identified by name. The specific content of the scenario then fixed two of the three factors varied across the experiments. Control over selection of subjects allowed the degree to which the conflict was polarised to be varied.

In this second phase, the facilitator engaged the group in a discussion of the expected policy response of the school board and informed the group that if they objected to it they could avoid its implementation only if they could reach a *group* consensus following one of three options. First, they could try to agree on an alternative package of budget cuts which might or might not include school closings. Second, they could try to agree to a set of objective criteria and formulas to be implemented by the school board in its budget reducing. Finally, they could try to agree on changes in the overall structure of decisionmaking in the school district, e.g. by changing the method of electing board members, the voting procedures followed by the board, the form of planning followed, or the amount and form of public input to the board's decisionmaking. Given our hypothesis that constitutional choice in a context of locational conflict should be dominated by a concern for procedural justice, we obviously were most concerned about the experimental conditions under which this option would be chosen. The facilitator clarified each of the options and urged the group to pursue the option that all subjects thought most likely to lead to a group consensus and yet resolve conflict. If they failed to reach consensus, they were to assume that the expected policy response of the school board would be implemented. The group could, however, abandon an option and shift to another at any time in the experiment, provided all in the group agreed. Once the group had decided on one of the three options, they were given more specific instructions to follow. These were designed so that comparison across experiments could be made and to facilitate their group decisionmaking. This second phase generally took from 15 to 30 minutes, leaving on average one hour for the group to reach a consensus.

The third and final phase of an experiment consisted of the group's deliberations in trying to reach consensus. Here the facilitator acted both as a moderator and facilitator, moderating discussion so that all points of view were heard, and facilitating so that the arguments were clarified and discussions remained productive. When deadlocks were reached, the group was reminded of the threat condition and urged to attempt agreement by following one of the other options.

Preliminary Results

The overall results of the experiments in terms of the frequency of agreements and types of agreement reached are both surprising and encouraging. Encouraging is the fact that in five of the eleven experiments, groups were successful in resolving conflict by following the third option (i.e., by reaching procedurally based agreements calling for changes in the school district's decisionmaking structures or procedures). All proposed changes involved redistributions of authority from the school district administration to the public. In four experiments, groups were unsuccessful in reaching any agreement, while in two experiments the groups were able to agree on some form of objective function to be employed in reaching budgetary reductions and school closures. In the aggregate, these results were as expected.

The surprise was that the patterning of agreement/non-agreement and of types of agreements across the levels of factors in the design were not as expected. In general, expectations were that:

1. Under high polarisation conditions, groups will either reach procedural agreemnts or fail to reach agreement altogether with (a) non-agreement predominating under the high threat condition and (b) procedural agreement predominating under the low threat condition.

2. Under the low polarisation/low threat conditions, agreements on either a specific package of budget cuts or on objective functions will predominate over both non-agreements and procedurally based agreements.

3. With regard to conflict level, the high conflict condition will tend to intensify the first and second tendencies (above). Namely, we expected:

a. High polarisation/low threat/high conflict to produce more procedural agreements.

b. High polarisation/high threat/high conflict to produce

more non-agreements.

c. Low polarisation/low threat/high conflict to produce other types of agreements.

As can be seen from Figure 5.1, these expectations were only partially realised. Most striking is that the expectations regarding agreements under low polarisation conditions were completely off the mark. In fact, it appears that low polarisation is a decided obstacle to conflict resolution, whereas high polarisation actually facilitates resolution. Procedurally-based agreements were the rule under high polarisation/low threat conditions (when only the numbers of schools slated for closure were specified in the scenario). In the polarised groups confronted with the threat of having *their* schools closed, there was a distinct tendency for a group to attempt to form a consensus on a set of objective criteria and formulas upon which to base budget reductions and school closures. Groups in two of the four such experiments were successful in their attempts. Preliminary analysis of the group discussions in these particular cases suggests that subjects were so inflamed by the threat of having their own schools proposed for closure that they were prone to enter into any group agreement that rationalised either the closure of fewer schools or the closure of no schools at all.

The finding that low polarisation over the issue of school closure led to a failure to reach any form of an agreement in three out of four experiments remains the most glaring anomaly. Thus far our analyses suggest that this finding may be more artifactual of the real dynamics of school closing conflicts in Cedar Rapids than it was induced by the factors manipulated in the experimental design. The low polarisation experiments were the only ones in the design that included subjects who took a more 'middle-of-the-road' position on school closing and these were also the subjects far more likely to be supportive of the existing school decisionmaking institutions. Both pro- and anti- school-closers were highly critical of existing institutions. Therefore, the institutional *status quo* had spokespersons only in these experiments and their presence seems to have served primarily to preclude the group from reaching a procedurally based resolution to the conflict (in most cases). It should also be noted that our survey uncovered relatively few persons in the district whose views on school closings could be construed as 'middle-of-the-road'.

Figure 5.1: Types of Agreements Reached Under the Experimental
Conditions

	CONFLICT LEVEL			
	High		**Low**	
	High Threat	Low Threat	High Threat	Low Threat
POLARIZATION **High**	2; N.A.	3; 3	3; 1&2	3
	Low Threat		**Low Threat**	
Low	3; N.A.		N.A.; N.A.	

1: Agreements on a specific package of budget cuts and school closures.

2: Agreement on objective criteria and formulas to be utilised in budget cutting and school closings.

3: Agreement on changes in the decisionmaking procedures and structures employed in the district.

N.A.: Non-agreement

Clearly, much more in-depth analysis of the experiments is necessary before firmer conclusions can be reached, but these preliminary results would seem to suggest that explorations into conflict-induced conceptions of procedural justice can indeed be a fruitful line of inquiry.

Concluding Remarks

Although this chapter has tended to champion a constitutional approach to what has elsewhere been referred to as the geography of social choice (Reynolds, 1981), it is both prudent and appropriate to conclude by pointing out more precisely what can and cannot be expected from the approach in a school retrenchment context. First, the approach does nothing to redress what many would call the more fundamental economic conditions that precipitated the conflict. Clearly, the identification and implementation of procedurally just institutions of decisionmaking will not cause the overall economic conditions in urban areas to improve. At best, such would only mitigate the effects of economic decline so that they are less freighted to the consistent disadvantage of certain groups. But in so doing, the effects would be felt by a broader spectrum of the population with the result that the more fundamental economic causes of the problem would more likely come to be politicised (correctly) as fundamental causes. At present, patterns of school decisionmaking are so rife with political inequities as to render the fundamental causes of conflict polemic.

Second, while a constitutional choice approach serves as a method for identifying alternative social choice institutions, it does not specify how such alternatives can be implemented. It does not create its own political dynamic. However, perhaps the alternatives identified through its application, if they are sufficiently different from existing institutions, can. It is this possibility which provides the ethical stimulus propelling our inquiry.

Notes

1. School boards are invariably dominated by citizens of high socioeconomic status. In a recent Iowa study only 2 and 23 per cent of school board members had 11 years or less of schooling and an income of less than $10,000 respectively (Paulsmayer, 1977). Candidates are often elected at large and are insulated from neighbourhood constituency politics. Hence, they tend to regard themselves not as politicians but as public guardians of a specific educational ideology. The consequence is a hegemony of the education professionals' interests over those of lay parents.

2. Distributive justice is defined as conformity to a principle of justice that requires allocation to achieve some specific distributional outcome or pattern.

3. Procedural justice is defined as conformity to a principle of justice that requires allocation to proceed according to some specific process or procedure without prior regard to the particular distributional outcomes of allocation.

References

Abramowitz, S., and S. Rosenfeld (1978) 'Setting the Stage', in S. Ambramowitz and S. Rosenfeld, (eds.), *Declining Enrollment: The Challenge of the Coming Decade,* US Government Printing Office, Washington, D.C.

Anderson, A. (1978) 'Use Decline as Opportunity to Advance', *American School and University,* **51,** 64-68 (3), 32-40 (5)

Berman, P., and M. McLaughlin (1978) 'The Management of Decline: Problems, Opportunities, and Research Questions', in S. Abramowitz and S. Rosenfeld, (eds.), *Declining Enrollment: The Challenge of the Coming Decade,* US Government Printing Office, Washington, D.C.

Bins, M., and A. Tounsel (1978) 'Changing/Declining Enrollments in Large City School Systems', in S. Abramowitz and S. Rosenfeld, (eds.), *Declining Enrollment: The Challenge of the Coming Decade,* US Government Printing Office, Washington, D.C.

Bishop, L. (1979) 'Dealing with Declining School Enrollments', *Education and Urban Society,* **11,** 285-295

Boyd, W.L. (1979) 'The Changing Politics of Changing Communities', *Education and Urban Society,* **11,** 275-284

Buchanan, J.M., and G. Tullock (1962) *The Calculus of Consent,* University of Michigan Press, Ann Arbor

Cohen, D.K. (1978) 'Reforming School Politics', *Harvard Educational Review,* **48,** 429-447

Davies, D., and R. Zerchykov (1981) 'Parents as an Interest Group', *Education and Urban Society,* **13,** 173-192

Erickson, K.L. (1975) 'Some Suggestions to Soften a Somber Economic Picture for Teachers', *Phi Delta Kappa,* **56,** 473

Grafstein, R. (1981) 'The Problem of Choosing Your Alternatives: A Revision of the Public Choice Theory of Constitutions', *Social Science Quarterly,* **62,** 199-212

Hasler, G., and G.R. Weldy (1977) 'How One District is Closing a High School', *NASSP Bulletin,* **64,** 35-46

Keough, F.W. (1978) 'Enrollment Decline: The Dilemma from a Superintendant's Chair', in S. Abramowitz and S. Rosenfield, (eds.), *Declining Enrollment: The Challenge of the Coming Decade,* US Government Printing Office, Washington, D.C.

National Center for Education Statistics (1975) *Digest of Education Statistics,* US Government Printing office, Washington, D.C.

Paulsmayer, D.L. (1977) 'Demand and Support Perspectives on Political Representation in the Municipal, County and Public School Legislative System', unpublished Ph.D. dissertation, Department of Political Science, The University of Iowa, Iowa City, Iowa

Plott, C.R. (1979) 'The Application of Laboratory Experimental Methods to Public Choice', in C.S. Russell, (ed.), *Collective Decisionmaking: Applications from Public Choice Theory,* Johns Hopkins University Press, Baltimore

Rawls, J. (1971) *A Theory of Justice,* Harvard University Press, Cambridge

Reynolds, D.R. (1981) 'The Geography of Social Choice', in A. Burnett and P. Taylor, (eds.), *Political Studies from Spatial Perspectives,* John Wiley, London

Reynolds, D.R., and F.M. Shelley (1981a) 'The Analysis of Constitutional Choice and the Provision of Locationally Specific Public Goods: The Decision to Seek Constitutional Agreement', Technical Report 130, Institute of Urban and Regional Research, The University of Iowa

Reynolds, D.R., and F.M. Shelley (1981b) 'Modeling the Choice of Constitutional Constraints on the Provision of Local Public Goods', Technical Report 132,

Institute of Urban and Regional Research, The University of Iowa

Shelley, F.M. (1981) 'Experimental Analysis of Constitutional Choice in the Provision of Local Public Goods', unpublished Ph.D. dissertation, Department of Geography, The University of Iowa, Iowa City, Iowa

Smith, V.L. (1976) 'Experimental Economics: Induced Value Theory', *American Economic Review*, **66**, 274-279

Timar, T.B., and J.W. Guthrie (1980) 'Public Values and Public School Policy in the 1980s', *Educational Leadership*, **38**, 112-115

Trotter, V.Y. (1976) 'Public Opinion, Legislation, and Declining Enrollments', in J.D. Bailey, (ed.), *Declining Enrollments and School Closings*, US Office of Education, Washington, D.C.

Valencia, R.R. (1980) 'The School Closure Issue and the Chicano community', *Urban Review*, **12**, 5-21

Wilken, W.H., and J.J. Callahan (1978) 'Declining Enrollment: The Cloud and Its Silver Lining', in S. Abramowitz and S.Rosenfield, (eds.), *Declining Enrollment: The Challenge of the Coming Decade*, US Government Printing Office, Washington, D.C.

Acknowledgements

The financial support of the National Science Foundation under Grant SES 81-20749 is gratefully acknowledged.

6

Jurisdictional Benefits and Local Costs: The Politics of School Closings

Rex Honey and David Sorenson

Introduction

School districts across the United States have been closing schools during the past decade, and in all likelihood many will continue to do so in the immediate future. Closing schools often is very traumatic, not only for those whose school is in jeopardy but also for those making the decision. The authors have embarked on a research project dealing with this acutely spatial political problem. The larger research programme has three distinct themes each of which is dealt with in this paper. First, what procedures are used in determining which schools are to be closed, if any? Second, what criteria are used in the decision-making process? And finally, whose schools get closed, i.e., do the burdens of school closings tend to fall upon certain classes or groups in society more than others? The focus of the study is avowedly American, although much that is said has relevance for many other societies, particularly those with falling numbers of school-aged children, high levels of residential mobility, and educational systems with decentralised power structures.

American School Governance

Several factors must be taken as given in any examination of education in the United States. For over 100 years the US has had compulsory universal education for all children. The view that any child may use education as a vehicle to rise in society is a cornerstone of American socio-political folklore. Handicapped children are provided with special educational support, and only under extreme circumstances are disruptive children prevented from attending school.

114

While the state must assure the provision of education for all children, children are not required to attend publicly operated schools. Private schools, especially those run by churches, are an integral part of the American educational system. These schools generally operate within guidelines determined by the states but with minimal or no financial support from public coffers. Education has been and remains a battlefield in the conflict of separation of church and state in the US Iowa courts, for example, permit the operation of Amish schools which do not meet state educational requirements because the Amish faith runs counter to the state's requirements. Iowa's courts have precluded spending public funds for furthering religious education, but they have authorised limited use of public funds to support non-religious curricula within parochial schools and to transport children to those schools.

The United States differs from many other countries in that the central government has a weak, indirect role in the field of education. Education is controlled by the states rather than the federal government. The federal government may cajole, entreat or otherwise try to influence education through a variety of means, however. Money is one of the chief means. The federal government funds a plethora of education programmes with states and local school districts having to follow federal guidelines in order to be eligible for these funds. Federal courts have also intervened to assure the fair treatment of all children, especially minority children. Nevertheless, education remains a function of state governments. The states establish teacher-training requirements, graduation requirements, control over expenditures, and even the way local school districts are organised.

Local school districts actually run the public schools, however. The discretion left to the local districts in terms of taxation, budget and curricula varies from state to state, but even in the most limited instance there is some considerable autonomy, much more than is typically the case in Europe. School districts certainly hire their own staffs and make construction decisions, although the latter often require voter approval as well. The districts also make the decisions to close schools.

Control over public education in the United States has centralised significantly in this century. As late as 1932, 127,000 school districts were operating in the US The number had shrunk to 15,000 by 1977, merely twelve per cent of the 1932 figure.

Reduction in school district numbers came about chiefly through amalgamation of old districts to merge with financial incentives (and penalties), but by and large the actual unions were worked out by the districts rather than being forced by the states. That is, the school districts were allowed to choose their new partners rather than having the states develop reorganisation schemes. Some states, mainly in the south, solved the problem differently, resorting to county school districts.

The centralisation of American education included many other factors besides larger school districts, though. The field of education became much more professional, and the states began to exercise much more control over the operation of schools, especially with regard to curricula and finance. By the 1970s many states required schools to purchase textbooks from approved lists; likewise, several states sharply curtailed districts' taxing options, the states at the same time taking over much of the responsibility for funding education. Power over education in the US consequently centralised not only into larger school districts but to state decision makers rather than locally elected school boards and locally hired school administrators (Sher, 1977).

Why Close Schools?

Clearly with the reduction in the number of school districts in the United States, especially one-school and even one-room school districts, the nation had excess schools, many of which were closed as a consequence of the school consolidation process. These were not the only schools being closed, however. Even larger school districts, those with several or even scores of schools, have been closing schools. Why have urban districts been closing their schools?

The most direct answer is that the United States has fewer school aged children. Births peaked at 4,258,000 in 1960, then slid to a low of 3,144,000 in 1975, a drop of over one million births in a year. Couple this with the tremendous construction of schools in the 1950s and 1960s, and one finds a collision between educators' expectations and demographic reality. All too many districts continued to build schools even after births began to decline. Iowa City, Iowa, for example, built four elementary schools in 1969 and 1970, increasing the supply of public elementary schools by 40 per cent. Within five years the district predictably had an excess supply of school places, a declining number of school children, and a dilemma concerning closing schools.

The American decline in the number of births is matched by similar declines in most of the advanced economies, especially European countries. Like the Americans, these societies experienced increases in total births after World War II (though usually not on such a sustained basis). Then their birth totals fell, and along with them fell the need for school spaces.

The numbers of births has been only part of the problem, of course. Equally important has been the distribution of children. The years since World War II have been the period of suburbanisation of the United States. Central city populations have actually declined, especially in the Northeast and Midwest. Until the 1970s, rural populations either declined or grew slowly, too. Growth was in the suburbs. Children were no longer where the schools were. Just as north-eastern schools lost their pupils to California and Florida, central city schools lost their children to suburban districts. Even within districts, children were moving from the old, central schools to peripheral sites. Districts often responded by building schools as new residential areas developed. Later, when decline set in, the districts had to choose which schools to close.

The districts' decision was eased by another factor which affected school closings even in areas within population declines or shifts. Some buildings deteriorated or became obsolete because of changes in educational procedures. Consequently, districts could easily justify closing their centrally-located old schools while retaining their new, modern, peripheral schools. The old ones often required major modification, such as enclosing stairwells to meet more stringent fire regulations. Often they required major repairs, such as to worn out heating equipment or faulty roofs. Rather than spend money on such non-educational expenses, districts often simply opted to close their old schools while retaining the new ones, even though the new ones probably should not have been built in the first place. School districts can, of course, replace obsolete facilities with modern ones on the same site. This was a strategy followed by the Cedar Rapids Community School District in Iowa during the 1950s and 1960s. More usual has been the replacement of an obsolete, deteriorated central building with a modern peripheral one.

One other major reson why schools have been closed in American cities has been a prevailing attitude among educational administrators that students learn better in schools large enough to provide for curricular and staff flexibility (Conant, 1959). The famous Conant report made the case for high schools with at least 100 pupils per grade. Similar studies cited the benefits of multiple sections even at the elementary level. While such thinking has been criticised strongly, enough school administrators and enough of the public accepted the positions that a number of school districts across the country moved toward larger schools. For a given number of children, larger schools equalled fewer schools, especially when coupled with enrollment decline. In order to maintain schools at a viable size, districts could overcome enrollment decline by closing excess buildings.

Even where the position of multiple section grades was not the ruling philosophy, fiscal retrenchment has forced many school districts to consider closing schools as ways to resolve financial crises. The late 1970s and early 1980s have been hard times in terms of school finance. After pruning away readily reducible costs such as extra supplies and staff coffee, school boards ordinarily have found themselves facing choices between cutting programmes and/or closing schools. The debates surrounding these choices have forced communities to face the purpose and role of education in modern society. The choices have not been easy, either on those responsible for making them or those who must live with the results. The choices have been highly political.

School Benefits

Understanding conflict over school closures in the US requires an understanding of the role of schools in American society. Schools, or more correctly education, have a hallowed position in American society. Education is widely seen as the vehicle for social and economic mobility. The local school is also typically the focus of community activity, with community identity defined by the school (Bowden, 1972).

Conflict over closing schools emerges largely because educational facilities generate two kinds of benefits, jurisdictional and local (Reynolds and Honey, 1978). Jurisdictional benefits accrue throughout a governmental unit's service area simply because of the quality of governmental performance. These can be user benefits, the chief of which accrue to all families with school children when educational services are being considered. Other user benefits would include after-hours use of school facilities, e.g. for meetings, recreation programmes, or adult education.

Jurisdictional benefits can also be indirect. Property values tend to be higher, for example, where services are perceived to be of a high standard. A 'good' school district may also inculcate in its pupils a sense of community value, an attitude of good citizenship rather than vandalism. The product of education is educated people, and even though post graduation mobility is high, further jurisdictional benefits may be enjoyed by communities with quality schools if the graduates are more self-sufficient, skilled and able to pursue advanced education. Jurisdictional benefits occur across a school district's territory and affect everyone within that territory, not just those attending school.

Quite different are those benefits accruing because one is close to a particular school building. These are local benefits, available only to those who live close enough to a facility to gain some additional advantage. While all children may benefit from quality schools, children living close to schools obtain extra user benefits. These children spend less time getting to school, can use the school more readily after hours, and possibly experience fewer safety hazards. Parents will likely have an easier time participating in school activities, too. All adults living near a school may benefit from having available meeting space or recreational options at hand. Schools also provide indirect benefits to their immediate neighbours. Schools, for example, often provide a park-like setting, complete with lawns and playing fields, which may especially be enjoyed on weekends. Schools also tend to make quiet weekend neighbours. Residences near schools tend to have higher values than equivalent homes elsewhere. These local benefits are available only for those who live near schools. Closing schools, of course, destroys these benefits while imposing additional costs on children and their parents when children are reassigned to more distant schools.

Figure 6.1 illustrates the relationship between jurisdictional and local benefits. Districts with superior school systems generate high levels of jurisdictional benefits while inferior districts generate low levels. Atop these levels of benefits come benefits available only to those residing close to the schools themselves. While the jurisdictional benefits are spatially uniform, local benefits exhibit strong distance decay effects, falling sharply as one moves farther from a school.

Locational Conflict Over School Closings

School closings are political decisions, fraught with all the power struggles of other politics. They are not exercises in achieving justice nor balancing acts for social scientists. The potential for conflict is high because people in one or more areas in a district face the prospect of losing their local benefits so that the district may raise (or retain) its jurisdictional benefits.

One could hypothesize that districts should close schools only when gains in jurisdictional benefits surpass losses in local benefits. Of course measurement problems immediately arise, especially with the introduction of indirect benefits. Setting the measurement problems aside, one would still have to sustain an argument that failure to close a school would be sufficiently injurious to the prime educational function of a school district that closing a school would be justified.

Imposing conditions of Pareto optimality or a Rawlsian approach would protect the interests of those at risk of losing a school (Rawls, 1971). A decision is Pareto-optimal only if no one becomes worse off. Likewise, Rawls would regard a decision as just only if the person affected most severely by a decision wound up at least as well off as before the decision. These conditions could be met in either of two ways. First, this would be attained if gains in jurisdictional benefits were so great that they surpassed losses in local benefits even for those whose school was closed. This could occur, for example, if a district faced a fiscal calamity such that several curricular programmes faced cancellation unless alternative funds were saved by closing a school. Second, the Pareto and Rawlsian conditions could be met by somehow compensating those losing their local benefits. The affected pupils, for example, could be assured preferential treatment in desirable classes, or extraordinary transportation options might be provided so children would not have to walk to their newly assigned school even if closer than normal busing requirements. Under such conditions, no school would be closed unless even those losing local benefits from that school were to emerge at least as well off as before. Considering indirect local benefits would complicate the situation even further, risking introduction of revealed preference and free rider problems, among others (Archer, 1981). One alternative would be to disregard the legitimacy of indirect local benefits altogether, arguing that these are incidental to the educational mission of a school district

Figure 6.1: The Relationship Between Jurisdictional and Local Benefits

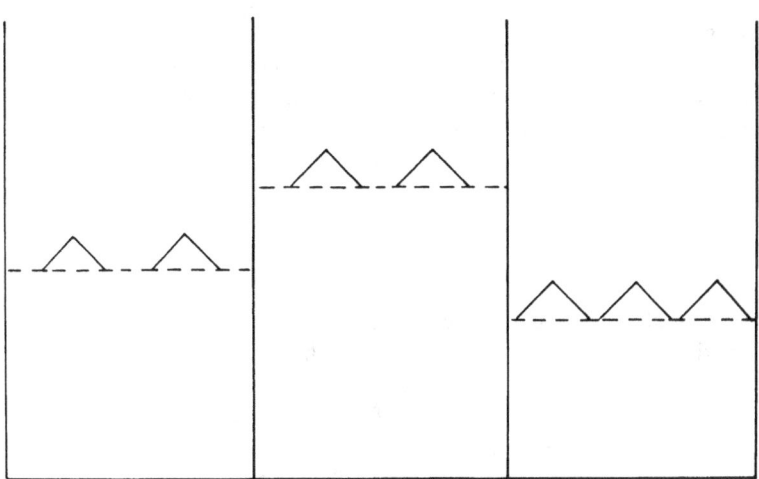

- – – JURISDICTIONAL BENEFITS

/\   LOCAL BENEFITS

and that they are unearned, stemming as they do from the financial base of the entire district, not just themselves.

Political decisions, of course, are not made under Pareto or Rawlsian conditions. Even with net positive utility, a majority could force inordinate sacrifice by a minority. For example, in order to fund a programme for 'gifted children' (generally from middle-class and above homes for a number of largely cultural reasons), a district could close an inner-city minority school. Alternatively, a district could expand its remedial programmes (generally benefitting lower class children, again largely for cultural reasons) by closing a school in a middle class neighbourhood.

Even worse, of course, are the political opportunities for a majority to exploit a minority. Similarly, those in power may simply exploit a situation for their own advantage. One in Iowa City, for example, used the subterfuge of needing an alternative educational programme which the district administration wanted to terminate. The district's superintendant succeeded in getting the district's oldest, smallest school closed; that school, of course, housed the experimental, alternative programme. Having closed the programme's building, the superintendant (and school board) refused to transfer the programme to another school without approval of staff and parents at the recipient school. No one else wished to house the experimental programme, all opting instead for the *status quo*. The administration succeeded in eliminating its wayward programme, the district achieving a modicum of savings at the expense of the adherents of the alternative school.

Programme Versus Buildings

School closing issues have become more sensitive — and more politicised — in recent years. Obvious targets for closing have often been closed already with the only choices left among sound buildings in neighbourhoods which still have children. Fiscal retrenchment, the consequence of stagnation of the American economy as well as suburbanisation, has left urban school districts, as well as many older suburban ones, with severe economic problems. All too often districts have had to cut deeply into their budgets. Sometimes choices have been framed as pitting programmes against buildings: should surplus space be reduced by closing schools so that programmes can be saved (or sometimes, added); or should educational offerings be reduced, possibly sacrificing entire programmes, possibly cutting across the board, so that all buildings may be kept open?

Several factors impinge on a district's decision. Many of these are spatial. Will indeed the jurisdictional benefits inherent in retaining or developing programmes balance the local costs of closing buildings? The answer will depend in part on the number, sizes and distribution of schools. Could a district, for example, close a building without generating increased transportation costs? If sufficient capacity is available in other schools within walking distance, a district could close a school without bearing additional transportation costs.

Closing schools may also depend on the match of programmes in neighbouring schools. In some districts individual schools or even teachers determine reading programmes, for example. Where adjacent schools have textbooks with different reading philosophies, merger would likely require additional expenditures on material, so savings would be reduced.

Possibly the greatest limitation on savings from closing schools is limitations on staff reductiSomewhere near eighty per cent of most school district budgets are for salaries, most importantly teacher salaries. Only if closing a school allowed staff reductions would a district be likely to achieve significant savings. When pupil-teacher ratios are held constant, savings would be limited to administrative and support positions — often much less than adherents of closing schools expect.

Desegregation is a further complicating factor affecting — sometimes even generating — school closings in the United States. Desegregation requirements may bring the issue of racial balance into school decisions (Lord, 1977). A particularly acute problem is that desegregation decisions unpalatable to whites may elicit flight responses from whites, whether by actually moving other school districts or opting for private schools (Adams and Brown, 1976). Desegregation programmes, of course, have often been implemented by courts after adjudging a school district's efforts inadequate.

Procedures for Closing Schools

Unlike desegregation issues, which have often fallen to the courts, school closing decisions have largely remained the prerogative of local school districts. As with any political decision, the procedures followed are critically important. States have tended to take a fairly distant stand, providing guidelines and hearing appeals but otherwise leaving school location and closing decisions to locally elected officials.

A review of dozens of school closing decisions reveals that districts have tended to follow two major decision strategies. In one, the district officers, perhaps aided by professional consultants, assess the situation, weight options, and develop recommendations. In the other, the district administration forms a special citizens review committee and acts only after receiving that committee's report.

The first strategy has been interpreted as an effort to de-politicise the decision, turning it into a technical issue to be decided by experts (Reynolds, 1982). Experts assess characteristics of buildings, transportation impacts, curricular implications, and costs. If the experts present an array of alternatives with supporting background data, this mode of operation need not yield a politically antiseptic result. On the contrary, it could lead to a more informed debate so that value choices can be discussed in full light of the facts.

The second alternative, often dubbed the 'Blue Ribbon Commission', has likewise been criticised, seen as an attempt to shift attention from the topic until the committee reports. Often these committees are packed with people committed to high levels of education, e.g., teachers and parents. The businessman head of such a commission in Milwaukee, for example, wrote a minority report deriding his colleagues for failing to consider the interests of the community as a whole (Brockel, 1978).

Whichever of the basic strategies is followed — experts or citizen committee — the school board is charged with making the decision, or more exactly, decisions. The order in which decisions are made is crucial. The problem may be equated with solving several simultaneous equations when answering one will affect answers to others. Consequently, control over the agenda is crucial. This gives significant advantages to those in positions of power, both administration and board, as well as those astute in political in-fighting. (In Cedar Rapids, Iowa, for example, inarticulate leadership seemed to doom one group's effort to save their neighbourhood school though by the district administration's avowed criteria another school should have been closed. That school, however, was in an upper middle-class neighbourhood home to many influential people.)

The depth and breadth of study is also important in school closing decisions. Are only direct effects to be considered, i.e., effects directly involving education? or should broader community impacts be considered? An administration proposal in Iowa City, Iowa, would have closed a school the existence of which was the cornerstone in a revitalisation plan by the municipal administration. Educational experts may tend to prefer to limit discourse to their areas of expetise than broaden evaluation into areas where others are better informed and better skilled.

Critically important issues include who determines the criteria to be used in deciding whether to close a school and if so which school or schools to close. Criteria selection is crucial because it may well determine the outcome. This depends of course on how the criteria are used. They could, for example, be technical requirements with their application actually determining results. Alternatively, they could be guidelines which decision-makers subjectively weigh in their decision calculus. Determining options for closure is important, too. Serious consideration of all buildings may result in generation of needless data and wasted labour if only a subset of schools is really to be considered. Limiting options obviously limits choice; protecting one's own local area can be accomplished by keeping a particular school off the target list.

School boards are elected bodies purportedly acting on behalf of their constituents. The boards hire professional educators to provide education. A chief question with regard to closing schools is the role of the public because the decision is not merely technical but very much political and value-laden. Experience shows that public input will be minimal until potential closure sites are targeted. Then response is likely to be mammoth when people see themselves threatened directly and no longer simply the subject of an abstract discussion.

Procedures are crucial in school closure decisions. The state role tends to be limited to ensuring fair procedures. The State of Iowa's Department of Public Instruction has issued guidelines for districts to follow (Table 6.1). If districts fail to follow these guidelines, opponents may appeal to the state. Decisions may be overturned, but only to force districts to repeat the decision process employing proper procedures. The state does not itself decide whether schools should be closed.

Table 6.1: Iowa Guidelines for Procedures to Be Followed in Determining Whether to Close Schools.

---

1. Establish a timeline for decisions in advance.
2. Keep everyone informed.
3. Solicit public output.
4. Conduct sufficient research.
5. Have open and frank discussion.
6. Keep proper records of proceedings.
7. Make the final decision in an open meeting.

Source: Larry Gustavson, Department of Public Instruction, State of Iowa

Whose Schools Are Closed?

Deductions and regulations aside, how do school districts actually go about determining which schools they will close? The authors examined school closure decisions in the central city school districts of metropolitan areas in three states: Minnesota, Wisconsin and Iowa. These cities form more of a class rather than a cross-section, but they do share sufficient experience in dealing with school closing problems to unveil a variety of responses to a shared problem. The districts tend to be large, geographically and in enrollment, and they tend to have experienced both enrollment decline and redistribution of enrollment within their boundaries.

Instructive with regards to differences in approaches are the various criteria used by the districts to select schools to be closed. Tables 6.2 through 6.5 list the criteria used by Milwaukee, Sioux City, Madison and Kenosha. Other districts were sometimes less explicit. The main concerns of the districts appear to have been potential savings, quality of the buildings, distribution of children, and curricular considerations. Seldom did the districts deal with impact on a neighbourhood losing a school in a formal way.

The cities in the study have all closed schools in the past decade. Given the districts overt emphasis on strictly educational criteria, one might ask what have been the consequences of closing schools in urban American — or at least this subset of urban America? Have certain identifiable groups been forced to bear disproportionate burdens in terms of lost local benefits so that jurisdictional benefits may be retained?

The literature on the location of noxious facilities documents the disproportionate burden carried by the economically disadvantaged and politically inert in the United States (Wolpert et al, 1972). Losing salutary facilities such as elementary schools is analogous to receiving a noxious facility, so one might logically expect a disproportionate amount of the local costs of school closings to strike the same population. In addition, given the criteria school districts cite (Tables 6.2—6.5), one would expect the same finding. Old school buildings in need of repair are more likely to be found in older neighbourhoods. Furthermore, mature areas with declining enrollments may have populations with little experience in political activity. So, whether one group is fighting for advantage over another or simply the interests of the larger number of children are being considered, the result expected is that poorer, older areas should lose their schools more frequently than more well-to-do, newer areas.

Attempting to step back a moment from the political fray, the authors sought to examine some of the consequences of school

Table 6.2: Milwaukee Criteria for Selecting Elementary Schools to be Closed

1. The costs associated with the facility as measured by:
   a. Per pupil costs which exceed the mean.
   b. Excessive costs for needed or desired modification.
   c. Energy costs which exceed the mean.

2. The adequacy of the facility and site as measured by:
   a. Access to the site/building is adequate.
   b. Close proximity to another school with similar programme.
   c. Structure is not fire resistive.
   d. School does not contain all facilities needed for educational programme.
   e. School has structural or mechanical deficiencies.
   f. Site size less than adequate for school programme.

3. The demographic considerations relating to the facility as measured by:
   a. Attendance area enrollment well below school use capacity.
   b. Use capacity of building below the level of board policies.
   c. Enrollment below the standards set in board policy.
   d. Enrollment in the school does not contribute to integration.
   e. Attendance area population trend exceeds city-wide trend.

4. The adequacy of the educational programme in the building as measured by:
   a. Building is not fully utilised for instructional purposes.
   b. Achievement level below the mean.
   c. Building is not accessible to the handicapped.
   d. School does not contain a recreational programme.

Table 6.3: Sioux City Criteria for Selecting Elementary Schools to be Closed.

1. Building enrollments and projections.
2. Age of building and parts of building.
3. Use as another educational facility to accommodate other high priority programmes.
4. Structural condition of the building.
5. Cost of maintenance and operation.
6. Location in relation to adjacent schools.
7. Adequacy of site.
8. Specialised instructional or support space.
9. Routes to school.
10. Accessibility to handicapped.
11. Influence on district's desegregation plan.
12. Provision of space for special education programmes.
13. Distance to school and impact on transportation.
14. Cost savings to the district.
15. Potential growth factor of the community.

Table 6.4:   Madison Criteria for Selecting Elementary Schools to be Closed

---

1. Enrollment minimum of two sections per grade.
2. Projected enrollment.
3. Students within walking distance to school.
4. Students within walking distance to adjacent schools.
5. Adjacent schools within walking distance can accommodate.
6. Operational costs ($ per square feet), maintenance, energy consumption.
7. Operational costs ($ per student, present enrollment), maintenance, energy consumption.
8. Cost per pupil of school operation (instructional and non-instructional costs; average costs used on salary items and adjusted for special programmes).
9. Potential for new or rehabilitative residences with elementary children.

Table 6.5:   Kenosha Criteria Elementary Schools to be Closed.

---

1. Physical facilities as they affect the educational programme (gym, library, lunchroom, special education, etc.).
2. Problems relating to transportation.
3. Per pupil cost factors (such as energy, maintenance, instructional, etc.).
4. Permanency of recommendation.
5. Effective utilisation of instructional personnel and programmes.
6. Population trends.
7. Make-up of student population.
8. Keeping families together in a K-6 elementary school.
9. Other uses for the building according to district needs.

---

closings, in particular how neighbourhoods losing their schools were expected to have larger minority populations than those retaining their schools. This is because of lower income, older neighbourhoods and lower levels of political participation by blacks. Areas retaining schools were expected to have higher percentages of their population below the age of eighteen. This is because school districts seem, through their decision criteria, to be sensitive to the residential distribution of children. Further, neighbourhoods retaining schools were hypothesised to have higher educational levels because this would be related both to propensity to participate in politics and to political skill. Likewise, median incomes were hypothesised to be higher in areas retaining schools. With regard to housing, neighbourhoods retaining their schools

Table 6.6: Characteristics of Census Tracts Losing and Retaining Elementary Schools.

Retaining Schools		Losing a School	Level of Significance
5.77	% population Black	6.83	
35.32	% population below 18 yrs.	34.33	
11.95	Median education	11.61	0.10
$10,678	Median income (1970 Census)	$9,754	0.04
68.80	% housing owner occupied	63.84	
77.08	% single family housing	73.92	
54.18	% housing built before 1950	65.68	0.03

were expected to have higher percentages of owner occupied housing and higher percentages of single family housing. These were because of an expectation that home owners and those with single family homes would feel a greater sense of belonging to a neighbourhood and have a greater stake in preserving the neighbourhood's resources. Conversely, areas losing their schools were hypothesised to have more housing built before 1950 because areas with older homes would likely have older schools and fewer children, each rendering them more vulnerable to school closings.

Lacking data on school attendance areas — because such areas change and districts maintain poor archives of data on past attendance areas — census tract data from the 1970 US census were utilised. Tracts were used as surrogates for neighbourhoods served by specific schools. Minneapolis, St. Paul and Milwaukee were excluded from the analysis because their size and racial makeup made them very different from the other cities in the study. A data set of census tracts was developed, 41 having lost a school and another 102 having retained their schools. Discriminant analysis was used to examine the hypothesised relationships (Table 6.6). In every case the relationship was as hypothesised; however, the strength of relationships was significant statistically in only three instances. The strongest was the age of housing with median income a close second. Somewhat weaker but still significant was median education.

Disadvantaged groups do appear to bear a heavier burden than middle class groups when schools are closed in medium-sized midwestern cities. This does not prove any attempt to discriminate against these groups, but the burden they pay in lost local benefits is there regardless of intent. Given the purported jurisdictional benefits justifying school closings, disadvantaged groups might legitimately ask for more equitable distributions of educational benefits, either in the form of reduced losses in local benefits or special programmes for the children to compensate for their losses.

References

Adams, J.S., and K.M. Brown (1976) 'Public School Goals and Parochial School Attendance in Twenty American Cities', in J.S. Adams (ed.) *Urban Policymaking and Metropolitan Dynamics*, Ballinger, Cambridge, Mass., pp.219-255

Archer, J.C. (1981) 'Public Choice Paradigms in Political Geography', in A.D. Burnett and P.J. Taylor (eds.), *Political Studies from Spatial Perspectives*, Wiley New York, pp.73-90

Bowden, L. (1972) 'How to Define Neighborhood', *Professional Geographer*, **XXIV**, pp.227-228

Brockel, H.C. (1978) *Minority Report of the Long Range Planning Commission to Study School Closings, Buildings and Sites*, Milwaukee Public Schools

Conant, J.B. (1959) *The American High School Today*, McGraw-Hill, New York

Lord, J.D. (1977) *Spatial Perspectives on School Desegregation and Busing*, Association of American Geographers, Washington D.C.

Rawls, J. (1971) *A Theory of Justice*, Harvard University Press, Cambridge, Mass.

Reynolds, D.R., and R. Honey (1978) 'Conflict in the Location of Salutary Public Facilities', in K.R. Cox (ed.), *Urbanization Processes and Conflict in Market Societies*, Maaroufa Press, pp.144-160

Sher, J. (1977) *Education in Rural America*, Westview Press, Boulder, Colorado

Wolpert, J., A. Mumphrey, and J. Seley (1972) 'Metropolitan Neighborhoods: Participation and Conflict Over Change', Association of American Geographers, Washington D.C.

7

Policy Evaluation and Selection: Can Formal Methods Help?

Bryan H. Massam

Introduction

Considerable interest is shown by academics, planners, politicians and the public in the topic of the generation and the evaluation of policies for the provision of public goods and services and the selection of a best policy. Interest ranges from the theoretical treatment of abstract optimisation problems to practical matters whereby actual conflicts have to be resolved. All recognise that the problem of defining and searching for the best alternative policy is complex because multiple criteria and goals must be considered, and not least of all because many individuals and groups will be involved in the determination of the criteria and goals. The search process which involves the collection of information may be lengthy and costly, opinions and preferences may shift during the study, and conflicts can arise. The scale of the study and the types of policies considered as well as the time horizon over which the search is made, the implementation of the policy undertaken, and the impacts evaluated all serve to complicate the problem further.

We might argue that given such a complex decision-making environment it is most unlikely that any formal method could be developed to identify a best policy; however we must recognise that attempts are being made to structure decision-making procedures and to incorporate measurements of impacts into the debate. A variety of procedures are being developed to help in the evaluation of alternatives, and in the general improvement in the quality of public planning and the use of public funds.

The purpose of this paper is to identify a number of issues relating to selected procedures which are being developed to compare policies and help in the definition and selection of a best one. Following this introductory section a general policy impact matrix is defined. There follow brief remarks on benchmark policies, an overview and application of a new procedure for classifying policies using data in a policy impact matrix, and a critique of a selection of alternate formal methods for analysing such a matrix.

The provision of public goods and services to urban dwellers is of interest to government officials, analysts and planners, and probably most of all to those who do or do not enjoy such goods and services. Government officials are concerned with the direct and opportunity costs of the services, the determination of priorities among services and the amount of each service offered, the impact of the investments on the local and national economies, the consequences on regional development policies, as well as the impacts on voting patterns and political stability. The complexity of the issues regarding the involvement of governments in the provision of public services is summarised in a White Paper by the British Government, *Development and Compensation: Putting People First* (1972, p.l) which clearly indicates that the heart of contemporary political debate (in most Western advanced industrialised market economies) is to strike a balance between

> ... the overriding duty of the state to ensure that essential developments are undertaken for the benefit of the whole community and no less compelling need to protect the interests of those whose personal rights or private property may be injured in the process.

It has been noted by Smith (1982) and Agnew (1982) that in many parts of the world we are caught between rising costs for services, and stable or declining revenues. Government responses tend to be pre-occupied with short-term expenditure and revenue policies. Recent articles in *Transatlantic Perspectives* on the role of governments in catering to contemporary social needs include the following comments:

> Partly they [governments] are slashing programs and benefits; partly, as these cuts wound affected groups, they are restoring programs and benefits and raising some taxes. But this approach represents a stop-gap course of action ...

and

> ... a basic reshaping of the traditional model, which postulates

a governmental agency financed by appropriations derived from taxes, providing services uniformly available and accessible without charge, with professionals accountable to elected officials and elected officials accountable to the voters (Kolderie, 1982, p.6)

The uniformity of availability and accessibility, and the zero price assumption clearly do not stand up to empirical verification and, we can ask, what kind of basic reshaping of the system is possible? From the monetarists we note that 'Lakerisation', and privatisation have been suggested (Frazier, 1981), whereas decentralisation with increased participation of individuals forms part of the emerging creed of the Social Democratic Party in the United Kingdom (Williams, 1981). Other suggestions which are being made to accommodate massive structural employment patterns of advanced industrialised countries, and to provide decent lives to individuals, include alternate versions to the market economy for distributing income and for providing services (Roberts, 1982; Clarke, 1982). The state of tension between the means of providing public services and the increasing demands for social services has been widely documented (*The Economist*, 1982).

Quantitative analysts attempt to structure relationships among components of the political economic system (parsing, using the terminology of Huggett, 1980), to try to understand what impacts emerge from alternate policies. Not infrequently analysts and planners attempt to suggest ideal patterns which have maximum efficiency or equity. For narrowly defined location-choice problems McAllister (1976), Hodgart (1978) and Hansen and Thisse (1981) have shown that different 'best' locations exist depending upon whether the definition of best considers equity, efficiency or is derived from a voting procedure. We should note that there is a large body of theoretical work which focuses on the problem of identifying a procedure to provide a consensus from individual preferences. While much of this work does appear to consider questions of reasonableness and fairness, it is difficult to apply any single numerical procedure to an urban public service provision problem, to accommodate accessibility, and to allow trade-offs among criteria. There are also severe difficulties associated with accounting for time and differential effect (Schaffer and Lamb, 1981). A complete operational definition of a numerical social welfare function remains to be provided.

It is obvious that formal practical policy analysis must involve the measurement of impacts, and we are reminded by Taaffe (Introduction to Smith, 1973) that, 'We really have no way of knowing if things are getting better or worse in view of the bewildering diversity of standards of measurement attached to most social problems', and Teitz (1968, p. 36) notes that, 'rules of thumb [for comparing alternate policies] have been developed but for the most part without ways to evaluate the results or to stimulate investigation of new systems'. He argues for a solid theoretical base to help determine the optimum size and location of public facilities. In a more practical vein Hatry (1972) offers a comprehensive table of workload measures and quality factors (often called measures of effectiveness or evaluation criteria) for a wide range of public services. A recent example of the application of formal measures of effectiveness and efficiency for public services is provided by Allen (1982). He quotes the empirical studies currently underway to improve public service provision in the City of Thunder Bay, Ontario, Canada. With the increasing use of social indicators Taaffe's criticisms have to some extent been answered.

Hatry (1972, p.783) comments that:

> Many new productivity improvement approaches need to be tried out in local governments if productivity is to be improved ... However, without adequate measurement, so-called evaluations are likely to be little more than public relations stories by the sponsors and of minimal practical use.

Measurement is clearly one of the keys to improving planning the provision of services, and Bracken (1981) emphasises the important role of evaluation in planning and policy-making: 'Evaluation can be regarded as the corner stone of attempting to improve the quality of planning activity and policies, and will involve making explicit value judgements about the worth of particular policies'. Without ways of evaluating or measuring alternate policies, rational policy-making will not emerge.

Within the framework of the system for providing public goods and services we can identify five structural features. They have been the focus of theoretical work and are usually referred to as:
(1) N — the number of facilities
(2) S — the size of each facility
(3) L — the location of each facility

(4) B — the location of the boundary enclosing consumers who are eligible to use or be supplied by a particular facility. (May be a *de facto* or *de jure* boundary.)

(5) NW — the network through which services are delivered.

It is combinations of these features which give rise to a system which in turn provides benefits and cause costs to be incurred. Clearly alternate configurations have different distributional effects of benefits and costs. The crux of the policy anaysis question is then to evaluate the alternatives in terms of the distribution of impacts, and with reference to some defined objectives in order to identify the most satisfactory alternative. In this chapter we will not consider the theoretical literature which deals with these five structural features and which attempts to characterise optimum conditions. A review of theoretical work which examines the relationships among the features within the context of a debate on centralisation versus decentralisation for public facilities in a rural context is provided by Massam and Askew (in press).

Finally in this section we can turn to recent work in management science and operations research which formulates the policy analysis problem in the following terms. We will refer to this statement as Stewart's problem (1981):

Given k criteria and N alternatives, the problem facing the decision maker is to select an alternative k such that the collection of criterion values ($Xkj, j = 1, 2, ... N$) is preferable to that of any other alternative.

The basic data set needed to address this problem is a policy impact matrix (PIM), and in the next section we will examine such a matrix.

A General Policy Impact Matrix

The essential details of a PIM are shown on Figure 7.1. The score:

$$t_j \times g_{,l}^i$$

is the impact value for policy i using criterion j, with respect to a social group g at a location l, during a time period t. Examples of such a matrix are shown on Tables 7.1, 7.2 and 7.3. Typically the

Figure 7.1: Sample Policy Input Matrix

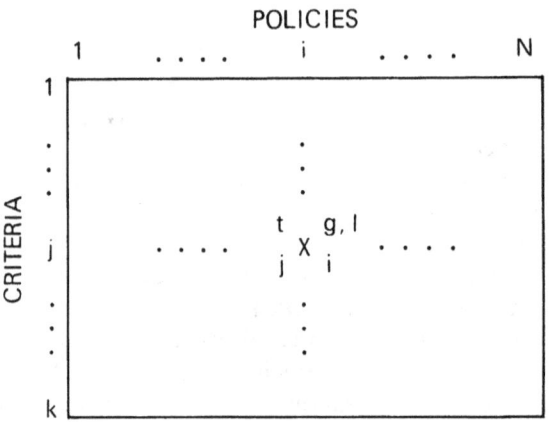

data available for practical exercises excludes the g, t and the l components, and this limits the validity of the results of the analysis.

McAllister (1980) provides a review of procedures for using such a matrix to calculate 'grand total' scores for each policy. The basic problem of this approach relates to commensuration, and while this has been recognised and documented by Nowlan (1975) and Lord *et al.* (1979), among others, we still find simple additive models using ordinal data being used. Some argue that the additive model is legitimate if the original data in the matrix are on interval scales and if each scale for each criterion is standardised. The problem of assessing the relative importance of criteria remains. A weighted additive model provides an easy response without considering the form of the indifference function among criteria. Attempts to determine the trade-offs among criteria and the shape of indifference curves exist and a variety of heuristic algorithms are now available (Siskos, 1982). An interesting interactive model for determing indifferences has been developed by Brown and Valenti (1982), using theoretical concepts developed in social psychology.

An alternate way of considering the criteria is to determine their relative importance or weighting. This is necessary if an additive utility model is employed for comparing policies (see, for example,

Table 7.1:   Hypothetical Town of Brove: Levels of Achievement of
Objectives by Alternative Policies

Policy	Coronary Deaths within		Infant Mortality	Old people's housing	Defective infants
	One week	Three years			
	(m)	(n)	(p)	(N)	(M)
1	100	200	100	0	20
2	100	200	100	1000	23
3	100	200	70	0	32
4	100	200	70	1000	35
5	100	200	20	0	30
6	100	200	20	1000	40
7	300	100	100	0	15
8	300	100	100	1000	19
9	300	100	70	0	18
10	300	100	70	1000	20
11	300	100	20	0	22
12	300	100	20	1000	28
13	250	150	100	0	15
14	250	150	100	1000	20
15	250	150	70	0	21
16	250	150	70	1000	22
17	250	150	20	0	23
18	250	150	20	1000	29
19	100	100	100	0	22
20	100	100	100	1000	28
21	100	100	70	0	23
22	100	100	70	1000	30
23	100	100	20	0	38
24	100	100	20	1000	40
25	100	100	20	1000	15

Benchmark 'best' policy: 25
Source: Rivett (1977)

Jacquet-Lagrèze and Siskos, in press). The weighting problem has
received attention particularly from psychologists in their
consideration of preference models (see Shanteau, 1980). Saaty
(1980) provides a novel way of determining the relative importance
of criteria using pairwise comparisons expressed in a positive
reciprocal matrix of the form shown on Figure 7.2. In this example
four criteria are compared. Saaty suggests that a nine point scale is
an appropriate one for assessing the relative attractiveness of pairs
of criteria. A score of 1 indicates indifference. In Figure 7.2 the

Table 7.2: Impact Matrix Values for Fire Station Location Problem in North York, Ontario, Canada

Alternatives: Given 5 sites, the problem is to select the best set of 3; there are 10 possible combinations

Criteria: Measures of accessibility in minutes to different land uses

| | Alternative Policies | | | | | | | | | | Benchmarks | |
	1	2	3	4	5	6	7	8	9	10	11 (best)	12 (worst)
1	1.65	1.66	1.63	1.67	1.63	1.64	1.65	1.64	1.63	1.63	1.63	1.66
2	1.88	1.92	1.85	2.40	1.88	1.94	1.87	1.92	1.91	1.81	1.85	1.94
3	1.50	1.50	1.57	1.56	1.59	1.59	1.54	1.61	1.59	1.63	1.50	1.61
4	2.79	2.73	3.19	2.73	2.89	2.63	2.71	3.23	2.92	2.63	2.63	3.19
5	2.42	2.40	2.36	2.33	2.44	2.40	2.31	2.44	2.38	2.40	2.33	2.44
6	3.15	2.90	3.08	3.08	3.12	2.94	3.08	3.06	2.98	3.00	2.94	3.12
Policies:	1	2	3	4	5	6	7	8	9	10		
Sites:	(1,2,3)	(1,2,4)	(1,2,5)	(1,3,4)	(1,3,5)	(1,4,5)	(2,3,4)	(2,3,5)	(2,4,5)	(3,4,5)		

Source: Massam (1981) p.26

Table 7.3: Facility Location Problem: Criterion Ratings

Criterion

Alternative	A	B	C	D	E	F	G	H	I	J	K	L	M	N	O	P
1	3	4	8	10	7	6	1	6	6	10	10	2	2	8	3	5
2	3	2	1	10	7	7	4	6	6	10	10	2	7	5	3	5
3	5	2	2	10	6	8	3	7	3	8	7	2	6	4	2	4
4	7	2	2	10	6	8	1	7	3	10	7	4	6	4	1	4
5	6	6	5	10	8	8	2	10	4	10	10	4	8	6	3	3
6	7	5	4	10	5	6	2	10	3	10	10	4	8	6	4	4
7	7	5	3	10	8	8	5	5	7	10	10	4	7	7	2	5
8	6	6	5	10	7	7	3	10	4	10	10	6	8	6	4	5
9	1	6	6	6	7	8	5	10	4	10	10	6	6	7	7	7
Ideal	7	6	8	10	8	8	5	10	7	10	10	6	8	8	7	7

Source: Stewart (1981)

Figure 7.2: Sample Positive Reciprocal Matrix

	A	B	C	D	Priority vector
A	1	5	6	7	0.61
B	1/5	1	4	6	0.24
C	1/6	1/4	1	4	0.10
D	1/7	1/6	1/4	1	0.05

score of 7 for the comparison of criteria A and D indicates that A is very strongly preferred to D. Data in such a matrix can be used to calculate a priority vector. That is the normalised principal eigenvector. The priority vector gives an indication of the relative importance of criteria. If the score in each cell of the matrix is 1, then the priority vector is (0.25, 0.25, 0.25, 0.25); all criteria are equally important. Saaty's method typically involves only one subject. The problem remains of assessing the relative importance of individuals and groups who express their preferences for criteria. One of the major characteristics of a public choice urban problem is surely that there are groups who have competing preferences, priorities and demands as well as varying levels of information and commitment to participation in a formal policy evaluation and choice exercise. These are the realities. For a narrowly-defined policy choice problem it may be reasonable to accept Stewart's definition of the problem. The task of the analyst becomes one of classifying the alternatives with respect to a benchmark policy. In the next section brief comments on benchmarks are provided and the following section provides a review of a general procedure to classify alternate policies using data in a policy impact matrix.

Benchmark Policies

The general notion of a benchmark is readily accepted in planning as it can represent a satisfactory or desirable level of achievement which the planning exercise is trying to match. Within the context of formal policy analysis a benchmark can be stated as an objective function or as a hypothetical reference policy with known characteristics, and for a classification exercise a benchmark, with the latter qualities, allows an interpretation of the classification. The alternate policies are compared to these benchmarks and the closer they are to an ideal benchmark the more attractive they are. The preferred policy is the closest to the ideal. For the analysis of a PIM an ideal benchmark can be defined (see Table 7.1: policy 25 is an ideal benchmark), or a pair of benchmarks, for example, a best and a worst can be used (see Table 7.2). In order to interpret the scale or space into which the policy options are mapped it is necessary to have some reference points. Consider the one and two dimension spaces in Figure 7.3. Without the location of the benchmarks on these patterns it would not be possible to interpret the classifications of policies to determine their relative attractiveness. For the one-dimension scale we do not know *a priori* how to interpret the end points, and for the two-dimension pattern, we have no clear indication of the meaning of the axes I and II.

A general procedure for classifying alternatives using a PIM and a set of weights for criteria is available and is discussed below. The procedure is computationally fast and allows a variety of sensitivity tests to be conducted.

Concordance and Scaling Model

A concordance and scaling model allows a classification of the alternate policies to be produced. The form of the classification is a geometrical pattern usually in a one or two dimension space of the form shown on Figure 7.3. Full details of the procedure and a practical example are given in Massam (1980) and will not be repeated here. For the purposes of this chapter we will consider the use of this model for analysing Table 7.3 using a set of five experiments. Details of the experiments are given in Table 7.4; different benchmarks and weighting schemes are used. The selection of the criteria weights is for illustrative purposes only. For a practical example Saaty's method could be used to determine a set of weights using information from an individual subject

A summary of the one-dimension classification is given in Table 7.5. Policies 8, 6, 5 and 9 are consistently at one end of the scale and, given the location of the benchmarks, we can infer that these four policies are among the best. Policies 3, 4 and 2 are consistently

Table 7.4: Facility Location Problem: Details of Experiments

Experiment	Benchmark Definition	Criteria Weights
1	Nil	all equal
2	Tie Best	all equal
3	Tie Best	'O' = 0.25; others = 0.05 each
4	Tie Best and Tie Worst	all equal
5	Tie Best and Tie Worst	'O' = 0.25; others = 0.05 each

Source: Massam (1982)

among the least preferred. According to Stewart's analyses of these data, using factor analysis and correspondence analysis, he suggests that policies 8 and 7 are the best ones. Alternative 9 is included only if criterion 'O' is exceptionally important.

We suggest that concordance analysis and scaling provides a formal model for tackling Stewart's problem which is more flexible than factor analysis or correspondence analysis. Four reasons are suggested for this claim. First, the model allows for the criteria to be weighted. By changing the relative importance of selected

Table 7.5: Facility Location Problem. One Dimension: Interval Values

				Experiments					
1		*2*		*3*		*4*		*5*	
8	-100.0	10	100.0	10	100.0	10	100.0	10	-100.0
6	-69.2	6	53.4	8	42.0	7	56.4	8	-60.5
5	-63.2	8	51.4	6	31.4	6	41.8	6	-49.5
9	-46.4	5	44.8	9	16.3	5	38.8	9	-39.7
7	-27.3	9	10.5	5	4.6	9	19.8	5	-31.5
1	7.9	7	1.4	7	-20.3	7	21.4	7	-16.1
2	15.5	1	-38.5	1	-32.4	1	5.8	1	-4.0
4	71.6	2	-46.2	2	-38.3	2	0.5	2	-3.9
3	100.0	4	-82.4	4	-71.7	4	-15.8	4	24.0
		3	-100.0	3	-100.0	3	-33.4	3	40.8
						11	-100.0	11	100.0
K_1	0.10		0.09		0.10		0.06		0.09
K_2	0.01		0.04		0.03		0.03		0.04

K_1: Kruskal's stress coefficient: one dimension
K_2: Kruskal's stress coefficient: two dimensions

Source: Massam (1982)

criteria, that is by assigning heavier weights to some criteria or a single criterion, it is possible to study the effect on the classification. This can be considered as a sensitivity test. With respect to this point Stewart (1980) notes:

> the main advantage of correspondence analysis is that various runs with different weights are not needed in order to judge their effect. In the correspondence analysis 'map', alternatives differ from the "ideal" (or any other hypothetical alternative if desired) along various directions which can be related to criteria or combinations of them. Thus by inspection it is possible to see
>
> (a) if one alternative is further from ideal than another along a similar direction, then no change in criterion weights can alter this fact
>
> (b) if one alternative is further from ideal than another along substantially different directions then sufficient weighting of criteria associated with the direction of the former will alter the relative distance.

Our model avoids the use of subjective interpretations implicit in inspections and the determination of similarity of direction.

Second, the model is based on pairwise comparisons of alternatives for each criterion and, in this step in the algorithm, we can define a threshold size which has to be exceeded in order for one alternative to be rated as different (superior or inferior) to another. If the impact values jXi are not subject to any measurement errors, and for any difference between jXi and jXi' where jXi is the value for alternative i for criterion j, jXi' is the value for alternative i' for criterion j, then the parameter defined as the just noticeable different (JND) is set to 100. If the difference has to be at least five per cent in order for one alternative to be preferred to another, the JND for this particular criterion is set to 95. Each criterion has an associated value for the JND.

Third, the level of agreement between the classification of the alternatives and the information from which it was derived is measured by an index; that is, Kruskal's stress coefficient (K). The use of this index provides an objective measure of the goodness of fit of the classification, it should not be interpreted as having statistical significance, rather as an objective function. The lower the value of K (minimum = 0; maximum = 1.0) the better the fit.

Figure 7.3: One and Two Dimension Policy Spaces

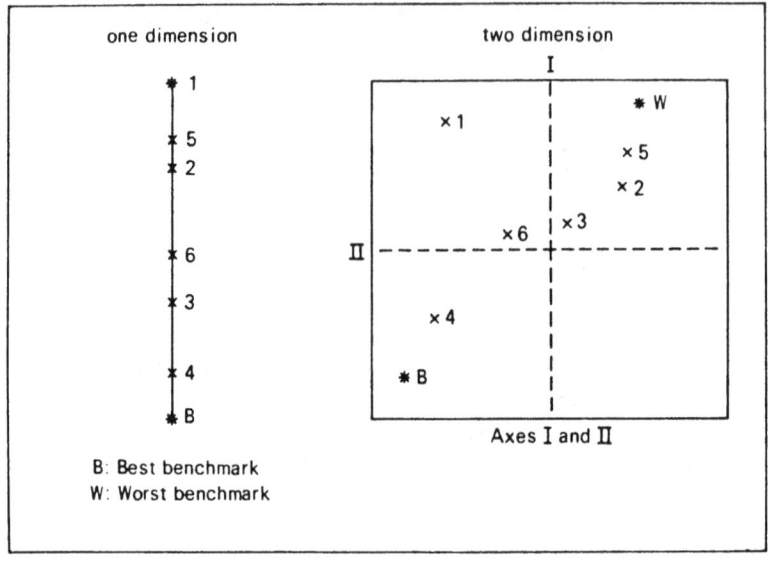

In the examples discussed here a maximum of two dimensions is used for the classification. However as $K \leqslant 0.10$ for the one dimension solution this is deemed to be a satisfactory classification. The K values for one and two dimension solutions are shown on Table 7.5. Fourth, the model provides a classification of all alternatives so that the magnitude of the differences between them and the benchmarks can be identified and portrayed. For these reasons we suggest that the model deserves close scrutiny as a viable way to tackle the policy selection problem as defined by Stewart.

A Comparison of Several Procedures

In the previous section brief comments on a comparison of the concordance and scaling model with factor analysis and correspondence analysis were made. It should be noted that there are a variety of formal procedures available for tackling Stewart's problem and for determining the utility of a policy using multi-criteria methods. The time is ripe for a comparison of these methods to determine which are appropriate. This leads into a general discussion on the identification of criteria for judging the worth of a model, and as a first attempt at this exercise the following points are suggested:

(i)   Can the model be incorporated into a planning process?
(ii)   Are the data available?
(iii) Can new data be added easily?
(iv)   Can sensitivity analyses be conducted?
(v)   Is the internal logic of the model acceptable?
(vi)   Is the model comprehensible to planners?
(vii) Can the results be displayed to non-experts?
(viii) Does the model demand sophisticated technology to be made operational?
(ix)   Is the model expensive to implement?
(x)   Can the model be used to teach, complement or improve judgement and intuition?

Moving from general principles to specific examples, two recent studies have been undertaken to compare models. The first, by Massam (1982), compared the concordance and scaling model to the following four models:
(1) An interactive additive utility model (AUM), as discussed in Marchet and Siskos (1979).
(2) A modified AUM, as discussed in Marchet and Siskos (1979).
(3) The Keeney and Raiffa (1976) model.
(4) The ELECTRE multi-criteria choice model after Roy (1977).

The second study, by Massam and Askew (1982), used the data presented by Rivett (1977) as shown on Table 7.1, to compare the concordance and scaling model to four other models. These models are:
(1) Structural mapping of indifferences as discussed by Rivett (1977).
(2) Additive utility model as discussed by Rivett (1977);
(3) The lexicographic ordering model.
(4) The factor analysis model

For this study a summary of the five best policies out of the set of 24 is given on Table 7.6. Among the eight best policies identified by Rivett's two models (24, 19, 21, 15, 11, 23, 22, 12), five were also identified by the concordance and scaling model (24, 23, 22, 21, 12), three by the lexicographic model (24, 11, 12) and only one by factor analysis (11). Table 7.6 illustrates that the choice of policy selection model determines the set of preferred policies.

Table 7.6:   A Comparison of Results Using Five Models and Rivett's Data

Rivett Structural Map	Utility Values	Lexicographic Ordering	Factor Analysis	Concordance and Scaling
Best				
24	24	24	13	24
19	23	7	7	23
21	22	13	9	20
15	21	11/12/8	11	22
11	12		1 (not ordered)	21/12

Source: Massam and Askew (1982)

It is worth evaluating the models, to identify any advantages or disadvantages that each may have. Comparisons of this nature are uncommon, although McAllister (1980) has looked at the overall framework of the evaluation process, and he produced a checklist of criteria by which to judge evaluation methods. It is with this list in mind that the following comments are made.

Factor analysis appears to be the least satisfactory model as not all the information available is used. As used by Stewart it would seem to be primarily a method for ordering criteria rather than policies, and this is one part of the decision-making process which should be carried out subjectively. Stewart (1981) states that the identification of factors reveals basic sources of conflict among the alternatives. In actuality the conflict is revealed among the criteria, a situation which should already be known by the decision-maker who formulated the criteria. Stewart himself (1981) shows that factor analysis can break down on problems where there are fewer alternatives than criteria. His discussion of, and analysis by, correspondence analysis indicates that it may be a more suitable multivariate technique to adopt.

Lexicographic ordering is also at fault through not necessarily considering all the information. It has the advantage of allowing the decision-maker to assign an ordering to the criteria, but using ordinal information means that the magnitude of the difference between ranks is not known, and the lexicographic principle can result in only the first few criteria being considered. The data set assumption of equal weighting for all criteria illustrated the binding nature of the ordering prerequisite, although a possible solution to this problem has been proposed by Massam and Askew (1982), using a JND value.

The drawbacks of the two methods proposed by Rivett — the use of indifferences and utility values — are as follows. First, in both cases the use of a subjective interpretation of the data prior to an objective analytic technique would seem to undermine the validity of using a scaling technique and an additive model. Second, both models assume that the analyst can correctly perceive the marginal rates of substitution between the criteria. For the indifference model this would be intuitive, but the utility value model needs commensurability between the scales by which the criteria are measured to allow the summation to be possible. Typically the additive utility model achieves this by data normalisation but the subjective approach is dependent again on the analyst's intuition. Together these models appear to violate two principles of decision-making procedures. Being subjective they are unsystematic and thus non-replaceable; further the nature of the models makes the data analyst also a decision-maker as the two roles are necessarily inseparable here. This situation is extremely rare in contemporary society.

None of the problems discussed here appear to apply to the concordance and scaling model. It is objective, permits incommensurable scales, and utilises all the data given. It allows sensitivity analyses to be easily included through varying different aspects of the model, and presents the set of best policies in a way that indicates the relative attractiveness of all the policies. Further disaggregation of the data to indicate the distributional characteristics of the impacts can in theory be incorporated into the model. The ability of a model to compare policies according to the individual groups or sectors of the population affected is an important quality. The common element of all the models reviewed here is that they aim to present a set of better policies from a larger set of feasible alternatives. As such the models should be seen as sieving devices for reducing the set of possible alternatives, rather than as a means of identifying the best policy. The most appropriate models need to be comprehensive, systematic, simple and quick, and be an aid in the decision-making process, not a means of making the decision. It is suggested that the concordance and scaling model meets these criteria.

Epilogue

Where do we go from here? Four avenues are suggested. First, with respect to formal models *per se*, there is clearly a need for a series of comparisons and the development of a set of criteria for evaluating the comparisons. Closely related is the need to broaden the definition of the policy choice problem to consider the full set of impacts as defined by the term

$$
{}^{t}_{j} X {}^{g,l}_{i}
$$

as well as to allow individuals to express their different opinions. Clearly, formal models cannot stand alone, they must be incorporated within the political system. Perhaps they can best serve to provide a framework for data collection, preliminary analysis and as tools for identifying preferred alternatives from different perspectives using different criteria and preferences. It is hard to imagine how discussions on the criteria and preferences can be reduced to objective technical steps. Second, while considerable progress in computer technology has been made in recent years, there is scope for improvements to algorithms to allow interactive programmes at decentralised locations to become much more widely available. Third, in order to judge the effects of the use of formal models and alternate urban political systems on the provision of public goods and services to urban dwellers, time series empirical analyses seem appropriate. Such analyses will require data on the quality of services and definitions of objectives. One such objective may refer to equality. For example, are public services being provided more equitably to urban dwellers? Within the context of Metropolitan Toronto, Frisken (1981) has undertaken a study on the equalisation of public services. She uses the following 'six separate (though interrelated) equalization objectives ...

(1) More uniform provision of capital work and other services deemed necessary to support continued economic growth.
(2) More equal distribution of taxable resources among separate taxing jurisdiction.
(3) More equal distribution of low and moderately-priced rental housing among central and suburban municipalities.
(4) Redistribution of income through increased provision of

services entailing income transfers (welfare, public housing) and more equal availability of these services to residents throughout the area.

(5) More equal provision of services thought to affect equality of opportunity (education, public health, public recreation).

(6) More equal accessibility to go by public transit for the outer parts of the area'.

Within the same vein we draw attention to the Toronto Area Survey (Atkinson 1981); this is a public opinion survey of evaluations of neighbourhood conditions and municipal services in Metropolitan Toronto and its boroughs. Results for three points in time — 1977, 1979 and 1980 — are compared. This leads to the fourth avenue, namely an advocacy role for the academic. Direct participation by academics may contribute to an enlightened debate among citizens and government officials on the search for appropriate ways of providing the goods and services to citizens which will improve the world in which we all must share.

Acknowledgments

The research reported in this chapter was partially supported by a grant from the Joint Program in Transportation (University of Toronto — York University)

References

Agnew, J. (1982) Federal policy and the possibility of urban triage, mimeo paper, AAG, San Antonio

Allen, J.R. (1982) 'Step One: measure municipal productivity', mimeo, Ministry of Municipal Affairs and Housing, Government of Ontario, Toronto

Atkinson, T. (1981) *Evaluation of neighbourhood conditions and municipal services in Metro-Toronto and its boroughs*, I.B.R. Report No. 3, York University

Bracken, I. (1981) *Urban planning methods, research and policy analysis*, Methuen, London

Brown, C.A., and T. Valenti (1982) *Multi-attribute tradeoff systems (MATS): user's and programmer's manual*, Environmental and Social Branch, Division of Planning Technical Services, Engineering and Research Center, Bureau of Reclamation, U.S. Department of the Interior, Denver, Colorado

Clarke, R. (1982) *Work in Crises*, St. Andrews Press, Edinburgh

The Economist (1982) 'The Withering of Europe's Welfare States', October 16-22, 67-71

Frazier, M. (1981) 'Private alternatives to public services', *Transatlantic Perspectives*, 5, July Frisken, F. (1981) 'Factors contributing to public service equalization in the restructured metropolis: the case of Toronto', mimeo paper, Canadian Political Science Association, Halifax, May 27

Great Britain (1972) *Development and Compensation: Putting People First,* Cmnd.5124, London, HMSO

Hansen, P. and J.F. Thisse (1981) 'Outcomes of voting and planning: Condorcet, Weber and Rawls locations', *Journal of Public Economics,* **16**, 1-15

Hatry, H.P. (1972) 'Issues in productivity measurement for local governments', *Public Administration Review,* **32**, 776-784

Hodgart, R.L. (1978) 'Optimizing access to public services: a review of problems, models and methods of locating central facilities', *Progress in Human Geography,* **2**, 17-48

Huggett, R. (1980) *Systems analysis in geography,* Oxford University Press, Oxford

Jacquet-Lagrèze,E. and J. Siskos(in press) 'Assessing a set of additive utility functions for multicriteria decision-making: the UTA Method' , *European Journal of Operational Research*

Keeney, R.L. and H. Raiffa (1976) *Decisions with multiple objectives: preferences and trade-offs,* John Wiley, New York

Kolderie, T. (1982) 'Government in the Eighties: Shifting Roles and Responsibilities' , *Transatlantic Perspectives,* **6**, 6-9

Lord, W.B., D.H. Dean and M. Waterstone (1979) Commensuration in Federal Water Resource Planning: problem analysis and research appraisal, Bureau of Reclamation, U.S. Department of Interior, Research Report 79-2

McAllister, D.M. (1976) 'Equity and efficiency in public facility location', *Geographical Analysis,* **8**, 47-63

McAllister, D.M. (1980) *Evaluation in Environmental Planning,* MIT Press, Cambridge

Marchet, J.C. and J. Siskos (1979) 'Aide à la décision en matière d'environment: application au choix de tracé autoroutier', *Sistemi Urbani,* **2**, 65-95

Massam, B.H. (1980) *Spatial search: applications to planning problems in the public sector,* Pergamon Press, Oxford

Massam, B.H. (1981) *The fire station location problem in North York: Ontario,* Urban Studies Working Paper No. 2, York University

Massam, B.H. (1982) 'The search for the best route: an application of a formal method using multiple criteria', *Sistemi Urbani,* **5**,181-192

Massam, B.H. and I.D. Askew (1982) 'Methods for comparing policies using multiple criteria: an urban example', *OMEGA,* The International Journal of Management Science, **10**, 195-204

Massam, B.H., and I. Askew (in press) A theoretical perspective on rural service provision: a system approach', in G. Enyedi and R.E. Lonsdale (eds.) *Rural Public Services: International Comparisons,* Westview Press, Boulder, Colorado

Nowlan, D.M. (1975) 'The use of criteria weights in rank ordering techniques of project evaluation', *Urban Studies,* **12**, 169-176

Rivett, B.H.P.(1977) 'Policy selection by structural mapping', *Proc. Royal Society,* **354**, 407-423

Roberts, K. (1982) *Administration, Unemployment and the Distribution of Income,* European Centre for Work and Society, Maastricht

Roy, B. (1977) 'ELECTRE III : an algorithme de classement fondé sur une representation floue des préférences en présence de critères multiples', *Cahiers du Centre d'Etudes de R.O.,* **20**, 13-24

Saaty,T.L. (1980) *The analytic hierarchy process : planning, priority setting, resource allocation,* McGraw Hill, New York

Schaffer, B. and G. Lamb (1981) *Can equity be organised?* UNESCO, Paris

Shanteau, J. (1980) *The concept of weight in judgement and decision making : a review and some unifying proposals,* I.B.S. Centre for Judgement and Policy, University of Colorado, Report No. 228

Siskos, J. (1982) 'Evaluating a system of furniture retail outlets using an interactive ordinal regression method' , *LAMSADE,* Université de Paris, **38**, 37

Smith, C.J. (1982) The urban services paradox : shrinking supply in times of rising demand, mimeo paper, AAG. San Antonio, March Smith, D.M. (1973) *The geography of social well being* McGraw-Hill, New York

Stewart,T. (1981) 'A descriptive approach to multiple criteria decision-making', *Journal Operations Research Society,* **32**, 45-53

Stewart, T. (1980) Personal communication

Teitz, N.B. (1968) 'Toward a theory of urban public facility location', *Papers, Regional Science Association,* **21**, 35-51

Williams, S. (1981) *Politics is for people,* Penguin, Harmondsworth

8

Urban Development and The Geography of Personal Services:
The Example of Medical Care in the United States

Paul Knox
James Bohland
and
Larry Shumsky

Introduction

Most research into urban service delivery has centred around issues of equity, efficiency, social well-being and community conflict surrounding the location of particular facilities and amenities. Such research has already gone a long way towards illuminating an important dimension of modern cities and, equally important, it has also generated valuable conceptual, methodological and theoretical insights. Conversely, the bulk of research in this area suffers from a significant weakness in being almost entirely ahistorical, with little or no attention being given to the evolution and locational dynamics of the services under consideration. This is doubly unfortunate, since the historical dimension not only provides a fuller understanding of contemporary organisational and geographical patterns but also offers considerable potential for linking ecological, locational and 'conflict' analyses to a broader and more flexible theoretical base. In this chapter, the evolution and locational dynamics of one particular group of services — medical care — is reviewed in order to illustrate the formative influence of changes in economic and social structure on subsequent spatial relationships between producers and consumers or, in this case, medical care professionals and their patients. The central argument is that, in order to understand the geography of medical care, it is essential to appreciate the interaction of changes in science, technology, residential segregation, medical care settings, economic cycles, professional structure and state intervention: all of which must be seen, in turn, as part of the overall dynamic of urbanisation.

The voluminous literature on the history of medicine has, however, virtually ignored the broader social and economic context of urbanising society. Much of the history of medicine consists of mere collections of facts arranged thematically or chronologically: usually without reference to any theoretical framework whatsoever. Written mostly by physicians for physicians, it was for a long time concerned mainly with famous personalities and key medical discoveries. Moreover, medicine and medical care were generally assumed to be independent variables in any relationship with social change, leaving the interactions between medicine, medical care, society and political economy to the periphery of an introspective and atheoretical discipline.

There have been some recent attempts to give greater prominence to these interactions in a more broadly conceived social history of medicine. The conventional account of the march of medical progress has been increasingly questioned as attention has been turned towards issues such as the implications of the shifting boundaries of professional and lay control over the the definition of health and disease, the changing relationships between different groups of medical care professionals, and the increasing degree of social control stemming from the practice and organisation of 'modern' medicine (see, for example, Cartwright, 1977; Grob, 1977; Reverby and Rosner, 1979; Starr, 1982; Vogel and Rosenberg, 1979; Woodward and Richards, 1977). What have not been systematically explored, however, are the social and economic consequences of the interaction between, on the one hand, the changing structure of cities and the changing nature of urbanism and, on the other, the changing structure of the medical profession and the changing nature of therapeutic practice. We know that the urban transition was characterised by profound changes in economic organisation, class, family and community structure, social values and municipal government. We also know that the same period (roughly between 1850 and 1930) was distinguished by several changes which together culminated in what Shryock (1947) described as 'the advent of truly modern medicine': the introduction of anaesthesia, the acceptance of germ theory, the expansion of the hospital system, the specialisation of medical care professionals, the radical reform of medical education and licensure, and the professionalisation of orthodox medicine. The question is: how were these economic, social and medical changes inter-woven, and with what consequences for the availability of medical care between different neighbourhoods, social classes and demographic groups? The purpose of this essay is to set out these issues within the dynamic framework of the urban transition and to point to some of the gaps in our present understanding of this dimension of urban service delivery.

The Context of Change

The dynamics of urbanisation subsumed a number of processes which are relevant to the evolution of medical care systems. The overarching process, of course, was the transformation of the economic base which brought an increasing division of labour, a new vulnerability to the periodicity of business cycles, and a new rhythm of daily life dictated by the factory and the office. In manufacturing, production shifted from the household through a series of distinctive stages: from sub-contracting via outside specialists to shop manufacture, small factory production and, finally, large-scale factory production (Starr, 1977). Personal services, while lagging behind this basic transition, followed a comparable pattern of development; though within the field of medical care the independent professionals equivalent to the 'shop' stage and the clinics and dispensaries equivalent to the 'small factory' stage have tended to survive alongside the big hospitals which are the equivalent of the large-scale production stage. As Starr points out, the result is not so much a series of distinct stages as a differentiation of *settings*. It is the changing importance and *relative location* of these settings which must be the focus of any consideration of the locational dynamics of medical care in cities.

Economic restructuring and specialisation also forged new social classes. Together with the basic realignment of society into owners and workers, there emerged the need for a secular bureaucracy: an army of clerks and agents to keep accounts and to attend to correspondence. Thus there emerged a middle class whose purchasing power, residential preferences and attitudes to the city were soon to have a profound effect on the social geography of the city (Knox, 1982a). Equally important were the changes which took place in the structure and role of the family. The imperatives of industrialisation and urbanisation required a rationalisation of everyday life. The new discipline of time was exacerbated by the constraints imposed by the increasing geographical separation of home and workplace, making it impossible for the family to fulfill its traditional roles (Pred, 1981). At the same time, increased residential mobility contributed towards isolating the conjugal family from the larger network of kinship, so that fewer relatives were available to perform informal service functions. Thus, in order to accommodate the routine of the new economic order, families not only gave up their economic function as a unit of production but also shed many of their responsibilities for educating the young, supporting the aged, caring for the sick, and being self-sufficient in a variety of economic activities. The corollary of this, of course, was the expansion of a whole spectrum of new service professions and service establishments: tailors, barbers and laundries as well as doctors, dispensaries and hospitals.

Meanwhile, innovations in technology precipitated changes in urban development and urban lifestyles which in turn promoted the expansion of the personal service professions and triggered successive changes in the economic and spatial relationships between the producers and consumers of personal services. By reducing the opportunity costs and transport costs of services, innovations like the electric tram, the telephone, paved roads and, later, the motor car, stimulated the effective demand for specialised services and increased productivity (and therefore profitability) in the service professions themselves (Starr, 1977). The same innovations also facilitated radical changes in urban ecology, releasing the pedestrian city to realign itself into a mosaic of distinctive communities sprawling over a much larger territory and providing a new logic for the locational preferences of every kind of enterprise.

Finally, as Polyani noted (1957), nineteenth-century urbanisation was characterised by the apparent contradiction of a movement towards free enterprise on the one hand and social protectionism on the other. The latter may be seen as the outcome of 'internal survival mechanisms' which evolved in order to protect industrial capitalism from its own internal conflicts and contradictions (Knox and Cullen, 1981). The central paradox was of course that while urbanisation was required by industrial capitalism to marshall goods and labour efficiently, it created dangerous levels of discontent, life-threatening environments, and a whole series of negative externalities which threatened business efficiency. Hence the paternalistic philanthropy of the late nineteenth century, the legitimation of liberal reform movements, and the emergence of the public health movement, town planning and municipal socialism.

All these were to influence the evolution of medical care systems in both Europe and the United States, though their relative importance was not always the same. It was in the United States that the initial relationships between urbanisation and the organisation of medical care were expressed most clearly, uncluttered as they were by pre-existing institutional or legal constraints.

Medical Care and the Social Order of the City

Attitudes to health during the early phases of metropolitan development in America were somewhat fatalistic. The emerging urban culture was still strongly influenced by the spiritual, existential and deterministic values of pre-industrial society: 'rational' and 'scientific' ideas were neither trusted nor respected. In medicine, this translated to a view of health and disease based on the idea of the body as a holistic system of intakes and outputs whose equilibrium was dependent on constitutional endowment and environmental conditions (Rosenberg, 1977). Implicit in this belief system — for both layman and physician — was the idea that every part of the body was inextricably related with every other. As a result, therapeutic practices were based on the idea of 'regulating' the equilibrium of the body, using a variety of time-honoured folk remedies to induce perspiration, urination, defecation or vomiting and so control the intake and output of the body. Most medical care was, accordingly, administered in the home by relatives and friends relying on cheap nostrums and traditional herbal cures (Harvey, 1979). In more serious cases, where physicians were consulted, therapeutics were simply more extreme versions of the same strategy. Leeching and cupping served to alter the internal balance of the body; blistering drew off unwanted toxins; and massive doses of mineral poisons were administered as purgatives, emetics and tonics. As with non-professional care, the *setting* for this 'heroic' therapy was generally the patient's home. Indeed, it was considered rather less than respectable to have to wait on the physician (Rosenberg, 1977). The majority of families, then, could afford medical care when it was necessary. 'Respectable' families who could not were treated free at dispensaries, which were originally set up as charitable institutions in order to keep honest folk from the almshouse, where they might be morally contaminated by the company of drunks, prostitutes and lunatics. The latter were kept clear of dispensaries by the simple gatekeeping device of requiring a certificate of recommendation from one of the sponsors of the dispensary. Those who could not acquire such a passport had to choose between the almshouse and the cheap services of a quack (Rosner, 1982a). Hospitals did exist in most large cities (although there were only just over 100 in the whole of the United States in 1873 (Vogel, 1979)), but most of these also required some certification of deservedness. In many cases hospitals were small, established and maintained by local religious or charitable organisations, and oriented to specific social groups (e.g. orphans, unmarried mothers) or neighbourhoods (Rosner, 1982b). Moreover, they were generally regarded, quite justifiably, as 'gateways to death'.

The role and status of medical care professionals in this environment were clearly constrained by the limitations of medicine itself. It is important to note, however, that they were also influenced by the dominant ethic of free enterprise and by the prevailing moral climate. The supply of family doctors, dentists, pox doctors, pharmacists, midwives, abortionists and other medical care professionals was almost completely unregulated by state or federal licensure. Commercial medical schools prospered, turning out graduates with rudimentary skills and a patina of professionalism, while diploma mills offered a large selection of 'qualifications' to those who were more impatient to enter the field. When the Illinois Board of Health was given the power to license physicians in the 1870s, it found that almost ten per cent of the doctors in the state admitted to having purchased their diplomas (Kaufman, 1976). Coupled with people's preference for self-treatment, the overall result was an oversupply of medical personnel. Consequently, many found it extremely difficult to support themselves from their practice. Some resorted to flambouyant behaviour and the extremes of heroic therapy in an attempt to publicise their business (Johnson, 1974); others were forced to pursue a second occupation — as a vintner, apothecary or a vetinarian — in order to supplement their income.[1]

Nearly all were part of the emerging group of 'marginal men' (Inkster, 1977) spawned by the changing structure of society: members of neither the working nor middle classes, but able to move freely in both social environments. Their role in this broad context was closely related to the moral and cultural order of the city: they reflected and transmitted prevailing moral values and social attitudes. A good example of the former is the way physicians translated Victorian attitudes to masturbation into the framework of medical theory, thus reinforcing social control over the moral offence. Masturbation was held to upset the equilibrium of the body, producing 'nerve shocks' which, in turn, led to everything from vertigo and loss of memory to rickets, acne and anaemia. Indeed, records show that some people were hospitalised for 'chronic masturbation', this even being pronounced as the cause of death for certain unfortunate individuals (Englehardt, 1978). Meanwhile, by assuming the role of general advisor and father confessor to the family, the physician also served as a medium through whom some families, at least, were able to resolve and clarify the conflicting demands and shifting values produced by the rapidly-changing city.

Urban Development and the Rise of Modern Medicine

The transition from this situation to the radically different system of medical care operating by the early decades of the twentieth century is conventionally ascribed to changes in science and technology: the introduction of anaesthesia, antisepsis, and so on. But, while these undoubtedly did exert a direct influence on medical practice and the organisation of medical care, it is important to recognise both the stimuli and the constraints provided by the overall process of urbanisation. One of the first significant impacts of urbanisation in this context was the great increase in demand for professional care and treatment. In the first instance, changes in the structure and role of the family, together with the increasing number of individuals living alone in the city, made for a much greater reliance on medical care as a commodity. The initial response of the medical care system was twofold. First, there was an expansion of the number and output of commercial medical schools and diploma mills. Second, there was a marked growth in non-orthodox therapeutics: Thompsonianism, eclecticism, homeopathy, osteopathy and, later, mesmerism, hydropathy, electro-magnetism and Christian Science.

This medical sectarianism was closely attuned to the changing cultural order of the city, appealing in particular to anti-intellectualism, romanticism and egalitarianism. Moreover, it represented the medical manifestation of *laissez-faire* and democratic ideals: 'If unorthodox religion was tolerated, why not also unorthodox medicine? If anyone could minister unto souls, why not also unto bodies? And if the success of churches depended on the judgement of the people, so too should the fate of rival medical professions' (Shryock, 1947, p.87). One of the earliest and most successful of the unorthodox therapeutics was Thompsonianism, which held that moderation was the key to health and relied entirely on botanical and herbal remedies. This appealed to a wide spectrum of the public not only because it avoided the traumas of heroic therapy but also because it was sensitive to certain social and intellectual currents. Its mildness and simplicity appealed in particular to women, who were increasingly the decisionmakers in family medical matters; while its condemnation of alcohol struck a chord with the moral tenor of mid-Victorian society and won the support of a broad spectrum of church and moral leaders (Kett, 1968). The appeal of homeopathy — the other major alternative to orthodox medicine — was broadly similar although it had a more scientific and sophisticated approach based on the doctrine of *similia simibulus curantor*, using as medicines minute doses of substances known to induce symptoms similar to those of the disease and relying heavily on the recuperative energies of nature. This tapped and unified the strands of sentimentalism and spiritualism among the constituency which had already been attracted to Thompsonianism, while earning grudging respect — as the 'Aristocracy of Quackery' — among the more worldly and scientifically-oriented supporters of orthodox therapeutics. The success of sectarian medicine is reflected in the results of a survey of 1200 households in Los Angeles just after the turn of the century. Only ten per cent employed orthodox, non-sectarian physicians as their family doctor, compared with 60 per cent who employed osteopaths, 10 per cent who employed Christian Scientists, and 10 per cent who employed chiropractors (Lawhead, 1926).

The challenge of sectarian medicine induced important changes in medical care. In terms of therapeutics, the response was to withdraw from the worst excesses of the heroic approach and to adopt a more rigorous attitude to theory and research (Rosenberg,

1977). In terms of competition for the patient's dollar, the response was an organised campaign to outlaw sectarian practice. Orthodox medicine was called upon to 'organise or perish' (Markowitz and Rosner, 1979), thus providing an important stimulus for professionalisation. The American Medical Association (AMA), together with numerous local societies, rapidly increased in membership during the third quarter of the nineteenth century and, from their inception, one of their primary aims was to control what was described as 'overcrowding' in the profession (Fishbein, 1946; Stevens, 1971). Medical education became an important issue in attempts to establish some semblance of professional stability, to exclude dissident theories of medical practice, and to generally restrict entry to the profession. It should also be acknowledged that concern with educational standards was also spurred by the need to cope with the advances in bacteriology, chemistry, pathology and physiology which had gained momentum during the 1870s.

Meanwhile, other forces increased the motivation of the profession to organise itself. The problem of 'overcrowding' was aggravated in the last quarter of the nineteenth century by the hardships of inflation (Burrow, 1977). Furthermore, the number of paramedical personnel working in the health field had increased, making certain skills of the family doctor obsolete as they began to

Table 8.1: Medical Care Practitioners in San Francisco, 1881 and 1911

	1881	*1911*
Nurses	86	707
Midwives	47	24
Patent Medicine Vendors	10	2
Druggists	152	217
Homeopathic Pharmacists	3	0
Opticians	13	41
Occulists/Aurists	5	55
Chiropodists	13	27
Dentists	120	440
Physicians (General)	413	874
Physicians (Homeopathic)	19	1
Physicians (Electromagnetic)	10	0
Physicians (Female)	31	103
Physicians (Eclectic)	2	0
Physicians (Dermatologists)	0	12
Physicians (Naturopaths)	0	55
Physicians (Osteopaths)	0	39
Physicians (Specialists)	0	26

delimit and defend their own professional turf (Levi, 1980). In San Francisco, for example, the number of nurses increasedfrom less than 100 in 1881 to more than 700 in 1911 (Table 8.1). Towards the end of the century, preventive medicine and public health provided a further spur: it has been estimated that such factors were responsible for a loss of nearly 40 per cent in the caseload of family doctors between 1887 and 1912 (Burrow, 1977). These pressures contributed to an even greater recruitment to the AMA (it grew more than sevenfold between 1900 and 1910 (Markowitz and Rosner, 1979)).

At this point we have to consider another of the key phenomena of nineteenth-century urbanisation: the paternalistic philanthropy of corporate capital. Just as the enlightened self-interest of philanthropic foundations influenced the course of housing, education and town planning, so did it intervene in the evolution of the medical care system. The first tangible product of this intervention was an investigation of medical education sponsored by the Carnegie Foundation and endorsed by the American Medical Association's Council on Medical Education. The outcome — the famous Flexner Report (1910) — directly precipitated the closure of scores of commercial schools, the widespread introduction of strict licensure, and a general increase in college entrance and course requirements. Within ten years of the report's publication, the Rockefeller Foundation alone had appropriated nearly $15 million for medical education (Brown, 1979). Meanwhile, of course, the increasing dominance of orthodox medicine was also fostered by the increasing rationalism pervading urban social and cultural values as industrial capitalism matured and the impact of formal education and the mass media took effect.

By 1918, the output of American medical schools was 2760 graduates, compared with almost double this figure immediately before the publication of the Flexner Report. This decrease in the supply of physicians coincided with a rise in the level of demand for their services as more people became aware of advances in orthodox medicine. The profession now found itself in a strong position, and its leaders were quick to urge colleagues to acquire 'business' methods. The April 1919 editorial of the *California State Journal of Medicine*, for example, lectured its readers on questions of physicians' fees:

For the answer to these questions we turn with authority to

the general principles of merchandising which are no whit different. It is no more incumbent on the physician to disburse his services free than it is on any other seller to disburse his wares or his services free ... Systematise, organise and be businesslike.

Within a short time, the AMA had followed the lead of industrial monopolies like the US Steel Corporation, introducing a systematic income maintenance and price uplift programme (Burrow, 1977).

In addition to medical education, the philanthropist had a major role in financing and administering many of the urban hospitals of the period. Revenue for hospitals came from varied sources, but fees from patients typically accounted for less than one quarter of total revenues in the 1880s (Rosner, 1982b). Contributions from charitable organisations and philanthropists were used to cover a large proportion of the operating expenses of many urban hospitals. The 1890s saw a radical shift in the fiscal conditions of hospitals: a change which had a major impact on the entire structure of the urban medical care system. During the 1890s hospitals found it increasingly difficult to balance their budgets using old revenue sources. Rising costs resulting from new medical technology were in part the source of the crisis. However, the severe economic cycles of the period also contributed to the problem. The period of depression not only led to higher utilisation of hospital facilities by the working class, but the severity of the recession reduced the support available from philanthropists. As a result, their role in financing and setting policies for the urban hospital was reduced.

In order to meet their new financial demands, hospitals had to increase the relative share of their revenues from patients. To attract fee-paying patients meant that the old image and role of the urban hospital had to change radically. Private rooms became more prevalent, the latest medical technology became an imperative, and recruitment of affiliated doctors was necessary if a hospital was to be successful. Hospitals became businesses, and in so doing the free care provided in the past was reduced in scope (Rosner, 1982). With the increased importance of hospitals and the expenses associated with new technology, the imperatives of scale and agglommeration economies became important in establishing the size of the hospital, its location, and the location of affiliated physicians. Hospitals became fewer in number, larger in size, and clustered in locations that were usually a short distance from the commercial centre of the city. Physicians, in turn, now found it advantageous to be located near major hospitals in order to perform daily rounds and to use the latest medical technology.

New Settings and New Spatial Relationships

These inter-related changes in urban social order and in the organisation of medicine and medical care were accompanied by significant shifts in the relative importance of different medical care settings and in the relative location of these settings to particular communities. Dispensaries, the cornerstone of medical care for the urban poor throughout the middle decades of the nineteenth century, began to change in function around 1880 and were well on the way to extinction by 1920 (Rosenberg, 1974). As medicine became more specialised in response to changes in science, medicine and professional organisation, dispensaries evolved from general-purpose facilities to a more specialist role, often run by medical schools as a source of 'clinical material' for their trainee specialists. Meanwhile, the bulk of the profession became alarmed at the example of free medical care represented by the dispensaries. In 1900, for example, 50 per cent of the residents of New York City received their medical care from free clinics and dispensaries (Brieger, 1977). The response, in line with the new business ethic, was to assert that free medical care 'demoralises the individual and encourages deceit, laziness and pauperism' (*Boston Medical and Surgical Journal*, 1905, p.303). Furthermore, it was asserted, 'Thousands of well-paid and prosperous patients crowd the clinics, some of them ... with the idea that they are getting a superior kind of treatment, but most of them ... because they can save money that should go to private practitioners of medicine' (editorial, *Indiana Medical Association Journal*, 1925). In the event, it was the expansion of the hospital system which dealt the most telling blow to the dispensary movement. Not only did new hospitals have outpatient facilities which made dispensaries redundant; they also provided an environment in which physicians could acquire prestige and status along with clinical skills, thus making neighbourhood dispensaries superfluous to the needs of the medical profession.

The expansion of the hospital system itself was, in the first instance, a product of science and technology which made hospitals

Figure 8.1: "Every Patient Looks for a Sterilizer" (*California State Journal of Medicine*, Feb. 1924)

safer and less forbidding, if not actually attractive. But urban political economy also played its part. It was the rationalisation of everyday life which provided the fundamental shift in demand for the new setting. The average family was no longer able to nurse the sick at home, even with the expertise of a visiting physician. Sick relatives were not only demanding in terms of manpower but also in terms of emotional strain, especially as the smaller unit of the conjugal family tended to be more emotionally intense than the traditional extended family unit (Parsons and Fox, 1952). At another level, it has been argued that the expansion of the hospital system can be interpreted as part of the emergence of the 'institutional state' in America during the second half of the nineteenth century; which in turn has been attributed to the humanitarian impulses that arose from the Second Awakening (Grob, 1973), to the breakdown of traditional communal controls (Rothman, 1971), and to the onset of urbanised capitalism which not only ended traditional ways of caring for dependants but also led to the absolute growth of the dependent population (via unemployment, industrial injuries, etc.) and to the creation of new types of dependants: the economically unproductive (Katz, 1978).

Meanwhile, family physicians had indeed begun to systematise, organise and be businesslike, and one result was a shift in the setting for primary care. Making house calls came to be viewed as an inefficient use of physicians' time. An office practice, on the other hand, made it possible to take on a much larger caseload. The office as a setting for primary care was also reinforced by the growing use of bulky clinical equipment (Figure 8.1), the increasing necessity for keeping systematic medical records, and a consequent dependence on clerical and paramedical assistants. 'The duties, legal exactitudes and other responsibilities of physicians', observed *California and Western Medicine* in 1926 (p.513), 'are becoming so numerous and complex that doctors must have competent technical assistants or devote a large share of their time to matters which ought to be attended to by less expensively trained assistants.' Medical offices quickly became designed to increase efficiency in providing care. New office designs compartmentalised functions in order to speed the movement of patients through the examination

Figure 8.2: "Sytematize, Organize and be Businesslike" (*California and Western Medicine*, Oct. 1934)

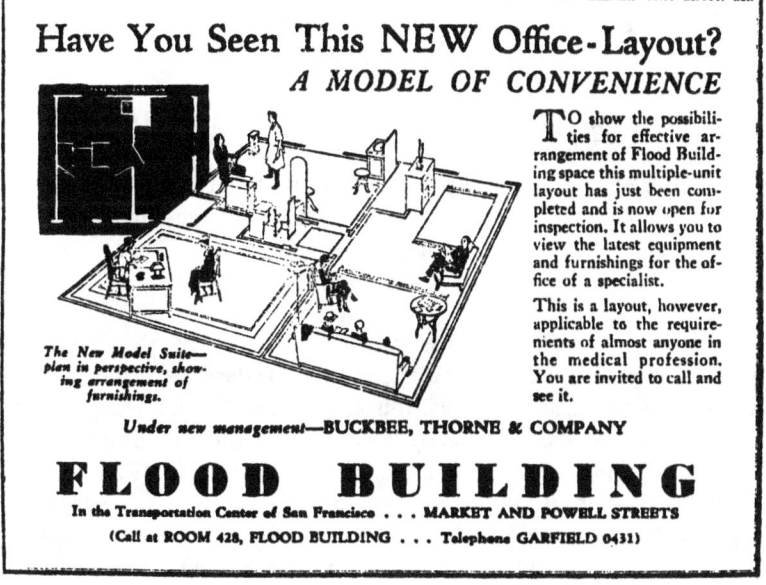

and treatment processes (Figure 8.2). These designs were part of the package one obtained with a location in the new medical arts buildings located in the central business district (Figure 8.3). The diffusion of the telephone, towards the end of the nineteenth century, had also reinforced the office setting, making it possible for physicians to establish orderly appoinment systems. The telephone also fostered co-operation between groups of physicians as they sought to become more efficiently organised. Some of the earliest telephone exchanges, for example, were organised on behalf of family doctors wanting to maximise their availability to potential customers. Such co-operation quickly spread to the practice of covering for one another during illness and vacations and this in turn helped to pave the way for the idea of group practices in which family doctors could reap some of the benefits of agglomeration and scale economies. Here again the leadership of the profession was active in promoting the idea as 'sound business' (Frederick, 1922; Johnston, 1923); though identical schemes organised by universities, medical associations, city governments and other 'lay managers' were quickly branded as 'cut-rate', 'socialistic' and somehow unethical (editorial, *California State Journal of Medicine*, March 1922).

It is important to note that not all physicians of the period supported the trends towards greater use of medical technology and towards the business orientation of medicine. H.D. Lawhead, a California physician, summarised an alternative view:

A generation ago the physician treated the patient. Today the tendency is strongly for the physician to treat the disease as a definite engrossing entity and either to forget the patient or treat him as a sort of secondary accompaniment or case ... Formerly the doctor studied the individual; today the physician investigates a case (Lawhead, 1926, p.321).

Similarly, Dr T.C. Edwards decried the loss of the personal relationship between doctor and patient: 'Modern medicine, by the use of hospitals, laboratories, nurses, specialists, has delegated so much of the work once done by the family doctor that the doctor of today is missing much of his patient's love' (Edwards, 1924, p.249). However, while it was common to find similar sentiments in medical trade journals of the time, the trend towards specialisation, medicine as business, and the increased use of medical technology

Figure 8.3: The influence of speculative finance capital: medical arts buildings in San Francisco's downtown (*California and Western Medicine*, July 1924)

Physicians Building

San Francisco

*Northwest Corner
Sutter and Powell Sts.*

A few desirable offices available

in a high class medical building with a professional atmosphere. Centrally located. Continuous service day and night. Automobile parking station near.

continued to dominate the profession.

The increasing importance of the office setting was accompanied by significant changes in the relative location of physicians' offices. The earliest offices had nearly all been simple affairs, usually part of the physician's living accommodation. With the need for larger, better-equipped offices with a suitably businesslike environment, however, there came a large-scale readjustment. Many physicians were attracted to new offices in central locations where they were able not only to maximise their accessibility to a large potential clientele but also to utilise the specialist facilities of nearby hospitals and to benefit from interaction with a large number of fellow professionals: factors which remain part of the conventional wisdom concerning physician location (Diseker and Chappell, 1976; de Vise, 1973).

The trend towards the centralisation of medical practitioners during this period was evident in the spatial pattern of physicians in San Francisco. A significant increase in the centrality of the location of medical services in the city between 1906 and 1913 was noted by Bowden (1967). Of the 23 urban services considered in his study, medical services were most affected by centripetal forces during this time. As a consequence, a medical specialty area within the central business district was clearly evident by 1913. The movement towards centralisation documented by Bowden had in

Table 8.2:   Home/Office Locations for Different Providers of Medical services in San Francisco, 1881-1911

	1881 Same Home/Office Location (% of total)	*1911* Same Home/Office Location (% of total)
Midwives	91.5	91.7
Nurses	99.9	97.7
Druggists	36.8	16.6
Dentists	67.5	33.6
General Physicians	69.0	46.8
Other Physicians[a]	86.1	46.7

Notes:
a. In 1881 the other physicians include: homeopathic, electromagnetic, female, eclectic and occulist/aurist. In 1911 the other physicians include: osteopathic, natural, female, specialist physician, homeopathic, dermatologist, and occulist/aurist.

fact begun somewhat earlier. Our own analyses of city directories show that between 1880 and 1910 doctors had become increasingly localised in the core of the city, in spite of the centrifugal pull of urban development in general. With the concentration of physicians in the central business district, a fundamental change in the geography of physicians' *residential* space also occurred. With centralisation, residences were separated from professional offices, and the earlier pattern of the physician working out of his home changed quickly. This change in residence and its relationship to the centralisation of physicians is illustrated by the office-residence geography of physicians in San Francisco. Between 1880 and 1910 the proportion of physicians who had separate offices increased by over 20 per cent. An even more dramatic change was recorded by 'specialists', where a 40 per cent increase took place (Table 8.2). The effect of a central business district location on the separation between home and office is evident from maps of physicians during the period (Figures 8.4 and 8.5). Physicians outside the core were

Figure 8.4: Distribution of physicians (all categories) in San Francisco, 1911

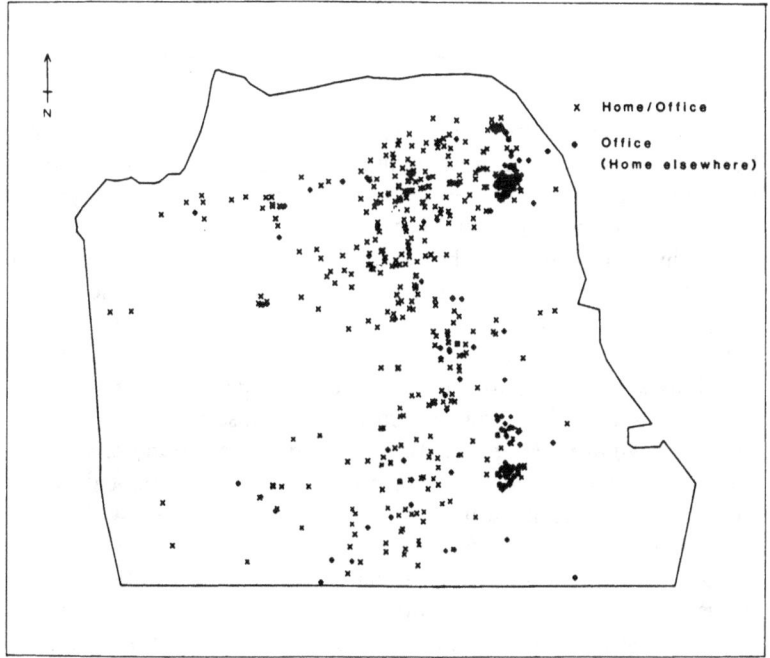

Figure 8.5: Home/Office vectors for physicians (all categories) with a separate office, San Francisco, 1911

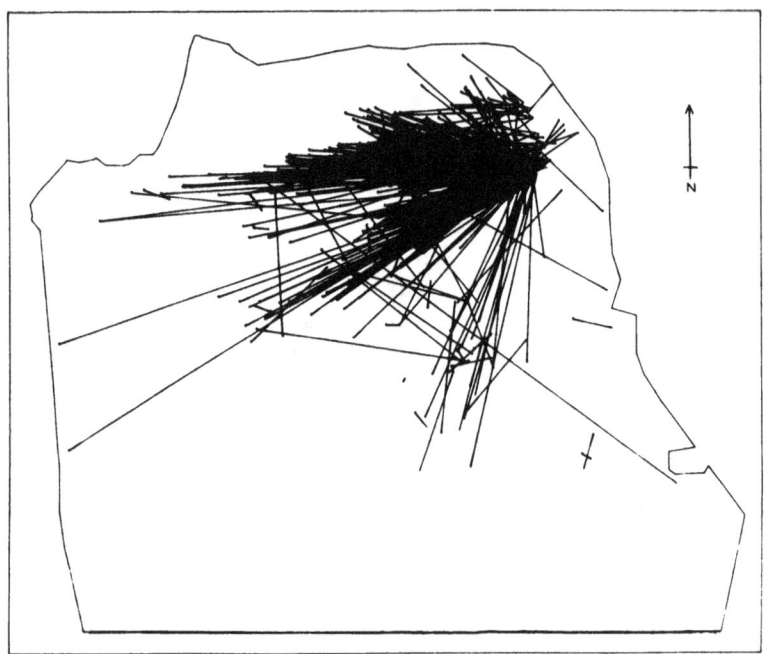

still tied to their home. Those who had office space in the central business district were now living in neighbourhoods scattered throughout the fringe of the city, a residential pattern which typifies the contemporary residential geography of medical professionals.

It is important to note, however, that broader factors were also important in precipitating centralisation. The advent of the motor car (Figure 8.6) and the development of public transport systems, for example, helped to weaken the logic of neighbourhood-based locations while central locations were encouraged by the speculative finance capital which spawned scores of purpose-built office blocks in downtown areas (Figure 8.3). At the same time, many physicians took advantage of the new transport technology to relocate their own residence in a suburban location more fitting with their increasing economic status. This, of course, was merely part of the broad realignment of urban social ecology which followed the diffusion of streetcar systems and the fostering of home ownership (as a 'Bulwark against Bolshevism') by the federal government. As a result, some physicians set up their new offices in the suburbs, seeking to capture the more lucrative (and less demanding) middle-class market and thus introducing another classic element of physician location patterns.

Figure 8.6: "Speed, Power and Dignity . . . It Saves Your Time. It Saves Your Money." (*California and Western Medicine*, July 1923)

Some Conclusions

The imperatives of urbanisation have been critical to the evolution of patterns of medical care delivery in the United States. By the 1920s, the foundations of modern medical care had been laid, and with them the template for subsequent patterns of medical care delivery. The arrival of the 'safe' hospital and the 'safe', and accredited, general practitioner had consolidated the transition from a home-oriented, family-centred system to a stratified system which was attuned to the new social and economic order of the city. Medicine itself was poised to become the focus of a major industry, while the medical profession had acquired a national political base and a much-improved public image. Equally important in terms of the implications for subsequent patterns of medical care delivery were the pre-conditions which had been set for state intervention (or the lack of it) and the divisions and conflicts which had been generated within and between medicine and its ancillary professions.

Setting urban services such as medical care against such a broad canvas should allow us to draw on the rich theoretical frameworks relating to urbanisation, professionalisation, and the role of the state. First, however, we need detailed historical research which will pinpoint the nature and the timing of the interactions which have been sketched in this essay. In addition, we need comparative analyses in order to draw out the salient processes under different conditions. The outcomes described in this chapter, for example, were broadly matched by those in Britain, and it seems reasonable to suggest that they were the product of interaction between the same economic, social, scientific and technological forces (Knox, 1982b). It would be dangerous, however, to lean too heavily on the idea that the two environments generated the same outcomes for the same reasons. For one thing, the *timing* of events was significantly different, with Britain experiencing the crucial urban transition much earlier, at a time when science, medicine and society were all at different stages from those obtaining during the urban transition in America. Another important difference was the existence within the medical profession of divisions controlled by Royal Colleges whose origins can be traced back to the sixteenth century. Thus at the onset of the urban transition there already existed a hierarchical structure within medical care which not only helped to shape the emerging pattern of medical care delivery but which also helped to structure the emerging relationships between the medical profession and the state (Cartwright, 1977; Honingsbaum, 1979). This relationship, in turn, became increasingly important as a determinant of the locational dynamics of medical care settings in British cities. A conditioning factor enveloping all these considerations has been the combination of collectivism and regionalism in British life (Dingwall, 1977; Eyles and Woods, 1983). One of the earliest influences on professional medical organisation in Britain was in fact the growing resentment of provincial rank-and-file at the power and autonomy of the London-oriented Royal Colleges (Parry and Parry, 1976). Thus the British Medical Association began life in 1832 as the Provincial Medical and Surgical Association. Subsequently, the profession mobilised itself in response to the same set of factors which had galvanised the AMA. In the process, however, the medical profession itself made a good deal of the running in getting socialised medicine off the ground. This was the result of its desperation in the face of the 'clubs' — friendly societies, provident clubs and trades unions with 'friendly' functions — which had been spawned by the collectivist movement of the late nineteenth century. Taking advantage of the still-overcrowded medical profession, these organisations were able to sign up large numbers of physicians for contract work at a fixed annual fee: 'not a pleasant matter for gentlemen of the medical profession' (editorial, *British Medical Journal*, 1875, p.484). The BMA struggled long and hard against this loss of control over a large portion of the marketplace, but eventually came to believe that some form of publicly-funded medical service was necessary in order to break the grip of the clubs and finally acceded to Lloyd George's National Health Insurance Act of 1911, which paved the way for socialised medicine in Britain.

Thus, although similar processes can be identified in different environments, it is the timing of the interactions between them which seems crucial to the outcomes. Similarly, we would expect that comparative analyses of different cities within the United States would reveal somewhat different outcomes to be associated with the east-west differential in the timing of the major phases of both urban development and medical practice.

Notes

1. One methodological problem resulting from this pattern is that of determining just which occupations constituted the practice of 'medicine'.

Acknowledgements

The research reported here was partially supported by grants from the Center for the Study of Science in Society, Virginia Polytechnic Institute and State University.

References

Bowden, M. (1967) 'The Dynamics of City Growth: An Historical Geography of the San Francisco Central District 1850-1931', Unpublished PhD dissertation, University of California, Berkeley
Brieger, G.H. (1977) 'The use and abuse of medical charities in late nineteenth-century America', *American Journal of Public Health*, **67**, 264-67
Brown, E.R. (1979) 'He Who Pays the Piper: Foundations, the Medical Profession, and Medical Education', in S. Reverby and D. Rosner (eds.) *Health Care in America*, Temple University Press, Philadelphia, 132-154
Burrow, J.G. (1977) *Organized Medicine in the Progressive Era*, Johns Hopkins University Press, Baltimore
Cartwright, F. (1977) *A Social History of Medicine*, Longman, London
Dingwall, R.W. (1977) 'Collectivism, Regionalism and Feminism: Health Visiting and British Social Policy 1850-1975', *Journal of Social Policy*, **6**, 291-316

Diseker, R.A. and J.A. Chappell (1976) 'Relative Importance of Variables in Determination of Practice Location: a Pilot Study', *Social Science and Medicine*, **10**, 559-564

Edwards, T.C. (1924) 'The Doctor, as he was, is and should be', *California and Western Medicine*, **22**, 249-252

Englehardt, H.T. (1978) 'The disease of masturbation' in J.W. Leavitt and R.L. Numbers (eds.) *Readings in the History of Medicine and Public Health*, University of Wisconsin Press, Madison, Wisconsin, 75-89

Eyles, J. and K.J. Woods (1983) *The Social Geography of Medicine and Health*, Croom Helm, London

Fishbein, M. (1946) 'History of the American Medical Association', *Journal of the American Medical Association*, **132**, 496-509

Frederick, E.V. (1922) 'Factors contributing to success or failure in group medicine', *California State Journal of Medicine*, **22**, 192-194

Grob, G.N. (1973) *Mental Institutions in America: Social Policy to 1875*, New York

Grob, G.N. (1977) 'The Social History of Medicine and Disease in America', *Journal of Social History*, **10, 391-409**

Harvey, K.A. (1979) 'Practising Medicine at the Baltimore Almshouse 1828-1850', *Maryland Historical Magazine*, **74**, 223-238

Honingsbawm, F. (1979) *The Division in British Medicine*, Kogan Page, London

Inkster, I. (1977) 'Marginal Men: Aspects of the social role of the medical community in Sheffield, 1790-1850', in J. Woodward and D. Richards (eds.) *Health Care and Popular Medicine*, Croom Helm, London, 128-163

Johnson, W.R. (1974) 'Education and professional life styles: law and medicine in the nineteenth century', *Historical Education Quarterly*, **14**, 185-207

Johnston, H.A. (1923) 'The Group Practice of Medicine', *California State Journal of Medicine*, **23**, 149-151

Katz, M.D. (1978) 'Origins of the Institutional State', *Marxist Perspectives*, **1**, 6-22

Kaufman, M. (1976) *American Medical Education: The Formative Years 1765-1970*, Greenwood Press, Westport, Conn.

Kett, J.F. (1968) *Formation of the American Medical Profession, 1780-1860*, Yale University Press, New Haven

Knox, P.L. (1982a) *Urban Social Geography*, Longman, London

Knox, P.L. (1982b) 'The Geography of Medical Care Delivery: An Historical Perspective', *Geoforum*, **13**

Knox, P.L. and J. Cullen (1981) 'Town Planning and the Internal Survival Mechanisms of Urbanised Capitalism', *Area*, **13**, 183-188

Lawhead, H.D. (1926) 'The relation between physician and patient', *California and Western Medicine*, **22**, 249-252

Levi, M. (1980) 'Functional redundancy and the process of professionalisation: the case of registered nurses in the United States', *Journal of Health Politics, Policy and Law*, **5**, 333-353

Markowitz, G.E. and D. Rosner (1979) 'Doctors in Crisis: Medical Education and Medical Reform during the Progressive Era, 1895-1915', in S. Reverby and D. Rosner (eds.) *Health Care in America*, Temple University Press, Philadelphia, 185-205

Parry, N. and J. Parry (1976) *The Rise of the Medical Profession*, Croom Helm, London

Parsons, T. and R. Fox (1952) 'Illness, Therapy and the Modern Urban Family', *Journal of Social Issues*, **8**, 31-44

Polyani, K. (1957) *The Great Transformation*, Houghton Mifflin, Boston

Pred, A. (1981) 'Production, family and free-time projects: a time-geographic perspective on the individual and societal change in nineteenth-century US cities, *Journal of Historical Geography*, **7**, 3-36

Reverby, S. and D. Rosner (eds.) (1979) *Health Care in America*, Temple University Press, Philadelphia

Rothman, D. (1977) *The Discovery of the Asylum: Social Order and Disorder in the New Republic*, Houghton Mifflin, Boston

Rosenberg, C.E. (1974) 'Social Class and Medical Care in nineteenth-century America: the rise and fall of the dispensary', *Journal of the History of Medicine and Allied Sciences*, **29**, 32-54

Rosenberg, C.E. (1977) 'The therapeutic revolution, medicine, meaning and social change in nineteenth-century America', *Perspectives in Biology and Medicine*, **20**, 485-506

Rosner, D. (1982a) 'Health Care and the "Truly Needy": Nineteenth-century origins of the concept', *Milbank Memorial Fund Quarterly*, **60**, 355-385

Rosner, D. (1982b) *A Once Charitable Enterprise: Hospitals and Health Care in Brooklyn and New York, 1885-1915*, Cambridge University Press, New York

Shryock, R.H. (1947) *The Development of Modern Medicine*, Knapp, New York

Starr, P. (1977) 'Medicine, economy and society in nineteenth-century America', *Journal of Social History*, **10**, 588-607

Starr, P. (1982) *The Social Transformation of American Medicine*, Basic Books, New York

Stevens, R. (1971) *American Medicine and the Public Interest*, Yale University Press, New Haven

de Vise, P. (1973) *Misused and Misplaced Hospitals and Doctors*, Resource Paper 22, Commission on College Geography, Association of American Geographers, Washington D.C.

Vogel, M.J. (1979) 'Machine Politics and Medical Care', in M.J. Vogel and C.E. Rosenbeg (eds.) *The Therapeutic Revolution*, University of Pennsylvania Press, Philadelphia, 159-176

Vogel, M.J. and C.E. Rosenberg, (eds.) (1979) *The Therapeutic Revolution*, University of Pennsylvania Press, Philadelphia

Woodward, J. and D. Richards (1977) *Health Care and Popular Medicine in Nineteenth Century England*, Croom Helm, London

9

Economic Determinism and the Provision of Human Services

Christopher J. Smith

Introduction

In this essay I shall be concerned with the provision of human services, those services in which the primary outcome is 'an interaction designed to change the characteristics or condition ... of the people involved' (Stevenson, 1976, p.78). Implicit in this definition is that individuals are experiencing problems that are of a social and, therefore, a relative nature. At times throughout the essay I shall refer to the more general terms deviance and social controls rather than social problems and human services. When I do this I shall be using the term deviance non-connotatively, to describe conditions or behaviours that deviate from societal norms; and social controls to refer to the ways individuals, groups, and societies regulate themselves.

At a general level, I shall be concerned with a wide range of social problems that elicit an equally wide range of responses, although two broad categories of response are evident: those providing services, such as education, medication, and protection; and those imposing controls, such as arrest, segregation, and punishment.[1] These responses fall into the category of formal social controls, those mechanisms by which 'society secures adherence to social norms ... specifically how it minimizes, eliminates, or normalizes deviant behavior' (Conrad and Schneider, 1980, p.7).

At a more specific level I shall concentrate my discussion on the range of problems associated with what has come to be defined euphemistically as 'substance abuse' — with an emphasis on alcohol and drugs. This decision is based on the realisation that a general discussion will necessarily ignore some of the important differences between the various problem categories. As we shall see, public responses to mind-altering substances, and the subsequent social policies, have changed dramatically through the years. It will come as no surprise to anyone to discover that social problems have, in recent years, become increasingly the responsibility of the state, mainly through its social welfare agencies. Managing social problems has in fact become a growth industry. For example, in the United States employment in education, health (including mental health), and welfare increased by almost 70 per cent in the 1960s; compared with a 13 per cent increase in manufacturing employment (Stevenson, 1976). *In spite of* this growth, there is little evidence that the human services actually 'work' in ridding society of its problems or reducing inequality. In addition, *because of* this growth, the business of solving (or not solving) human problems has become increasingly costly.

In this essay I shall argue that the human services do not 'work' because they are not supposed to 'work', at least not in the sense of preventing or reducing the prevalence of social problems. As we shall see, the provision of human services fulfills some other, perhaps equally important, functions. I shall also argue that even if problem prevention were the goal, the human services could not possibly 'work', because they could not control problems at a fast enough rate to offset the incidence of new problems. Before presenting the major arguments, it is necessary to make some rather general remarks about the nature of social problems and the need for social controls.

Social Problems and the Need for Formal Social Controls

At any point in time we can assume that the number of individuals experiencing physical, social, or psychological problems is several times greater than the number receiving formal services. The most recent estimates of the prevalence of serious psychological distress in the United States, for example, puts the figure at 25 per cend of the population (Dohrenwend *et al.*, 1980); whereas estimates of mental health 'episodes' show that, at most, only 2-3 per cent of the population use mental health facilities, and an unknown but probably large number of these individuals are multiple users. It is also clear that prevalence estimates vary depending on who is making the definition and what criteria are involved. As Durkheim (1938) observed, deviance in some form or another is universal, although there are no universal definitions of a deviant act.

Deviance is also a social definition of an individual's status, so it is usually defined *for* individuals rather than *by* them. Deviance is also contextual, in other words what is defined as a problem depends on the time, the place, and the sub-culture. In the field of alcoholism, for example, what has been defined as a deviant act has varied substantially over time. Only in the last ten years has the *per capita* level of alcohol consumption reached the boozy heights of the late eighteenth and early nineteenth centuries, when the United States was appropriately nicknamed the 'alcoholic republic' (Rorabaugh, 1979). At this time, however, public condemnation of drunkenness was rare. There was no alcohol problem (Levine, 1978); just as there was no cocaine problem in the late nineteenth century when Freud was prescribing it as a cure for digestive ailments, asthma, and melancholia (Reinarman, 1979). As the years rolled by these two drugs experienced different fates. Alcohol has led a charmed life — it is addictive and deadly, but cheap and still legal; cocaine, on the other hand, is non-addictive and relatively harmless, but it is expensive and illegal. As we shall see later, the societal response to drug use and overuse is clearly independent of the drug's chemical properties.

Spatial variations in both the consumption of alcohol and the prevalence of drinking problems are well-known (Smith and Hanham, 1982). Suburban Americans drink more than their urban counterparts, with rural dwellers far behind; but the ratio of drinking problems to drinkers is higher in the 'dry regions' than in the 'wet regions' (Cahalan and Room, 1974). Clear differences in prevalence rates also exist between sub-groups of the population, according to age, race, and sex. Some of these differences represent a considerable problem for the development of social policies. Among Native Americans, for example, the mortality rate from liver cirrhosis, an illness that is strongly correlated with heavy alcohol consumption, is 99 per 100,000; in comparison to a rate of 20 per 100,000 for whites. It is evident from these few examples that alcoholism is a relative concept and, as such, societal responses to heavy drinking are likely to vary significantly from one place to another. At the present time heavy alcohol consumption is considered to be a serious social problem in most developed countries around the world (Smith and Hanham, 1982); but it is clear that some individuals and groups are able to keep themselves out of the prevalence data by restraining their own behaviour. This observation is not limited to 'bible belt' abstainers. For example,

American Jews are continually upheld as a group among whom alcohol problems are virtually unknown, even though very few Jewish people are actually abstainers (Snyder, 1978). It seems that Jews identify sobriety as a Jewish trait, as opposed to other ethnic groups that have defined their cultural distinctiveness, or had it defined for them, in terms of their heavy drinking practices (Stivers, 1976). Informal social controls on drinking habits develop over a long period of time, usually during periods of social and cultural stability. Jews, for example, learn to drink moderately during childhood, when they are exposed to alcohol in religious and secular rituals. In later life the sobriety habit is reinforced by patterns of social interaction — in other words moderate drinkers generally choose to interact with other moderate drinkers, which for Jews invariably means other Jews (Skog, 1980). As a recent survey showed, the vast majority of Jewish respondents said they did not know *anyone* who was a heavy drinker (Glassner and Berg, 1980).

It is obvious from this discussion that one solution to the 'alcohol problem' is through informal social controls — mechanisms operating at the individual and group level. The policy implications are considerable, because if heavy drinkers can learn to drink moderately or 'responsibly', the problem would be solved by making alcohol more rather than less available, in the hope that good sense will prevail. This strategy would please all the interested parties and it would not infringe upon the behaviour of millions of individuals for whom drinking is not a problem (Beauchamp, 1976). Obviously this solution is both overly optimistic and potentially dangerous. As cultural practices, drinking habits are slowly acquired; they can hardly be altered overnight. As many observers have predicted, letting alcohol flow more freely through the veins of society may well bring about a substantial increase in the prevalence of heavy consumption and problem drinking (Popham *et al.*, 1975; Schmidt, 1977).

A further observation is that in some cases it is difficult to distinguish between the social problem and the social control. High rates of alcoholism among some Native American tribes can be interpreted, in part, as a response to the collapse of informal controls on drinking habits during periods of rapid cultural change.[2] The societal response to Indian alcoholism may be to accept the high rate of prevalence as a culturally or ethnically determined fact, and one that essentially solves the 'Indian problem' by defining it as an 'alcohol problem' that can best be dealt with through the correctional system or the medical/psychiatric system. As Maloff *et al.* (1979) have observed, this type of response deals primarily with the symptoms rather than the causes of the breakdown of informal controls over drinking. As such, the response may be perceived, by Indians, as yet another branch of repression and cultural enslavement. At a broader level it is intriguing to extend this argument to consider the roles that alcohol and societal responses to alcohol have played in international development. There is evidence, for example, that imperial interests in Africa found it convenient to stimulate heavy drinking among the indigenous population:

> In most African societies, the brewing of beer had been carried out within 'traditional' modes of production ... Beer drinking was literally a celebration of the economic surplus ... [but] ... From the colonial period onwards ... the social character of drinking began to change. Among migrant laborers the reasons for taking a drink turned on the alleviation of personal suffering and alienation ... their consumption of alcohol had become totally divorced from the kind of production in which they now engaged. For both these reasons the inbuilt contraints which had formerly controlled drinking tended to disappear ... [because it] ... improved the overall health of the workers by making good some of the basic deficiencies in their diet ... [and because] ... the availability of alcohol provided an outlet for boredom and frustration which might otherwise have exploded in more coherent forms ... [and also because] ... the presence of local brewing ... [was] ... a useful mechanism for stabilizing the workforce (Doyal, 1979, pp.114-115).

From this example we have some indication that colonial interests were reinforced by heavy alcohol consumption, the encouragement of which can actually be interpreted as a branch of social control. In other words the 'problem' from our perspective was also the 'solution'. It is not surprising, therefore, that mass alcoholism has been 'an almost invariable companion of headlong and uncontrolled industrialization' (Hobsbawm, 1973, p.248). Following McNeill's (1976) hypothesis about the reciprocal relationship between the spread of disease and the spread of civilisation, it is reasonable to suggest that heavy alcohol consumption may have facilitated the imperial mission by effectively narcotising the local population. The net effect, as McNeill might have predicted, would be a significant reduction in the overall level of cultural diversity in drinking practices around the world, a phenomenon that is in fact occurring at a rapid pace (Edwards, 1979; Sulkunen, 1976; McAndrew and Edgerton, 1969).

The Creation, Evolution, and Maintenance of Social Problems

As we have seen, what is defined as a social problem is culturally, temporally, and spatially determined; and it follows that the provision of services to either 'treat' or 'control' problem populations is equally variable. In the United States and the United Kingdom, however, in recent times public policy responses have been converging on a service provision model that is increasingly dominated by a medical and/or a welfare state ideology (Cohen, 1979; Conrad and Schneider, 1980).

It is evident that this convergence conceals considerable diversity in the theoretical explanations of the creation and maintenance of social problems. These explanations can be broadly grouped into positivist, interactionist, constructionist, and structuralist camps — and from each camp comes dramatically different implications for social policy. It is worth noting, before considering these four camps, that from an intellectual perspective there are some clear trends in the recent literature that social scientists, including geographers, are eschewing the strictly positivist line (Cox, 1981; Pred, 1981). From the perspective of service provision, however, positivist explanations remain not only credible, but dominant, even though there is no shortage of literature describing alternatives. That there should be such a sharp discrepancy between theory and practice will surprise nobody; but, as we shall see, the impact on those who receive services — the clients — may be substantial.

The Positivist View of Social Problems

The positivist or absolutist view holds that the problems encountered are real and objectively experienced by the individual. Society has defined what is deemed to be appropriate behaviour, and these views are widely shared. Scientists of all persuasions (social, physical, and medical) search for causal explanations. For professionals in the alcoholism field, gaining scientific recognition has been a long and arduous task,[3] and it is not surprising to find that these workers cling doggedly to variations of a medical model of alcoholism. For them, the alternatives are not only poor substitutes, they are anachronisms. Accepting that alcoholism is an environmental or a social problem, or, even worse, a political problem, would imply that the field is unscientific and therefore not respectable. This situation is similar to the dilemma that has faced the medical profession in the twentieth century. The discoveries of the 'microbe hunters' like Koch, Pasteur and Roux, had liberated medicine from its environmental and public health roots. It is hardly surprising, therefore, to find in recent times a marked reluctance to seek non-medical or non-individual explanations for the rising prevalence of chronic disease mortality and morbidity (Eyer and Sterling, 1977; Pyle, 1979).

A positivist view of a social problem or a disease involves what Renaud (1978) has called a 'medical engineering' model which:

> transforms the potentially explosive social problems that are diseases and death into discrete and isolable commodities that can be incorporated into the capitalist organization of the economy in the same way as any other commodity on the economic market (p. l09).

From this perspective a disease is explained by any number of *endogenous* causes. There is a norm of functioning against which the physiological symptoms of the disease can be compared, invariably by medical observers. In the alcoholism field the disease concept evolved slowly into a set of generally-agreed propositions, which, in the light of recent empirical scrutiny, cannot be defended (Watts, 1981). The major propositions, each of which has significant implications for service provision, are:

1. *Alcoholics have predisposing characteristics that are significantly different from non-alcoholics.* The search for an 'alcoholic personality' has failed to substantiate this claim (Freed, 1979), and the only unequivocal fact is that alcoholics drink more than everyone else. Statistically, drinking habits within the population can be described most accurately by a unimodal rather than a bi-modal curve.

2. *Alcoholics develop an allergic reaction to drink, and are unable to stop once they start drinking.*[4] The 'loss of control' hypothesis obviously fits some alcoholics, but reviews of the literature show that this trait is nowhere near universal (Shaw *et al.*, 1978; Pattison, 1976).
3. *Alcoholism is a progressive, chronic, and irreversible process, evolving inexorably toward death.* As Cahalan (1970) has shown, this piece of crude social Darwinism simply does not fit the facts. Many individuals move backwards and forwards along the consumption curve, with a corresponding waxing and waning of the major symptoms (Smith and Hanham, 1982).
4. *Alcoholism can only be treated if the individual abstains completely.* Evidence accumulated within the last decade shows that many alcoholics can and do successfully return to moderate drinking (Armor, *et al.*, 1976).

As Watts (1981) has observed, the adoption of the disease model of alcoholism is an example of the social construction of reality, in which a concept, in this case disease, is borrowed from another field. Through time 'the borrowed concept will determine what subjects or things or processes are to be considered for treatment or study under the heading "alcoholism" ' (Bacon, 1976, p.93). The implications of the disease model for the treatment and social control of alcoholism are clear. Alcoholics cannot help themselves; they cannot stop drinking; but they are to be treated as patients not as criminals. They are sick; they have a cast-iron alibi; and they must be restored to wellness by the available technology, which may be medical, psychological, or chemical in nature. They must also, of course, abstain from drinking completely.

Some people, particularly the alcoholics themselves, look upon this as a humane and dignified response, especially in comparison to being treated as degenerates, sinners, or criminals, as they have been in the past. Unfortunately, however, treating alcoholism as a disease tends to preclude a search for other causes and alternative solutions. Pred (1981) has recently observed that most geographers, even behavioural geographers, have looked at human processes in an essentially positivist fashion, treating individuals in a fragmented and 'thingified' way with, at best, a marginal consideration of the social and political constraints under which they operate. Geographical analysis is often conducted, as Pred observes, 'at the individual level as self-contained behaviours "explainable" in terms of personal and environmental attributes or variables at the moment of observation, but somehow completely unconnected either with past actions, experiences, or feelings, or with the functioning of particular institutions and society in general' (p.3).

The Interactionist View of Social Problems

Partly as a result of the empirical inadequacies of the positivist view, many sociologists have argued that deviance is a relative concept, one that is related only marginally to an individual's characteristics or predispositions. In this sense deviance, or 'having' a social problem, is a status conferred upon or ascribed to an individual. It is, in other words, an emergent outcome of social interaction, resulting from the contacts made between rule breakers and the social actors who define their behaviours as deviant acts. Once the label is designated it often becomes fixed, so that individuals gradually acquire a deviant self-image and drift into an increasingly deviant lifestyle. Pittman and Gordon (1958) have described how public drunks brush up against the law and the other social control agencies who create the categories of deviance and provide the facilities for processing drunks. At first they may not be alcoholics, but they tend to fit into the niche created for them. Through repeated trials in the community and after making the rounds of all the available programmes, these individuals slip through the 'revolving doors' many times, until they are firmly established as chronic drunkenness offenders. Before the widespread decriminalisation of public drunkenness during the 1970s, arrests in this category represented up to one third of all arrests in the United States (Morris and Hawkins, 1969).

It is implicit in the interactionist perspective of deviance, and it was made explicit in some studies (Wilkins, 1964; Ditton 1979), that the actions of social control agencies could amplify or reinforce the deviance and consequently increase the prevalence rate of what became known as secondary deviance. Consider, for example, the societal response to marijuana smokers in Notting Hill in the late 1960s. As Young (1971) has argued, public stereotypes about marijuana are exaggerated out of all proportion by the individuals who negotiate between the community and the potential deviants — the police. From positions of power, the police negotiate the evidence to fit society's preconceived stereotypes. As a result of continual interactions between smokers and the police, the former intensify their deviance, amplifying it to fit the stereotypes. Fantasy becomes reality in the following way:

> when society defines a group of people as deviant it tends to react against them so as to isolate and alienate them from the company of 'normal' people ... the group ... tends to develop its own norms and values, which society perceives as even more deviant than before. As a consequence of this increase in deviancy, social reaction increases even further, the group is even more isolated and alienated, it acts even more deviantly, society acts increasingly strongly against it, and a spiral of deviancy amplification occurs (Young, 1971, p.33).

The Constructionist View of Social Problems

In its simplest form the relativist or interactionist view assumed a general consensus in society about what ought to be defined as a social problem. Some of its most influential exponents showed that it was unrealistic to suppose that the agents of social control merely carried out the majority wishes of society (Becker, 1963; Matza, 1969). They argued that deviance designations and subsequent actions emerge from the interactions between a plurality of different groups within society. Those with the most power or influence are able to impose authority that would reflect their own interests. Thus, as we shall see later, some relatively molehill-like problems can be stretched into mountainous social responses, and vice versa. The pluralist studies also helped to skirt another of the criticisms of the simple form of interactionism, its focus on individual transactions. The pluralists showed how groups interacted to forge collective definitions of deviance. Their studies also allowed a consideration of the macro-sociological aspects of labelling, by showing how particular social or political trends in society at large might produce changes in the definitions of deviance.

Becker (1963) first used the term 'moral entrepreneurs' to describe groups that have a vested interest in the social control of deviance. Typically they include both rule *creators*, who are outraged about a particular problem and are morally committed to bringing it under control; and rule *enforcers*, who carry out the controls on an everyday basis. As Becker's study of the passage of the Marijuana Tax Act illustrated, sometimes the rule creators were also the enforcers. Until the 1930s there had been little or no public interest in marijuana, but an intense campaign was launched by the Bureau of Narcotics. In the absence of any organised opposition from marijuana smokers, and in the presence of a largely apathetic but impressionable public, the Act was passed in 1937, making the sale and use of marijuana a deviant act. The moral outrage notion provided an acceptable explanation for launching what would eventually be a successful campaign. In other cases material interests rather than moral outrage would fuel the campaign, resulting in a new class of individuals or groups who are essentially 'social control entrepreneurs' (Warren, 1981). In a re-interpretation of the Marijuana Tax Act, Dickson (1968) argued that the Bureau's campaign was motivated largely by organisational concerns, which is an example of what Warren referred to as 'program entrepreneurship'. According to Dickson the agency was facing a potential budget cut, in response to which it decided to challenge a deadly foe, to demonstrate its powers and its social usefulness.

It is clear from the literature that some of the successful moral enterprise endeavors were exclusively products of their time, and that they could probably never be replicated. The passage of the Eighteenth Amendment in 1919, prohibiting the public sale and consumption of alcohol, is an example. The Prohibition movement was largely a moral crusade, initially led by a group of women who were mostly rural, middle-class Protestants (Gusfield, 1963). Drinking within this group was not a problem, so explanations for the fanaticism and the success of the Women's Christian Temperence Movement (WCTU) have to be sought in the historical/cultural context. In the first two decades of the twentieth century the demographic character of the United States was changing irreversibly. From being dominated by native-born Protestants living on or closely tied to the land, the demographic balance of power was shifting toward foreign-born, Catholic city-dwellers. The former group was watching its influence on the mainstream of American culture fade. Realising that on the whole they were powerless to alter this trend, the Temperance crusaders focussed on prohibition as a symbol of their cultural values, which were rapidly being diluted in an ocean of intemperance. As Gusfield argues, the movement was an exercise in status politics in which one group was able to stamp its moral standards on the entire country. As Conrad and Schneider (1980) have suggested, the crusaders were not concerned with the mechanics of enforcing the legislation. They merely wanted to see it passed, and they wanted everyone to know *whose* law it was. From a geographical perspective the Temperance Movement was one expression of regional tension within the

United States.[5] The Movement was strongest in the 'dry' regions of the South and the Great Plains, and its success dealt a blow to the other regions. This tension was also fueled by another typically American source of geographical conflict, that between cities and towns. Temperance groups had their power base in small-town America, so it was hardly accidental that they associated alcoholism with the moral degeneracy of large cities (Howland and Howland, 1978).

It should be evident from this discussion that the individuals and groups making deviance designations may not be concerned with the problems of the people whose behaviour they have condemned. For example, few in the Temperance movement were concerned with the pain associated with alcoholism. They were obsessed with the way the problem was perceived, and their strategy was to persuade others to adopt their views. Such groups attempt to legitimate their deviance designations through their 'claims-making' activities (Spector and Kitsuse, 1973). Claims are made by groups who feel they have a valid grievance. From this perspective the diverse groups on all sides of an issue are much more than passive reactors — they are in fact acting, making demands on the existing institutions, usually for higher wages or better treatment. The recent changes in care for the mentally ill have been, in part, explained in this way. In the last decade mental patients as both individuals and in groups have made a series of claims on the service providers that have helped to shape mental health policy (Chamberlin, 1978). Recent critiques of this phenomenon, however, point out that it is naïve to think of the official agencies simply as passive reactors in the changing picture of service provision. Brown (1981), for example, has argued that the patients' demands were etched into law only because what they wanted happened to be consistent with the state's desire to reduce *per capita* expenditures on mental illness through deinstitutionalisation. In other words, there is evidence that the service agencies themselves operate as powerful interest groups, defining the problems, and their own responses, to ensure their successful future operation. In this sense public concerns about social problems are essentially *created* at the agency or governmental level, and *then* legitimated by public acceptance and recognition of the problems. There is evidence that in the mental health and alcoholism fields, agency attempts to create a public consensus about the definitions and causes of the problems have been moderately successful. Over the last two to three decades public attitudes toward mental illness have changed considerably. Segal (1978) has observed that the improvements have occurred in five general areas:

1. Members of the public accept a broader range of symptoms of mental illness today than they did twenty years ago.
2. Attitudes, particularly negative attitudes, no longer appear to be determined primarily by the mere label of mental illness or the specific diagnoses. Recent studies have demonstrated that attitudes are most closely related to the actual behaviours associated with mental illness (Kirk, 1973).
3. People now tend to require less social distance between themselves and the mentally ill.
4. Little evidence exists to demonstrate a direct link between negative attitudes and overtly hostile behaviour toward the mentally ill living in the community.
5. If the mentally ill are viewed in normal roles, most community residents will eventually begin to evaluate them positively and accept their right to live in the community (Smith and Hanham, 1981; Dear *et al.*, 1981).

A similar trend can be detected from changes in public attitudes toward alcoholism (Smith and Hanham, 1982). Although in both areas there is room for improvement, members of the public are now more likely to define mental illness and alcoholism as serious, but not dangerous, illnesses for which help is available and effective. These are considerable achievements, and they have contributed greatly to the 'selling' of mental health and alcoholism services in recent years.

The public legitimation of officially designated problems does not occur automatically. For example, consider the experiences of the agency that was given the federal responsibility for managing the 'alcohol problem', beginning in the early 1970s, the National Institute of Alcohol Abuse and Alcoholism (NIAAA). In recent years NIAAA has identified special populations that have been earmarked for particular emphasis, which generally means priority funding and greater availability of research funds (NIAAA, 1978; 1981). Presumably alcoholism or heavy drinking is a particular concern within these sub-groups of the population. In some instances, however, it is difficult to find empirical evidence for this higher level of concern. One of the special populations is women, but there are very few data to show that alcoholism among women is increasing rapidly, or at a faster rate than for men (Smith and

Hanham, 1982). The evidence suggests that the slight increase in utilisation rates among women may result from an *uncovering* process in which true prevalence rates remain the same, but more women enter treatment programmes. We can only assume that more services are being used as a result of greater public awareness and a reduction in community hostility toward women alcoholics; although the explanation may simply be that there are more facilities offering services for women (Shaw, 1980).

One of the special populations on which considerable public scrutiny has been focussed is teenagers. More teenagers drink today than ever before, but there is no unequivocal proof that this drinking has resulted in a higher prevalence of alcohol-related problems (Chauncey, 1980). In spite of this, teenage drinking has become a growth industry within the field, to such an extent that in 1977 NIAAA announced the development of a five year $83 million National Teenage Alcohol Education Program. The new emphasis has left its mark on the literature: with some 675 citations on teenage drinking between 1972 and 1975; compared with 475 from 1960 to 1971 (Chauncey, 1980). A review of this literature, however, shows no evidence of a *growing* problem for teenagers who drink (Blane and Hewitt, 1977). The FBI Uniform Crime Reports show a decline in arrests for juvenile drunkenness between 1970 and 1975; and membership in teen-based AA groups has been short-lived. One conclusion is that:

> This manipulation of teenage drinking as a public and political issue by the NIAAA offers self-preservation as a dominant motive behind the campaign. This is not to demean the agency or its employees, but merely to emphasize the entrepreneurial aspect of welfare organizations ... (Chauncey, 1980, p. 51).

As Trice and Roman have observed (1972, p. 44):

> the aim of various problem industries is the accumulation of new programs, jobs and resources, which in turn may yield greater social prestige and power. Thus, we warn against ready acceptance of definitions of the scope of problems from those whose future authority and power hinge heavily on public acceptance of these definitions.

To explain why an agency like NIAAA felt it necessary to push the teenage drinking issue, we have to consider its status vis-à-vis other agencies, particularly those within the parent organisation.[6] NIAAA has the lowest budget within the Department of Human Services. As one response to the threat of being subsumed within the more general 'substance abuse' umbrella, NIAAA bureaucrats may have felt it incumbent upon them to carve out their own turf within the teenage drug field. The alcohol treatment industry has also faced the problem of continual public apathy, bordering on opposition. This apathy is in part an outcome of widespread cultural ambivalance toward alcohol. Many people like to drink, and most of them do so without problems. To overcome such ambivalance NIAAA bureaucrats felt it necessary to overstate certain parts of the 'alcohol problem'. In the case of teenage drinking this was not difficult to do, because once the agency set the ball rolling, the media took over, and the result was a near-epidemic!

The evidence suggests that the problem of teenage drinking was to some extent created, but a question remains as to whether it has been validated and legitimated by society. In other words, do members of the public agree that the problem exists, and are they willing to support the newly created programmes? As Chauncey (1980) has noted, 'the legitimacy of an officially created social problem ... is established by the arousal of public controversy or discussion coupled with the popular participation in some ameliorative program' (p. 53). To date, the evidence for such a legitimation is slim, and what does exist is contradictory. Public *attitudes* toward alcoholism in general have improved to the extent that most people agree with a disease definition of alcoholism (Smith and Hanham, 1982). On the other hand the majority still see self-help and Alcoholics Anonymous as the solution to alcohol problems, rather than formal treatment programmes, which implies a view of alcoholism as a 'folk illness' (Rodin, 1981). Public *behaviour* toward the alcohol problem, especially for teenagers, seems to reflect this ambivalence. Referrals have been slow, and new programmes are often running at less than full capacity (Chauncey, 1980). Where are all the teenage drinking problems? It seems they may be much less prevalent than has been reported; or perhaps they are being syphoned-off by other agencies such as drug clinics and diversion programmes; or they are simply being absorbed in the community as a result of informal coping mechanisms, or through parental, medical, and police ambivalence. It is also possible that by defining its own turf as being 'alcohol-only', NIAAA may have found itself on a lawn the size of a postage stamp.

On the positive side, it is worth noting that nobody is hurt when agencies construct their own reality of social problems. The service programmes help those people who enter them; jobs are created; and an aura of prevention and education, in this case in the schools, is created. On the other hand, programme expansion drains federal and state resources; it may foster or at least support the growth of an increasingly avaricious class of professional service providers (the helping professionals, see Stoesz, 1981); and it may also erode the public's confidence in social programmes of all types. In a hypothetical example of the recent trend toward multiplication of social programmes, Cohen (1979 pp. 358-9) has described the brave new world of the helping industries. The story is fictitious and obviously it is meant to be amusing, but all of the programmes actually exist:

Mr. and Mrs. Citizen, their son Joe and daughter Linda, leave their suburban home after breakfast saying goodbye to Ron, a fifteen year pre-delinquent who is living with them under the LAK (Look After a Kid) scheme. Ron will later take a bus downtown to the Community Correctional Center, where he is to be given two hours of Vocational Guidance and later tested on the Interpersonal Maturity Level Scale. Mr. C. drops Joe off at the School Problems Evaluation Center from which Joe will walk to school. In his class are five children who are bussed from a local Community Home, four from a Pre-Release Facility and three, who, like Ron live with families in the neighborhood. Linda gets off next — at the GUIDE Center (Girls Unit for Intensive Daytime Education) where she works as a Behavioral Contract Mediator. They drive past a Threequarter-way House, a Rape Crisis Center and then a Drug Addict Cottage, where Mrs. C. waves to a group of boys working in the garden. She knows them from some volunteer work she does in RODER (Reduction of Delinquency Through Expansion of Opportunities). She gets off at a building which houses the Special Intensive Parole Unit, where she is in charge of a five year evaluation research project on the use of the HIM (Hill Interaction Matrix) in matching group treatment to clients. Mr. C. finally arrives at work, but will spend his lunch hour driving around in the car again as this is his duty week on patrol with TIPS (Turn in a Pusher).

Unfortunately, in spite of the growth in the level of service provision, there is little evidence that the magnitude of the societal response is determined by the actual severity of the problem in question. The penalties for possessing and using cocaine, for example, are inconsistent with the drug's effects (Reinarman, 1979). This point is critical when we compare cocaine (or marijuana) with other drugs that are still legal, either by cash purchase or prescription. Alcohol is legal in spite of its proven ability as an incompetence producer, for a variety of historical, cultural, and economic reasons (see Smith and Hanham, 1982). Other drugs, including tranquilisers and depressants, are palatable socially, and they remain legal in spite of substantial evidence of their damaging effects (Hills, 1980; Conrad and Schneider, 1980). From the perspective of radical critiques of Western medicine, the prescribed drugs are acceptable because they help to reproduce the social relations of production in capitalist society. Valium, for example, helps workers overcome their day-to-day problems, leaving them better able to function in the work world. By comparison, most of the currently illegal drugs do not help individuals conform to reality. In fact they change reality, causing people to challenge authority and contradict social norms, all of which challenges the work ethic. As we shall see, there is evidence that the 'drug and alcohol problem' is more of a 'battlefield of material and ideological conflicts than a symbol of concern for public safety' (Reinarman, 1979, p. 250).

A Structuralist Perspective on Social Problems

The previous discussion illustrated how policy responses to social problems have been interpreted from a pluralist perspective. The studies falling within this category view society as a mix of competing interest groups fighting for dominance, status, wealth or power. To this point, however, we have looked only at deviance designations as they are negotiated through the mechanisms of partisan politics. Critics of this perspective argue that the definitions and rules governing social behaviour are not negotiated in this way, but are inherent in capitalist society, and are integral parts of a society's 'superstructure', its culture and knowledge, which in turn is largely determined by its economic 'sub-structure' (Quinney, 1980). The rules and definitions of deviance protect the interests of the capitalist class, thereby helping that class continue its domination. Thus, instead of describing a process in which *groups* seek a consensus from the existing diversity within society, this perspective deals with *classes*, and essentially defines the state as being largely in the pocket of a particular class. As the simplest interactionist studies presupposed, there is indeed a consensus within society, but one that is imposed by the ruling class in its own interests (Ryan, 1978). From this perspective it is unrealistic to assume that individuals float through society exerting their free choices. As Young has pointed out:

> By granting men freedom in an absolute sense without acknowledging any material constraints, human purpose was reduced to the level of whimsy. By characterizing society as a simple diversity of values, they [the pluralists] blinded themelves to the existence of a very real consensus — the hegemonic domination of bourgeois values. By pointing to power without analyzing its class basis and the nature of the state, they transformed the actions of the powerful into an arbitrary flexing of moral muscles (1976, pp.12-13).

To outline briefly a conflict perspective on the production of social problems and the consequences for service responses, I shall look firstly at how social problems are generated in capitalist society; and secondly at how those problems become serious enough to warrant official intervention.

The Prevalance of Social Problems in Capitalist Societies. Individuals in a capitalist society may encounter or experience social problems in two general ways: *directly*, as a result of contradictions in the capitalist mode of production; and *indirectly*, as a result of disturbances in the system of class rule (Spitzer, 1975).

(a) Contradictions in the capitalist mode of production. Capital accumulation requires fit and healthy workers, but systematically debilitates workers and makes them unfit to offer their services in the market place. Eyer (1977) has observed that the sources of worker stress derive from both *external* and *internal* controls over the labour force. External controls result from the need for increased labour mobility, which has consistently broken up familes and communities, and created pools of surplus labour; and the

division of labour which has resulted in increasingly boring and alienating work. By internal controls, Eyer was referring to the familiar patterns of socialisation associated with capitalist production, in which workers are rewarded for being competitive but not too individualistic, and in which they are encouraged to spend their rewards on the acquisition of material possessions. These sources of stress are endemic in the capitalist system, but they are unequally allocated between the classes: workers experience more than their share of the costs or stresses, and less than their share of the benefits. It is no surprise, therefore, that the working classes are disproportionately represented in the prevalence data for mental illness, drug and alcohol abuse, and crime; in addition to accidental deaths and mortality and morbidity rates for a wide range of chronic and infectious disease (Doyal, 1979). The importance of the work environment in the etiology of stress-induced illness has been recognised: there is evidence, for example, that only about a quarter of the mortality from heart disease, the leading cause of death, can be explained by 'individual' factors such as diet, exercise, medical care and genetic inheritance (Renaud, 1978). The rest is unexplained, although a strong case can be made for the importance of social and environmental factors, including the nature of the work environment. The same study concluded that 'the strongest predictor of longevity was work satisfaction ... [and] ... the second ... was overall "happiness" ' (p. 114). Navarro (1975) has observed that conclusions such as these tend to be systematically ignored because they fail to reflect the individualistic, bourgeois biases of the medical research establishment; and because they fundamentally threaten the interests and demands of the capitalist class (Kirby, this volume).

Another set of contradictions inherent in capitalism involves the production of a surplus population that is both *vulnerable*, in the sense of being powerless; and yet sometimes *dangerous*, because its members are increasingly alienated from and resentful of the ruling classes. As a *vulnerable* group the 'reserve army' can sometimes be exploited by the capitalists in the interests of profit. For example, until recently, high levels of unemployment could exert a downward force on wages and inflation. This helped to maintain profits because unemployed workers will accept lower paying jobs, reduce their workplace demands, and work more productively in fear of being laid off and replaced by members of the 'reserve army'. As a *dangerous* group, on the other hand, the 'reserve army' has to be maintained and provided for, in other words kept 'under control'. This implies a substantial *social expense* that chips away at the process of *capital accumulation*. Not only will the costs rise, thus reducing profits; but the increased level of worker security provided by income maintenance programmes and other welfare entitlements may also reduce worker productivity (Piven and Cloward, 1981). In this sense the welfare state acts against the interests of the capitalist class, which explains the demand for substantial cuts in entitlements made by the current administration in the United States. From the perspective of deviance production, the surplus population will be increasingly likely to encounter serious social problems, resulting either from the stress of unemployment and alienation; or from the repression and degradation of being supported by the welfare state at an increasingly marginal level.

(b) Disturbances in the system of class rule. As we have seen, some of the state's attempts to guarantee and maintain the interests of the capitalist class may serve counter to those interests, and may encourage further challenges to the ruling class. Navarro (1975), for example, has argued that the creation of the National Health System in Britain was at least partly a result of the radicalisation of the working class — it was a bribe, in other words, to defuse the rising level of class struggle. After more than thirty years, it is evident that class inequality, at least in health terms, is as great if not greater than it was in 1948 (Doyal, 1979). So, the conflict between labour and capital continues, with increasing demands to raise 'social wages' and provide ever higher welfare payments to 'cushion the dislocation, uncertainty, and diswelfare created by the process of capital accumulation' (Navarro, 1975, p.77). The development of mass education has a similar contradictory effect (Spitzer, 1975). It is clearly in the interests of capitalism to train, evaluate, and sort labour in the education system. On the other hand, education has allowed some people to see how alienated they are, and how much they have been exploited. Their responses may be to 'drop-out', become radical (i.e. deviant), or make further service demands on the capitalist class. In this sense the provision of one service, education, makes it necessary for the state to spend more and more on other services, which might include repression and formal controls. It is worth noting here that in late capitalism the proportion of the population that is 'stagnant', in other words permanently redundant and unwanted, continues to rise (Spitzer, 1975). Most of these people cannot be co-opted back into the

system by employment, so they either have to be served or controlled. Thus, almost by definition, the state's 'social expenses' grow as capital becomes increasingly spatially and organisationally concentrated. O'Connor (1973) showed that this has also been accompanied by a socialisation of more of the costs of production ('social capital'), but at the same time most of the profits have been going to individuals and corporations. The net effect is that the state continues to experience a deficit in transactions between itself and the other sectors of society. As O'Connor (1979) noted, 'The state budget grows because it grows' (p. 65) as social capital financing requires more social expenses to mop up the casualties of capital accumulation. As the 'structural gap' widens, the social problems are exacerbated, partly because fewer resources are available to provide the necessary human services.

These disturbances in the system of class rule have been exacerbated in recent years because some of the policies designed to provide services to the growing problem population have increased *per capita* costs. This is a topic worthy of an entire paper in itself, but at this point it is necessary only to outline some of the major issues. In the first place, the strategies of social control that have dominated the human services during the last two decades, those that can be referred to as 'dispersed-integrative' rather than 'concentrated-segregative', have shifted the burden away from the state and toward a basic free-for-all. The federal government foots the bills, through its welfare payments, but a hodge-podge of public and private providers offer the services (Rose, 1979). As Scull (1981) has observed, the clients often lose out in this 'new trade in lunacy'. Second, the expected savings from deinstitutionalisation, decarceration, decriminalisation, and diversion programmes have not materialised; partly because providing adequate community alternatives turned out to be at least as costly as keeping people in the institutions; and partly because the overall dispersal has been accompanied by a mushrooming of services at all levels (Cohen, 1979). Third, many of the individuals who are left in the institutions, particularly those in mental hospitals, are much more costly to serve than the average patients of two decades ago. This is true both in the short run because closer supervision and more medication are required; and also in the long run because the fastest growing group, the young chronic patients, in all probability, are facing a lifetime of institutional care (Pepper *et al.*, 1981). As the demographic structure of public mental hospitals changes, costs to the state will rise even further: because the shrinking numbers of elderly patients will deprive the state of federal (Medicaid) contributions; and also because the increasing group of younger patients is not eligible for Medicaid (New York State, Office of Mental Hygiene, 1981). Fourth, the trend toward medical and psychiatric treatment of social problems means that individuals are entering more humane but much more costly forms of care. Thus as the decriminalisation of public drunkenness results in more alcoholics coming under the umbrella of the welfare state (Regier, 1979), and as more criminals are treated in mental hospitals (Melick, *et al.*, 1979), the costs continue to escalate. Evidence of the rising costs of maintaining the welfare state has been skillfully used by politicians to provide a mandate for extensive cuts in the human services. In doing this the political right has been able to forge an unusual alliance between the in-work members of the working class and the capitalist class — both of whom can easily see the threat presented to them by out of work 'welfare chisellers'. This is part of what Piven and Cloward (1981) have referred to as the 'new class war' and, as Navarro (1975) forewarned, it has been made possible, in part, by putting ever increasing numbers of people on the politically-vulnerable perch of 'welfare'. It is much more acceptable to argue for a reduction in welfare payments than it is to argue for releasing criminals from prison or throwing mental patients out of hospitals.

Converting the Problem Population into Objects for Social Control. The rate at which individuals in the large problem population pool are converted into 'proper objects for social control' (Spitzer, 1975), is determined by a number of variables. Most noteworthy among these are the following:

(a) The ability of the health and welfare systems to keep problem prevalence rates in check. State expenditures on welfare medicine and income maintenance payments can be interpreted as attempts to socialise and control the working classes. Being sick, poor, or unemployed does not necessarily constitute a serious social problem for an individual; in fact for many people it has become the norm. There is a threshold point, however, in everyone's life, beyond which an individual is forced into desperation — a life of crime, permanent illness, mental illness, or drug abuse. From this perspective state-supported health and welfare programmes have a preventive role. Providing diversion programmes for teenage offenders is intended to prevent a lifetime of contacts with the

criminal justice system (Cohen, 1979; Van Dusen, 1981). In the same way, decriminalisation of public intoxication is an attempt to steer heavy drinkers away from one too many trips through the 'revolving door' of chronic drunkenness (Fagan and Mauss, 1978).

However beneficial and humane these trends are, the capitalist mode of production will continue to create physical and psychological casualties at a faster rate than the medical and welfare state services can patch them up and put them back to work, or otherwise keep them out of harm's way. The inexorable increase in prevalence rates in almost all categories of medical and mental illness, in spite of the ever increasing expenditures, gives testimony to this depressing fact (Illich, 1975; Zola, 1978; Doyal, 1979; Eyer and Sterling 1977). Those individuals who are helped earn the right to return to work, thereby reproducing one of the major inputs of production. For those who can not be put back to work, medical treatment still performs a useful service because it helps to reproduce the relations of production, by shaping attitudes and beliefs that are consistent with the capitalist organisation of society (Navarro, 1975). This is essential to hold society together, as Cockburn (1977) has observed: 'Workers must not step outside the relation of the wage, the relation of property, the relation of authority. So "reproducing capitalist relations" means reproducing the class system, ownership, [and] above all reproducing a frame of mind' (p. 56).

Services that are organised along the general lines of the medical model can help to reproduce this 'frame of mind' in a number of ways:

(i)   Allying medicine to service provision brings science and high technology to the helping professions, which helps to legitimate the existing character of capitalist society. As Doyal (1979) notes, this helps to provide 'important window-dressing in maintaining support for the existing system' (p. 43).

(ii) Treatment is dominated by individual helper/client interactions, which serves to maintain the class-based hierarchies found in society as a whole. Dear (1981) has shown how doctor/patient relationships in the mental health field serve this purpose; and as Doyal (1979) observes it also helps to justify the mechanisation and excessive division of labour that pervades capitalist production techniques:

The idea that it is only the doctor who can cure, and the belief that one's mind and body can be separated and treated according to the laws of science; both serve to emphasize the loss of individual autonomy and the feelings of powerlessness so common in other areas of social and economic life. People come to believe that they have little control over their own bodies, just as ... they have so little control over the conditions in which they spend their working lives (p. 43).

(iii) The belief that there is a benevolent state somewhere 'out there' helps to depoliticise and carry the working class through all but the most stressful times.

As Navarro (1975) has suggested, medicine (and to this we can add many of the state-supported social welfare programmes) is destined to 'fail' because it has been given an impossible task. Perhaps, like prisons, medicine and social welfare are supposed to fail (Foucault, 1977). Perhaps they are simply expected to 'manage' rather than 'reduce' the problems they encounter. Or, as some would argue, perhaps they simply do not even attempt to tackle the problems they are, in name, intended to tackle. They do, however, have a function, as Navarro has argued for medicine:

to the degree that the majority of people believe and accept the proposition that what are actually politically caused conditions can be individually solved by medical intervention ... from the point of view of the capitalist system, this is the actual utility of medicine, it contributes to the legitimation of capitalism (Navarro, 1975, p.69).

(b) The availability and effectiveness of alternative coping mechanisms. As noted earlier, informal methods of social control are often able to curb the excesses of certain individuals and sometimes entire sub-groups of the population (Maloff *et al.*, 1979). The extent to which informal controls are effective will help to determine how many individuals need to make use of the formal services that are available. It is also possible that informal social support networks can be useful in preventing entry into formal programmes, particularly in the case of the elderly and the mentally ill (Smith, 1978; 1982c). Another partial solution lies in the operation of self-help groups that are organised by individuals who share certain problems, for example, alcoholics, child abusers, and the mentally ill. In recent years, the proliferation of these groups has been remarkable (Smith 1978); but it can be argued that self-

helping has become so popular only because the state is unwilling to tackle some of the root causes for societal ills. In this sense many self-help groups are effectively co-opted by the state. Their own rhetoric, claiming that self-helping is more effective than official agency intervention, contributes to the process.

(c) Current political and economic circumstances. Recent attempts to cut back income maintenance programmes, coming during high levels of unemployment, are likely to exacerbate the insecurities and stresses among the working classes (Ehrenreich, 1982). In addition, budget cuts in all categories of the human services will threaten to worsen the already dismal performance of these programmes by cutting back services, and 'dumping' individuals into the greedy hands of the growing class of private care operators (Rose, 1979; Scull, 1981). It seems likely that the remaining funds will be reserved almost exclusively for the most traditional treatment programmes, while even the most rudimentary attempts at preventive and educational programmes will be threatened.

One of the major concerns about the current economic situation is that programme cuts are occurring just when such programmes need to be expanded (Smith, 1982a). The early retirements, higher levels of unemployment, and greater levels of insecurity among the workforce are likely to increase the prevalance of many health and social problems. In other words demand is increasing, but the state can not afford to expand any services because all spare capital is needed for suplus-producing activities. The current 'slash and burn' approach to social welfare programmes is based on the neo-conservative view that the war on poverty has been successful, and that it is time to hand over a larger share of the existing welfare programmes to the private sector (Stoesz, 1981). Such a strategy will help to reduce overhead costs, increase efficiency and accountability, and shrink the role of 'big government' in the health and welfare fields. However, in these difficult times the state would normally appear to be neutral or 'classless' in the conflict between labour and capital by helping to buffer some of the stresses inflicted on the workforce. The current administration has, of course, suspended even the pretence of being classless, and it remains to be seen whether this has the effect that theory would predict, namely that in the absence of adequate social expenditures, the state's legitimacy will be threatened, and force or repression will be needed to carry out the existing economic programmes.

One of the most publicised consequences of the current fiscal crisis has been the impact of unemployment on the prevalence of social problems. In the last decade some impressive evidence has been gathered to demonstrate a significant and positive relationship between unemployment and a range of medical, psychological, and social problems: including mental hospital admissions (Brenner, 1973); suicides (Pierce, 1967; Stack, 1981); child abuse (Steinberg, *et al.*, 1981); depression and stress Dooley, *et al.*, 1981); and alcoholism (Brenner, 1975). This work, particularly Brenner's, has been very influential in both Britain and the United States, but the major policy implication — manipulating the unemployment level to reduce the level of stress and hence the level of social expenditures — has so far been impossible to implement.

Brenner's work has been questioned: on methodological grounds (Eyer, 1976a); as a result of contradictory findings (Eyer, 1975; Marshall and Dowdall, 1981); because of his oversimplistic model of causation (Michaels, 1976); and also because unemployment may simply 'uncover' existing conditions rather than 'create' new illness (Smith, 1982a). It is also evident that Brenner's conclusions are too general to be useful in a policy sense. We know very little, for example, about the differential effects of unemployment in different sectors of the economy; and Brenner and most of his followers ignore the possibility of regional or even local variations in the unemployment effect (see Dooley *et al.*, 1981, for exceptions). Perhaps the most telling criticism, however, is that Brenner overemphasises the importance of economic downturns, so his policy implications only go as far as suggesting that attempts be made to smooth out the business cycle. In other words, Brenner is not critical of capitalism as a whole, only of unemployment. Eyer (1976b) argues that the boom phase of the business cycle is perhaps more pathogenic. Consistent with the major arguments described in this section of the paper, Eyer believes that economic growth under capitalism is the major stress producing phenomenon of our times.

(d) The characteristics of the problem population. As the overall prevalence of a particular social problem increases, so does the probability that official agencies will intervene by offering formal services. The current level of unemployment in both the United States and Britain, for example, might help to create a greater demand for health, mental health, and other services. At the same time, the existing programme cuts, and the drive to keep people out of institutions, may encourage some creative social control

entrepreneurship, such as the creation of new deviance categories
— a process that has been referred to as 'relabeling' (Van Dusen,
1981; Cohen, 1979). This may occur at the client level, for example,
when an individual adopts a criminal, suicidal, or drug strategy to
ensure his or her entry into a facility; but it is more likely to occur
at the programme level, when individuals are processed into
whatever services have vacancies.

In addition to the size of the problem population, other factors
may alter the rate of deviance processing, such as: the relative
power of the group; its level of organisation and visibility; and the
spatial and temporal context of the problems. The elderly in Britain
and America are an increasingly vocal and visible political power,
so even the Reagan administration is unlikely to launch an all-out
attack on Social Security in the face of their inevitable opposition
(although in non-election years the situation may easily change). In
recent years the mentally ill have also been able to influence policy,
although the success of patients acting as individuals and in groups
can be interpreted as co-optation (Brown, 1981). Increases or
decreases in the provision of services may also be partly a function
of the actual and perceived 'utility' of problem populations.
Alcohol consumption, for example, provides revenue and jobs, so
state agencies need to weigh the costs of treatment against the
considerable benefits of the alcohol industry. State mental hospitals
and prisons provide an enormous economic boost to their local
communities (Moore, 1981); so any attempts to cut back or
eliminate services are usually hotly contended. The continued
presence of particularly deviant groups, notably criminals, may also
serve an important political function, especially for administrations
that derive much of their support from their stance against crime.

The location of problem populations can also be an important
determinant of service response. Obviously the bulk of the social
problems discussed in this essay are concentrated in cities, a
tendency that has been accelerated by the recent moves toward
dispersal and community care. In addition, recent demographic and
economic shifts at both the intra-urban and inter-regional levels
may have resulted in an increasing concentration of social problems
in the inner cities, particularly the older cities of the manufacturing
core. It is no surprise then, to find that the supply of many human
services are heavily skewed towards urban areas (NIMH, 1976):
partly because they are most needed in such locations; but also
because the abilities and wherewithal necessary to apply

successfully for funds to establish services are also concentrated in cities (Smith, 1982b).

One final consideration at this point is the tendency for the supply of services to influence local demand. It is well known, for example, that community mental health centres now offer services for individuals who were not previously receiving them (Brown, 1979; Levine, 1981). There is also a tendency for the level of admissions, for example to mental hospitals, to increase as hospital capacity increases (Marshall and Funch, 1979). In addition, as we have seen, there has also been a tendency for social programmes to expand and multiply as a result of welfare entrepreneurism in recent years. There are reports of service providers scouring the landscape ever more diligently for new clients, 'bagging' them either from other agencies, or from the ranks of previously unserved individuals in the community. As Van Dusen (1981) has noted such examples of 'net widening' are common.

As we have seen then, the processes that could reduce the problem prevalence rates are, in general, unable to do so. Most of the social problems we have considered here are socially, environmentally, or politically caused, but the responses to those problems remain based on explanations that are individual and mainly medical in character. These responses are justified because (i) they support the prevailing economic and social organisation of society; (ii) they are consistent with the medical-engineering approach to social problems; and (iii) because the agencies providing services tend to be mainly concerned with self-preservation and economic survival. The services offered can, at best, gnaw away at the prevalence rates at a glacial pace; but with the incidence of new cases and the reentry of the 'failures' (readmissions, repeat offenders, etc.), the problems continue to grow. In other words, the human service programmes 'fail' to 'solve' the problems, at least in terms of lowering the prevalence rates. On the other hand it is clear that other, presumably more important, goals are achieved.

The 'Alcohol Problem' and Social Policy in the United States

The United States government has launched a serious attempt to deal with the 'alcohol problem'. The creation of the NIAAA in 1970 firmly placed the official response to alcoholism under the auspicies of the welfare state. At approximately the same time the Uniform Intoxication Act (1971), a version of which has been passed in about three quarters of the states, began the move toward decriminalisation of public drunkenness. Slowly but surely the 'alcohol problem' has been redefined as a medical rather than a criminal (or a moral) problem (Smith and Hanham, 1982; Beauchamp, 1980). Consistent with this trend, most state alcohol agencies have begun making plans to provide a 'continuum' of alcoholism programmes in the community (Anderson, 1979; Glaser *et al.*, 1978). In other words, wherever possible the social control of alcoholism is to be dispersed into the community, with a minimal emphasis on institutional care.

The majority of the programmes created under these new guidelines, and consequently the bulk of NIAAA's budget, has been directed toward funding alcoholism treatment programmes, with only a secondary focus on public education and prevention (Glaser, *et al.*, 1978). This orientation reflects the dominance of the disease model of alcoholism, which defines alcoholism as primarily an individual problem, but one that only affects a small proportion of the drinking population. Other models of alcoholism are featured frequently in the literature, but at the present time their influence on policy and service provision is, at best, peripheral (Whitehead, 1979; Siegler *et al.*, 1968; Roebuck and Kessler, 1972). It is a great irony, therefore, that just when the federal role in combatting alcohol abuse has been institutionalised, 'the de facto policy of the Congress has been to promote consumption of alcoholic beverages through lower taxes' (Cook and Tauchen, 1981, p.1). Between 1960 and 1980 the real price of alcohol in the United States fell: for liquor by 48 per cent; for beer by 27 per cent; and for wine 20 per cent (Cook, 1981). During this period federal taxes remained at the 1951 level of $10.50 per proof gallon of alcohol. As Cook points out, if this tax had been tied to the Consumer Price Index, it would have been $28.00 by 1980. Federal alcohol policy shows no evidence of any interest in supply-side controls, including price (tax) increases, reducing availability, or limiting accessibility. This apathy is matched at the state level, where Alcoholic Beverage Control administrators are loath to try anything other than a policy of 'regulated maximum availability'. Alcohol policy simply attempts to maximise revenues and control the market — public health goals are not even on the horizon (Beauchamp, 1976; Bunce *et al.*, 1979). The alcoholic beverage industry is obviously not about to regulate itself in the direction of reducing availability; so it is hardly surprising that the industry actively supports the medical model of alcoholism.[7] Their argument, and that of the medical model proponents, is that because only a few individuals consistently abuse alcohol, it is unfair to penalise the millions of individuals who enjoy drinking and are able to drink without damage. On balance, the apathetic and ambivalent public is also happy with the *status quo*.They can get a drink at a low price pretty much whenever and wherever they want. In some states there are local 'dry' options or some limits on availability that will satisfy the local band of moral crusaders. In other words, everyone is happy with things the way they are.

By shifting the responsibility for alcoholism away from the substance to the individual, the 'alcohol problem' has been redefined, and the solution is pre-determined. In this sense the treatment of alcoholism can be interpreted as yet another way to renew labour power and reproduce the basic bourgeois philosophy of the capitalist system of production (Morgan, 1980). The perceived value, to the capitalist class, of alcoholism treatment programmes, is reflected in the widespread adoption of industrial alcoholism programmes, which are as much in the employers interests as the workers (Trice and Roman, 1972). By separating the responsibilities for control and prevention, and redefining prevention almost exclusively as tertiary prevention, or treatment, the state has organisationally solved the contradiction of trying to collect revenues from alcohol consumption, while at the same time treating alcoholics for drinking too much. The contradiction remains, but the agencies are now clearly separated, and as Morgan observes: 'This enabled control policies to develop relatively unfettered by old moralistic or temperance arguments against greater availability, lower taxes, and state supported production policies' (1980, p.135).

Alcoholism came under the welfare umbrella during an era of 'liberal' expansionary views about social problems and ideas about how they could best be treated (Levine and Levine, 1970; Williams *et al.*, 1980; Toews, 1980). A medical rather than a criminal response to alcoholism can be interpreted in the same light as the desire to deinstitutionalise the mentally ill or the elderly. Implicit in all of these trends has been the creeping encroachment of the state into an ever-widening range of medical and welfare problems. In prosperous times such encroachments can be interpreted as serving the interests of capital accumulation, by keeping the casualties relatively happy and therefore unlikely to revolt against the system. The state's new role in the alcoholism field was even more consistent with the interests of the capitalist class, because it did not significantly interfere with the production, distribution, and consumption of alcohol.

This brief summary illustrates how the state acts as a 'mediator' between the varying groups that are competing to control or manage the 'alcohol problem' (Morgan, 1980). A solution based on the medical model is acceptable to all parties: it is clearly dissociated with Prohibition moralism; it allows the market to operate freely; it is scientifically respectable, unlike the public health model of alcoholism; and it is 'liberal' in that it allows adults to choose for themselves how, when, and where to drink. On the other hand, in reaching a compromise, the state's solution of the 'alcohol problem' guarantees its failure. As Room (1978) has noted, to make significant inroads into the problem, the incidence rate must be reduced by preventing moderate drinkers from becoming problem drinkers. It has been estimated that incidence rates of serious alcohol related problems are in the range of 500,000 new cases per year (Keller, 1975). Programmes and mortality rates will chip away at the overall prevalence rate; but as Keller has calculated, about 9 per cent of all moderate and heavy drinkers are likely to become alcoholics each year. It seems likely that the nascent alcoholism movement has no more hope of succeeding than its more elderly relatives, the prison systems, mental hospitals, and general hospitals. None of these systems can hope to perform much more than acts of philanthropy. At best they can help the ever increasing army of the debilitated and demoralised workers to sober-up or straighten-up, and get back to work. At worst they will stand idly by as the former soldiers become flotsam and jetsam in the stagnant pool, lifetime casualties of the swim of capitalism.

References

Ahr, P.R., M.J. Gorodezky, and D.W. Cho (1981) 'Measuring the Relationship of Public Psychiatric Admissions to Rising Unemployment', *Hospital and Community Psychiatry*, **32**, 399-401

Anderson, D.J. (1979) 'Delivery of Essential Services to Alcoholics Through the "Continuum of Care" ', *Cancer Research*, **39**, 2855-58

Armor, D.J., M.J. Polich, and H.B. Stamboul (1976) *Alcoholism and Treatment*, Rand Corporation, Santa Monica

Bacon, S.D. (1976) 'Concepts' in W.J. Filstead, J.J. Rossi and M. Keller (eds.) *Alcohol and Alcohol Problems: New Thinking and New Directions*, Ballinger, Cambridge, Mass., 57-134

Beauchamp, D.E. (1976) 'Exploring New Ethics for Public Health: Developing a Fair Alcohol Policy', *Journal of Health, Politics Policy and Law*, 1, 338-54

Beauchamp, D.E. (1980) *Beyond Alcoholism: Alcohol and Public Health Policy*, Temple University Press, Philadelphia

Becker, H.S. (1963) *Outsiders*, The Free Press, New York

Berliner, H.S. (1977) 'Emerging Ideologies in Medicine', *The Review of Radical Political Economy*, 9, 116-124

Blane, H.T. and L.E. Hewitt (1977) *Alcohol and Youth: An Analysis of the Literature, 1960-75*, Final Report prepared for the National Institute on Alcohol Abuse and Alcoholism; Contract No. ADM 281-75-0026

Brenner, M.H. (1973) *Mental Illness and the Economy*, Harvard University Press, Cambridge, Mass.

Brenner, M.H. (1975) 'Trends in Alcohol Consumption and Associated Illness', *American Journal of Public Health*, 65, 1279-1292

Brenner, M.H. (1977) 'Personal Stability and Economic Security', *Social Policy*, May/June, 2-4

Brown, P. (1979) 'The Transfer of Care: US Mental Health Policy Since World War II', *International Journal of Health Services*, 9, 645-662

Brown, P. (1981) 'The Mental Patients' Rights Movement and Mental Health Institutional Change', *International Journal of Health Services*, 11, 523-540

Bunce, R.P., P. Morgan, J. Mosher, L. Wallack and F. Wittman (1979) 'The Structure of the Alcohol Market: A Conceptual Framework', Unpublished paper (mimeo) , Social Research Group, School of Public Health, University of California at Berkeley

Cahalan, D. (1970) *Problem Drinkers: A National Survey*, Jossey-Bass, San Francisco

Cahalan, D. and R. Room (1974) *Problem Drinking Among American Men*, New Brunswick, N.J., Rutgers Center of Alcohol Studies, Monograph No. 7

Catalano, R., D.Dooley and R. Jackson (1981) 'Economic Predictors of Admissions to Mental Health Facilities in a Nonmetropolitan Community', *Journal of Health and Social Behavior*, 22, 284-297

Chamberlin, J. (1978) *On Our Own: Patient-controlled Alternatives to the Mental Health System*, Hawthorn Books, New York

Chauncey, R.L. (1980) 'New Careers for Moral Entrepreneurs: Teenage Drinking', *Journal of Drug Issues*, 10, 45-70

Cockburn, C. (1977) *The Local State: Management of Cities and People*, Pluto Press, London

Cohen, S. (1979) 'The Punitive City: Notes on the Dispersal of Social Control', *Contemporary Crises*, 3, 339-363

Conrad, P., and J.W. Schneider (1980) *Deviance and Medicalization: From Badness to Sickness*, C.V. Mosby, St. Louis

Cook, P.J. (1981) 'The Effect of Liquor Taxes on Drinking, Cirrhosis and Auto Fatalities', in M.H. Moore and D. Gerstein (eds.) *Alcohol and Public Policy*, National Academy of Sciences, Washington, D.C., 255-285

Cook, P.J. and G. Tauchen (1981) 'The Effect of Liquor Taxes on Alcoholism', Unpublished paper (mimeo) , Duke University, Center for Demographic Studies

Cox, K.R. (1981) 'Bourgeois Thought and the Behavioral Geography Debate', in K.R. Cox and R.G. Golledge (eds.) *Behavioral Problems in Geography Revisited*, Methuen, New York, 256-280

Dear, M. (1981) 'Social and Spatial Reproduction of the Mentally Ill', in M. Dear and A.J. Scott (eds.) *Urbanization and Urban Planning in Capitalist Society*,

Methuen, London, 481-497

Dear, M., S.M. Taylor, and G.B. Hall (1980) 'External Effects of Mental Health Facilities', *Annals of the Association of American Geographers*, **70**, 342-352

Dickson, D.T. (1968) 'Bureaucracy and Morality: An Organizational Perspective on a Moral Crusade', *Social Problems*, **16**, 143-156

Ditton, J. (1979) *Contrology: Beyond the New Criminology*, Macmillan, London

Dohrenwend, B.P. et al. (1980) *Mental Illness in the United States: Epidemiological Estimates*, Praeger, New York

Dooley, D., R. Catalano, R. Jackson, and A. Brownell (1981) 'Economic, Life, and Symptom Changes in a Non-metropolitan Community', *Journal of Health and Social Behavior*, **22**, 144-154

Doyal, L. (1979) *The Political Economy of Health*, Pluto Press, London

Durkheim, E. (1938) *The Rules of Sociological Method*, E.G. Gatlin (ed.), Free Press, New York (originally published 1895)

Edwards, G. (1979) 'Drinking Problems: Putting The Third World on the Map', *The Lancet*, August 25th, 402-404

Ehrenreich, P. (1982) 'Entitlements — for whom?: Where the Health Dollar Really Goes', *The Nation*, **234, 19**, 586-588

Elling, R.H. (1981) 'The Fiscal Crisis of the State and State Financing of Health Care', *Social Science and Medicine*, **15c**, 207-217

Eyer, J. (1975) 'Hypertension as a Disease of Modern Society', *International Journal of Health Services*, **5**, 539-558

Eyer, J. (1976a) 'Review of Mental Illness and the Economy', *International Journal of Health Services*, **6**, 139-148

Eyer, J. (1976b) 'Rejoinder to Dr. Brenner', *International Journal of Health Services*, **6**, 157-168

Eyer, J. (1977) 'Prosperity as a Cause of Death', *International Journal of Health Services*, **7**, 125-150

Eyer, J. and P. Sterling (1977) 'Stress Related Mortality and Social Organization', *Review of Radical Political Economy*, **9**, 1-44

Fagan, R.W. and A. L. Mauss (1978) 'Padding the Revolving Door: An initial assessment of the Uniform Alcoholism and Intoxication Treatment Act in Practice', *Social Problems*, **26**, 232-247

Foucault, M. (1977) *Discipline and Punish: The Birth of the Prison*, Pantheon, New York

Freed, E.X. (1979) *The Alcoholic Personality*, Charles B. Slack, New York

Glaser, F.B., S.W. Greenberg, and M. Barrett (1978) *A Systems Approach to Alcohol Treatment*, Addiction Research Fondation, Toronto

Glassner, B., and B. Berg (1980) 'How Jews Avoid Alcohol Problems', *American Sociological Review*, **45**, 647-664

Gusfield, J.R. (1963) *Symbolic Crusade*, University of Illinois Press, Urbana, Illinois

Hills, S.L. (1980) *Demystifying Social Deviance*, McGraw-Hill, New York

Hobsbawm, E. (1973) *The Age of Revolution*, 2nd Edition, Cardinal, London

Howland, R.W., and J.W. Howland (1978) '200 Years of Drinking in the United States: Evolution of the Disease Concept', in J.A. Ewing and B.A. Rouse (eds.) *Drinking*, Nelson-Hall, Chicago, 39-62

Illich, I.(1975) *Medical Nemesis: The Expropriation of Health*, Calder and Boyars, New York

Keller, M. (1975) 'Problems of Epidemiology in Alcohol Problems', *Journal of Studies on Alcohol*, **36**, 1442-1452

Kirk, S.A. (1974) 'The Impact of Labeling on Rejection of the Mentally Ill', *Journal of Health and Social Behavior*, **15**, 108-117

Levine, H.G. (1978) 'The Discovery of Addiction: Changing Conceptions of Habitual Drunkenness in America', *Quarterly Journal of Studies on Alcohol*, **39**,

143-174

Levine, M. (1981) *The History and Politics of Community Mental Health*, Oxford University Press, New York

Levine, M. and A. Levine (1970) *A Social History of Helping Services: Clinic, Court, School and Community*, Appleton-Century-Crofts, New York

MacAndrew, C., and R. B. Edgerton (1969) *Drunken Comportment: A Social Explanation*, Aldine, Chicago

McNeill, W.H. (1976) *Plagues and Peoples*, Anchor Press/Doubleday, New York

Maloff, D., H.S. Becker, A. Fonaroff, and J. Rodin (1979) 'Informal Social Controls and Their Influence on Substance Abuse', *Journal of Drug Issues*, 9, 161-183

Marshall, J.R. and G.W. Dowdall (1982) 'Employment and Mental Hospitalization: The Case of Buffalo, New York, 1914-55', *Social Forces*, 60, 843-853

Marshall, J.R. and D.P. Funch (1979) 'Mental Illness and the Economy: A Critique and Partial Replication', *Journal of Health and Social Behavior*, 20, 282-289

Matza, D. (1969) *Becoming Deviant*, Prentice-Hall, Englewood Cliffs, New Jersey

Melick, M.E., H. J. Steadman, and J.J. Cocozza (1979) *Journal of Health and Social Behavior*, 20, 228-237

Michaels, R.J. (1976) 'Noncriminal Deviance and Mental Hospitalization: Economic Theory and Evidence', *Journal of Legal Studies*, 5, 387-437

Morgan, P. (1980) 'The State as Mediator: Alcohol Problem Management in the Post-War Period', *Contemporary Drug Problems*, 9, 107-140

Moore, G.A. (1981) 'Mental Health Deinstitutionalization and the Regional Economy: A Model and Case Study', *Social Science and Medicine*, 15c, 175-189

Morris, N., and G. Hawkins (1969) *The Honest Politician's Guide to Crime Control*, University of Chicago Press, Chicago

National Institute of Mental Health (1976) *A Study of Deficiencies and Differentials in the Distribution of Mental Health Resources in Facilities*, Superintendent of Documents, U.S. Government Printing Office, Washington D.C., Series B, No. 15, DHEW Publiciations (ADM) 79-517

National Institute on Alcohol Abuse and Alcoholism (1978) Third Special Report to the U.S. Congress on *Alcohol and Health*, U.S. Department of Health, Education and Welfare, Rockville, Md.

National Institute on Alcohol Abuse and Alcoholism (1981) Fourth Special Report to the U.S. Congress on *Alcohol and Health*, U.S. Department of Health and Human Services, Rockville, Md.

Navarro, V. (1977) 'Political Power, the State and their Implications in Medicine', *The Review of Radical Political Economy*, 9, 63-80

New York State Office of Mental Health (1981) The 1982-83 Office of Mental Health Program/Budget Overview, Albany, New York

O'Connor, J. (1973) *The Fiscal Crisis of the State*, St. Martins Press, New York

O'Connor, J. (1979) 'Some Reflective Criticisms on Mosley's "Critical Reflections on the Fiscal Crisis of the State" ', *The Review of Radical Political Economy*, 11, 60-65

Pattison, E.M. (1976) 'Nonabstinent Drinking Goals in the Treatment of Alcoholics', in R. J. Gibbins *et al.* (eds.) *Research Advances in Alcohol and Drug Problems*, Wiley, New York, 3, 401-456

Pepper, B., M.C. Kirschner, and H. Ryglewicz (1981) 'The Young Adult Chronic Patient: Overview of a Population', *Hospital and Community Psychiatry*, 32, 463-469

Pierce, A. (1967) 'The Economic Cycle and the Social Suicide Rate', *American Sociological Review*, 32, 457-462

Pittman, D.J. and C.W. Gordon (1958) *Revolving Door*, The Free Press, Glencoe, Ill.

Piven, F.F. and R.A. Cloward (1982) *The New Class War*, Pantheon, New York

Pollack, E.S. (1974) Review of 'Mental Illness and the Economy', *American Journal of Public Health,* **64,** 512-513

Popham, R.E., W. Schmidt, and J. de Lint (1975) 'The Prevention of Alcoholism: Epidemiological Studies of the Effects of Government Control Measures', *British Journal of Addiction,* **70,** 125-144

Pred, A. (1981) 'Social Reproduction and the Time Geography of Everyday Life', *Geografiska Annaler B,* **63,** 5-22

Pyle, G.F.(1979) *Applied Medical Geography,* V.H. Winston, Washington D.C.

Quinney, R. (1980) *Class, State, and Crime,* Longman, New York

Regier, D.A., I.D. Goldberg, and C. Taube (1978) 'The de facto U.S. Mental Health Service System: A Public Health Perspective', *Archives of General Psychiatry,* **35,** 685-693

Reinarman, C. (1979) 'Moral Entrepreneurs and Political Economy: Historical and Ethnographic Notes on the Construction of the Cocaine Menace', *Contemporary Crises,* **3,** 225-254

Renaud, M. (1978) 'On the Structural Constraints to State Intervention in Health', in J. Ehrenreich (ed.) *The Cultural Crisis of Modern Medicine,* Monthly review Press, New York, 101-122

Rodin, M.B. (1981) 'Alcoholism as a Folk Disease: The Paradox of Beliefs and Choice of Therapy in an Urban American Community', *Journal of Studies on Alcohol,* **42,** 822-836

Roebuck, J.R. and R.G. Kessler (1972) *The Etiology of Alcoholism:Constitutional, Psychological and Sociological Approaches,* C.C. Thomas, Springfield, Illinois

Room, R. (1978) 'Evaluating the Effect of Drinking Laws on Drinking', in J.A. Ewing and B.A. Rouse (eds.) *Drinking,* Nelson-Hall, Chicago, 267-289

Rorabaugh, W.J. (1979) *The Alcoholic Republic: An American Tradition,* Oxford University Press, New York

Rose, S.M. (1979) 'Deciphering Deinstitutionalization: Complexities in Policy and Program Analysis', *Milbank Memorial Fund Quarterly,* **57,** 429-460

Ryan, M. (1978) *The Acceptable Pressure Group,* Saxon House, Farnborough, Hants

Schmidt, W. (1977) 'Cirrhosis and Alcohol Consumption: An Epidemiological Perspective', in G. Edwards and M. Grant (eds.) *Alcoholism: New Knowledge and New Responses,* Croom Helm, London, 15-47

Scull, A. (1981) 'A New Trade in Lunacy: The Recommodification of the Mental Patient', *American Behavioral Scientist,* **24,** 741-754

Segal, S.P. (1978) 'Attitudes Toward the Mentally Ill: A Review', *Social Work,* **17,** 211-217

Segal, S.P., J. Baumohl, and E.W. Moyles (1980) 'Neighborhood Types and Community reaction to the Mentally Ill: A Paradox of Intensity', *Journal of Health and Social Behavior,* **21,** 345-359

Shaw, S. (1980) 'The Causes of Increasing Drinking Problems Among Women', in Camberwell Council on Alcoholism (ed.) *Women and Alcohol,* Tavistock, London, 1-40

Shaw, S., A. Cartwright, T. Spratley and J. Harwin (1978) *Responding to Drinking Problems,* University Park Press, Baltimore

Siegler, M.H., H. Osmond, and S. Newell (1968) 'Models of Alcoholism', *Quarterly Journal of Studies on Alcohol,* **29,** 571-591

Skog, O.J. (1980) 'Social Interaction and the Distribution of Alcohol Consumption', *Journal of Drug Issues,* **10,** 71-92

Smith, C.J. (1978) 'Self-Help and Social Networks in the Urban Community', *Ekistics,* **45,** 106-115

Smith, C.J. (1982a) 'The Urban Services Paradox: Shrinking Supply in Times of Rising Demand', Paper presented at the annual meeting of the Association of American Geographers, San Antonio, Texas (April)

Smith, C.J. (1982b) 'Geographical Approaches to Mental Health', forthcoming in

H. L. Freeman (ed.) *Mental Health and the Environment*, Churchill Livingstone, London

Smith, C.J. (1982c) 'Home-based Mental Health Care for the Elderly', in A.M. Warnes (ed.) *Geographical Perspectives on the Elderly*, Wiley, London, 375-398

Smith, C.J. and R.Q. Hanham (1981) 'Proximity and the Formation of Public Attitudes Towards Mental Illness', *Environment and Planning*, 13A, 147-165

Smith, C.J. and R.Q. Hanham (1982) *Alcohol Abuse: Geographical Perspectives*, Resource Publications in Geography, Association of American Geographers, Washington D.C.

Snyder, C. (1978) *Alcohol and the Jews*, Southern Illinois University Press, Carbondale, Ill.

Spector, M. and J. I. Kitsuse (1977) *Constructing Social Problems*, Cummings, Menlo Park, California

Spitzer, S. (1975) 'Toward a Marxian Theory of Deviance', *Social Problems*, 22, 641-651

Stack, S. (1981) 'Divorce and Suicide: A Time Series Analysis, 1933-1970', *Journal of Family Issues*, 2, 77-90

Steinberg, L., R. Catalano, and D. Dooley (1981) 'Economic Antecedents of Child Abuse and Neglect', *Child Development*, 52, 260-267

Stevenson, G. (1976) 'Social Relations and Consumption in the Human Service Occupations', *Monthly Review*, July/August, 78-87

Stivers, R. (1976) *The Hair of the Dog: Irish Drinking and American Stereotype*, Pennsylvania State University Press, University Park, Pa.

Stoesz, D. (1981) 'A Wake for the Welfare State: Social Welfare and the Neoconservative Challenge', *Social Service Review*, 55, 398-410

Stratton, R., A. Zeiner, and A. Paredes (1978) 'Tribal Affiliation and Prevalence of Alcohol Problems', *Journal of Studies on Alcoholism*, 39, 1166-1177

Sulkunen, P. (1976) 'Drinking Patterns and the Level of Alcohol Consumption: An International Overview', in R. J. Gibbins *et al.* (eds.) *Research Advances in Alcohol and Drug Problems*, Wiley, New York, 3, 223-282

Toews, J. (1980) 'Mental Health Service Priorities in a Time of Restraint', *Canada's Mental Health*, 28, 2-4

Trice, H.M. and P.M. Roman (1972) *Spirits and Demons at Work: Alcohol and Other Drugs on the Job*, New York State School of Industrial and Labor Relations, Cornell Univ. Ithaca, N.Y.

Van Dusen, K.T. (1981) 'Net Widening and Relabeling: Some Consequences of Deinstitutionalization', *American Behavioral Scientist*, 24, 801-810

Warren, C.A.B. (1981) 'New Forms of Social Control: The Myth of Deinstitutionalization', *American Behavioral Scientist*, 24, 724-740

Watts, T.D. (1981) 'The Uneasy Triumph of a Concept: The "Disease" Conception of Alcoholism', *Journal of Drug Issues*, 11, 451-460

Whitehead, P.C. (1979) 'Public Policy and Alcohol Related Damage: Media Campaigns or Social Controls', *Addictive Behaviors*, 4, 83-89

Wilkins, L.T. (1964) *Social Deviance*, Tavistock, London

Williams, D.H., E.C. Bellis and S.W. Wellington (1980) 'Deinstitutionalization and Social Policy: Historical Perspectives and Present Dilemmas', *American Journal of Orthopsychiatry*, 50, 54-56

Young, J. (1971) 'The Role of the Police as Amplifier of Deviancy, Negotiators of Reality and Translators of Fantasy: Some Consequences of our Present System of Drug Control as seen in Notting Hill', in S. Cohen (ed.) *Images of Deviance*, Pelican, London, 27-61

Young, J. (1976) Introduction to Frank Pearce's *Crimes of the Powerful*, Pluto Press, London, 12-13

Zola, I.K. (1978) 'Medicine as an Institution of Social Control', in J.Ehrenreich (ed.)

The Cultural Crisis of Modern Medicine, Monthly Review Press, New York, 80-100

Notes

1. It should be clear that the division between service and control is not hard and fast. Some institutions, for example mental hospitals, both serve and control; and it is also reasonable to argue that some services, e.g. state-based education and tranquilising drugs, also control individual attitudes and behaviours.

2. As Stratton *et al.* (1975) have observed the prevalence of alcohol-related deaths among native Americans varies both by tribal affiliation and location, with some tribes, notably the five 'civilised' tribes (Choctaw, Chicasaw, Creek, Seminole and Cherokee) having lower rates than whites.

3. It was not until 1958 that the American Medical Association officially recognised alcoholism as a disease (Smith and Hanham, 1982).

4. Some alcoholics are able to stop drinking altogether for varying lengths of time although they still refer to themselves as alcoholics.

5. This particular expression of regional tension was just one in a long and continuing series of such events in American history. In recent years we have witnessed new variants on this theme, based on energy endowments, presidential voting patterns, and variations in economic growth.

6. The National Institute of Mental Health (NIMH), and the National Institute of Drug Abuse (NIDA) are both housed with the Department of Health and Human services.

7. One of the industry organisations, the Distilled Spirits Council of the US, provides funds for alcohol research projects. Not surprisingly, the emphasis of these projects is heavily skewed toward biochemical and medical research.

10

Health Care and the State:
Britain and the United States

Andrew M. Kirby

Introduction

This chapter is an attempt to contrast two distinct traditions in the analysis of medicine. The first places its emphasis upon the organisation of health-care at the national scale; the second focuses more firmly upon the distribution of resources at the local scale.

In the first category can be found several distinct strands of emphasis. Alford, for example, has discussed in the American context the role of health institutions in the shaping of national policy (1975). Illich, in a more populist vein, has aimed his invective at the medical profession, in an attempt to argue that the latter's members are in fact counter-productive in the attempt to reduce levels of mortality and morbidity within advanced societies (1975). A more recent perspective has been pioneered by Navarro, who harnesses materialist state theory to the provision of medicine; more will be said of this perspective below (e.g. Navarro, 1976b).

This type of literature is in contrast to the focus of much health-care debate. Many studies of local funding, state-local jurisdictional financial transfers, the organisation of provision and the geographical distribution of particular facilities have little to say regarding the nature or role of medicine within society, but far more to contribute concerning the relationship between health-care and individual health histories or futures (Shannon and Dever, 1974; Pyle, 1979).

In the next section, an attempt is made to sketch the organisation of health-care in both the USA and the UK, in order to begin to reconcile these two distinct strands of medical and more general social science literature.

Health and health-care in the USA and UK

It would be possible to caricature the health economies of the USA and the UK as private and public respectively. Figures 10.1 and 10.2 indicate however that this would be only partially correct. As Alford has argued, the increasing technology residing within American medical practice, and the tendency for demand to fall in step with the resultingly higher price of care, produced in the 1960s a political climate within which the state subsidy of health provision was possible. The introduction of Medicare and Medicaid, plus a long series of organisations and items of legislation, has clearly increased the use made of professional services by the poor, but has in no way reduced medical expenditure (Rice and Wilson, 1976). We thus find that the American case is now represented by a mixed health economy (Figure 10.1), in which the public input is expected to carry on growing (Figure 10.2: Mitchell, 1981). The corollary is the case in Britain. In the recent past, the structure of health provision has been virtually exclusively via state organisations (Figure 10.3). However, private health, financed via individual medical insurance, is growing rapidly. The most recent data for 1981 indicate that in excess of 4 million persons are so insured, and that approximately $250m was being spent annually on care and treatment (Laurance, 1983; Lee, 1978, pp.7-9). Although this total represented only some two per cent of total state expenditure on health, this should not be taken as an indication of the unimportance of private medicine. In one sense, the data on costs and expenditure are not strictly comparable, as the private sector does not have to bear the costs of training its staff, most of whom receive qualifications overseas or at the expense of the state. Similarly, much high-cost equipment is bought by the state services, but used relatively cheaply by private practitioners. Finally, there is evidence that recent trends have been towards a major upturn in private insurance registration, whilst the use of private abortion facilities is still on the increase.

Medicine and the state in capitalist societies: ideology

Our ability to characterise these tendencies — which have been portrayed here as converging — depends clearly enough upon our theoretical perspective. As already argued, many interpretations

Figure 10.1: The US Health Care System

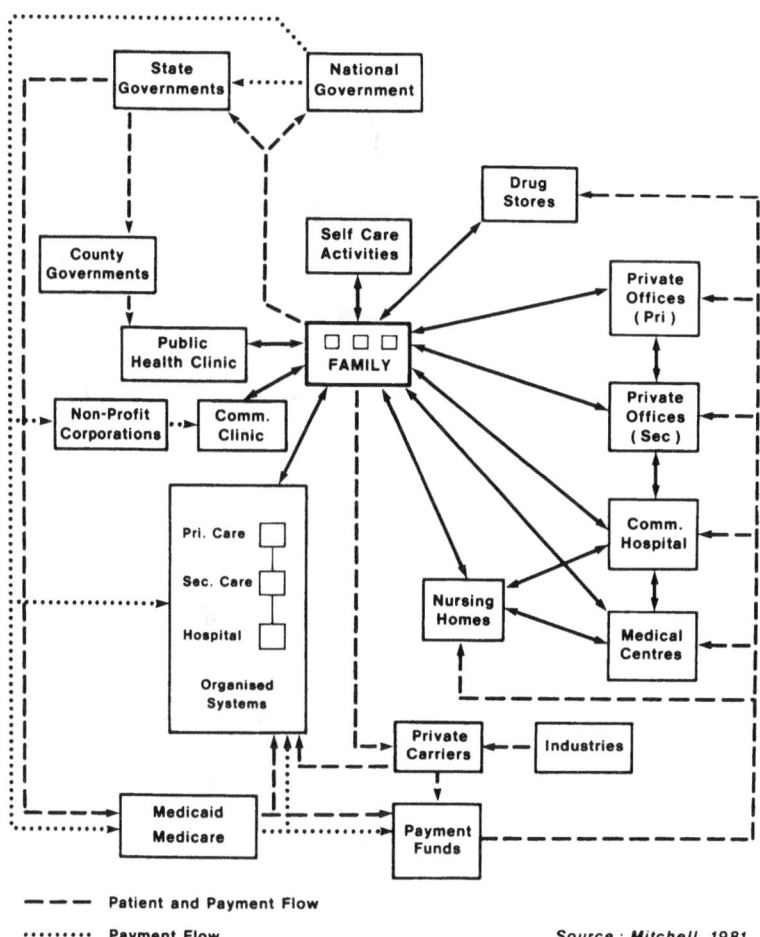

— — — Patient and Payment Flow

·········· Payment Flow

Source : Mitchell, 1981

focus upon the medical profession itself, with the results that both the nature of medicine and the role of the state (which is spending extremely heavily upon the latter) tend to become lost (see for example Weller, 1977).

This problem is partially solved by Navarro, who inverts the focus of interest, so that the differences between public and private health-care are played down (Navarro, 1976; 1977b). He achieves

Figure 10.2: US Health Care Costs

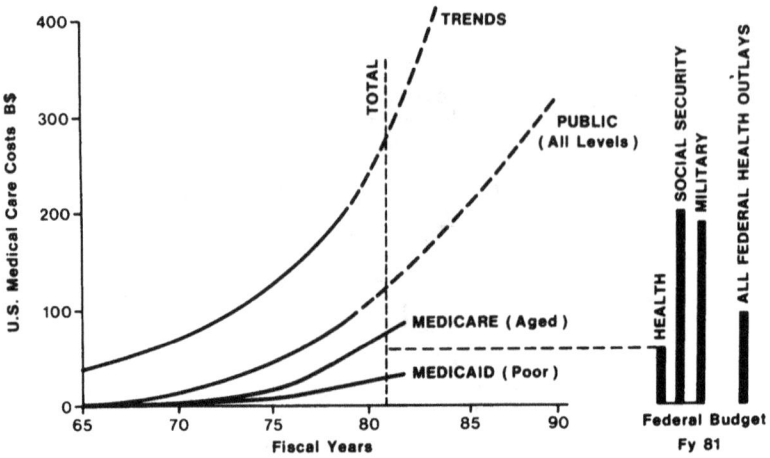

Source : Mitchell, 1981

this by directly considering the role of medicine within the capitalist societies. Using O'Connor's typology of social investment, social consumption and social expenses, or Navarro's own trichotomy of the infrastructure of production, the defence of the capitalist system, and control against internal and external threats (Navarro, 1976, pp. 268-269; O'Connor, 1973), we can identify an important role for medicine.

In other words, it has always been consistent with the state's interests for the medical profession to promote a mechanistic view of health, in which the onus of day-to-day living is placed upon the individual, and the responsibility for aberrant symptoms is borne by the physician. This Flexnerian perspective (Navarro, 1976, p. 277), is of course at odds with much that we know about the etiology of disease, which is generally environmental in its creation (Giggs, 1979). However, it is also equally obvious that a perspective upon health that focussed upon structural problems would both undermine the role of medical professionals and the economic system that either directly (via the negative externalities of production) or indirectly (via the failure of urban and regional planning) produces such etiologies. It is therefore not against the state's interests to support the medical profession if 'the cause of the problem is perceived as individual and the nature of intervention is individually oriented' (Navarro, 1976, p.278) As a consequence, medical expenditure has a key ideological role: 'from the point of view of the capitalist system, this is the actual utility of medicine: it contributes to the legitimation of capitalism' (Navarro, 1976, p.279). Of importance too with such a perspective is that it negates the distinction between public and private health economies: 'the ideological influence of the state far transcends what we usually refer to as the public sector. And medicine is very much a part of it, regardless of whether those medical institutions are, largely speaking, private or public' (Navarro, 1976, p. 283).

Navarro's interpretation is valuable therefore insofar as it encourages us not to become mesmerised by the public/private health distinction. This notwithstanding, it would be unsatisfactory if we did not attempt to account for the different historical paths that have been taken by the UK and the USA with regard to health-care.

Medicine and the state: reproduction and accumulation

Although health-care is most easily categorised as an aspect of consumption — part of the social wage — it would be negligent to overlook the fact that provision is also part of the accumulation process within capitalism; in other words medicine is not simply a service, but also a commodity. That said, it becomes less surprising that private medicine should be increasing within the United Kingdom; simply, it exists as a profitable alternative to the public arena in a sector of financial stringency. Indeed, it is probably more sensible to ask why it is that the British medical economy has been so slow to follow the American model, which has long had a tradition of large financial returns (see Klein, 1981 for a sarcastic evaluation).

Any discussion of the British case must of course confront the existence of the National Health Service, which has assumed shibboleth status in the annals of British political history (Navarro, 1978). What is clear however is that the NHS was not a major concession wrung from the state by working class action. Not surprisingly, in an era of deep unemployment, trade union activity between the wars focussed primarily upon issues in the factory, not the home: production and not consumption. Most importantly, the real beneficiaries of the NHS proved to be the middle classes, who had not enjoyed free hospital and practitioner care previously. The innovation stimulated by the NHS, namely the emergence of general practitioners as the key to primary care (rather than hospitals and clinics), has ever since been exploited far more widely by middle-income groups (Walters, 1980).

A more fundamental point lies beneath these interpretations. Apologists for the NHS imply that the arrival of a publicly-provided health-care service can be equated with the arrival of good health for all. This is of course over-optimism. As Harvey observes: 'a national health-care system which defines ill-health as inability to go to work (to produce surplus value), is very different indeed from one dedicated to the total mental and physical well-being of the individual in a given physical and social context' (Harvey, 1981, p.116).

In other words, medicine is also a key part of the reproduction of labour. Although Navarro, as we have seen, emphasises the ideological factor, it is self-evident that health-care is important to the maintenance of certain health standards, both public and private. This then becomes the key to the interpretation of the creation of the NHS immediately after the Second World War. Although it is possible to promote spurious claims concerning organisational goals ('efficiency was emphasised above all else': Walters, 1980, p.106), it is clear that the standard of adult health during the war had — once again — taken the Government by surprise. There exists a direct parallel between the introduction of public housing in 1919 and the introduction of public health provision — the NHS — in 1946. As Burnett has chronicled, the deplorable standard of army recruits during the First World War was a particularly important strand in the justification of state housing provision, as one way of improving living standards and thus wellbeing (Burnett, 1978). Similarly, the recurrent problem in the Second World War had indicated that more direct steps were required to ensure suitably fit men and women in the troubled era ahead should another war become a reality: as a Minister of Health stated in 1944, the NHS was 'a plan to raise national health to a higher plane' (quoted in Walters, 1980, p. 105).

This interpretation does of course conflict with the more usual argument — such as that provided by Navarro — which emphasises the importance of class struggle at a national level to the achievement of working class gains: 'the level of militancy of the working class and the far-reaching demands put forth by Labour clearly represented once again a threat to the British establishment and its political arms, the Conservative and Liberal parties' (Navarro, 1978, pp.28-29). Navarro's argument is unsubstantiated; as he himself however goes on to demonstrate, whilst the question of the success of labour's demands remains speculative, it is clear that the British Medical Association was keen to restructure the state support of medical finances, because economic circumstances were reducing profitability within the profession. It is interesting that both the BMA and the AMA (with its support for the Blue Shield package) were moving in similar directions. If this facet of analysis is added, it thus becomes possible to see state intervention in order to maintain profitability levels, or to maintain standards of labour production. Either (or both) of these elements is thus more convincing than the assertion that working-class struggles alone have obtained health provision as part of the social wage (a point to which I return below).

To bring this section to some conclusion, two inferences will be made. The first is that some understanding of the state is vital to an interpretation of health-care. Discussion here has focussed upon ideological issues, and the role of public provision in both the accumulation process and the reproduction of the labour force. In this, I follow Navarro: 'if we are to understand the nature, composition, distribution and function of the medical care sector in Western developed capitalist societies, we must first understand the distribution of power in those societies, and the nature, role and instrumentality of the state' (Navarro, 1976, pp.511-2).

The second inference is less clear-cut, and returns us to the theme of this paper, i.e. does one analyse medical provision solely from the top down, or also from the bottom up? I reintroduce this question here because it is clear that as one focusses upon reproduction (rather than, say, accumulation or ideological issues), then the emphasis shifts from the state — the national scale — to the local state: the point of reproduction.

Health-care at the local scale

One of the key findings of contemporary health research is a belated recognition that the major variations that exist between classes (in the UK) and between races (more typically in the USA), can also be expressed in terms of morbidity and mortality variations between geographical locations (see for example Townsend, 1982).

This issue has been most directly addressed in the British context, due to the way in which the financial organisation of the National Health Service focusses attention explicitly upon the different geographical units (see Figure 10.3). During the early 1970s, major financial discrepancies emerged between the largest units of organisation, the Regional Health Authorities; indeed, the rate of expenditure varied per capita by a factor of approximately two (Kirby, 1982). Moreover, there is superficial evidence that the RHAs with the highest rates of expenditure were also the ones with, in the main, the most favourable SMRs: i.e. the lowest standardised mortality ratios corrected for the age and sex balance within the area. As Table 10.1 indicates, the range of SMRs between regions is on the whole as large as the range between socio-economic categories.

Interestingly, these relationships have now become officially linked, as a result of the work of the Resource Allocation Working Party (1976). As a means of 'rationally' distributing scarce financial resources, SMRs are used as a target against which to direct funds;

Table 10.1: A Comparison of Standardised Mortality Ratios by Socio-Economic Group (A) and by Region (B)

A. Socio-Economic Groupings and SMRs (1972)

	I	II	III (non-manual)	III (manual)	IV	V
Respiratory TB	26	41	84	89	124	254
Stomach Cancer	50	66	79	118	125	147
All Causes	77	81	99	106	114	137

B. Range of Regional SMRs and Standard Deviations

Nervous System	87-119	3.4-5.0
Circulatory	86-116	0.8-0.5
Respiratory	77-122	0.9-1.4
Digestive	86-117	2.2-3.5
Perinatal	76-115	3.8-5.4

Source: Extracted from Walters, 1980; Palmer, *et al.*, 1980.

Figure 10.3: The Reorganised Health Service in Britain

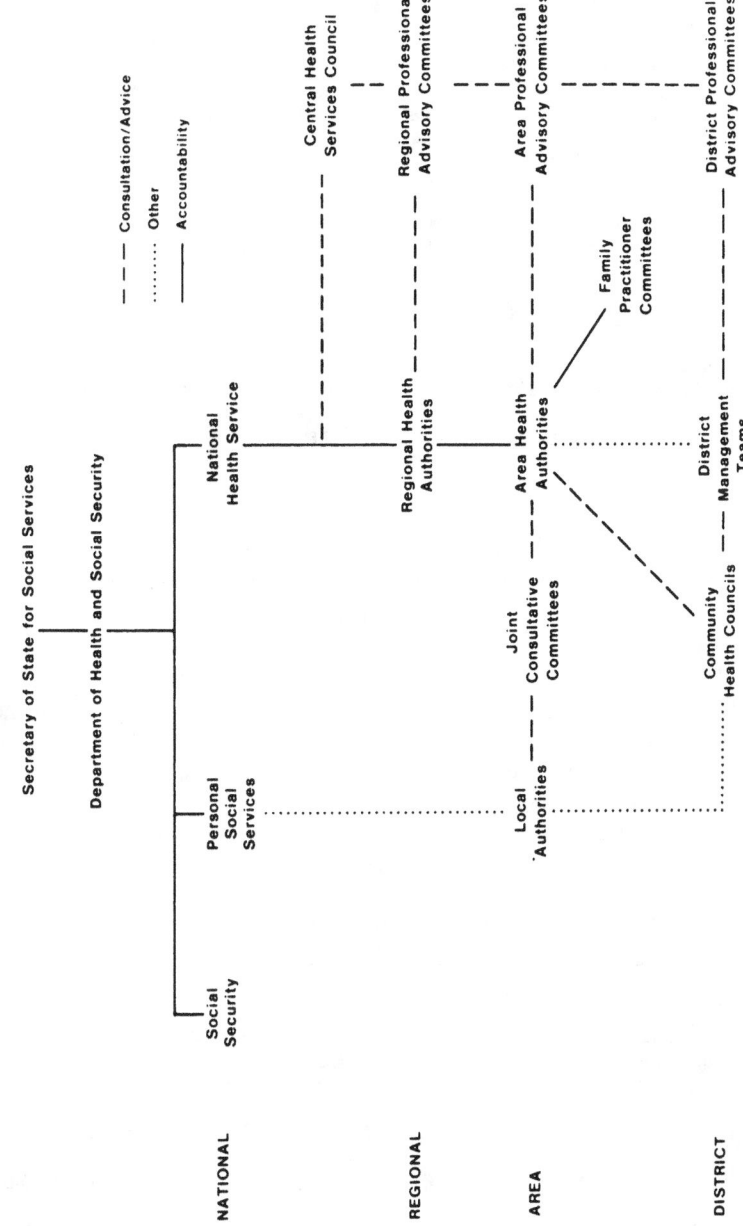

Table 10.2: Selected SMRs:[a] Liverpool AHA(T) and Mersey RHA, 1974-76

Condition[b]	LIVERPOOL		MERSEY	
	Male	*Female*	*Male*	*Female*
Infectious diseases	150	99	105	110
Cancers	140	120	107	103
Anaemia, etc.	136	122	121	115
Respiratory diseases	144	129	119	115
Digestive diseases	130	105	109	96
Arthritis	129	146	71	88
Accidents	131	147	94	95

Notes:
a. Standardised Mortality Ratios, taking into account demographic characteristics; 100 is the norm.
b. Based on International Classification of Diseases

Source: DHSS, unpublished data

it is also intended that the allocations within individual Regional Health Authorities will take place on a similar basis, despite the extreme unreliability of the data (Palmer and West, 1980).

As can be expectd, the variations in both financial provision and SMRs at small spatial scales are large. Vetter *et al.* have examined both inputs and outcomes for counties in Wales, although given the essentially low economic status of the country, the range of variation is not as large as if a wider range of counties had been chosen; nor unfortunately does the restricted sample size permit statistical testing.

Table 10.3: Social Area Analysis, Liverpool AHA

Indicator	1	2	3	4	5	6	7
Illegitimacy	2.04	0.13	0.23	1.43	0.66	1.01	1.02
Infant Mortality	1.51	0.28	0.81	0.33	0.37	4.00	1.01
Long-term Unemployment	2.29	0.15	0.30	1.27	0.70	0.88	1.68
Higher Education Grants	0.37	2.70	2.65	0.65	0.81	0.72	0.94
Population Aged 75 +	0.74	0.67	1.17	0.93	1.16	0.99	0.67
Crude Birth Rate	1.31	0.72	0.72	1.04	0.89	0.95	2.74

(city = 1.00)

More interesting data, although they do not include financial inputs, are shown in Tables 10.2 and 10.3, which reveal SMRs and other indicators for a progression of spatial scales. Table 10.2 begins this process with a contrast of SMR data for the Merseyside Regional Health Authority (which receives approximately 5.6 per cent of the national health allocation), and the Liverpool Area Health Authority. As may be expected, the extremes of the SMR data are to be found in Liverpool, which as a metropolitan centre possesses concentrations of deprivation (DoE GB, 1977). These are highlighted in Table 10.3, which shows variations about the city average for selected indicators; the data relate to a social area analysis undertaken by Scott-Samuel (Kirby and Scott-Samuel, 1981).

Parts of this argument, concerning class inequalities and medical care need little rehearsal, and this is also the case with inner area deprivation. In Table 10.3, column 1 highlights the concentrations of disease and medical need in Liverpool's inner city, a finding which is broadly replicated throughout cities in the developed world (Paine, 1978). In the American case, inner urban health problems are discussed by Pyle (1979), and the paucity of health-care in such areas has been well documented; a recent study for example illustrates the way in which poor hospital standards in Washington DC have been at least partially responsible for high neo-natal mortality levels amongst the black population (Madans, 1981).

A framework for analysis

It should be clear from this illustrative material that any analysis of health and medicine must focus upon scales other than the national, if any understanding of particular life chances is of importance. Strangely however, there is little evidence — in terms either of academic or community concerns — of such a focus.

As a broad generalisation, the majority of social science studies of local health-care focus upon either the basics of provision, or the attendant patterns of consumer use. Once more, this material is readily accessible, and need not be reevaluated at length here (for reviews, see Kirby, 1982; Knox, 1982).

In both the British and American cases, attention has been aimed at the variations in provision that exist at different spatial scales.

These essentially descriptive studies document the concentrations of facilities in particular locations: such as hospitals in central cities; general practitioners on the fringes of British inner areas or in high-status neighbourhoods; and the shortage of health-care in other contexts — such as rural areas and public housing neighbourhoods. At the broader scale, major regional disparities are also evident, in step with economic performance. In addition, the structuring of space has been examined, notably the ways in which catchment systems operate (see Dear, 1981; Knox, 1979; Shannon *et al.*, 1979).

This research (which has also involved this author), may be faulted at various levels. The first is that it has been slow to demonstrate the importance of the patterns that it describes; i.e. the relationships between health-care and health have not been made explicit, which leaves some of the work open to charges of relative triviality. More importantly, little has yet been said about the underlying structures of health-care location. Accounts of geographical distributions have tended to focus upon descriptions; such as either central place theory or the ways in which individual perceptions (of perhaps general practitioners) produce a particular residential location decision.

What is clear is that these do not add up to an explanation of the structuring of space by health-care professionals. Underlying the latter's motiviations is the commodification of health, which reduces all locations to potential sources of personal and corporate profit. Similarly absent is any mention of the ways in which local political demands shape and manipulate locational outcomes, in the manner that is normal in the contexts of other services such as education. The only studies which attempt a political economy of local health-care have focussed upon negative reponses: exclusionary politics practised by communities which do not require particular facilities in the neighbourhood. Dear has articulated this with respect to mental illness and attendant facilities (Dear, Taylor and Hall, 1980), and preliminary examinations in Britain suggest that these hypotheses may be equally valuable there (Jones and Kirby, 1982).

This paucity does not reflect however a glaring weakness of research per se. Rather, it constitutes a mirror image of the reality it seeks to understand. In other words, the inability to address health, in the way that other services have been subsumed into analyses of urban politics, represents the reality of health-care within the local state. Essentially, the preoccupation with the organisation of health at the national scale extends throughout the system. In the USA, the dramatic failings of medicine in particular neighbourhoods has been fought out politically over the funding of Medicare and Medicaid. In Britain, health has been taken out of the local government system in such a way that it is merely tangential to the latter; in consequence, the political links between the two systems are tenuous in the extreme (see Figure 10.3). Not only does this mean that direct political pressure upon health professionals is extremely difficult (with the result that the consumer [or group of consumers] is hard pressed to complain effectively about levels of provision or standards of care); it means moreover that localised shortages within the public sector, of services such as abortion (due to localised decisions against such a service) can only be reconciled in one of two ways: via national campaigns relating to women's rights, or the use of private facilities, which emerge to fill the demand.

In addition, one further point is to be stressed *vis-à-vis* the British case, where it is important to note that the spatial organisation of care is essentially — in Sayer's phrase — 'a chaotic conception'. The Regions, Districts and Areas employed within the NHS do not constitute 'meaningful' spatial units: note for example the way in which London's inner areas, with their distinctive health needs, are parcelled out amongst four quadrants of suburban areas (Paine, 1978). In these contexts, concerted political responses to service shortages are not to be expected.

The American situation is necessarily different from the British case, although the same general remarks can be made about the political response. In the first instance, local shortages of supply have been resolved at a higher level, typically via the courts, and ultimately via the Supreme Court. Abortion legislation has been challenged, and the cases of Roe in Texas and Doe in Georgia have both succeeded in securing the right to abortion, but not of course the availability of suitable medical facilities (Kemp *et al.*, 1976).

This of course remains at the core of the American dilemma: why is it that local political struggles have been so ineffective in securing what one might regard as basic levels of medical provision? Recent accounts attempt to point to the achievements of innovations like the Regional Medical Program and Comprehensive Health Planning (set up as part of the Great Society initiative), and the Health Task Force, which was created by the National Urban Coalition (Silver, 1973; Mooney, 1977). In each case, it is clear however that energy has been directed into financial matters (which as we have noted stimulates demand but does not necessarily improve supply), and that initiatives have been handed down, not created in response to specific bouts of community activity:

> in sum the Urban Coalition undertook to give communities a voice in program design for health services, by setting up a power centre (the Health Task Force) and giving the poor and deprived an important role in its deliberations. The coalition then proceeded to use the power of this community structure to influence existing health decision-making bodies ... community action created health programs (Silver, 1973, pp.128-129).

Moreover, it is worth noting that the health programs in question are token programs, depending in large measure upon voluntary inputs rather than federal or local funds. In short, neither the community action, nor the state response, is particularly significant.

The paucity of community response to health-care shortages (particularly in the US, where a greater tradition of neighbourhood activism is typical) must be explained and can be addressed in two ways. First, the weakness of response in working class communities is typical, and extends across fields of public provision from housing to transportation. An inability to access the political machine is usual (see Kirby, 1982, chapters 6,7), although in this context it is also the case that working class neighbourhoods have traditionally attempted to solve their own health problems: the use of 'patent medicines' has a long history on both sides of the Atlantic, and more specifically the localised provision of unlicensed (and illegal) abortions has always been a common feature of British cities.

Second, the question of community attitudes to health-care in wealthier areas is to be explained in the context of a rather different interpretation of the relationship between health and provision. Historically, it has been the middle classes who have been responsible for the development of public health legislation, as a result of their recognition of the relationship existing between poor standards of social control (*vis-à-vis* housing density, refuse disposal, water quality) and levels of both endemic and epidemic disease. Schwartz, for example, shows in great detail how middle class communities in the Eastern United States reacted to the threats of cholera and tuberculosis:

> the public health movement of the nineteenth and early twentieth centures was one of the earliest expressions of the desire of the upper and middle classes to impose a rational structure dictated by business values and practices on what appeared to be an increasingly unruly and threatening society (Schartz, 1977, p.81).

This development, often fallaciously discussed as one aspect of the increased enlightenment of city governments at the end of the nineteenth century, was of course achieved at the expense of a great deal of social disruption (following the removal of tenements without their replacement by alternative accommodation); interestingly, it was also achieved in the teeth of fierce opposition by the medical 'profession' at that time, which resented the (correct) implication that its ability to deal with urban health problems was strictly limited. It is not surprising that the Flexnerian view of medical practice discussed above can be traced back directly to this period, when many physicians regarded epidemic disease as an indicator of moral failing on the patient's part, rather than a professional failing of their own.

In my view, this precedent of emphasising the origins of health problems — rather than the need for health-care professionals to pick up the pieces — can still be identified within middle class communities. The preparedness of the latter to contest stressful externalities, like roads, airports or nuclear power plants is well documented, and does of course reflect a great maturity of causal reasoning. Navarro is quite right to point out that human health problems are essentially the byproducts of capitalist organisation — stress, pollution and contamination. He fails to follow his own inexorable logic however when he emphasises the need for 'a change in the sex and class composition and the system of governance of the agencies in the health sector and its institutions' (Navarro, 1976b, p. 176). What is of course necessary is the reorganisation of the problem, not the symptoms; in other words a radical alteration (by all classes and types of community) of attitudes to stress, industrial safety, drug consumption (particularly alcohol) and food production, rather than simply a rejigging of those responsible for caring for those already sick. In this sense, the emphasis upon public or community health indicates the way in which struggles over collective consumption should most usefully be directed; this in turn dictates also the most useful focus of academic attention.

Conclusions

In the Introduction, I argued for the need to reconcile two very different strands of research, which can be summarised as the 'top-down' and 'bottom-up' approaches. The argument presented here is that the former is vital for an understanding of the relationship between the state and the medical economy: in other words, medicine is part of the capitalist process *vis-à-vis* accumulation, reproduction and ideology. This notwithstanding however, it is also vital to examine the relationship between health and health-care within the context of the local state, for it is here that provision is organised, and inequalities engendered. Most importantly, it is at the local scale that individual life chances can be changed. The experience of the different underclasses (like women) in both the UK and the USA is that battles over medicine are not won within the national political arena. Even a radical restructuring of the health profession and its institutions will not achieve any alteration in the general environment (in its widest sense), which is responsible for health problems. It is through the medium of public health that this can be done, and at the local scale that this must necessarily be attempted, although all communities must be involved, in order to avoid 'salami politics': in other words, the route to better health lies in the reorganisation and control of the environment via local political struggles.

Acknowledgements

The subject of this paper was suggested by Jocelyn Cornwell at the Geography Department, Queen Mary College, London, and redirected — also in discussion — at Virginia Polytechnic and State University; I would like to thank those responsible, particularly Paul Knox and Sara Rosenberry. The paper was written on leave from the University of Reading, and my thanks go to that institution for allowing me to desert my desk. I would also like to thank the Faculty and Staff of IURD at UC Berkeley, who in innumerable ways helped my research.

References

Alford, R.R. (1975) *Health-care politics: ideological and interest group barriers to reform*, University of Chicago Press, Chicago

Burnett, J. (1978) *A social history of housing*, David and Charles, Newton Abbot

Dear, M. (1981) 'Social and spatial reproduction of the mentally ill', in M. Dear and A.J. Scott (eds.) *Urbanization and urban planning in capitalist society*, Methuen, London

Dear, M., S.M. Taylor and G.B. Hall (1980) 'External effects of mental health facilities', *Annals, Association of American Geographers*, **70**, 342-52

DoE, GB (1977) *Change or decay?*, HMSO, London

Giggs, J.A. (1979) 'Human health problems in urban areas', in D.T. Herbert and D.M. Smith (eds.) *Social problems and the city*, Oxford University Press, Oxford

Harvey, D.W. (1981) 'The urban process under capitalism', in M. Dear and A.J. Scott (eds.) *op. cit.*

Illich, I. (1975) *Medical nemisis: the expropriation of health*, Calder and Boyars, London

Jones, K. and A.M. Kirby (1982) 'Provision and wellbeing: an agenda for public resources research', *Environment and Planning* **14a**, 297-310

Kemp, K.A., R.A. Carp and D.W. Brady (1976) 'Abortion and the law', *Journal of Health Politics, Policy and Law*, **1**, 318-337

Kirby, A.M. (1982) *The politics of location*, Methuen, London

Kirby, A.M., and A. Scott-Samuel (1981) 'Health and health-care in the inner city', *Reading Geographer*, **8**, 31-42

Klein, R. (1981) 'Reflections on the condition of American health-care, *Journal of Health Politics, Policy and Law*, **6**, 188-204

Knox, P.L. (1979) 'The accessibility of primary care to urban patients', *Journal of the Royal College of General Practitioners*, **29**, 160-168

Knox, P.L. (1982) *Urban social geography*, Longman, London

Laurence, J. (1983) 'The collapse of the BUPA boom', *New Society*, February 24, 295-296

Lee, M. (1978) *Private and national health services*, PSI XLIV, Policy Studies Institute, London, 578

Madans, S.H. (1981) 'Differences among hospitals as a source of excess neo-natal mortality, *Journal of Community Health*, **7**, 101-117

Mitchell, F. (1981) Health-care delivery and primary care in the US, mimeo, School of Medicine, UC Davis

Mooney, A. (1977) 'The Great Society and health', *Medical Care*, **15**, 611-619

Navarro, V. (1976) 'Social class, political power and the state', *Journal of Health Politics, Policy and Law*, **1**, 256-284

Navarro, V. (1976b) *Medicine under capitalism*, Croom Helm, London

Navarro, V. (1977) *Health and medical care in the US*, Baywood, New York

Navarro, V. (1977b) 'Social class, political power and the state (III), *Journal of Health Politics, Policy and Law*, **1**, 499-513

Navarro, V. (1978) *Class struggle, the state and medicine*, Robertson, Oxford

O'Connor, J. (1973) *The fiscal crisis of the state*, St. Martins, New York

Paine, L.W.H. (1978) *Health-care in big cities*, St. Martins, New York

Palmer, S.R., and R.A. West (1980) 'Randomness in the RAWP formula, *Journal of Epidemiology and Community Health*, **34**, 212-216

Pyle, G. (1979) *Applied medical geography*, Winston, Washington

Resources Allocation Working Party GB (1976) *Sharing resources for health in England*, Department of Health and Social Security, HMSO, London

Rice, D.P., and D. Wilson (1976) 'The American medical economy', *Journal of Health Politics, Policy and Law*, **1**, 151-172

Schwartz, J.I. (1977) Public health: case studies in the origins of government responsibility for health services in the US, mimeo, City and Regional Planning, Cornell, New York

Shannon, G., and G. Dever (1974) *Health-care delivery: spatial perspectives,* McGraw-Hill, New York

Shannon, G., J. Lovett and R. Bashshur (1979) 'Travel for primary care', *Journal of Community Health,* 5, 113-125

Silver, B.E. (1973) 'Community participation and health resource allocation, *International Journal of Health Services,* 3, 117-132

Townsend, P., and N. Davidson (eds.) (1982) *Inequalities in health,* Penguin, Harmondsworth

Walters, V. (1980) *Class inequality and health-care,* Croom Helm, London

Vetter. N.J., D.A. Jones and C.R. Victor (1981) 'Variations in care for the elderly in Wales', *Journal of Epidemiology and Community Health,* 35, 128-132

Weller, G.R. (1977) 'From pressure group poitics to medical industrial complex: the development of approaches to health', *Journal of Health Politics, Policy and Law,* 1, 441-470

11

Inequality in Pre-School Provision:
A Geographical Perspective

Steven Pinch

In the last decade geographers have examined many areas of public policy including housing, the elderly, immigrants, education and health care. One set of services which has been almost totally ignored are those for children under five. Many of the fields hitherto studied, such as housing and health care, obviously have an important impact of the welfare of young children but, with a few exceptions (Holmes, Williams and Brown, 1972; Freeman, 1977), there has been little systematic geographical study of services directly concerned with care of the under-fives. These services involve places where children can spend time outside their own homes with people paid to take care of them. In Britain today such services are an enormously complex mixture of day nurseries, nursery schools, childminders and playgroups. Such facilities are sometimes collectively termed 'nurseries' (Hughes, *et al.*, 1980), 'day-care' facilities or 'pre-school' services. The latter term is most common in Britain and is generally employed here, although it is something of a misnomer because nursery schools, nursery classes and reception classes for rising-fives are provided by local education authorities.

The aim of this paper is to illuminate the neglected geographical dimensions of the problems of pre-school provision. There are three basic reasons for a geographical perspective upon the distribution of public services. The first reason is because of *jurisdictional partitioning* — the division of nations into local governmental or administrative units and the consequent inequalities in service provision levels between these areas. The second reason is because of *'tapering'* — the decline in the use of point specific facilities within these local areas with increasing distance from the facilities. Third, there are the problems of the *positive and negative*

231

externalities imposed upon areas by the desirable or undesirable aspects of service infrastructure. The third issue is generally not relevant to pre-school facilities; nurseries and playgroups cannot be regarded as noxious facilities in the same league as motorways, refuge tips or heavy industries, while the possession of pre-school facilities is unlikely to radically increase house values in an area in the same manner as 'good' primary and secondary schools. As this paper will demonstrate, however, jurisdictional partitioning and tapering effects are important in the case of pre-school services and raise issues which are central to an understanding of service allocations in cities.

There are two main parts: first, a description of basic patterns of provision at various scales, and second, a consideration of explanations for these patterns. The discussion is based primarily upon the British experience, although reference will be made to North America and other nations where relevant. First is is necessary to describe the services.

Pre-School Services in Britain

An understanding of the issues involved in the field of pre-school provision is immediately impeded by the enormous complexity of existing patterns of care. As Hughes and his associates note:

> ' ... like Topsy the services "just grew" each starting at a different period in response to differing needs and following different lines of development. The result has been a chaotic mismatch of anomalies, gaps, overlaps, inequalities and feuds'.

Indeed, such is the complexity of the service structure that confusion abounds; consumers are often ignorant of what services are available or even their correct names (the term 'playschool' may often be heard although this has no official status being the name for a popular BBC television programme for the under-fives).

There is also considerable controversy over just what functions these services actually fulfil and what functions they ought to provide. Since the nineteenth century the level of state pre-school provision in Britain has been related to the need for women in the workforce and associated attitudes to the desirability of women taking up paid employment. Women were needed in munitions factories during the First World War and nurseries were established to look after young children. The inter-war period saw little extension of pre-school sservices and it was only again with the Second World War and the urgent demand for female labour that nurseries were developed.

The development of pre-school facilities was also related to changing attitudes to the role of children in society. The pioneering work of early psychologists undermined the Victorian attitude that children were 'young adults' who needed to be 'civilised' and gave rise to the view that childhood was a distinctive part of human development. The various Factory Acts thus precluded children as active participants in the productive forces of the economy and led to compulsory schooling. As Blackstone (1971) notes, initially parents had the right of admission for their children if over three, but the rigid methods of instruction led many to conclude that such forms of schooling were undesirable for the under-fives. The Report of the Consultative Committee to the Board of Education argued that the best training for children aged between 3 and 5 was at home with their mothers provided that home conditions were satisfactory. Some argued that special schools be established for the very young but resources were limited and the education authorities were concerned with extending education for older children. In 1905 the authorities were given discretionary powers to withdraw the right of admission for the under-fives and after this date their numbers in schools began to dwindle rapidly. However, concern was expressed for the welfare of young children when home conditions were poor and public provision for the under-fives was recommended by the Consultative Committee in such circumstances. This was left to the discretion of the local authorities and was primarily motivated by a concern for basic welfare needs rather than educational motives. This contrasts with the experience in the United States where nursery education originated as a 'form of psychological laboratory in a middle-class setting' (Cusden, 1937).

Thus, the particular value of pre-school provision from a developmental point of view has only come into prominence in the last twenty years. The 1950s were generally a period of stagnation in the field and this policy was justified by the belief that nurseries were harmful to young children since they would lead to 'maternal deprivation'. This theory was propounded by John Bowlby who argued that it was essential that young children should experience intimate and continuous relationships with their mothers or mother-substitutes. In recent years these ideas have been subject to enormous criticism. Bowlby's theories were derived from studies of children who were totally separated from their mothers and had grown up in poor quality residential institutions. They were not derived from experience of day nurseries and day schools. Consequently, there is now a tremendous concern in many families to provide sufficient stimulation for children by some form of pre-school experience. A more recent strand in the evolution of pre-school services in Britain has been a growing awareness of the role which these facilities can play in helping parents, and in particular mothers. There is now a greater awareness that the needs of the mother (or mother substitute) and child cannot be separated and that both should be catered for. A distinction between 'welfare' and 'educational' functions is therefore almost impossible with these services.

A list of the major forms of pre-school provision currently available in Britain is shown in Table 11.1. It should be noted that they involve both public and private agencies. Local authority provision is divided into two basic forms. Social Services departments are responsible for what are termed the 'caring' services — the local *day nurseries* which operate on a highly selective basis coping with those children 'who cannot be adequately cared for at home'. These take priority cases from frequently long waiting lists. The education departments of local authorities provide *nursery schools* and *nursery classes* on a non-selective basis. However, the majority of places are provided by the private sector. *Private nurseries* are, in contrast to the US, relatively unimportant in terms of size and greatly exceeded by *playgroups*. This voluntary movement began in 1966 with the initiative of a single mother who organised neighbours with other young children into a group which met regularly in each others homes, sharing the tasks of child care. Today this has expanded into a widespread movement coordinated by the Pre-School Playgroups Association (Crowe, 1974). Most controversial however, has been the rapid growth of *childminders* — persons who look after children in their homes for profit. Such persons are required to register with their local social services department but it is known that many (of unknown numbers) do not (Jackson and Jackson, 1979). These are of course only the 'official' forms of pre-school care, and there are

Table 11.1: Main forms of Pre-School Provision in Britain

LOCAL AUTHORITY SERVICES

Day Nurseries	Administered by local Social Services Departments to provide care as a substitute for that they would otherwise receive at home where they or their parents are considered to be in spcial need.
Nursery Schools and Classes	Administered by Local Education Authorities to provide educational experience for children below school age.
Reception Classes	Administered by Local Education Authorities to provide a first class for children starting infant school (discounting nursery classes where they exist).

PRIVATE AND VOLUNTARY SERVICES

Private Nurseries	To provide care - sometimes with particular social, educational or other purposes in mind for children whose parents can pay the fees or meet other admission criteria.
Playgroups	Administered by committees of parents to provide children with the opportunity to mix and play with other young children.
Childminders	To provide care in the minders home for children whose parents can meet the cost.

Source of Definitions: Hughes *et al*, 1980.

in many communities complex self-help networks of friends, relatives and minders (both registered and unregistered) who look after young children.

The net effect of this complex structure is a pattern of provision which is unsatisfactory for both parents and children. Parents vary enormously in their needs for pre-school services and ideally a wide range of types of service should confer flexibility and choice. In reality, however, the enormous divesity of pre-school services in Britain is bewildering to many parents and is likely to impede their access to the most suitable forms of provision.

More important in preventing parents having any realstic choice in the field of pre-school provision is the overall low level of places available. In 1977 the estimated total pre-school population of England and Wales was 3.4 million, and studies suggest that some form of alternative care is wanted for two thirds of all children

(Bone, 1974). However, local authority day nurseries, playgroups, nursery classes and nursery schools amounted to only 162,000 places. In 1977, for example, the national waiting list for local autnority day nursery places was some 12,000 and the vast majority of these children have little or no hope of obtaining a place (Jackson and Jackson, 1979). In an inner-city borough like Lambeth the provision of maintained day nursery places exceeded the DHSS guidelines by four fold, yet the borough could still provide for only half of its priority children (Bruner, 1980). This restricted state provision has led to a proliferation of facilities in the private and voluntary sectors through private nurseries, playgroups and childminders. In 1977 these amounted to 495,000 places — about three times the number of places provided by the state — but there are still only enough plces for just over half the parents who want them.

Many have argued that it is the fragmentation of the services which impedes their development. It would also seem that the structure of the present system is such that those in greatest need do not obtain the most suitable form of pre-school provision. Since council day nurseries take priority cases, this results in many disadvantaged children in one type of institution with all the stigma that this entails. Nursery education, in contrast, is available on a non-selective basis but is offered only in school term-time and for short sessions. This is of little use to the mother working full-time and favours the middle-class mother who is more likely working part-time than her working class counterpart. The most widely used service — playgroups — are also only available for short sessions and again have a disproportionately high number of middle-class children. The children least likely to obtain nursery education are those who might benefit from it most, the children of the low-paid, immigrants and single-parent families, whose mothers are more likely to be in full-time employment, and who are therefore more likely to be cared for by childminders, or local authority day nurseries if they are priority cases. However, it is attitudes towards the widespread phenomenon of childminding which are most controversial. The bulk of the available evidence indicates that parents are largely forced to use childminding and that the majority who do so would prefer some other communal form of pre-school care, usually in a nursery (Bone, 1974). The Department of Education and Science (DES) and Department of Health and Social Security (DHSS), in contrast, see childminding as the inexpensive and practical way in which to meet the enormous demand for pre-school care, and are concerned at what they see as parental prejudice against minders. Others have argued that childminders are cheap and flexible compared with nurseries and, since they are a 'fact of life', local authorities should become more positive in their attitudes to childminding providing real benefits at registration by linking minders with playgroups, and offering access to training schemes, toy libraries and free milk (Jackson and Jackson, 1979).

Certainly, many recent developments, including the television programme *Other Peoples Children,* and the formation of the National Childminding Association, would seem to indicate a change of attitude towards minding and a lessening of the stigma associated with this form of care. Nevertheless, critics assert that while childminding is cheap compared with other forms of care, this only appears to be the case because most of the hidden capital costs are born by the minders themselves (who in many cases appear to work for a net loss). A number of studies have also highlighted the low levels of physical, emotional and intellectual care provided by some childminders (Mayall and Petrie, 1977; Bryant, Harris and Newton, 1980), and it seems clear that it is the privacy and isolation of this form of care which many parents dislike (Hannon, 1978).

Given this complexity of service structure it does not make sense to restrict analysis to the public sector, for these services are to varying degrees substitutable and therefore inter-related. If one is concerned with describing 'who gets what?' then clearly they must be considered together. In order to understand the reasons for variations in the provision levels in the public sector, it is also essential that reference be made to the activities of the private and voluntary sectors. Furthermore, although the number of places provided by the local state may in many cases be small, local social services departments have an important regulatory function. They are responsible for ensuring that all private nurseries, playgroups and childminders in an area provide adequate standards of care and this can give considerable discretion to local officials. (This point is discussed below).

Before examining the results it is important to highlight the limitations inherent within the data for there can be few fields in which official statistics are as unreliable as in the realm of pre-school services. This is, of course, hardly surprising given the enormously fragmented and illogical pattern of pre-school facilities which exists in Britain. There are enormous differences in the quantity and quality of care (hours of availability, cost, number of facilities etc.), both within and between services, which are not revealed by official statistics. The data are most reliable in the case of those services such as the day nurseries and nursery classes that are directly provided by the local authority, although these are not without problems of interpretation. The unreliability of data is rather more questionable in the realm of private and voluntary forms of care since there are inevitably problems involved in coordinating information from such a wide range of informal organisations, even with coordinating bodies such as the Pre-School Playgroups Association.

It is in the field of childminding, of course, that the data is most questionable. Since 1948 childminders have been obliged to register with their local authority social services department if they mind children for profit, but many minders are not registered. This is the sector of pre-school provision where there is least information but it is known to be the area where standards are most variable. The extent of this illegal childminding is almost impossible to estimate. Detailed investigation of small inner areas of British cities (involving following the travels of young children to minders at 5.30 in the morning) have indicated that there are far more unregistered than registered minders (Jackson and Jackson, 1979). The Jacksons claimed that the ratio of unregistered to registered minders was 10:1 in certain areas of British cities. Recent estimates have put the ratio at a much lower level between 2:1 to 6:1 but no one can be sure of the precise figure and this is likely to vary considerably between different areas (Bryant, Harris and Newton, 1980). There has certainly been an enormous increase in the number of registered childminders in recent years, and although this coincides with an increased rate of participation by women in the workforce, it is difficult to assess the extent to which this reflects a genuine increase in childminding or an increased rate of registration by social services departments. There are certainly considerable variations between local authority areas in the numbers of registered childminders which seems difficult to relate to the number of working women. The assumption must be, therefore, that these figures reflect the extent to which the local authority is prepared to publicise the need for registration. Many childminders are ignorant of the need to register but the registration procedure is typically cumbersome, lengthy and negative in character and often of relatively little benefit to the childminder. An inspection is made before registration with the local authority to ensure that basic standards of safety, health and space are provided for. However, these standards may vary between local authorities and it is claimed that some authorities may be reluctant to refuse registration as this may be the only way to keep a check on the minders (Bryant, Harris and Newton, 1980; Jackson and Jackson, 1979).

Finally, it must be appreciated that, from the consumers viewpoint, many of these services are not separate. Many children, and especially those aged three and four, are passed between a complex network of nursery classes, playgroups and minders, so that an element of 'double-counting' inevitably exists in the official statistics.

Inter-Jurisdictional Variations

British local authorities are under no statutory obligation to provide pre-school services and, as with other discretionary services, have varied enormously in the extent to which they have developed facilities. The source of this variation is highlighted by Blackstone (1971) in her excellent review of the evolution of local authority nursery schools and nursery classes in the latter half of the nineteenth century.

She points out that, whereas the private forms of care in nurseries and kindergartens purchased by the middle classes in the late nineteenth century were influenced by the philosophies of educational pioneers such as Froebel and Montessori, the origins of state nursery education were rather different. The various Factory Acts passed in the Victorian era led to a greater awareness of the plight of young children in poor working class homes and education was seen as a way of removing young children from these harmful environments. Eventually the 1908 Report of the Consultative Committee of the Board of Education argued that, although the best training for children was at home when conditions were satisfactory, the state should intervene where this is not the case. It was argued that the amount of nursery education for the under-fives should vary from area to area depending on 'the industrial and social conditions of the area, and the proportion of children under five years in conditions of whose homes are unsatisfactory' (Consultative Committee p.48, quoted in Blackstone, 1971, p.31). As Blackstone notes, this concept of local discretion has been of crucial importance:

'It has dominated policy directives in the field of pre-school education from its initial introduction in 1908 to the 1950s and has been an important factor in the patchy development of nursery schools, in that it allows those in power at local levels wide powers of interpretation as to what the needs of the area involve' (Blackstone, 1971, p.31).

Indeed, although local authorities have been progressively stripped of many of their powers in the realm of primary and secondary education, nursery education has remained in something of a unique position. The impact of this local discretion can easily be demonstrated by examining variations in total pre-school provision in the English local authorities. Figure 11.1 shows the total number of places in all forms of local authority nursery schools, nursery classes, reception classes and day nurseries, together with all forms of registered private and voluntary playgroups, nurseries and childminders in 1976 per 1000 of the population under five. With a few exceptions (notably Hertfordshire, Isle of Wight, Northamptonshire, Warwickshire and Cambridgeshire) the highest providers are the London boroughs and metropolitan districts. Thus, Richmond, Brent, Redbridge, Kingston, Bromley and Merton emerge as the highest providers together with the cities of Manchester, Liverpool and Newcastle. Conversely, the authorities with the lowest provision levels are predominantly the non-metropolitan counties, notable exceptions being Bradford, Wigan, Barnsley, Trafford, Wakefield, Rotherham, Wolverhampton, Kirclees, Knowsley and Dudley (for more detailed results see Pinch, 1983)

This total pre-school provision is, of course, made up of the wide range of services described above. Table 11.2 shows the inter-relationships between the various state services and private and voluntary forms of provision in a correlation matrix. All the forms of local authority provision are correlated with one another but the coefficient is largest (0.46) between nursery school provision and day nursery provision. Thus, by and large, local authorities which provide relatively high levels of nursery schools and nursery classes through their education departments also provide relatively large amounts of day nursery provision through their social services departments. In contrast, voluntary playgroups are negatively correlated with all types of local authority provision. Private and voluntary day nurseries have small correlations with the local state

Figure 11.1: Total number of places in all forms of pre-school care in the English local authorities in 1976 per 1,000 population aged under five

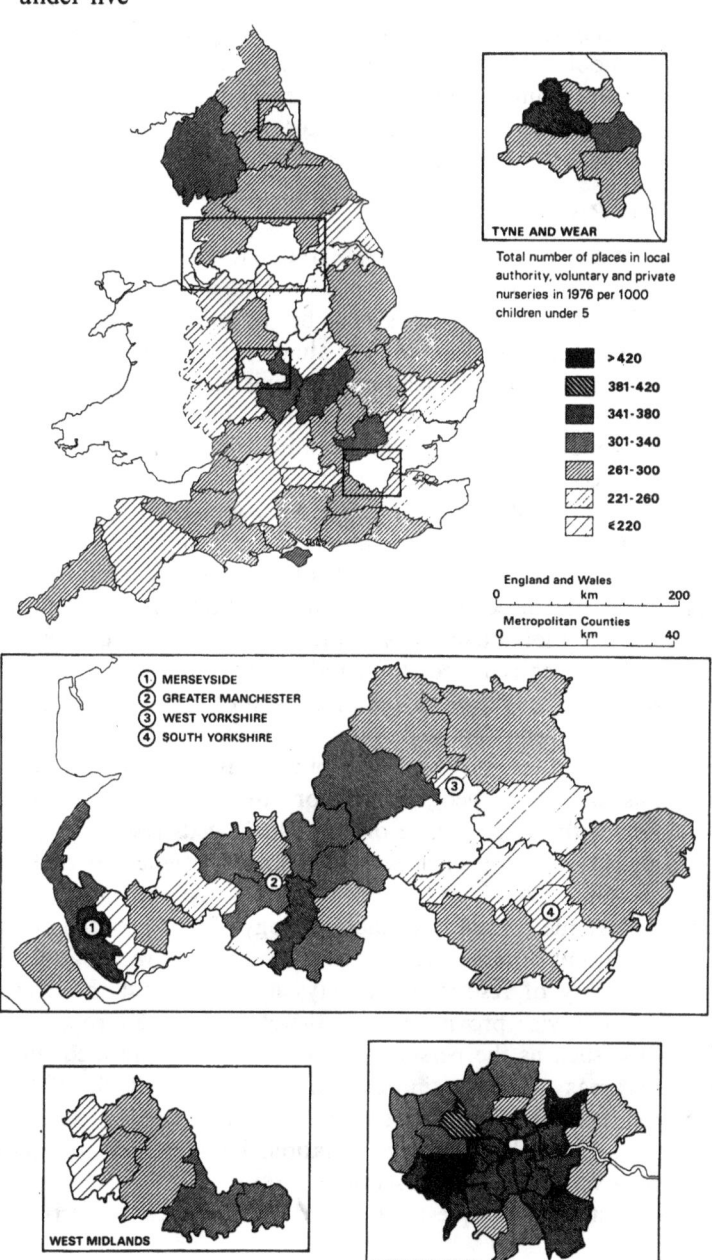

TYNE AND WEAR

Total number of places in local authority, voluntary and private nurseries in 1976 per 1000 children under 5

■ >420
▨ 381-420
▧ 341-380
▨ 301-340
▨ 261-300
▨ 221-260
▨ ≤220

England and Wales
0 ——— km ——— 200

Metropolitan Counties
0 ——— km ——— 40

① MERSEYSIDE
② GREATER MANCHESTER
③ WEST YORKSHIRE
④ SOUTH YORKSHIRE

WEST MIDLANDS

GREATER LONDON

services but childminders are negatively correlated with the provision of local nursery classes and nursery schools.

The overall pattern is therefore fairly clear. Where there are relatively large levels of local authority provision, and in particular nursery schools and nursery classes, there are relatively low levels of private and voluntary services. Conversely, where local authority provision is deficient, playgroups, and to a lesser extent registered childminders, can be expected in larger numbers.

Needs and Resources

It is of course of relatively little use to document spatial variations in provision levels without reference to some criteria by which the desirability of these variations may be judged. In this analysis a crude attempt has been made to evaluate the extent of 'territorial justice' — the degree to which service provisions meet the 'needs' of areas for these services (Davies, 1968). This is undertaken by correlating indices of service provision in administrative areas with indices of needs for these services. Ideally a situation of territorial justice should result in a perfect positive association.

It should be noted that, because of the 'ecological fallacy', a pattern of territorial justice   between a set of administrative areas does not necessarily imply a situation of social justice amongst the individuals *within* the areas. Davies' concept of territorial justices is based upon individuals, however, the needs index being the aggregate of the needs of all the individuals in the area. It has been pointed out that often externalities and indivisibilities in the provision of public goods and services leads to situations in which geographical or areal need may not be coincident with the aggregate of individual needs (Bennett, 1980). However, Davies' approach was specifically designed to evaluate those personal social services delivered at the individual level. Nevertheless, the correlational methodology of the approach means that his concept of territorial justice measures *relative* variations in the availability of resources and says nothing about the overall shortfall in service provision. It is therefore most appropriate in situations (such as the personal social services) where inequalities between areas are large in relation to the overall shortfall in provision. Pre-school services in Britain are a complex mixture for not only are there large relative variations between areas but there is a large overall shortfall in services.

The most difficult questions posed by the idea of territorial

Table 11.2: Inter-Relationship between Types of Pre-School Provision in the English Local Authorities. Data refer to number of places per 1000 of population under five in 1976.

	1	2	3	4	5	6	7	8	9
PROVIDED BY LOCAL AUTHORITY									
1. Nursery Schools and Classes	1.00								
2. Reception Classes	0.29	1.00							
3. Day Nurseries	0.46	0.27	1.00						
4. Total Local Authority	0.97	0.32	0.66	1.00					
PRIVATE AND VOLUNTARY SECTORS									
5. Play Groups	-0.64	-0.51	-0.40	-0.66	1.00				
6. Childminders	-0.32	-0.35	-0.08	-0.24	0.41	1.00			
7. Day Nurseries	0.02	-0.23	0.22	0.08	0.17	0.33	1.00		
8. Total (Excluding Reception Classes)	-0.03	-0.43	0.16	0.01	0.67	0.65	-0.04	1.00	
9. Total (Including Reception Classes)	0.23	0.48	0.40	0.30	0.20	32.00	0.08	0.59	1.00

Data Source: Hughes *et al* 1980.

justice are:

1) How does one measure adequately indices of needs and standards of services?
2) Is 'need' the most suitable criteria against which their service distributions should be judged?
3) Are these services most appropriate in meeting the needs (however defined)?

Again Davies' approach was tailored for those services which, within the overall tenets of the British welfare system, are intended for allocation on the basis of need, such as social services for the elderly. Controversy arises of course over detailed definitions of need in situations of shortage and also over whether the services actually provided are the most suitable. For example, should we provide residential-based or community-based services for the elderly or simply dispense with much of the welfare state apparatus and provide larger pensions?

Such issues are brought into sharp focus in the field of pre-school provision. As described in greater detail below, the concept of women staying at home and looking after young children is central to the definition of the female role in Western societies and there is often considerable hostility to the idea of mothers with young children taking up full-time paid employment. It is often asserted that this is a dereliction of parental responsibility and that such mothers do not 'need' the additional income being preoccupied with obtaining consumer goods at the expense of the welfare of their children. However, evidence suggests that many women are compelled to return to paid employment to raise the low living standards of their families. Continuing high levels of inflation, among the lowest levels of child allowances in Europe (Lister, 1980), and a taxation policy which discriminates against children, have all contributed towards the economic pressures upon women to take up employment. Even so, the financial rewards available to women are typically low (especially when the cost of child care are discounted). Not surprisingly therefore, the evidence suggests that financial reasons alone are frequently not claimed to be the major factor determining the return to paid employment. Recent social change has produced a decline in the possibilities of support for mothers from friends or relatives in the immediate neighbourhood. Increased residential mobility and household formation rates means that families and friends are now much more likely to be separated geographically. Rehousing schemes have also served to increase the dislocation of familial support and the growth of flats has increased the social isolation of many mothers. There has also been growing evidence in recent years that the experiences of motherhood fall far short of the idealised state portrayed in advertising. Women with young children suffer from particularly high rates of depression (Brown and Harris, 1978) and the accident rate amongst children with depressed mothers is considerably increased. Increased workforce participation rates must therefore also be seen as related to an increased desire amongst women to enjoy the independence, status and companionship which work can provide, and which motherhood can frequently undermine.

It is theoretically possible that radically increased child allowances or other types of social policy designed to make looking after young children more acceptable would be an alternative policy which would lessen the demand for certain types of pre-school care. However, recent social changes in Britain suggest that, not only is such a policy unlikely to be implemented, but it is unlikely that it would have the desired effect. As Bruner (1980) argues, moral indignation is unlikely to 'wish away' the phenomen of working mothers and it is far more preferable that adequate pre-school provision be planned instead. In this context, despite the absence of consensus over objectives, the evaluation of territorial justice can be a useful approach.

In recent years researchers have stressed the ways in which all chldren can benefit from some form of pre-school care outside their own home, and this would suggest that pre-school places be provided simply on the basis of the numbers of the under-fives in each area. However, there is evidence to suggest that children from certain backgrounds are most able to benefit from pre-school services or have a greater need for care.

A crucial factor determining the need for care and the type of service required is whether or not the mother of an under-five works full-time. In these circumstances day nurseries and or childminders are the only viable solution which provides care for a sufficient number of hours. Nursery schools, nursery classes and playgroups are usually only available in two and a half hour sessions which cannot be fitted into a full-time working schedule without a group of friends or relatives willing to help.

The first variable selected as an indication of 'need' for nursery provision was thus the number of married women working full-time (i.e. more than 30 hours per week) with at least one child under five, per 1000 married women with chldren under five. These data should be treated with caution because they are derived from the 10 per cent sample census. Where numbers are small in certain areas sampling error is likely to be large and the data will be unreliable, but this should not be a problem with the large local authority areas considered here. A more important problem may be the tendency for working mothers to understate their working hours or simply refuse to provide accurate information in the belief that they can avoid enquiries concerning taxation. The extent to which this is likely to vary between areas is difficult to assess but may increase in low social status areas. By far the largest proportions of working mothers with young children occur in the major conurbations and particularly in the inner London boroughs.

Another limitation of the data relating to working mothers is that they exclude the single, widowed, or divorced. This deficiency can partly be overcome with a second variable — the number of single-parent families with children, per 1000 of all families with children. Single-parent families are much more likely to have a low income, a parent working full-time and a correspondingly greater need for pre-school care. In recent years the proportion of single mothers with young children who are working has increased considerably to 14 per cent full-time and 18 per cent part-time. According to the latest estimates there were in 1980 at least 920,000 one-parent households in Britain with one and a half million children. Once again, the metropolitan districts and the London boroughs have the largest proportions of single-parent families.

In those situations in which mothers do not work, or only on a part-time basis, then nursery schools, nursery classes and playgroups are a much more acceptable form of provision. In these circumstances it is the child from a poorer low status background who frequently has most to gain from the stimulation which good quality pre-school care can provide, but who sadly is often more likely to miss such an experience (Bell, 1976). However, information on the number of low-status families was not directly available, so the final need indicator was a surrogate measure of socio-economic status — the proportion of unskilled workers in each local authority.

The relationships between these three 'need' indicators and the indices of pre-school provision are shown in Table 11.3. The proportion of working mothers with children under five is positively related with all forms of local authority provision but especially with the local day nurseries. As might be expected, the correlations with the nursery schools, nursery classes and reception classes are small since these are largely unsuitable for mothers working full-time. Somewhat surprising, however, are the small correlations with the number of places provided by childminders and private day nurseries. This might result from the widespread use of unregistered childminders and the inability of working mothers to afford care in private nurseries. Private and voluntary playgroups are negatively correlated with the proportion of full-time working mothers while total provision has a near zero correlation.

A broadly similar pattern of correlations is revealed by the proportion of one-parent families with chldren, but in this case the associations with local authority provision are (with the exception of reception classes) much stronger. The young children of single-parent famiiles are more likely to be given priority status in local day nurseries and this form of provision has a high positive correlation (0.85) with the incidence of single-parent families. Nursery schools and classes also have a relatively high correlation with single-parent families but this is likely to result from the tendency for authorities to provide large amounts of both day nurseries and nursery schools and classes, rather than the relevance of the latter for single-parent families. In most areas there is enormous demand for places in local authority day nurseries and it is of note that private day nurseries are also positively correlated with the incidence of single-parent famiiles. Private playgroups are once again negatively correlated with the need variable while childminders have only a small positive association. Inspection of the scatter diagrams revealed that London has an important influence upon the results. Here large proportions of single-parent families are associated with large rates of nursery provision but limited numbers of playgroups and childminders.

The correlations between pre-school provision and socio-economic status are amongst the most interesting because both the 'underclass' hypothesis (Lineberry, 1977) and the so-called 'inverse-care law' (Hart, 1971) would suggest that poorer groups in society are least likely to receive services. The evidence derived from a wide

Table 11.3: Correlations between indices of need and pre-school provision in the English local authorities.

	% Married Women with Children under 5 Working more than 30 hours in 1971	% Single Parent Families with Children in 1971	% Unskilled Workers in 1971
*PROVIDED BY LOCAL AUTHORITY			
1. Nursery Schools and Classes	0.26	0.51	0.44
2. Reception Classes	0.37	0.28	0.28
3. Day Nurseries	0.59	0.85	0.26
4. Total Local Authority	0.37	0.63	0.45
*PRIVATE AND VOLUNTARY SECTORS			
5. Playgroups	-0.32	-0.28	-0.61
6. Childminders	0.27	0.21	-0.39
7. Day Nurseries	0.24	0.50	0.13
8. Total (Excluding Reception Classes)	0.06	0.17	-0.56
9. Total (Including Reception Classes)	0.29	0.41	-0.22

*   Data refer to number of places per 1000 population in 1976

range of services is rather inconsistent and contradictory (Kirby and Pinch, 1983) but in the pre-school field the aggregate correlations derived for local authorities would support the assertation that lower- status families are relatively disadvantaged. The association of nursery schools and classes with low-status areas arises, of course, because of their concentration in the major conurbations. What is surprising in this context therefore is that the association is not stronger. The extent of a linear relationship is diminished by a number of authorities that provide relatively small numbers of places in nursery schools and classes in relation to their socio-economic structure (Humberside, Knowesley, St. Helens and

Gateshead) and a number of authorities that provide relatively high numbers in relation to their need (Merton, Hertfordshire, Barnet, Kingston and Sutton). Day nursery provision has an extremely small positive correlation with the percentage of unskilled workers. Inner London boroughs, including Tower Hamlets, Southwark and Newham, have less day nursery provision than might be expected given their socio-economic structures but, in general, there is wide variation in the extend of day nursery provision which has little connection with social class. Indeed, when the London boroughs are removed, any relationship with socio-economic status disappears almost completely. Playgroup provision is negatively correlated with the socio-economic status, there being relatively small amounts of playgroup provision in the major conurbations and a similar pattern applies in the case of childminders. This might reflect a greater use of unregistered childminders or friends and relatives in low-status areas. Private day nurseries have only a weak association with unskilled workers while total provision (excluding reception classes) has a strong negative association.

These results should be interpreted carefully because they refer to relative rather than absolute variations in levels of pre-school provision. Some areas have large amounts of provision compared with others but still have an overall shortfall. There is evidence from these results that in areas where there are large proportions of working mothers and single-parent families local authority forms of care, and in particular local day nurseries, have developed on a scale larger than elsewhere (even if there is still insufficient supply to meet demand). Nevertheless, the overwhelming impression left by these results is one of generally weak correlations between provision and needs indices. This is especially true in the case of private and voluntary forms of provision upon which many mothers are dependent. To a large degree then, these results from an aggregate level confirm those derived from individual studies. The crucial point is that many of the decision making processes responsible for these patterns are made at the local authority level and these provide an appropriate level through which explanation of these patterns must be sought. Furthermore, the problem is not simply one of an overall shortfall in pre-school provision but also one of enormous inequalities in provision levels between different areas.

Intra-Authority Patterns

Problems of data collection mean that, as with most other types of urban service, our knowledge of relationships between need and provision in the pre-school field is most deficient at the intra-authority level. Nevertheless, once again, there are strong reasons for providing a geographical perspective on the distribution of these services within cities. These services as defined here take place outside the home (in-home arrangements with nannies or *aupairs* are not considered). Hence they are not 'outreach' but 'place specific' or 'fixed point' facilities (Wolch, 1979) to which consumers must travel. The universally observed phenomena of 'distance decay' or 'tapering' means that the use of facilities tends to decrease with increasing distance away from the facility. Thus, the ease of access to pre-school services depends greatly upon the locality in which the family lives. Mothers with young children are amongst the most immobile sections of society and can generally only travel short distances each day (Holmes, Williams, and Brown, 1971). Even relatively small variations in the location of facilities can therefore affect the extent to which they are enjoyed by families.

It is therefore hardly surprising that in the first of their eight recommendations for reform of pre-school services Tizard, Moss and Perry (1976) note:

> 1. *The services should be local.* In urban areas at least, pre-school services should normally be within walking distance of the home — the sort of walking distance that is feasible with two small children in tow. This means not having to cross roads or walk very far. If each pre-school centre served a small catchment area most of the children who came to it would live nearby (Tizard, Moss and Perry, 1976, p.207).

This section examines geographical variations in pre-school services within the City of Southampton, a medium-sized free-standing urban centre in Southern England with a recorded population of 204,000 in the 1981 Census. In keeping with other 'sunbelt cities' (although this may be stretching the term somewhat in the British context) Southampton has had an above average rate of population growth since the Second World War. It is a relatively prosperous commercial and industrial centre with a famous port and, despite a range of social problems, lacks the degree of deprivation and chronic unemployment of more northerly conurbations.

The city is an administrative district within the County of Hampshire — a local authority whose pre-school policies are similar to other Conservative-dominated non-metropolitan counties. In relation ot other non-metropolitan counties Hampshire ranks high in terms of total pre-school provision. However, the county is amongst the lowest ranks in terms of both nursery schools, nursery classes and day nurseries. The vast majority of places are in playgroups amongst which Hampshire ranks highly. The county also emerges high in the ranks of registered childminder places but has an intermediate position in terms of private nursery places. Hampshire therefore represents an extreme case of an authority which is essentially concerned to promote pre-school provision through the private and voluntary means with minimum levels of intervention from the public sector.

Table 11.4 shows the distribution of pre-school services within the major urban centres of Hampshire. Southampton provides rather more day nursery and nursery schools than other areas (although its level of provision is far behind Portsmouth) but provides lower levels of childminders and playgroups. Southampton and Portsmouth also have the largest concentrations of poor social conditions in the county and are under-represented in terms of the higher income groups. The inequalities of pre-school provision at the inter-authority level would therefore seem to be replicated at the intra-authority scale with playgroups and other forms of voluntary provision positively related with higher socio-economic status.

Figure 11.2 shows the geographical distribution of pre-school facilities within the district of Southampton. The key to this map serves to emphasise the enormous diversity of services, and to appreciate the differences in location of facilities it is necessary to consider the various types separately. In the case of officially registered childminders the pattern must be regarded as only a 'snapshot' of the distribution at one particular point in time, since the number and location of registered minders fluctuates considerably in a short period. This reflects the desire of many minders to undertake the job for a short period (possibly while their own children are young) but also many short-term variations in the demand for minders in different areas. Nevertheless, the overall pattern at any period is likely to replicate the most notable feature of Figure 11.2 — the high degree of clustering. It is known that

Table 11.4: Variations in Pre-School Provision within Hampshire

	Population[a]	PLACES IN DAY NURSERIES		PLACES IN NURSERY SCHOOL		PLAYGROUPS		CHILDMINDERS	
		Total	Rate Per 1000 Pop.	Total	Rate Per 1000 Pop.	Total	Rate Per 1000 Pop.	Total	Rate Per 1000 Pop.
Southampton	221,700	90	0.40	367	1.73	1,827	8.24	444	2.00
Portsmouth	191,200	215	1.12	566	2.91	1,524	7.97	644	3.37
Basingstoke	127,000	30	0.24	58	0.38	2,384	18.77	655	5.15
Andover	93,600			52	0.28	1,529	16.33	387	4.13
Winchester	91,400			37	0.13	1,512	16.54	175	1.91

Notes:
a. *Source:* Hampshire County Council

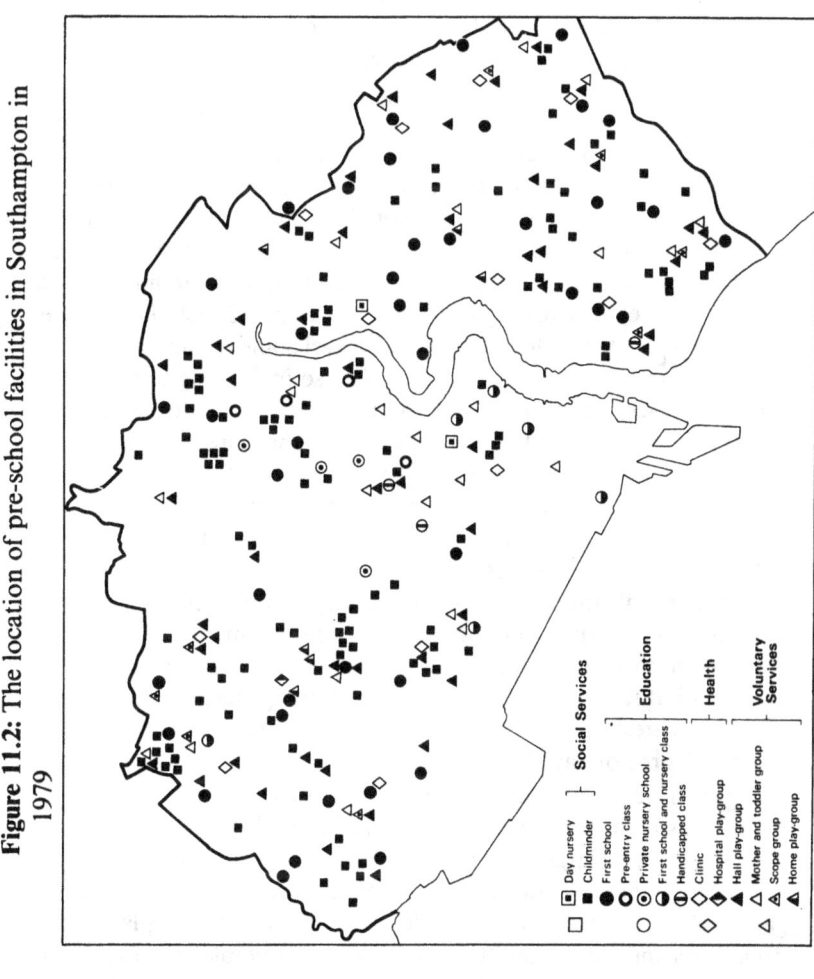

Figure 11.2: The location of pre-school facilities in Southampton in 1979

many minders are prompted into this type of work by demand from someone in the immediate vicinity (Bruner, 1980) and there would clearly seem to be some kind of 'neighbourhod effect' in operation here. It may also be that knowledge of the requirement to register with the local authority is unevenly distributed. The largest numbers of minders are to be found on the peripheral local authority estates. Anecdotal evidence suggests that these are the areas with large numbers of single-parent families and thus a high local demand for care, but they are also areas where there are women (many with young children) who find that minding is one of the few ways they can supplement their income. However, not all the children, and in many cases not the majority, come from the immediate locality of council estates. Interviews with local authority organisers and minders suggests that many minders cater for the children of working professional parents. Some of these live outside the Southampton district and travel some distance each day to receive day care. In this instance it is also interesting to note that many of these local authority housing areas are in peripheral locations close to higher status estates. The spread of minders around the University is generally accepted as related to the large proportion of working women with small children employed on the campus. Conversely, near the city centre, there is a distinct absence of registered childminders. This is also the area which has the largest concentration of immigrant groups, young children and a tradition of mothers taking up paid employment. There is a concentration of state-funded day nurseries and nursery classes in this area but it is probable that the use of unregistered childminders is also greatest in this district. It is also possible that there is a greater degree of care by local relatives.

Figure 11.2 shows that the distribution of voluntary playgroups is also clustered, but generally well distributed throughout the city. This reflects to a large degree the vigour and enthusiasm of the Pre-Schools Playgroups Association in attempting to ensure an even geographical spread of facilities. Interviews with playgroup organisers indicates that the availablity of suitable premises is a crucial factor. Virtually all the playgroups are located in church halls and community centres. Playgroup organisers suggested that the areas where it is often most difficult to provide playgroups are the new peripheral estates in the private sector which have a high birth rate and high demand for care, but frequently lack suitable premises.

Quantitative support for these inferences is provided by Table 11.5 which shows the simple correlations between indices of pre-school provision and corresponding measures of need for these services, at a ward level in Southampton. Early results from the 1981 Census made it possible to select measures of married women and single-parent families working either full-time or part-time with at least one child aged between 0 to 4 years. At the time of writing, results were not available for the socio-economic status of areas but indices of housing structure and car ownership provided an alternative yardstick of social compostion.

These results should be treated carefully since many of the facilities were on the border of wards and these are in any case large and relatively hetereogeneous spatial units. However, such was the complexity of service centres with complex overlapping catchment areas that re-calculation of alternative catchment areas on the basis of enumeration districts was not considered to be an efficient or desirable research strategy. The simple ward-based correlations should therefore provide a broad measure of the correspondence between overall service levels and the social structure of the city.

The concentration of nursery units in the inner-city areas means that the number of session places, in both playgroups and nurseries combined, are strongly associated with married women working full-time with children aged 0-4, the proportion of immigrants from the New Commonwealth, private renting, households lacking amenities and the absence of a car. This replicates the broad pattern observed previously at the inter-authority and inter-county level. However, these nursery and playgroup facilities are better suited to mothers working part-time rather than full-time and it is noticeable that married women and single parents working part-time have negative associations with this 'total provision' variable. Furthermore, when the total number of children rather than session places are considered, these negative correlations increase in magnitude. The number of childminders is positively associated with both married women and single parent families working full-time with at least one child aged between 0-4, but the coefficients are, as with most of the remaining variables, rather small.

In the case of playgroups there are differing results depending upon the measure of provision used (Table 11.6). For example, although the total number of children attending playgroup facilities is negatively related with ethnic status, the number of session places available is positively related (albeit mildly) with ths variable.

Table 11.5: Correlations between indices of need and provision for pre-school services in Southampton wards (N = 15)

	Number of session places in nursery classes and play-groups per 1000 pop. 0-4 in 1979	Number of children attending nursery classes and play-groups per 1000 pop. 0-4 in 1979	Number of child-minders per 1000 pop. 0-4 in 1979
Proportion of Population[a]			
Married women working full-time with at least one child aged between 0-4.	0.59	0.20	0.30
Married women working part-time with at least one child aged between 0-4.	-0.22	0.19	
Single-parents with at least one child aged between 0-4.	-0.16	-0.37	-0.26
Single parents working full-time with at least one child aged between 0-4.	-0.00	-0.46	0.13
Single parents working part-time with at least one child aged between 0-4.	-0.09	-0.22	
Proportion of population New Commonwealth immigrants	0.81	0.00	-0.14
Proportion of private households[a]			
Owner occupied	-0.24	-0.03	0.37
Rented from council	-0.34	-0.09	-0.25
Privately rented (furnished and unfurnished)	0.78	0.19	0.02
Lacking bath and inside W.C.	0.55	0.87	0.42
Without the use of a car	0.63	0.10	-0.37

Notes:
a. Data Source: 1981 Census

Overall, playgroups are negatively associated with areas with large proportions of local authority housing and over-represented in the inner wards with larger proportions of privately rented accommodation lacking amenities. Although, in absolute terms, the peripheral estate areas often have considerable numbers of places, these are relatively small in relation to the large numbers of children below five. Other variables relating to single-parent families, car ownership, and owner-occupied housing have small and inconsistent associations.

Another method employed to gauge equality of access to pre-school facilities was to examine the location of all enumeration districts whose centroid was more than half a mile from either a playgroup or a nursery class (see Figure 11.3). Various threshold distances were considered including 1 kilometre, but although many parents walk considerable distances to visit the playgroup of their choice, a half mile was considered to be the maximum desirable limit on a cold and wet day before lunch. Such is the spread of pre-school facilities in Southampton that only 49 of the 450 enumeration districts lie outside the half mile threshold. There is some tendency for these enumeration districts to predominate in peripheral wards while the inner areas are relatively accessible to facilities. However, given the tendency for playgroups to concentrate in centres with suitable premises, the least accessible areas just happen to be in the 'watersheds' between these clusters of playgroups and nursery classes. It is hardly surprising therefore, that these districts have little in common in terms of their housing and social composition. Taken as a whole they have slightly fewer children below five, fewer owner occupiers, commonwealth immigrants and car owning households than the Southampton average, but the differences are not important. Indeed, a detailed comparison of the enumeration districts in each ward in comparison with the ward average revealed considerable variations which would undermine the view that certain areas are systematically disadvantaged in terms of obtaining access to pre-school facilities.

At this finest scale of analysis much of the regularity previously observed in the geographical distribution of facilities at the inter-urban scale tends to break down. Superficially there is some correspondence of state nursery provision in the poorest inner-city areas but, as elsewhere, the whole system is dominated by the private and voluntary sectors. Here the efforts of the Pre-School

Figure 11.3: The distribution of enumeration districts beyond half a mile from either a playgroup or a nursery class in Southampton

Playgroups Association have ensured that there is no gross inequality in provision levels between areas which would support any 'underclass' hypothesis. The most suitable type of explanation in this context might be termed 'ecological' or related to the physical and spatial structure of areas. As in the case of certain health care facilities, it is the peripheral estates which lack facilities, largely because of the absence of suitable premises. They also tend to be somewhat further from the older centres, with their abundance of church halls, where facilities tend to cluster. Conversely, the demographic structure of peripheral estates results in a large proportion of children requiring pre-school services. This may however, be a time-lag effect as service provision adjusts to a more decentralised city form. In Southampton there has been a considerable improvement in pre-school service provision in certain peripheral areas as community centres and schools have caught up with the initial wave of residential construction.

What is clear from interviews with various individuals however, is that the system of pre-school care is complex, inter-dependent and to a large degree vulnerable and fragile. The structure is dependent upon a great deal of cooperation, hard work and often make-shift organization which can easily be threatened by relatively small events such as loss of particularly enthusiastic organisers, a sudden drop in local demand, or difficulties in obtaining local premises. These factors create a close inter-dependence between various forms of service at the micro-level. However, documentation of such processes, together with details of need, demand and supply, are virtually impossible throughout a large area such as Southampton without an enormous research team which would have to engage in almost clandestine research methods (Jackson and Jackson, 1979).

Explanatory Frameworks

The crucial issue facing urban analysts is of course how to explain such variations in service provision. This is a daunting task, not only because of the numerous scales or levels at which inequalities may be identified, but also because of the numerous theoretical perspectives currently available. We have already referred to the value of 'ecological' explanations but in Britain there has been a growing recognition of three other broad positions: the 'pluralist',

Table 11.6: Correlations Between Indices of Need and Playgroup Provision in Southampton Wards (N = 15)

	Number of session places in playgroups per 1000 population 0-4 in 1979	Number of children attending play-groups per 1000 population 0-4 in 1979
Proportion of Population[a]		
Married women working part-time with at least one child aged between 0-4.	0.08	0.25
Single parents working part-time with at least one child aged between 0-4.	0.03	-0.25
Proportion of population New Commonwealth immigrants	0.30	-0.28
Proportion of private households[a]		
Owner occupied	0.06	-0.18
Rented from council	-0.51	-0.16
Privately rented (furnished and unfurnished)	0.65	0.10
Lacking bath or inside W.C.	0.51	0.82
Without the use of a car	0.06	-0.21

Notes:
a. Data Source: 1981 Census

'managerialist' and 'structuralist', to which in the case of pre-school services must also be added various 'feminist' perspectives. What then do these approaches have to offer as explanations of pre-school services?

Pluralism

The pluralist view is based upon an analogy with private markets. Local politics is envisaged as a political marketplace in which politicians respond to the wishes of the publc. Pluralists argue that these responses will not reflect any overall class bias for the local state is a neutral arbiter between competing interests. This diversity of interest groups is seen as a guarantor of broad equality of outcomes, for individuals will find themselves in very different and non-overlapping groups according to different issues. Coupled to this are the ever present periodic elections through which politicians may be brought to account.

This perspective has been subject to enormous criticism in the past for reasons which are by now well known, although recently there has been a restatement of pluralist positions in somewhat revised form. Saunders (1979) for example, makes a distinction between the corporate and non-corporate (or pluralist) sectors of state policy-making. The corporate sector is concerned with production and involves the state taking a directive role in conjunction with big business and organised labour. The 'pluralist' sector is mainly concerned with social consumption and involves the state responding to pressures from the locality for housing, social services and the like.

As shown above, local authority services for the under-fives *have* developed to the greatest extent in the cities with the greatest need for these services, and this might suggest that the authorities have responded in some measure to 'demands' from the local environment. Prominent amongst the high providers are metropolitan districts in the North and Midlands including Manchester, Salford, Barnsley, Bolton, Rotherham, Walsall, Liverpool and Newcastle. This pattern serves to emphasise historical factors and past decisions affecting current distributions. The demand for care was inevitably greater in the northern textile towns with large proportions of women at work in the factories. Poverty was widespread in these cities created by the Industrial Revolution and, as Rowntree observed, was especially concentrated amongst families with young children. Many mothers were therefore forced to seek employment in order to increase their household income. Day-care facilities for young children were, however, grossly inadequate. In the absence of relatives or neighbours who were willing to care for their children mothers were forced to rely upon either childminders or the notorious 'dame' schools. Contemporary reports depict a bleak picture of care by many childminders at this time, while in the dame schools large numbers of children were crammed into what were frequently unhealthy conditions.

The emphasis placed upon social conditions by the Board of Education meant that the early progress in nursery education was made in these northern industrial cities. This early progress developed an ethos favouring provision while other authorities have sought do little. Bradford, for example, was one of the first local authorities to stress the educational value of nursery schools maintaining that they should be a universal experience. The rate of provision of nursery schools and nursery classes in Manchester is worthy of particular note for it is over twice the extent of the second highest provider (which is neighbouring Salford). There is a long history of interest in nursery education in Manchester which may be traced back to the middle of the nineteenth century. Following the European uprisings of 1848, a relatively large colony of wealthy German immigrants settled in Manchester and they provided a fertile seedbed for the new kindergarten movement. This movement in turn influenced some of the more liberal minded of the upper middle-class merchants in the city (and especially those from the Jewish community) to sponsor nursery education schemes (Blackstone, 1971). Over the years the local authority has done much to sponsor nursery education and did much to foster nursery classes in the 1930s while other authorities dragged their feet.

However, there is little evidence which would suggest that this local authority development was a response to pressure group activity 'from below'. Indeed, as will be suggested in the next section on managerialism, it would appear that this was largely a policy imposed 'from above' through the efforts of the Victorian social reformers. Similarly, when in 1905 education authorities were given discretionary powers to withdraw the right of admission of under-fives to primary schools, this trend was the result of changes in the policy of education authorities rather than the wishes of parents. Significantly there was no middle-class involvement in the state education system to act as a pressure for improvement.

Evidence of pressure group activity upon pre-school provision, can, however, be derived from a contemporary study at the intra-authority level. Saunders (1979) cites as the best example of a successful campaign by a pressure group in Croydon the campaign for a day nursery. Croydon has an extremely low level of local authority provision but the protesters managed to obtain a new day-care centre. Saunders notes how, despite demonstrations, the campaign organisers managed a careful balance between conciliation and coercion. They were careful not to use any tactic which could have been defined by the local authority as irresponsible or illegitimate.

Nevertheless, in general terms it is difficult to find much recent evidence for the effectiveness of pressure groups affecting the level of pre-school services in Britain. Indeed, to the contrary, pre-school services represent a wide difference between the wishes of the public (more specifically mothers) and the attitudes of public policy makers. The most comprehensive study was undertaken by the Office of Population Censuses and Surveys (Bone, 1974). The results are complex, for what is desired by parents depends upon the type of day care (if any) which is currently being used. The hypothetical nature of the questions also means that the preferences expressed in the study must be treated with some caution. Given the complexity of existing services for the under-fives, and the fact that the full range of facilities is unlikely to have been available in certain areas in which the respondents lived, it is also likely that there was considerable misunderstanding about the nature of pre-school provision. Nevertheless, the overall pattern of the results is remarkably clear. Most striking is the enormous shortfall in provision levels. Provision was wanted for twice as many children as were receiving it so that whilst 32 per cent of children were using facilities, some form of day-care was desired for a further 33 per cent who were not using services at the time of the survey. With the exception of childminding, preferences were expressed for more of all types of provision, but especially those of an educational character. Disaggregated by age, some form of day-care was wanted for 20 per cent of all children under 1 year of age, 41 per cent under 2 years, 72 per cent under 3, 87 per cent under 4 and 91 per cent under 5. Perhaps more significantly, less than half of the mothers interviewed wanted part-time hours of less than four hours per day. Given the tendency for supply to create demand, it seems that many mothers would utilise facilities if they were available.

These preferences, which are supported by other studies, contrast sharply with the official view of the two departments responsible for pre-school services, the Department of Health and Social Security and the Department of Education and Science, which is that children under three should not be separated from their mothers and then for only a few hours each day (D.E.S. and D.H.S.S., 1976).

It must therefore be concluded that, despite considerable strength of feeling in favour of more pre-school provision, mothers lack sufficient 'purchasing power' of both an economic and political kind to achieve their objectives. In the private sector, with the exception of a small minority, most families are unable to command incomes sufficient to pay the cost of full-time nursery care so that such facilities are limited in Britain. Within the political sphere mothers lack sufficient organisation to mobilise for a widespread system of pre-school services. Looking after young children is typically a time consuming, exhausting and isolated activity and as such tends to inhibit collective organisation for political ends. Although many women's groups have been formed in the last decade, these are typified by a concern with a diverse set of aims, including 'consciousness raising', which are not always overtly concerned with government policy. Many groups have purposely distanced themselves from conventional policies and have tended to build their own alternatives (Coote and Hewitt, 1980). This is not to argue that women are not involved in local campaigns for nurseries, playgroups and the like. Indeed, these are the campaigns they are most likely to be found in, although as Hanmer (1977) points out, paradoxically this serves to confirm their primary definition as child minders.

Saunders (1979) notes that the successful day nursery campaign in Croydon was largely organised and supported by middle-class residents who could invest the considerable time, money and effort necessary to influence the local council. He also observes that in overall terms the new day nursery was relatively insignificant; the overall low level of nursery provision in the borough was unaffected. Indeed, it could be argued that this campaign was successful at the expense of others in more needy but politically disorganised areas.

Generally speaking, however, even the middle classes have been unable to reap significant rewards from the political system in terms of pre-school provision. In Southampton the widespread growth of the voluntary playgroup movement was largely a response to the lack of nursery education. Thus playgroups were initially seen as some form of interim arrangement until extensive nursery education could be developed. The playgroup movement was not an aggressive campaign for well developed state facilities but rather a patient substitution of faciities until a state initiative emerged. Thus many of the members readily accepted the reasons forwarded by the local authorities why extensive state provision was not possible. Since then many of those involved in the playgroup movement have accepted that the Pre-School Playgroups Movement — with its emphasis upon parental involvement — has advantages that the state system cannot provide. Indeed, the movement is now actively encouraged by local authorities through the provision of paid organisers and the provision of premises. Many would undoubtedly still like a system of state nursery education with purpose-built premises and trained staff but there is a widespread recognition that this would be 'expensive' and that the 'country cannot afford it'. Participation in the voluntary sector has therefore served to reinforce the existing lack of provision, legitimising the existing system without securing any major concessions. In this context it should be noted that Nursery Schools Association founded in 1923 has gradually become less visionary in its aspirations as it has been incorporated into policy making.

It is therefore hardly surprising that Saunders qualifies his 'pluralist' sector (in which the state responds to pressures from the locality) with the observation that these pressures are mediated by bureaucratic definitions of what is possible and the financial constraints imposed by both the local revenue base and central control.

Managerialism

The emphasis placed in legislation upon local discretion suggests that the managerialist perspective, which places emphasis upon the role of key officials in the public sector, has much to offer in this context. Pahl's (1970) original version has been subject to considerable criticism and amendment over the years. Managers are now no longer seen as independent variables but key 'agents' allocating resources whose scale is determined by central government and those who control the private sector (Pahl, 1977). The early managerialist perspectives also tended to ignore the role of local politicians in affecting resource outcomes and this cannot be discounted in the context of pre-school services.

Generally speaking the Labour Party with its ideology of state provision has been in favour of local authority day nursery and nursery school provision. It is this tradition of 'municipal socialism' and public provision which determined the response to the pressures in northern industrial towns. In contrast, Conservative councillors have generally been against pre-school provision both on the grounds that it will encourage women with young children to return to work and also that it will incur unnecessary public expenditure. The former argument is used even in the case of nursery schools and nursery classes, even though the hours these provide are unsuitable for mothers working full-time.

The non-metropolitan county of Hampshire again illustrates these tendencies in a striking manner. A recent policy document recognises the scale of the problem:

> Most of the services reach only a small proportion of children, typically those from the higher socio-economic familes ... To a certain extent the geographic distribution of resources is uneven ... The families that do not make use of the services are often found to be the same families that experience problems of low income, poor housing conditions and chronic child illness or handicap (Hampshire County Council, 1978).

However it is quite clear that the major theme running through the report is the need to minimise public expenditure. The priority objective of the report is stated as: 'To help those parents with children under five years of age to fulfil and enjoy their parental role to the maximum' (Hampshire County Council, 1978, p.2). The prime emphasis of services is seen as developing the involvement of parents in 'the family setting'. The major implication of this is that little or nothing will be done to encourage mothers with children under five to return to work. Instead emphasis is placed upon private and voluntary forms of provision through playgroups. In those cases in which a mother wishes to return to work the document endorses central government policy which is to encourage 'low cost' care through childminders rather than in day nurseries (despite the fact that childminders are the form of care least preferred by parents).

A second object of the report is: 'To help every child to realise to the full his or her development potential' (Hampshire County Council, 1978), 3). However, there is no consideration of the value of the favoured voluntary services in meeting this role in comparison with alternative forms of provision. The report acknowledges that 'in Hampshire the County Council has not in recent years allocated resources to allow any significant expansion of nursery education'. It is also acknowledged that in view of central policy that nursery education be expanded for 3 and 4 year olds that 'it will be necessary in the years ahead — when hopefully financial constraints are a little easier than they are at present — to extend nursery education to meet government policy guidelines'. It is clear that no great enthusiasm for this policy is expressed.

Another influence which has been neglected in the managerialist debate has been the influence of professionalism rather than bureaucracy. Throughout most of the twentieth century the pattern of pre-school services in Britain has been affected by a conflict between the medical and nursing professions on one hand and educationalists on the other. The former expressed an interest in the physical needs and dominated the day nurseries and grant-aid voluntary nurseries established by the 1918 Maternity and Child Welfare Act. The education profession were concerned with the education and social development of children and operated within the local authority nursery schools and voluntary schools established by the 1918 Education Act. Conflict between the medical and educational groups made it difficult to evolve a national policy during the Second World War but the decision was eventually made in favour of nurseries. However, after the Second World War the distinction between educational and health needs was maintained. The 1944 Education Act empowered education authorities to provide nursery schools and nursery classes for the under-fives and the 1946 National Health Act empowered local authorities to provide day nurseries. However, the Ministry made it clear that nursery schools and nursery classes were the preferred form of pre-school provision with day nurseries acting as small scale supplements for those mothers with particular needs. Many of the nurseries established in wartime were therefore transferred to local education authorities to be run as nursery schools, and the number of day nurseries was reduced. Many have argued that the legacy of this system and the absence of any single department in charge of pre-school services leads to a vacuum of responsibility (Challis, 1980). Those wishing to obtain increased levels of service in an area may therefore be passed between the two departments each denying responsibility for further extension of facilities. This would seem to be a classic case of the separation of powers helping to supress demand for services.

Whatever the influence of politicians and professionals, there are still grounds (and some evidence) for believing that local managers do have considerable influence upon both the overall level of pre-school services in an authority and the distribution of facilities to specific neighbourhoods within the authority. Striking evidence of the former is provided by Blackstone (1971). She observed that Hertfordshire has a much higher level of nursery class and nursery school provision than its position as a relatively high status non-metropolitan district would suggest. In fact, before the Second World War there was no nursery provision in Hertfordshire, but to cope with evacuation 42 wartime nurseries were established. After the war however, these were either closed or taken over by the education department and used as nursery schools. Blackstone attributes this shift to the relative power of officials in the bureaucracy:

> The powerful chief education officer at the time was convinced of the value of nursery provision and believed that it belonged to the province of the education department rather than that of the health department ... The medical officer of Health was considerably less powerful in the hierarchy of chief officers and consequently his own departments bid to take over the wartime nurseries was quashed early on without a prolonged fight, although it did succeed in wresting three of them from the education departments grasp, which subsequently became health department day nurseries. The sharing out of war nurseries merely shows that the power wielded by the officials concerned can affect the nature and extent of provision in a demonstrable way (Blackstone, 1971).

In this context it is also interesting to note that Cusden (1937) in a much earlier study attributed the variations in levels of nursery education to: ' ... the vision of an enlightened director here, the driving power of an enthusiastic local organiser there, and the tireless devotion of a group of teachers elsewhere ... (Cusden, 1937, p.25). She also suggests that the early rapid progress made in Bradford and Manchester was largely the result of their active Directors of Education.

The influence of intermediate and lower level personnel upon service outcomes is also likely but much more difficult to demonstrate. The extent to which departmental rules and conventions provide guidelines and give discretion to lower level officers is likely to vary between local authorities and between departments within local authorities. Webster (1977) notes that the nature of service organisation and the way in which this is delivered to areas may affect the nature of provision. It may be that different practices are employed in different social services divisions and that the provision of services is shaped by professional and personal attitudes and values rather than the needs and preferences of neighbourhoods. A good deal of the local authority work in this context is regulatory, inspecting standards of childminders and nurseries. There is a good deal of anecdotal evidence concerning the attitude of such fieldworkers to facilities but systematic analysis of their impact awaits further study.

Today most researchers who point out the influence of local agents upon resource allocations would also accept that the activities of these persons must be incorporated into some broader framework of political economy (Williams, 1982). The crucial issue therefore, is how to specify the constraints under which these local managers have to operate. In Britain, in the pre-school field, these constraints have certainly been considerable. Although considerable discretion has been given to local authorities to enable them to determine the extent of local needs, this has taken place within a straightjacket of financial and legal constraint. It is certainly true that, given sufficient will, some authorities have shown considerable resourcefulness and ingenuity in discovering loopholes in legislation. Hertfordshire is again an example of an authority which was able to thwart many central pressures after the Second World War in order to replace inadequate accommodation and to maintain its existing stock of nursery schools and classes (Blackstone, 1971). Nevertheless, the history of pre-school provision is characterised by episodes in which initial aspirations (in most cases not particularly high) have been blocked by Treasury demands for fiscal restraint. The 1944 Education Act led many to think that an era of universal nursery education was about to begin but during the 1950s and 1960s a succession of Ministry circulars prevented this happening. Given the continuing overall shortfall in provision levels any consideration of inequalities in pre-school provision must therefore address this central issue of the role of these services in capitalist economies.

In attempting to answer this question one is faced with two basic types of explanation — the neo-Marxist, and the feminist approaches — with various sub-divisions, hybrids and combinations of radical, liberal and sociaist feminist theory.

Neo-Marxist Explanations

Contemporary neo-Marxist theories stress the role of the state and its local representatives in supporting the capitalist mode of production. One of the most widely cited examples is O'Connor's (1973) distinction between 'social investment', 'social consumption' and 'social expenses'. Social investment (such as roads) and social consumption (such as housing) are seen as forms of expenditure by the state which are necessary to maintain the rate of profit in the private sector. In contrast, social expenses (such as education) do not directly affect capital accummulation but are envisaged as necessary to maintain social cohesion and to legitimise the existing social order by offsetting problems which would threaten its ideological stability.

Clearly, these functions need not be exclusive to particular types of expenditure or service. Thus, pre-school services might be envisaged as a part of social consumption lower the costs of class reproduction, but like social expenses might perform a legitimising role of 'buying off' popular discontent and inculcating values to the very young. Nevertheless, this does not invalidate the core of O'Connor's argument which is that conflicts and tensions arise because of the need to satisfy these differing functions. In particular, welfare policies designed to create popular support for the system may undermine social investment which is directly necessary to maintain profitability in the private sector.

As Saunders (1979) points out, one does not have to be a Marxist to accept this type of taxonomy or to see the numerous conflicts of interest which emerge in the modern state — indeed, such problems are a major concern of liberal and conservative perspectives. The crucial issue is whether one envisages these functions as inevitably tied to the interests of capital or some notion of the 'collective national interest'. What makes pre-school services so interesting in this context is that their form and extent varies so enormously between different capitalist economies. Many western European societies with their extensive services stand in marked contrast to the lack of provision in Britain and the United States. Sweden has especially well developed facilities and Adams and Winston (1980) argue that the system there has more in common with China than North America.

In Britain pre-school services have been particularly vulnerable to expenditure cuts aimed at diverting resources away from consumption and into investment. Indeed, it is somewhat ironic that the largest increases in pre-school services in Britain since the Second World war were planned by Margaret Thatcher when she was Secretary of State for Education. Following from the recommendations of the Plowden Report, full or part-time nursery education was planned for 50 per cent of three year olds and 90 per cent of all four year olds (Department of Education and Science, 1972). However, the increase in oil prices and subsequent recession and expenditure cuts (largely imposed by the following Labour administration) meant that these targets were not attained. In 1977 there was the equivalent of nursery provision for 16 per cent of three year olds and 50 per cent of four year olds.

The Marxist response to such variations in provision between capitalist economies is, in essence, to argue that the class struggle can take various forms in different places at different times. The contradictions between the need for social consumption and social investment necessary for profitable production are claimed to produce lacunae in vast areas of consumption. Offe (1972) argues that:

> This seems to be symptomatic of a phase of capitalist development in which areas of crisis peripheral to the central group of problems, however segregated and insignificant they may be with the institutional system, are hindered from generating further disturbances to the system ... This would mean that the pauperism of the early capitalist proletariat has given way to the modern pauperism of depressed areas: the areas of education, transportation, housing and health which affect the entire population are obvious cases in point. Institutions that are marginal to the mainstream of life, *such as the pre-school socialising phase,* unemployment, old age after retirement, mentally ill and criminals are further examples ... (emphasis added, Offe, 1972, p.102).

It follows therefore that within capitalist economies, low levels of pre-school provision, the ease with which plans for expansion may be reduced or abandoned, and the vulnerability of existing services to closure, is made possible because these services are not directly responsible or necessary for maintaining profit accumulation in the same manner as roads or public utilities. In communist societies with a strong need for female labour to support the productive infrastructure a widespread system of nurseries is more often provided. In capitalist economies, however, widespread female employment has only been necessary to ensure national survival in times of war. Female participation in the paid workforce is of course important in capitalist economies in times of peace, but although the state has intervened to provide accommodation for those under-fives in most need, and is ostensibly concerned to provide certain minimum standards, there is an avoidance of responsibility for the working mother. Thus Offe argues:

The capicity for conflict refers to the capacity of an organisation or the corresponding functional group, to collectively refuse to perform, or to present a plausible threat of such a refusal to the system in a relevant way. A collection of status groups and functional groups is indeed organizable but not capable of conflict ... Groups consisting of *housewives,* secondary school pupils, college students, the unemployed, the mentally ill, and ethnic minorities may be cited as examples. The capacity of these groups to bring their influence successfully to bear is small in as much as their functional utility is minimal (emphasis added, Offe, 1876, p.87).

The major problem with such explanations based on the 'needs of capital' is that in one sense they explain 'everything and nothing' for there is little or no specific indication of why pre-school services should vary so considerably between societies. Indeed, there would seem to be no reason why capitalism should be associated with any particular level of pre-school provision. Humphries (1977) argues that it is possible to envisage a system of state childrearing agencies which would benefit from economies of scale and which could provide the 'docile' workforce in a similar manner to that currently provided by the family. Although undeniably expensive, the centralisation of support involved in the substitution of state for family services would give capital greater control over the administration of resources which could be streamlined in the interests of capital production. Barrett (1980) claims it has yet to be demonstrated that capitalism could not survive without the present system of domestic labour and childrearing, and that explanations based around the smooth reproduction of capitalist social relations run the risk of ignoring conflict and political struggle.

Furthermore, Saunders (1979) argues that these theories face the same problems as functionalist sociology in explaining causes in terms of effects. Low levels of pre-school provision in Britain may be compatible with class interests but there is little evidence that the policy was deliberately created with these interests in mind. Concern was expressed at the time of the Boer War about the poor quality of British conscripts, and inadequate nutrition and poor childrearing standards in the working class were blamed (Lewis, 1980). Thus emerged the campaign to 'glorify, dignify and purify motherhood' which included infant welfare clinics, health visitors and hospital facilities for women and infants. These policies were based upon the underlying assumption that needs were due to individual moral failure rather than broader social conditions — hence the emphasis upon education. This focus upon motherhood strengthened the role of women in the home and helped to undermine the needs for pre-school provision. Hall (1979) argues that the ideology of domesticity was strongly advocated by the Evangelical Movement and initially adopted by the new bourgeoisie during the rapid industrialisation of Britain between 1780 and 1830. This ideology was not developed primarily to subordinate women in the home but it was subsequently moulded by economic forces to achieve this end when disseminated amongst the working classes.

In a similar vein Barrett notes that, although industrial capitalism brought about sweeping changes in the position of women, many changes related to the increased possibilities of divorce and the rise of notions of romantic love are less plausibly related to specifically capitalist modes of production (Barrett, 1980). Other developments, such as protective legislation for working women and the limited growth of pre-school services, are not explicable strictly within the logic of capitalist development. The initial state involvement in nursery education also arose from a concern with health needs but there is little indication that this policy was primarily motivated with the interests of business in mind. Indeed, following in the wake of the Factory Acts, the early legislation introducing educational provision threatened the profitability of the private sector by removing a cheap source of labour. The introduction of the relatively early starting age of five meant that education would be accomplished quickly and children of ten would be able to enter the workforce (Blackstone, 1971). Although nursery education may have contributed to the creation of a healthier workforce, the initial impetus came from the zeal of the early social reformers — teachers, social workers and Medical Officers of Health. Similarly, in the 1960s when the value of pre-school experience was rediscovered, the primary movers were not industrialists concerned to create a workforce more compatible with the needs of industry but educationalists, psychologists and social reformers attempting to create greater 'equality of opportunity'.

Feminist Approaches

The factor conspicuously absent from these Neo-Marxist theories of the state is the role of women in society and it is therefore to feminist approaches that one must turn for further elaboration of the role of pre-school services. Such approaches suggest that pre-school services are vulnerable and limited in scope because the role of women in modern industrialised societies is primarily identified with looking after children in the home (Oakley, 1972). This 'female' role within the family is not biologically linked with motherhood but is a culturally ascribed 'gender-role'. Thus:

> Far from being womans 'natural' role, the allocation of the responsibility for the full-time care of pre-school children to the biological mother alone is a phenomenon peculiar to twentieth century industrial society (Ginsberg, 1977, p.75).

In pre-industrial Britain the family was the main unit of production and women undertook a wide range of functions to support their families (Oakley, 1974). Industrial capitalism called for the concentration of economically productive effort into large organisations outside the family and this led to the distinction between the private world of economically non-productive work and the public world of wage-earning work. Of course initially many women and children were recruited to work in the new factories. However, the second half of the nineteenth century saw a progressive decline in the numbers of working married women. Amongst the most important reasons for this decline were increasing male earnings and the growing hostility to the idea of women taking up employment. The textile industries in which women were highly represented were overtaken by mechanisation and the growth of heavy engineering industries from which women were largely excluded. Thus, throughout the nineteenth century women found their roles increasingly confined to housework and childrearing. In recent years, however, this childbearing has been spread over a much shorter period with women marrying younger and having smaller families (Garland and White, 1980). Consequently, the proportion of their lives devoted to bringing up children is much smaller than in the past and increasing numbers of women, many with young chldren, have taken up paid employment outside the home.

Nevertheless, for a variety of reasons, including inadequate child-care facilities, a generally unequal division of labour in the home, socialisation into conventional gender roles and discrimination against women by employers and trade unions, women are severely constrained in the forms of employment they can obtain, typically being restricted to low-paid semi- or unskilled occupations, frequently on a part-time basis with little security of employment.

A radical feminist perspective suggests that at the root of this oppressed position is the system of patriarchy. This is generally defined as a system of male supremacy which pre-dates capitalism having existed in many diverse forms for thousands of years. It is maintained by sexist ideology, this being defined as situations where differences between men and women are consistently emphasised to the detriment of women (Allen and Barker, 1976).

The case for the influence of patriarchy as a determinant of pre-school services is put forcefully by Hughes and associates:

> ... those who hold political and economic power are predominantly men with little understanding of the realities of motherhood and no day-to-day responsibilities themselves for pre-school children. Imagine the reaction of government and employers to a situation where all civil servants, managers and professional men with pre-school children suddenly found themselves actually responsible for the daily care of their children. Would they be left to make their own arrangements as best they could? Or be given an outdated list of childminders and be told to find a vacancy as best they could? Or be told to choose between a family and a career? Or would nursery schools and employment measures suddenly become a major item on the political and economic agenda, an essential feature of the industrial strategy, whle company nurseries and child care allowances joined the company car and BUPA membership and help with school fees as a standard fringe benefit?' (Hughes *et al.*, 1980).

This emphasis upon patriarchal forms of power relationships suggests a more general form of explanation which is applicable to pre-school services than the 'needs of capitalism' arguments. Given that gender divisions preceded the rise of capitalism, these divisions (and the position of pre-school services) would not necessarily be altered by a transformation of capitalist modes of production. In the case of the system of patriarchy, however, any radical transformation must inevitably have a crucial impact upon pre-school facilities.

Of course, pre-school services are only one aspect of the oppression of women. The women's liberation movement has a wide range of other concerns including equal pay and opportunities, abortion on demand, adequate birth control facilities and the stereotyped representation of women in advertising. It is therefore possible to have extensive pre- pre-school services but considerable dimensions of inequality between men and women on other spheres. For example, in many communist societies, despite widespread nursery provision, there is typically a highly unequal division of labour between men and women both in the home and in the formal economy. A similar situation exists in capitalst economies in which extensive nurseries have been provided. In Sweden there is evidence that the expansion of services for working mothers may have served to reinforce occupational segregation and sexual stereotypes between men and women. The development of nurseries, home-helps and other welfare services has created a strata of relatively low-paid public sector jobs primarily undertaken by women performing the tasks they have traditionally undertaken on an unpaid basis in the home — cooking, cleaning and child care (Adams and Winston, 1980). Nevertheless, the importance of adequate child care is crucial, for while alone not sufficient, it is a necessary condition for greater sexual equality. As Adams and Winston (1980) note, women are currently caught in a viscious circle. Husbands and policy makers see the role of women as secondary, and economically this is the case. In this situation women will continue to identify themselves primarily with domestic responsibilities. A rearrangement of household roles will not therefore emerge until both husband and wife identify themselves as both breadwinner and homemaker, but women cannot expect to obtain more than relatively marginal jobs until they receive help with these domestic responsibilities. The logical conclusion from this situation must be that the equal participation of women in the workforce cannot await a massive change of attitudes to household responsibilities (such a policy would in any case not help the growing numbers of single-parent families). It will only come about when women have more than marginal jobs and this is critically dependent upon adequate child care.

There is enormous controversy at present as to how this may be achieved. The crucial issue is the extent to which the oppression of women is independent of material economic factors or grounded in ideology. Liberal feminists have emphasised the ideological basis of women's oppression and believe that social equality can be achieved within democratic capitalist societies without a class revolution. Socialist feminists have tended to stress a material analysis in which the struggle of women is part of the broader struggle against the dominant mode of production. This controversy has led to many attempts at a fusion between perspectives of gender and class. There is now a growing recognition that although patriarchy existed prior to the rise of industrial capitalism, this in turn shaped patriarchal relations in crucial ways. There was not a complete break with the past for there had always been a degree of separation between work and family before the Industrial Revolution — not all work was done in or near the home and women did a great deal of work concerned with the care of children. Indeed, the beginning of the Industrial Revolution prompted a rise in home working as the newly mechanised industries required increased capacity in other unmechanised sectors. Nevertheless, what distinguished the rise of capitalism was the privatisation of domestic labour by women in the home and their exclusion from the world of social labour. Many would therefore assert that society can only be adequately understood in terms of *both* capitalist and patriarchal relations. The capital accumulation process has accommodated itself to patriarchal structures and at the same time helps to perpetuate them. This does not mean, as many have asserted, that capitalism and patriarchy are one and the same thing, but that although conceptually distinct they are in reality highly interdependent.

This is still far from satisfactory for it leaves many questions unanswered. As Barratt (1980) notes, the crucial task for the future is how to conceptualise the role of women in a way that is not either completely autonomous from, or totally determined by, the economic relations of the capitalist mode of production. What is clear however, is that pre-school services are but one aspect of the constraints upon women, and that extensive pre-school services need not be incompatible with the interests of capitalism. It is true that in Sweden pre-school facilities served an economic function, allowing women to satisfy a need for labour in the economy which, in other capitalist economies, has been satisfied by immigrants. Nevertheless, the crucial factor which has permitted the Swedes to adopt this solution has been differing attitudes to the role of motherhood which have been translated into political processes. This contrasts with Britain and the United States where, at the level of government, motherhood and full-time employment are generally considered to be fundamentally incompatible. It is therefore difficult to escape the conclusion that, when considering pre-school services (rather than the position of women in society as a whole), the ideology of femininity has been a crucial determinant affecting the overall scope of provision.

Conclusions

With a few notable exceptions geographers and other urban analysts have ignored the allocation of pre-school services. There are numerous possible explanations for this state of affairs, not the least important being the fact that study of the under-fives has been dominated by psychologists concerned with the intellectual, emotional and social development of young children. Furthermore, as this paper reveals, numerous elements need to be integrated to analyse this problem from a spatial perspective: accessibility indices within cities, the social structure oof neighbourhoods, the operation of the local political system and the development of social policy at the national and international level. Various authors have examined these issues in isolation but few have brought the necessary synthesis for a spatial view of pre-school services. It must also be remembered that there are in any case relatively few 'official' pre-school facilities so that inevitably the major items of expenditure in the fields of housing, transportation, social services and the like have received the lion's share of attention. Indeed, although there has been some controversy over the closure of nurseries in certain local authorities, the provision of pre-school services is not a major political issue in the same manner as inflation, housing and unemployment. However, the major reason for the neglect of these services must be the fact that they primarily affect the lives of women and, in common with all similar issues, have been neglected by social scientists (Monck and Hanson, 1982).

Of the two major contributors to service inequality discussed in this chapter — jurisdictional partitioning and tapering — it would seem that juridictional partitioning is the more important reason, for there appears to be greater inequality of pre-school provision levels between local governments than within their boundaries. This conclusion is of course derived from one case study, and Southampton may be an exception by virtue of its diverse social structure and vigorous playgroups movement. Patterns of intra-city provision might be different in a larger northern conurbation with greater social deprivation. Nevertheless, there seems little doubt that decisions made at the local government level are vitally important and require further study. The relative immobility of mothers with young children means that 'tapering' effects are also important, although experience in Southampton indicates that considerable ingenuity and determination displayed by those transporting their children considerable distances to partake in the desired form of pre-school experience. At this level it is therefore more difficult to match the correspondence between needs of areas and provision. Measuring the degree of 'territorial justice' in the allocation of services is most appropriate in situation (such as the personal social services) where inequalities between areas are large in relation to the overall shortfall in provision. Large though the area-inequalities may be in the pre-school field, it should always be remembered that the crucial source of deprivation is the absolute shortage of such facilities in the nation as a whole.

The present Conservative government is (at the time of writing) planning to reduce the level of nursery school provision between 1982 and 1985 at a rate faster than the projected decline in the numbers of nursery-aged children. Cuts planned in recent White Papers would have been even more severe but for stout resistance from local councils. Leaks from the secret committee of cabinet ministers known as the Family Policy Group suggest that the government would like to see a return to Victorian ideology with respect to the role of women in the family. With increasing female unemployment the demand for full-time day care is certainly diminishing in certain areas. In Southampton for example, some registered childminders have been unable to obtain children to care for because of insufficient demand. (This may of course have arisen because they are being 'undercut' by unregistered minders offering services at cheaper rates). But whatever the explanation some makeshift form of solution will emerge to both full-time and part-time day care. The important point is that this is not the type of solution which many parents appear to want or what is most desirable in the interests of young children.

Drawing together the evidence presented above it is also possible to make some speculations about the link between these scales of inequality and the various modes of explanations. Saunders (1979) has made a vertical division of explanatory modes, depending upon the type of service, with 'pluralist' influences most pertinent to housing and social services. However, within a particular set of services such as pre-school facilities it is possible to envisage a geographical division of explanatory influences. As suggested above, pluralist bargaining-type explanations seem generally inappropriate in the pre-school context but their influence is most likely to be found in particular areas *within* local governments affecting an isolated nursery here or playgroup there. The most plausible explanation of spatial variations at the intra-authority, however, can be labelled 'ecological' depending upon the availability of premises, demographic structure and physical location of estates. In contrast, 'managerial' influences, in the broad sense of the term, are most likely to be useful in understanding the overall level of service allocations made by the authority and the administrative milieu in which the diverse voluntary and private organisations have to operate. Finally, aggregate social theories can help to specify some of the constraints within which local agents operate and the total amount of resources allocated at the national level.

From the policy perspective, a spatial analysis can help to illuminate, at various scales, the areas of relative deprivation where local campaigns can be directed for further service provision. However, the more important absolute level of deprivation will only be countered with a radical shift in the position of women in British society, which in turn depends upon greater provision of pre-school facilities - a situation somewhat reminiscent of Catch 22.

References

Adams, C.T., and K.T. Winston (1980) *Mothers at Work: Public Policies in the United States, Sweden and China*, Longman, New York

Allen, S., and D.L. Barker (1976) *Sexual Divisions and Society*, Tavistock, London

Barrett, M. (1980) *Women's Oppression Today*, Verso Press, London

Bell, L. (1976) *Underprivileged Under-Fives*, Ward Lock Educational, London

Bennett, R.J. (1980) *The Geography of Public Finance*, Methuen, London

Blackstone, T. (1971) *A Fair Start*, Allen Lane, London

Bone, M. (1974) *Preschool children and the need for day care*, Office of Population Censuses and Surveys, London

Brown, G., and T.O. Harris (1978) *Social Origins of Depression*, Tavistock, London

Bruner, J. (1980) *Under Five in Britain*, Grant McIntyre, London

Bryant, B., M. Harris and D. Newton (1980) *Children and Minders*, Grant McIntyre, London

Challis, L. (1980) *The Great Under-Fives Muddle*, Bath Social Policy Papers, University of Bath

Coote, A., and P. Hewitt (1980) 'The stance of Britain's major political parties and interest groups, ' in P. Moss and N. Fonda, (eds.) *Work and the Family*, Temple Smith, London

Crowe, B. (1937) *The Playgroup Movement*, Allen and Unwin, London

Cusden, P.E. (1937) *The English Nursery School*, Routledge and Kegan Paul, London

Davies, B.P. (1968) *Social Needs and Resources in Local Services*, Michael Joseph, London

Department of Education and Science and Department of Social Security (1976) *Low Cost Provision for the Under Fives*, HMSO, London

Freestone, B. (1977) 'Provision of child care facilities in Sydney' , *Australian Geographer*, 13, 318-325

Garland, C., and S. White (1980) *Children and Day Nurseries*, Grant McIntyre, London

Ginsberg, S. (1977) 'Women, Work and conflict' , in N. Fonda and P. Moss, (eds.), *Mothers in Employment*, Brunel University, Uxbridge

Hall, C. (1979) 'The early formation of Victorian domestic ideology', in S. Burman, (ed.), *Fit Work for Women*, Croom Helm, London, 15-32

Hanmer, J. (1977) 'Community action, women's aid and the women's liberation movement' , in M. Mayo, (ed.), *Women in the Community*, Routledge and Kegan Paul, London

Hart, J.T. (1971) 'The inverse-care law' , *The Lancet*, i405-411

Hampshire County Council (1978) *Provision for the Under-Fives*, The Castle, Winchester

Holmes, J., F. Williams, and L.A. Brown (1972) 'Facility location under a maximum travel restriction' , *Geographical Analysis*, 4, 258-266

HMSO (1972) *Education: a Framework for Expansion*, Department of Education and Science

Hughes, M., B. Mayall, P. Moss., J. Perry., P. Petrie and G. Pinkerton (1980) 'The class struggle and 'The persistence of the working class family' , *Cambridge Journal of Economics*, 1, 241-258

Jackson, B., and S. Jackson (1979) *Childminder*, Routledge and Kegan Paul, London

Kirby, A.M., and S.P. Pinch (1983) 'Territorial justice and service allocation' , in M. Pacione, (ed.), *Progress in Urban Geography*, Croom Helm, London

Lewis, J. (1980) *The Politics of Motherhood*, Croom Helm, London

Lineberry, R.L. (1977) 'Equality, public policy and public services: the undercllass hypothesis and the limits to equality' , *Policy and Politics*, 4, 67-84

Lister, R. (1980) 'Family policy' , in N. Bosanquet, and P. Townsend, (eds.), *Labour and Equality*, Heinemann, London

Mayall, B., and P. Petrie (1971) *Minder, Mother and Child*, Institute of Education, London

Monck, J., and S. Hanson (1982) 'On not excluding half of the human in human geography' , *Professional Geographer*, 34, 11-23

Oakley, A. (1972) *Sex, Gender and Society*, Temple Smith, London

Oakley, A. (1974) *The Sociology of Housework*, Martin Robertson, London

O'Connor, J. (1973) *The Fiscal Crisis of the State*, St. James Press, London

Offe, C. (1972) 'Advanced capitalism and the welfare state' , *Politics and Society*, 2, 479-488

Pahl, R.E. (1970) *Whose City?*, Longman, London

Pahl, R.E. (1977) 'Managers, technical experts and the state' , in M. Harloe, (ed.), *Captive Cities*, John Wiley and Sons, Chichester

Pinch, S.P. (1983) *Inequality in pre-school provision: a geographical perspective*, University of Southampton, Department of Geography, Discussion Paper No. 16

Saunders, P. (1979) *Urban Politics*, Hutchinson, London

Sylva, K.D., Roy, and M. Painter (1980) *Childwatching at Playgroup and Nursery School*, Grant McIntyre, London

Scott, J.W., and A.W. Tilley (1975) 'Women's Work and the family in nineteenth century Europe' , *Comparative Studies in Society and History*, **17, 1**, 36-84

Tivers, J. (1977) *Constraints on spatial activity patterns: women with young children*, Kings College London Department of Geography Occasional Papers, **6**

Tizard, J., P. Moss, and J. Perry (1976) *All Our Children*, Temple Smith, London

Webster, B. (1977) *The distributional effects of local government services*, mimeo

Williams, P. (1982) 'Restructuring urban managerialism: towards a political economy of urban allocation' , *Environment and Planning A*, **14**, 95-105

Wolch, J.R. (1979) 'Residential location and the provision of human services: some directions for geographical research' , *Professional Geographer*, **31**, 271-7

12

Social Change, Turf Politics, and Concepts of Turf Politics

Kevin R. Cox

Introduction

A variety of conflicts in cities — conflicts over zoning, residential displacement, the location of public facilities, etc. — and the accompanying consciousness which emerges from anecdotal evidence suggest the contemporary prevalence of a politics of turf in the living place. Residents come together and form civic associations, residents' associations and the like in order to keep certain types of land use off the local turf; or to attract different types of land use on to it.

Concomitant with these real world events is a social science literature which reflects them and attempts to give them meaning in wider theoretical contexts. There are abroad, in other words, in political science, economics, sociology, geography and urban planning *concepts* of turf politics. This literature is a very recent one. Probably the earliest evidence we have of it is Tiebout's (1956) contribution which sparked so much subsequent research in economics. Appropriately enough, the real world events which this literature tries to shed light on appear also to be of recent vintage.

This chapter seeks to characterise the literature on turf politics and to understand it as a reflection of changes in the way the world appears. While at one level it can be understood as a reflection of the real world emergence of turf politics in the post-war period, the argument here is that this would allow only a very limited understanding. Rather we should be interested in the concepts through which understandings are fashioned — the means of producing knowledge — as well as the objects about which knowledge is sought.

It is the contention of this chapter that not only is the object of knowledge defined by the way the world appears — specifically by the appearance in the 1960s and 1970s of locational conflicts, resident groups and their exclusionary tactics and the like; but so are the means through which knowledge is produced — such concepts as 'residential preference', 'objective characteristics of neighborhoods' and 'externality effects'. By postulating a set of generative mechanisms through which those appearances are produced, it is the ultimate aim of this chapter to elucidate not only turf politics but also the concepts through which attempts have been made to grasp the phenomenon. These concepts can then be demonstrated as affording only limited insight into the real world emergence and development of turf politics.

The chapter is divided into two major sections. In the first section, the literature dealing with turf politics is characterised both in terms of its focus (i.e., its object of knowledge) and its concepts (i.e., the means of producing knowledge in this substantive area). The historical specificity of the object of knowledge is validated, and that of the concepts through which one attempts to understand it is outlined. In the second and longer section of the chapter we proceed to an investigation of the historical emergence of turf politics. Here we demonstrate how both it and the concepts employed by orthodox social science to understand it are embedded in phenomenal forms, and how these phenomenal forms are produced, reproduced, and transformed by much more fundamental generative mechanisms, the nature of which is belied by the contemporary literature.

The Turf Politics Literature

Turf politics assumes the form of a politics conducted by coalitions of residential households, as in a neighborhood organisation; or by a local government representing those residential households. The object of the coalition or local government is to manipulate the environment of externalities impinging in the living place through appropriate land use, public expenditure and taxation policies. Land uses regarded as providing positive externalities for current residents will be attracted in while attempts are made to exclude those imposing some form of external cost. At the same time, public expenditure decisions may signal the availability of a particular bundle of public goods and so discourage the location of those who would prefer some different bundle and so vote against it.

Theories of turf politics, both positive and normative in emphasis, abound in the social sciences. Noteworthy on the positive side has been the work of the political scientist Oliver Williams. He has identified urbanism as 'an instrument for facilitating human interaction' (1971, 12) and hence the first objective of urban political analysis is to identify the control mechanisms manipulating social access. While the individual can manipulate social access through relocation strategies, he/she also joins place-based coalitions designed to control social access.[1] Relocation is itself a form of coalition-joining behaviour since local governments are seen as coalitions. These coalitions at both neighbourhood and municipal scales are often competitive one with another.

A remarkably similar and apparently independent formulation of urban politics (though both reference Tiebout) has come from an urban planner, Lowdon Wingo:

> Experiential environments are analogous to 'clubs' as economists have come to use the term. One can join such a club for a 'price' which entitles him (1) to quasi-property rights in the environmental goods offered by the club, as well as (2) to join with others to determine how the collective resources of the club will be used, i.e., what collective goods the environment will embody (Wingo, 1973, 14).

The relative desirability of the bundles of goods provided by such 'clubs' is reflected in competitive bidding behaviour in the housing market. The value of the right to a club membership, therefore, is apparent in that fraction of market price attributable to a particular experiential environment or 'club'. Conversely:

> The decision *not* to move, then, is a political as well as an economic decision reflecting confidence (1) that the locality's collective choice mechanisms are representing well what its members want, and (2) that the majority of the members want pretty much the same collective output as a given individual does at approximately the same cost he is willing to pay. Hence, the performance of the collective choice processes becomes a key element in the ability of an environmental club to hold on to its membership and to preserve, if not enhance, the economic rent attributable to membership (Wingo, 1973,

16).

Yet other theories of turf politics incorporate an explicit normative element defining whether or not it is a vehicle for good or bad. These are arguably more stimulating since their confrontation with each other throws into relief underlying assumptions about individuals and society in general and paves the way for a more general critique. Both conservative and liberal poles can be recognised (Cox and Nartowicz, 1980).

The conservative view has the advantage of a strong and explicit basis in theory: public choice theory is an attempt to apply concepts of marginal economic analysis to the public sector (Ostrom, Tiebout and Warren, 1961; Bish and Ostrom, 1976). Furthermore, it is firmly rooted in transparently clear assumptions about human nature and about society. In this conception individuals have pregiven preferences for bundles of public goods which they can satisfy by coming together under the same local government umbrella with those sharing similar preferences. Since they all share the same preferences, nobody will have to pay for public sector output which they do not want. Hence, the organisation of cities into a large number of separate jurisdictions, each providing a public service menu catering to a specific type of preference function, maximises individual freedom — specifically individual freedom to realise preferences for public sector outputs. As tastes change, of course, there need be no loss of freedom since the individual can relocate to a jurisdiction the local government of which provides a bundle of goods more appropriate to changed tastes.

The realisation of individual freedom has, of course, always been central to the philosophy of modern conservatism. The obstacles to such realisation embedded in social structures perpetuating inequality of opportunity has been equally strategic in the viewpoint of liberal reformism (Danielson, 1972; Harvey, 1973, Ch. 3; Newton, 1975). The argument here is that jurisdictional fragmentation represents a means by which wealthier households can maximise their well being by: (i) sharing out the positive externalities they can provide each other — behavioural, fiscal and status, for instance; (ii) excluding others from realising the *same* preferences for good schools, public safety, neighbourhood aesthetics, etc. In contrast to conservatives, therefore, liberals argue for a much more homogeneous preference function for public sector output; and instead of favouring fragmentation as a means to the realisation of individual freedom, they advocate jurisdictional integration as a means to greater equality of opportunity. Thus, by (e.g.) state funding of education local disparities in school funding could be eliminated, while (e.g.) regional land use planning would democratise access to favoured residential enclaves. In this view, the public choice literature on jurisdictional fragmentation is pure ideology: an attempt to explain as in the general public interest an institutional structure which obviously redounds to the benefit of a few (Neiman, 1975).

These theories of turf politics have led to a fairly predictable programme of empirical research. This has included studies of home values.[2] Especially popular among the urban economists, they have attempted to identify the particular characteristics of Wingo's (1973) experiential environments which form the focus of collective choice processes and also the basis of the economic rent acting as entrance fee. Home value studies have, in addition, been employed in attempts to evaluate the degree to which exclusionary mechanisms are effective: do they in fact result in higher home prices than would occur in their absence (Maser, Riker and Rosett, 1977)?

A second area of research has been into segregation. In his original formulation of turf politics, Oliver Williams (1971) identified as questions for future research: whether or not sociospatial segregation was increasing or decreasing; and whether or not political fragmentation affects the degree of sociospatial segregation. Addressing himself to both of these questions, Williams finds an increase over the 1950-1970 period in inter-municipal segregation by social status in Philadelphia (Williams and Eklund, 1978). Similar research, also explicitly rooted in conceptions of turf politics, has been undertaken elsewhere (Pack and Pack, 1977; Hamilton, Mills and Puryear, 1975).

A third area of research has been into intra-metropolitan inequalities in public provision. This has embraced both inter-neighbourhood (Baron, 1971; Webster and Stewart, 1974) and inter-jurisdictional levels (Davies, 1968; Pinch, 1979). With respect to the latter, particular attention in the US has been given to metropolitan fiscal disparities (Neenan, 1972; Cox, 1973, Ch.2). At both scales, however, the burgeoning area of social indicators research has made clear and self-conscious contact (Knox, 1983).

In addition, there have been innumerable case studies drawing

Table 12.1: Instances of Localised Conflict Over the Built Environment: Columbus, Ohio, 1900-1980

Year	High Density Residential Rezoning	Non-Residential Rezoning	Roads	Annexation	Urban Renewal	Services	N
1970-8	38.3 (66)[a]	25.0 (43)	16.3 (28)	5.8 (10)	5.2 (9)	9.3 (16)	172
1960-68	32.2 (48)	26.8 (40)	12.1 (18)	6.0 (9)	4.0 (6)	18.8 (28)	149
1950-8	8.6 (5)	29.3 (17)	25.9 (15)	5.2 (3)	—	31.0 18)	58
1940-8	10.0 (2)	10.0 (2)	25.0 (5)	5.0 (1)	—	50.0 (10)	20
1930-8	3.6 (3)	12.0 (10)	19.3 (16)	—	—	65.1 (54)	83
1920-8	3.0 (2)	1.5 (1)	26.9 (18)	4.5 (3)	—	64.2 (43)	67
1910-8	—	10.0 (3)	20.0 (6)	6.7 (2)	—	63.3(19)	30
1900-8	—	5.7 (2)	34.3 (12)	11.4 (4)	—	48.6 (17)	35
	20.5 (126)	19.2 (118)	19.2 (118)	5.2 (32)	2.4 (15)	33.4 (20)	614

Notes:
a. Row percentages are given, with the figure in parentheses referring to the number of distinct cases of political activism recorded for the even years, within each category.

upon some sort of turf politics paradigm. These include the very large number of studies of locational conflict undertaken in geography[3] and those of broader policy issues examined by political scientists. Danielson (1976) undertook a lengthy study of residential exclusion in American metropolitan areas. Young and Kramer (1978) examined similar issues of 'opening up the suburbs' in a study of public housing policy in the London metropolitan area.

Finally, but fewer in number, have been studies of those who get active in turf politics. The goal here is to shed light on the forces — expressed at an individual level — which engender a politics of turf. These studies have been fewer in number and, oddly enough, almost entirely the work of geographers (Agnew, 1978; Cox and McCarthy, 1980; Ley and Mercer, 1980) though the work of Orbell and Uno (1972) should be noted.

The Object of Knowledge

The first theoretical statement of a politics of turf, partial to be sure, that I have been able to identify is that of Tiebout in 1956. Subsequent statements and, indeed, empirical studies are slow to appear until after the mid-sixties. Momentum picks up considerably in the seventies. This timing is significant, it seems to me, because it is matched by what we know about the historical emergence of a turf politics in the residential sphere. Although the evidence is limited to Columbus, Ohio, and needs to be replicated for a number of other cities, it is, at the very least, highly suggestive.

Using a content analysis of the local newspaper over the period 1900-1980, [4] 614 separate controversies over the built environment were identified (Table 12.1). Significantly, neighbourhood activism has increased dramatically during this period especially since the Second World War[5] (Table 12.2). The marked increase during the 1960s and 1970s far exceeds that which would be expected on the basis of Columbus's population increase. For example, prior to the 1960s observed neighbourhood activism was less than expected given the population of the Columbus metropolitan area: there were in fact only half as many protests as one would expect. In the 1960s and 1970s, however, observed levels of neighbourhood activism exceeded by about 40 per cent what one would expect.

Especially interesting in Table 12.1 is the increasing stress on rezoning away from an earlier orientation towards conflicts over the provision of services. These latter were particularly prominent before 1950 and largely assumed the form of petitioning for

Table 12.2: Expected and Observed Neighbourhood Activism[a]

Decade	Expected % (based on metropolitan population)	Observed % (excluding activism over services)
1970s	29.8	38.9
1960s	23.4	32.1
1950s	16.0	10.7
1940s	11.0	2.8
1930s	9.3	5.9
1920s	7.7	3.6
1910s	5.4	2.5
1900s	3.6	

Notes:
a. Only protests were included in the compilation of this table.

improvements — better roads, mass transit, street cleaning, sewage provision, fire stations, street lights, and so on. Since 1950, rezoning issues have been dominant, testifying to the exclusionary character of contemporary activism. This shift to a more exclusionary focus is further evidenced by the increasingly controversial nature of multi-family projects in single-family residential neighbourhoods (Table 12.3). We find, for example, only one protest per 815 building permits in the 1920s compared to one protest per 56 permits in the 1970s. And the exclusion of higher density residential developments has dominated recent neighbourhood activism.

Concepts

There are, then, some grounds for believing that the experiential basis of the object of knowledge in studies of turf politics is fairly recent and corresponds in its timing with the literature under review. To that degree, the literature is a reflection of phenomenal forms. It is our view, however, that the literature is a reflection of the world of appearances in a much more fundamental sense: the concepts extant in it are likewise a reflection of how the world appeared and, indeed, continues to appear.

Consider, for example, the following concepts which appear central to the turf politics literature: 'residential preference function'; 'objective characteristics of neighbourhoods'; 'externality effects'; 'the relation between mobility and coalition'. In an attempt to understand turf politics there is a concerted effort to project onto residents a certain view of their relation to the neighbourhood. Specifically, it is argued, individuals have residential preference functions through which they relate to certain characteristics of neighbourhoods independent of those prefernces. These characteristics are externalities. Further, it is through the application of this simple conceptual apparatus that one seeks to understand why in some circumstances, people decide to stay and fight (Orbell and Uno, 1972; Wingo, 1973) and why in other circumstances people choose to move; or alternatively how the problems people experience in the living place and which cause them to organise can be traced to the mobility decisions of others.

Debates on turf politics are confined within this paradigm. Controversy between conservative (public choice) and liberal views, for example, revolves around the homegeneity or heterogeneity of preference functions (Cox and Nartowicz, 1980). That preference functions are separable from objective characteristics is not treated as problematic by either of these perspectives. People are assumed to exist in a highly privatised world ready to instantly respond to perturbation of the 'quality of life' (Wingo, 1973) afforded by a particular experiential environment through either mobility or some form of collective action. Implicit in this view is the notion of residents as *de*tached relative to the neighbourhood in which they reside; the notion that they might be *at*tached in any way which would not permit the concept to be forced into the preference function-objective characteristics duality remains untheorised.

To marxists this is not surprising. Essential to their ontology is a world of appearances or phenomenal forms generated by unseen, hidden mechanisms embedded in the relations through which people produce their material life. At the epistemological level the concrete is always grasped through certain preformed concepts. To the extent that the ontology is marxist, these concepts will be in terms of prevailing notions of generative mechanisms. To the extent that the ontology is bourgeois, they will respond to the way the world appears since, at the ontological level, bourgeois social science makes no such distinction. Facts speak for themselves and it is in the observable facts that explanation is ultimately sought. Epistemologically the factual is pre-theoretic.

It is our argument that the separability of residential preferences and objective characteristics, externalities, and privatised individuals searching in a detached manner for an enhanced 'quality of life' are concepts grounded in a world of appearances

Table 12.3: Neighbourhood Activism over Multi-Family Projects:
Columbus, Ohio, 1900-1980

Year	Ratio of Protests to Projects	Multi-Family Conflicts as % of All Neighbourhood Activism
1970-78	1:56	38.3
1960-68	1:41	32.2
1950-58	1:127	8.6
1940-48	1:220	10.0
1930-38	1:156	3.6
1920-28	1:815	3.0

generated, in turn, by the production relations of generalised
commodity production.[6] Object of knowledge and concepts,
therefore, are to be referred to a world of appearances ultimately
referable to relations of production: in this instance, generalised
commodity production. This, however, presents a problem since
most would assume generalised commodity production to date
back at least to the beginnings of the nineteenth century. It is the
argument of this paper, however, that the world of appearances
supporting both the object of knowledge of turf politics and the
conceptual apparatus through which it can be grasped does not
appear until the post-1945 period. Until then the concepts of
externality, preference function and the like had only very limited
applicability to specifically living place relations. This suggests that
the answer to our enigma — why turf politics and why the
particular concepts through which bourgeois social science has
attempted to understand it — must be referred to a delayed
extension of the relations of generalised commodity production to
the living place. It is to that possibility that we now turn.

The Emergence of Turf Politics

Necessary for the emergence of turf politics is the commodification
of the neighbourhood. [7] This allows people to relate to
neighbourhood as some*thing* from which others can be excluded.
At the same time, the separability of needs and 'objective'
characteristics wrought by the commodity relationship implies the

pervasiveness of externality effects; and it is the externality effects which become the arguments in residential preference functions once neighbourhood has in fact been commodified.

Commodification, however, while necessary for turf politics, is not sufficient. Given commodification as a background condition, the critical catalyst is the relation between needs and the ability to satisfy the needs of others through the provision of desirable externality effects. On the one hand, one can postulate a convergence in the needs which people feel for the 'objective' characteristics of neighbourhoods — social status, a certain aesthetic, good schools, for example; and on the other hand a spread in the degree to which people are able to provide the externalities satisfying the needs or preferences of others. Consequently, while everyone positively evaluates a certain type of neighbourhood above all others, not everyone can provide the externalities which will reproduce it as that type of neighbourhood for other residents.

Neighbourhood as a commodity, and externalities as political issues in the living place are, however, historical products. It is this which accounts for the historical character of the concepts through which social scientists have attempted to understand turf politics. We need to consider, therefore: the processes through which the neighbourhood becomes a commodity and, conversely, those processes which prevented its commodification for so long; and the processes through which needs converge on a common set of externalities while abilities to provide those externalities remain widely divergent. This will be done here through a consideration of the relation between capitalist development and the living place: it will involve both a general consideration of the contradictions labour has sought to resolve in the living place and the scope afforded such resolution by the separation of production from consumption processes; and an historical reconstruction of the changing relation to neighbourhood over the past eighty years or so. The first part of this section of the paper, therefore, considers the concepts of commodification of neighbourhood, externalities, and their relation to turf politics. The second part seeks to place these processes in the context of capitalist development.

Commodification, Externalities and Turf Politics

In relating to neighbourhood as a commodity, people are seen as, and experience themselves as, bringing certain pregiven preferences into contact with so-called 'objective' characteristics of neighbourhoods — quietness, good schools, public safety, etc. . These traits are traded off against one another according to a common scale of value enshrined in an individual preference function, and within a budget constraint, to yield a purchase or sale decision. This conception has received particular expression in property value studies (Ball, 1973), wherein all manner of objective characteristics receive dollar values based on regressions of home values upon diverse independent variables.

To the extent that neighbourhood is commodified, one relates to it therefore through individual needs experienced as separate from 'objective' characteristics. These objective characteristics may be regarded as 'social' in character (e.g., publicly safe, good schools) or 'physical': quiet with good views.[8] How one uses a particular set of objective characteristics is a function of purely *individual* needs: depending upon what one's needs are, one may (e.g.) alter the physical structure to obtain a better view, at the same time impeding the view of other residents; or, alternatively, convert it into a restaurant or souvenir shop. In other words, given the imperfect degree to which neighbourhood is commodifiable (Hooper, n.d.), relating to the neighbourhood as a commodity engenders a profusion of *externality effects*. And to the extent that *everyone* relates to the neighbourhood as a commodity, it will be the externality effects — of public behaviour, of children's peer groups, of private landscaping, etc. — which provide the arguments in preference functions.

The commodified neighbourhood should be contrasted with the case in which the social and physical characteristics of neighbourhoods are *not* sensed as separate from needs: the case in which, that is, people have an *at*tached rather than a *de*tached relation to neighbourhood. Webber has described it well in his description of the relation to neighbourhood in the traditional working class community:

> The physical place becomes an extension of one's ego. The outer worlds of neighbourhood-based peer groups, neighbourhood based family, and the *physical* neighbourhood place itself, seem to become internalised as inseparable aspects of one's inner perceptions of self. In the highly personalised life of the working-class neighbourhood, where one's experiences are largely limited to social contacts with

others who are but minutes away, the physical space and the physical buildings become reified as aspects of the social group. One's conception of himself and of his place in society is thus subtly merged with his conceptions of the spatially limited territory of limited social interaction (Webber, 1964, 63).

In other words, instead of the disunity between individual, society and place presupposed by commodification, there is a unity. The individual experiences the social bond as internal rather than external. Relations to others and to place are sensed as presuppositions for individual existence. Individual needs and living space experience are so intertwined and organically related that the very concept of 'preferences' and 'objective characteristics' as externally related lacks meaning. The individual can differentiate only with great difficulty between his needs and those of the specific others to whom he related in the living place. The notion of a separation of individual and society, and hence of an independent self, are only weakly developed.[9]

As a consequence, in the non-commodified neighbourhood the concept of 'externality' has little meaning. The individual does not differentiate between his needs and those of the community: to act on behalf of the community is to act on behalf of oneself and *vice versa*. Interestingly, the absence of an externality problem is often referred to as 'a strong sense of obligation' or 'the strength of social sanctions' in the traditional working class community. However, this is to fundamentally misread the character of such communities since it interprets them in terms of categories more appropriate to the disunity of individual and society — society as an external, dominating force, for instance — rather than in terms of categories appropriate to a more typical unity.

Commodification of the neighbourhood, therefore, implies some separation of the elements of a unity: individual, society and place or of individual, community and neighbourhood. Commodification, moreover, is prerequisite to turf politics. In order for turf politics to be possible, people have to relate to neighbourhood as a thing apart: a thing apart from their needs for specific use values, a thing apart from other neighbourhoods, and a thing apart from certain processes — developmental and planning — regarded as impacting on the neighbourhood in an external, non-necessary fashion. Only then can people conceive of space as a thing whose quantitative aspects (more or less respectable, more or less desirable as a place to bring up children, more or less safe) can be regulated by regulating the planning and developmental processes which, in turn, interact with the neighbourhood and determine the quantities relevant to people's use values. In other words, 'spatial fetishism' — conceiving of social relations as moulded by areal characteristics or spatial structure — is a necessary precondition for the emergence of a politics of turf. Only then do exclusionary policies become meaningful for those engaging in them.[10]

And secondly, commodification implies that not only do people relate to neighbourhood as a thing apart from other neighbourhoods and from their needs for specific use values but, equally important, they relate according to their *own individual* needs apart from the needs of others. This opens up the possibility of externality effects; and to the extent that those externality effects are negative in character, of a politics of turf.

The literature on turf politics is emphatic upon the central significance of externality effects. Conceptions such as those of Wingo (1973) and Williams (1971) see turf-based coalitions as regulating land use policy in accord with preferences for particular types of externalities. In geography, the locational conflict literature has given pride of place to the negative externality (Wolpert, 1970; Dear, Taylor and Hall, 1980; Robson, 1983).

Commodification, we have seen, contains within it the concept of externality effect and so makes a turf politics possible. It does not make it necessary, however. To the extent that people provide in the living place the same externality effects which they demand of others there can be no conflict, and, therefore, no politics of turf: people will cluster together and share out their (positive) externalities with each other without any necessity for the regulation of inflows and outflows, except insofar as economies of scale in the provision of public services are at issue. Locational issues emerge, however, when there is homogeneity in preference functions across households while the ability to provide the externalities demanded of others varies substantially.[11] It is at that point that turf politics becomes necessary rather than merely possible.

For example, one can postulate a not unrealistic situation in which all households chase status by desiring to reside in reputable neighbourhoods. A low status household in a high status neighbourhood, however, represents a negative externality to the high status households living there (Downs, 1973). Likewise with respect to the congestion issue. To the extent that people living in densely settled parts of the city desire to live in low density sections, the spaciousness of those neighbourhoods and their uncongested character for existing residents will be threatened. It is for reasons such as these, of course, that the politics of turf has acquired its redistributional reputation among liberals.[12]

Given commodification, therefore, the critical catalyst to a politics of turf is the emergence of the negative externality. This we have traced to a homogenisation of preferences for externalities in the context of variation in the ability to provide those self-same externalities. This homogenisation, however, like commodification, is an historical product. It is to an understanding of the processes through which these emerged that we turn next.

Capitalist Development and the Living Place

Our problem is to explain the historical emergence of the neighbourhood as commodified, and the homogenisation of needs for particular types of externality. Our approach is to examine the various ways in which capitalist production relations have affected living place experience. This is treated first in general terms by a scrutiny of the *possible* consequences of the capitalist mode for relations in the living place. This will set the stage for an understanding of the *actual* unfolding of events in the traditional working class community over the last eighty years or so.

In commodity production, use values are obtained only to the degree that one has an equivalent or an exchange value. People produce use values for exchange and relate to them as their own; the individual is free to dispose of them as he sees fit. This allows us to deduce, first, an orientation to exchange value since it is only through exchange value that use values can be obtained. And secondly, it establishes an indifference to specific buyers or sellers; commodity exchangers relate contingently rather than necessarily, according to whether or not the price is right. The buyer searches for that seller willing to accept the minimum price, just as the seller searches for that buyer willing to pay the maximum.

Under capitalism, commodity production is generalised so that labour power also becomes a commodity. This is because labour is separated from (i.e., does not own) the means of production and so must enter into an exchange relation with capitalists: the exchange of their labour power for a money wage. Labour power becomes a commodity, therefore, of which its owner cannot be divested by force: the labourer is free to enter into a contract with whatever capitalist he chooses. Likewise money capital is a commodity which the capitalist can use to hire whatever labourers *he* chooses.

Both wage labourer and capitalist have an orientation to exchange value. The ultimate goal, however, differs. For the labourer it is the exchange of the wage for the *use values* through which his labour power can be reproduced. For the capitalist it is *the accumulation of capital* (i.e., exchange value); without accumulation, continued ownership of the means of production is threatened and reduction to the position of wage labourer therefore more likely. Further, orientation to exchange value and voluntary divestment of property results in a mutual indifference of labourer and capitalist. The labourer is indifferent to who employs him so long as the wage is right. Likewise with respect to the capitalist; the only critical difference between wage labourers is the wage they are prepared to accept in exchange for making over control of their labour power.

Thus defined, the relations of production of the capitalist mode have certain critical implications for the process of reproduction of labour power; i.e., for those processes which in bourgeois society we normally associate with a living place spatially distinct from a workplace. These implications are: i) the separation of production from reproduction; ii) the contradiction between production and reproduction; iii) contradictions experienced in production which the worker seeks to resolve in the reproduction sphere. We consider each, briefly, in turn.

1.   Separation of Production from Reproduction: Under the capitalist mode of production, the production process is separated from the process of reproduction. While in production the worker sells his labour power to the captalist to do what he wants with it, the worker enjoys a freedom to dispose of the wage as he sees fit in the reproduction of his labour power. The individual capitalist, therefore, does not regard the reproduction of the labour power of any individual worker as a precondition of his captalist production; likewise the individual worker does not regard working for any particular capitalist as a precondition for reproducing his labour power. This is in contrast to, say, slavery where the slave owner relates to the slave as the inorganic condition of his own existence and must therefore reproduce the slave much as he reproduces other

inorganic conditions of his subjectivity such as farm animals or fruit trees.[13] Or alternatively, to subsistence farming, where production and reproduction are likewise sensed as mutually presupposing.

2. The Contradiction between Production and Reproduction: Needs, preferences, motivations of individuals are defined in and through the relations in which those same individuals stand to each other. It is the need of the capitalist to infinitely expand exchange value regardless of the consequences this might have for labourers *as a class* upon which capital *as a class* must ultimately depend: profit maximisation is the criterion of the individual capitalist regardless of the consequences this may have for the reproduction of labour power.

In the middle years of the nineteenth century, this was the background for concurrent debates over the length of the workday and public health. Successive extensions of the workday under the competitive pressures experienced by capitalists threatened the process through which labour power reproduced itself; labour was not given the time in which to reproduce, through rest and recuperation, its power to labour. The result was a progressively worsening wage labour crisis characterised by increased mortality rates and susceptibility to disease. Likewise, with respect to public health. Factory production made the crowding together of large masses of people highly profitable. And to the extent that capital could resist the need to spend money on improved housing, sanitation, and water supplies, profits would be further enhanced.

While legislation on workday length and public hygiene measures suspended these particular expressions of the contradiction, others remained. Low wages and infrequent work, poor health care, for example, made reproduction of the working class family a chronic problem. Only with the implantation of the welfare state did it seem as if some resolution had been attained.[14]

3. Contradictions in Production: In production itself, man experiences a number of contradictions which Marx defined as alienations. Thus man is alienated from himself, from his activity as a worker and from other men. Man is alienated from himself in that he relates to his activity as something that is external to himself and which is forced upon him by circumstances beyond his control. He is alienated from nature in that nature is

experienced as something external rather than a necessary
presuppostion for individual existence, and as something to
which man relates in the context of a labour process forced upon
him by conditions not of his own choosing. And finally, the
worker is alienated from his fellow men. They are not seen as
presuppositions for individual being through, say, a division of
labour in which people self-consciously work for each other.
Rather one relates to them externally as agents who through
their own activities force one to do things one would not
otherwise have done. They are experienced in other words as an
external, dominating force.

All these are instances of the alienation of man under capital
from his social being. The alienation of the product under
commodity exchange externalises the social bond as something
separate from the individual: as exchange value, money or capital it
dominates men, frustrates their socially defined purposes and
conceals from them the necessarily social character of themselves,
their activity, and of nature.

Endemic to the capitalist mode, therefore, are contradictions
within the sphere of production itself and between production and
reproduction. At the same time, production is separated from
reproduction. The history of capitalist development, however,
suggests that it is this very same separation of production from
reproduction that has allowed a resolution of sorts of these
contradictions.

In the first place one can see how relations of reproduction might
evolve to some degree separately from relations of production as a
solution to labour reproduction problems. It is widely recognised,
for example, that in contemporary South Africa, future generations
of labour power are reproduced not so much through wages
derived from commodity production. Rather, their reproduction
depends upon the working for subsistence of peasant plots held on
the basis of tribal membership. Damaris Rose (1981) has similarly
described the significance of small subsistence plots for the
reproduction of tin miners and their families in West Cornwall.
They may have been quite common in rural areas in the nineteenth
century,[15] though it was obviously not a solution which could be
resorted to in urban areas.

Secondly, it may well be that the separation of reproduction from
production permits a resolution of sorts of the alienations
experienced in the workplace; that is, they are resolved in the living

place. A number of writers, both marxist and non-marxist, have argued for this type of relationship. Noteworthy among these is David Harvey's explanation of the emergence of a certain concept of nature which divorces it from production: a conception of nature that has penetrated deeply into the consciousness of all segments of society and which 'conjure(s) up images of mountains and streams, seas and lakes, trees and green grass far from the coal face, the assembly line and the factory, where the real transformation of nature is continually being wrought' (1978, 27). Harvey is quite clear as to the relationship he sees between the remarkable allure of this image and workplace alienations:

> Industrial capitalism, armed with the factory system, organised the work process in a manner which transformed the relation between the worker and nature into a travesty of even its former, very limited self. Because the worker was reduced to a 'thing' so the worker became alienated from his or her product, from the manner of producing it, and, ultimately, from nature itself ... Faced with the brutalising and degrading routine of the work process in the factory, the workers themselves sought ways to ameliorate it. In part, they did so by resorting to the same mystifications of the bourgeoisie, and, thus, came to share a common Romantic image of nature (1978,26-27).

This goes a long way towards explaining the attractiveness of suburbia and what Werthman *et al.* have called the 'social class aesthetic'.[16] Similar arguments, however, have been used to explain the attractions of the nuclear family in its own home. The notion here is the familiar one of the family and home as 'haven in a heartless world'. To the extent that suburbanisation has been linked to child raising, owner-occupying families (Modell, 1979), its attractions have therefore received added impetus. With respect to the nuclear family, Young and Willmott have argued how its:

> ... advantages offset some of the disadvantages of the sort of society that technology has created. People who are not much valued by their employers, and are paid a wage that shows it, can still be valued at home, their bad and good qualities combining to make up a whole personality, in the round: not a machinist or a park-keeper, a solicitor or a sociologist, but a

person. Whether or not leisure activities are a compensation to people who do not fulfil themselves in their work, the family certainly is. As a multi-purpose institution ... it can provide some sense of wholeness and permanence to set against the more restricted and transitory roles imposed by the specialised institutions which have flourished outside the home. The upshot is that, as the disadvantages of the new industrial and impersonal society have become more pronounced, so has the family become more prized for its power to counteract them (1975,269).

Rakoff (1977) has presented arguments regarding the values of home ownership[17] and one can see additional directions in which the general logic could be extended. For example, the estrangement of the individual from his social being results in a crisis of personal significance: people no longer feel that their activities are either important or seen as important in the reproduction of society. They see themselves as working for themselves rather than for others and that is also how they see others seeing them. One way in which this contradiction has been resolved is by a redefinition of personal significance in terms of a status hierarchy: one feels significant to the degree to which one appropriates value and to the degree that it is recognised by others. And it is recognised in the reproduction sphere: in the house one lives in and the reputation of one's neighbourhood.[18]

All these responses, however — the Romantic image of nature, the pursuit of social significance through status, the family as haven in a heartless world — are fundamentally mystified. They are responses to the world of appearances rather than to the production relations which generate them: responses to the seeming separation of the natural from the social, of reproduction from production, and of individual from society. And they are, therefore, responses contained within that world of appearances and within those production relations: 'Nature' becomes an object of consumption which the commodity form can penetrate; neighbourhood in its social aspects becomes a vehicle by which the career prospects of the children of so-called child-centred families can be advanced, etc. The result is consequently a reproduction of the alienations to which Romantic images of nature, and the 'symmetric family' (Young and Wilmott, 1975) were responses and a sense of frustration and inadequacy with the responses themselves ('the sterility of the suburbs', 'the problem of the family', etc.).[19]

In sum, we have seen how capitalism divorces production from reproduction. At the same time, it engenders a contradiction between production and reproduction and an alienation of man from his necessary sociality. The divorce of production from reproduction, however, facilitates resolution of the production/reproduction contradiction through the development of relations of reproduction at variance with relations of production; we might envisage in this context the retention of pre-capitalist social relations in the reproduction sphere. Likewise, the divorce of production from reproduction allows some resolution in the living place, albeit in a mystified manner, of the alienations experienced in the workplace. These propositions now allow us to fashion a more specific argument regarding the delayed commodification of the living place and the concomitant delay in the homogenisation of neighbourhood preferences. We do so in historically specific terms by examining the character and development of the traditional working class communities so widespread in North American and in Western European cities at the beginning of this century: the community form dubbed here 'the classic community'.

My argument is that as a result of the contradiction between production and reproduction, and the separation of the production sphere from the reproduction sphere, the commodity form did *not* initially penetrate the relations of reproduction to the same degree as it did the relations of production. In particular, and for the working class, pre-capitalist elements assumed an importance in the relations of reproduction: this is associated above all with the role in the reproduction of labour of mutual aid structured by the extended family. This 'solution' to the reproduction problem, however, brought the relations of production and reproduction into contradiction with each other: worker alienation deriving from the workplace could not be resolved in the living place due to its non-commodified form. However, a *new* resolution of the production/reproduction contradiction in the form of the welfare state *does* allow the commodification of neighbourhood and the emergence of those responses which Harvey (1978), Young and Wilmott (1975), Rakoff (1977) and others have identified. In the late nineteenth century most working class people — and most people were working class — related to each other in the living place through necessary, highly particularised relations of personal dependence. These relations were kin relations within an extended family. They contrast with the social relations characteristic of the commodity form: relations of a contingent, personally independent, abstractly universal character.[20]

The material basis for the significance of the extended family was mutual aid. Mutual aid, in turn, stemmed from the chronic and pervasive material insecurity of the working class: ill health, periodic unemployment, an old age without pensions, necessitated some form of primitive insurance; i.e., mutual aid was an attempt to resolve the production/reproduction contradiction.[21]

The social vehicle chosen can be regarded as pre-capitalist in character. In pre-capitalist social formations people depend for access to the means of production upon specific others: access to tribal hunting grounds, for example, is mediated by membership of the tribe. In this instance, however, what we have is people depending to a very considerable degree upon specific others — their respective extended families — for access to the means of *re*production. In other words the contradiction between production and reproduction was resolved, at least in part, by the exploitation of a pre-capitalist form of social relationship: mutual aid within an extended family.

Pre-capitalist social relations engender a unity of individual, society, and place. This case is no exception. Given the uniqueness and non-substitutability of a person's extended family, these relations have a necessary quality to them. Extended families are not traded off against one another in the same way that one trades off one employer against another. The extended family is sensed as a necessary presupposition for individual being in a way in which the individual capitalist is not, and cannot be.

Within the extended family, people exist for each other in terms of concrete use values: they are imprisoned, in Marx's terms, within a certain definition of themselves. Children are socialised into the role of looking after parents when they retire; sisters into helping each other clothe their children through hand-me-downs. These roles are allocated by tradition rather than chosen by people relating to each other as abstract values. The identity of individual and society — the extended family as necessary presupposition for, and product of, one's individual activity — is thereby reaffirmed.

Pre-capitalist communities are characterised not only by a unity of individual and society but by a unity of individual and nature; it is, after all, through membership of a specific community that one obtains access to the means of production. Hence, just as the individual has no sense of self apart from a specific community, so he/she has no sense of self apart from the specific locale of that community: a specific place in terms of means of production and of reproduction is as much a presupposition of his being as the community he belongs to. And community is sensed as much a place as that place is a community.[22]

It is in these terms that it becomes possible to understand the attachment of the traditional working class to what must to bourgeois eyes seem the most depressing of physical environments: unrelieved, streetscapes, corner shops, views of distant chimneys, shipyard gantries and slag heaps, or atmospheres pervaded by the smell of coal tar. In a study of the steel town of Middlesborough at the turn of the century it was observed:

> Many of the dwellers in the place have as deeply rooted an attachment to it as though it were a beautiful village. There are people living in these hard-looking, shabby, ugly streets, who have been there for many years and more than one who has left it has actually pined to be back again.

And she adds, groping for an explanation:

> It is not, after all, every man or woman who is susceptible to scenery and to the outward aspect of the world around him; there are many who are nourished by human intercourse rather than by natural beauty (Bell, 1907, 126).

It was this local attachment, embedded in pre-capitalist relations of reproduction which, I am arguing, provided the critical obstacle to commodification of the living place; and at the same time, therefore, inhibited conceptualisation of that externalised social bond in terms appropriate to a resolution of workplace alienations. This is not to say, however, that all in the traditional working class community felt the same degree of identity of self with society. Marx noted, for example, that it is at the boundary of pre-capitalist communities that people begin to relate to each other as personally independent, in a contingent and external rather than necessary, internal fashion, and in abstractly universal rather than in concretely particular ways.

The obvious place to look for these relations is the capitalist workplace. Here the indifference of the commodity relation provided a sense of the externality of the social bond, at the same time posing the problem of resolving that contradiction in a manner consistent with their production relations. Yet the point here is that for most women there were no such relations. They were confined to the sphere of reproduction. Accordingly it is among the women of the traditional working class community that we should expect to find the most intense identification with community and with neighbourhood. What evidence we have suggests that this was so.[23] Conversely, it is to men that we should look for signs of a weakening of the unity of individual and society and the emergence of a sense of the social bond as external and manipulable in accord with a vision of the private life designed to counter the alienations of the workplace (Young and Wilmott, 1975, 93). It may also be in these terms that we can understand the strength of the daughter-mother bond in the traditional working class community as opposed to, say, that of the son-father or son-mother bond.

This suggests a contradiction between relations of production and relations of reproduction felt more severely by some than by others. What provides the possibility for resolving the contradiction is a new resolution of the original contradiction between production and reproduction. This assumes the twin forms of the welfare state and women's work. In turn, it allows the breakup of the extended family and the commodification of the neighbourhood. We consider in turn, therefore, the role of the labour movement and of the women's movement in the disintegration of a unity in the sphere of reproduction.

1. The Labour Movement: The welfare state is critical in facilitating the disintegration of the extended family and allowing full weight to privatising impulses nurtured in the workplace: old age pensions, unemployment compensation and aid for dependents, as in family allowance policies or the American Aid to Families with Dependent Children, and some measure of assistance in health care, all greatly reduce the need for mutual aid and therefore dependence upon the extended family. The scope of these measures varies from one country to another as does their timing. They can all be traced, however, either to the platforms of the direct political representatives of the labour movement, as in the British Labour Party, or to those of liberal reform parties — such as the US Democratic Party — supported by organised labour.

Some have noted that the redistributional element in these programmes has been very modest. Rather, they represent a redistribution within income strata, perhaps between those at different stages in the life cycle.[24] It seems not unfair, therefore, to regard the welfare state as the formalisation, and securing on an actuarially sounder basis, of that mutual aid mechanism which the working class has developed in their struggle against material uncertainty. At any rate, its significance for us is that by eliminating the need for more informal types of mutual aid it released the nuclear family from dependence on an extended family.

2. The Women's Movement: Complementing the effects of the labour movement has been the women's movement. Crucially, emancipation has brought women out of the living place and into the workplace. In 1900 only 20 per cent of women went out to work; the proportion of married women going out to work was much lower. By 1977 this had increased to 49 per cent, the larger part of this increase (from 29 per cent) occurring since 1940 (Kolko, 1978). Since the war, the rate of increase has been especially marked among married women and among women of the working class; i.e., precisely among those groups in the population who one might have expected to be most immersed in the traditional, particularistic, and localised working-class community.

One significant consequence of this has been an additional contribution to amelioration of the reproduction problem of the working class.[25] Additionally, however, has been its effect upon consciousness. Immersion in the world of the commodity has prised women away from that sense of unity between themselves and society, weakened their identification with a local community and externalised the social bond: the critical prerequisite for commodification.

With the deliquescence of mutual aid and, therefore, the material basis for dependence on an extended family, the way lay open for the disintegration of the unity of individual, community and neighbourhood. Neighbourhood could now be commodified for the working class and free rein given to those privatising impulses aimed at resolving in the living place the alienations experienced in the workplace. The pursuit of status, privacy, the Arcadian ideal, and the family as haven in a heartless world was now generalised. It was in this context that turf politics became not only possible but also necessary.

Of course suburbanisation of the middle class in the nineteenth and first half of the twentieth century had been substantial. It was, as others have recognised, part of an attempt to get away from a central city that was increasingly working class and given over to production (Walker, 1978). Until after 1945 these retreats were relatively secure from threat. Only with the privatisation of living place relations for the working class do the suburbs come under seige from those who, likewise, are seeking a retreat — yet who were themselves unable to contribute towards providing the sort of retreat middle class residents were looking for. Moreover, the working class was by no means homogeneous in terms of its ability to provide externalities in the living place in terms of public safety and social status. There is, in other words, a stratification of the working class which yields a politics of turf quite as intense as that which pits middle class resident against working class newcomer.

Conclusions

In the 1960s and 1970s there appeared in the social sciences a literature dealing with turf-based politics: a politics of experiential environments in the living place. The phenomenal basis for this appeared virtually simultaneously. This is true both in terms of the object of knowledge pursued by students of the politics of turf, and in terms of the concepts through which understanding of that object of knowledge was sought. These concepts included those of: 'residential preference functions'; 'objective characteristics of neighbourhoods'; the separation of objective characteristics from preference functions; 'neighbourhood externalities'; and the interrelation of mobility and coalitional forms of residential action. In other words, there were changes in the way people related to the living place which supported both the idea of a politics of turf and the concepts through which the social sciences attempted to come to terms with it.

We have sought an explanation of these changes in the commodification of the neighbourhood and an associated homogenisation in the sorts of neighbourhoods people were looking for. Although these processes had worked themselves out for the middle class long before 1945, this was by no means true of the working class. Rather, for the working class instead of the disunity of individual, community and neighbourhood presupposed by commodification and residential negative externalities, there was a unity. Neighbourhood and community were sensed as internal rather than external to the individual. In traditional working class communities residential preference functions, objective character-istics of neighbourhoods and externality effects had, therefore, no reality in everyday experience. Behavioural forms supported notions neither of a politics of turf nor of the concepts through which understanding of a politics of turf has subsequently been sought.

The unity of individual, community, and neighbourhood we have traced to mutual aid through an extended family which was necessitated, in turn, by the severe material insecurity faced by the working class. Only with the elimination of the need for mutual aid, consequent to the achievements of the labour movement and of the women's movement, does dependence on an extended family in the reproductive sphere disappear. This makes possible the commodification of the neighbourhood and affords to the working class the opportunity of resolving workplace alienations in the living place in the same, albeit mystified, manner as the middle class before them. What is a resolution for the working class, however, is a threat to middle class suburban retreats. It is here, given the commodification of the neighbourhood, that we have sought the critical catalyst for a politics of turf.

Primary for bourgeois social science is the category of experience. At the level of the object of knowledge it is this which makes it appear as 'relevant' to its supporters and so ·'faddish' to its detractors. At the level of concepts it means that, since it is the same world which is being experienced, the categories employed merely mimic, perhaps in a slightly more abstracted form, the categories through which agents in the real world — real residents and real neighbourhood activists — attempt to make sense of events around them. What I have attempted to do in this paper, however, is to demonstrate that experience is not enough: that underlying the events which bougeois social scientists define as co-extensive with the real are hidden generative mechanisms. These generative mechanisms are the relations through which people come together to produce and reproduce their material life. They are apparent neither to the agents involved nor to the social scientists; but when postulated, they are able to explain both those events *and* bourgeois social science.

Acknowledgements

The research on which this paper is based is supported by a grant from the National Science Foundation (SES-8112324). This support is gratefully acknowledged.

Notes.

1. For reasons of readability, I have not stuck rigidly to the 'he/she' convention. Except in those instances where context indicates otherwise, 'he' should be taken to mean 'he/she'.

2. A good review of a number of these is provided by Ball (1973).

3. For example, Janelle (1977), Ley and Mercer (1980) and Robson (1983).

4. Procedures are discussed in greater detail in Sutcliffe (1982).

5. Only protests were included in examining the intensity of neighbourhood activism because of both problems in the reporting of neighbourhood meetings *and* the decrease in petitions for urban services consequent to the introduction of a capital improvements programme.

6. This is not a point which will be expanded on further in this paper. For further elaboration, see Bologh (1979, Chapter 3).

7. 'Neighbourhood' cannot be in the strict marxist sense a commodity since it cannot be regarded as the objectification of human labour; it cannot, therefore, have a value. However, '[T]hings which in and for themselves are not commodities can be offered for sale by their holders, and thus acquire the form of commodities through their price' (Marx, 1976, 197).

8. Hence, not only is society grasped as separate from the individual, the physical is grasped as separate from the social.

9. This is a major conclusion in another study of a traditional working class community, that by Gans (1962).

10. Case study evidence suggests that the spatial imaginations that develop in the context of embracing spatial fetishism can show considerable subtlety and sophistication. Neighbourhoods or local government jurisdictions, for example, are often seen as in competition for 'desirable' residents (Wolf and Lebeaux, 1969; Molotch, 1972), the 'thin end of the wedge' implied by a low income housing project, say, upsetting whatever spatial equilibrium exists and touching off massive and localised neighbourhood change. It may well be that here lies the true significance of the widely noted concern of residential households for property values when confronted with some threat to the neighbourhood: rather than indicating a concern for the value of one's own house, it expresses concern for that equilibrium in the local housing market which maintains existing use values; i.e., one is not so much concerned with the value of one's own house as with the values of houses in the neighbourhood in general since they determine who one's neighbours are likely to be in the future and hence one's use values.

11. Bruce Hamilton, for example, has used this idea as a rationale for zoning and a concomitant critique of Tiebout: ' ... in the absence of the [zoning] constraints which will be built into my model, the Tiebout Hypothesis seems to be a formula for musical suburbs, with the poor following the rich in a never-ending quest for a tax base' (Hamilton, 1975, 205).

12. Smolensky and Gomery (n.d.) clearly see this when they argue for increased income equality as a means of creating a more spatially compact city.

13. The term 'inorganic' is used in the sense Marx uses it in his discussion in the *Grundrisse* of pre-capitalist social formations. For example: ' ... just as the working

subject appears naturally as an individual, as natural being — so does the first objective condition of his labour appear as nature, earth, as his inorganic body; he himself is not only the organic body, but also the subject of this inorganic nature. This condition is not his product but something he finds to hand — presupposed to him as a natural being apart from him' (1973, 488). And: 'In the relations of slavery and serfdom ... one part of society is treated by the other as itself merely an inorganic and natural condition of its own reproduction. The slave stands in no relation whatsoever to the objective conditions of his labour; rather, labour itself, both in the form of the slave and in that of the serf is classified as an inorganic condition of production along with other natural beings, such as cattle, as an accessory of the earth' (1973, 489).

14. I say 'seem' since many would argue that the contradiction has merely been displaced into the political sphere where it appears as a conflict between the demands of capital for government spending and/or reduced taxation aimed at enhancing accumulation and the demands of labour for use values provided through the welfare state.

15. See, for example, the evidence adduced by Mair (1982).

16. By 'social class aesthetic' Werthman *et al.* signify a cluster of elements in the physical environment symbolising the socio-economic status of the residents. This includes: trees, hills and views; quiet cul-de-sacs; tree-lined curved streets; underground utilities; well-kept lawns; and a separation of residential from commercial and industrial facilities.

17. In his discussion of the meanings of homeownership, Rakoff has emphasised 'the importance of the individual's increasing search for a realm of personal control in a world where he or she generally feels impotent' (1977, 101).

18. There appears to be, in fact, a general tendency to use residential location as a shorthand for social status. A study of stratification in Kansas City concluded that '[r]esidential address was considered [by respondents] the quickest index to a family's social status — the foremost sign of the breadwinner's financial competence and his or his wife's social ambitions' (Coleman and Neugarten, 1971, 30).

19. I realise that the argument recounted in the paragraphs immediately above raises a number of thorny issues around the marxist conception of human nature. Marx argued that the essence of man was his character as a social being: his nature was defined by the social relations in which he found himself and which he reproduced and transformed. Yet in the instances I have identified above there is a sense of a pre-social impulse towards an unalienated relation with other men, with oneself and with nature. Nor is this sense of the problem confined to the writers I have referred to. Harvey, for example, draws heavily upon Raymond Williams who sees capitalism as divorcing a 'necessary materialism' from a 'necessary humanity' and producing a 'conflict of impulses' (p. 297). This is clearly a very large issue which needs to be examined in its own right. It is interesting to note, however, that Marx himself comes very close to a formulation in terms of an impulse towards the establishment of unalienated relations:

> Firstly, the fact that labour is *external* to the worker, i.e., does not belong to his essential being; that he therefore does not confirm himself in his work, but denies himself, feels miserable and not happy, does not develop free mental and physical energy, but mortifies his flesh and ruins his mind. Hence, the worker feels himself only when he is not working; when he is working, he does not feel himself. He is at home when he is not working, and not at home when he is working. His labour is therefore not voluntary but forced, it is *forced labour*. It is therefore not the satisfaction of a need but a mere *means* to satisfy needs outside itself. Its alien character is clearly demonstrated by the fact that as soon as no physical or other compulsion exists, it is shunned like

the plague. External labour, labour in which man alienates himself, is a labour of self-sacrifice, of mortification (Marx, 1975, 326).

And:

> [T]he result is that man (the worker) feels that he is acting freely only in his animal functions — eating, drinking and procreating, or at most in his dwelling and adornment — while in his human functions he is nothing more than an animal (Marx, 1975, 327).

20. For an excellent account of contrasting social relations in capitalist and pre-capitalist social formations based on Marx's *Grundrisse*, see Gould (1980, Chapter 1).

21. The extended family has very substantial advantages over mere friends and neighbours. An enduring mutual aid relation- ship depends upon social control. In a context of generalised commodity production in the workplace people must have felt the attractions of throwing off the domination of a larger group, particularly when personal fortunes were on the rise. There had to be a sanctioning mechanism to discourage such backsliding: the extended family was a more effective mechanism in this regard than an ad hoc group of neighbours since neighbours can always detach themselves from the communication network through which control is exerted (e.g. by relocation): relatives are much less easy to escape.

22. Much of the intractability of the neighbourhood-community relationship encountered in the literature on community may stem from the inability to recognise precisely this unity and to theorise its disintegration.

23. Consider, for example, the evidence which Young and Wilmott (1957,Chapter 9) bring together on the reactions of home-bound women to leaving a traditional working class community.

24. 'Social security contributions in most welfare states tend to be either regressive, by requiring a flat rate payment, or proportional to income. The effect of this is to impose a relatively greater burden on lower-income groups than does direct taxation. It seems to be the case that much of the redistribution which does take place is of a 'horizontal' rather than a 'vertical' kind. That is, it is contributions from groups like the young or the unmarried which are largely subsidising payments to the sick or the elderly or those with large families. It is in other words, a form of 'life cycle' transfer, which does not necessarily entail much movement of resources from one *social class* to another' (Parkin, 1972, 125).

25. ... the rise of the working class woman was a direct response to the inability of the traditional male-dominated working class to thrive and meet its obligations with its own participation alone ... Post-war American prosperity was not the consequence of the traditionally male-dominated working class's rising fortunes so much as that class's capacity to find solutions to problems which it could not resolve with traditional means' (Kolko, 1978, 274).

References

Agnew, J.A. (1978) 'Market relations and locational conflict in cross-national perspective', in K.R. Cox, (ed.) *Urbanization and Conflict in Market Societies,* Methuen, Inc., New York, 128-143

Ball, M.J. (1973) 'Recent empirical work on the determinants of relative house prices', *Urban Studies,* 10, 213-233

Baron, H.M. (1971) 'Race and status in school spending: Chicago, 1961-66', *Journal of Human Resources,* 6, 3-24

Bell, F. (1907) *At the Works: A Study of a Manufacturing Town,*

Bish, R.L. and V. Ostrom (1976) 'Understanding urban government: metropolitan reform', in H. Hochman, (ed.), *The Urban Economy,* W.W. Norton, New York, 95-117

Bologh, R.W. (1979) *Dialectical Phenomenology: Marx's Method,* Routledge and Kegan Paul, London

Coleman, R.P., and B.L. Neugarten (1971) *Social Status in the City,* Jossey Bass., San Francisco

Cox, K.R. (1973) *Conflict, Power and Politics in the City: A Geographic View,* McGraw-Hill, New York

Cox, K.R., and J. McCarthy (1980) 'Neighborhood activism in the American city: behavioral relations and evaluation', *Urban Geography,* **1,** 22-38

Cox, K.R., and F.Z. Nartowicz (1980) 'Jurisdictional fragmentation in the American metropolis: alternative perspectives', *International Journal of Urban and Regional Research,* **4,** 196-211

Danielson, M.N. (1972) 'Differentiation, segregation and political fragmentation in the American metropolis', in A.E.K. Nash, (ed.), *Governance and Population: Governmental Implications of Population Change,* US Government Printing Office, Washington D.C., 143-176

Danielson, M.N. (1976) *The Politics of Exclusion,* Columbia University Press, New York

Davies, B. (1968) *Social Needs and Resources in Local Services,* Michael Joseph, London

Dear, M., S.M. Taylor, and G.B. Hall (1980) 'External effects of mental health facilities', *Annals, Association of American Geographers,* **70,** 342-52

Downs, A., and R.J. Monsen (1971) 'Public goods and private status', *The Public Interest,* **23,** 64-76

Downs, A. (1973) *Opening Up the Suburbs,*   *Yale University Press, New Haven and London*

Gans, H. (1962) *The Urban Villagers,* The Free Press, New York

Gould, C. (1980) *Marx's Social Ontology: Individuality and Community in Marx's Theory of Social Reality,* MIT Press, Cambridge, Mass.

Hamilton, B.W. (1975) 'Zoning and property taxation in a system of local governments', *Urban Studies,* **12,** 205-11

Hamilton, B.W., E.S. Mills, and D. Puryear (1975) 'The Tiebout hypothesis and residential income segregation', in E.S. Mills and W.E. Oates, (eds.), *Fiscal Zoning and Land Use Controls,* Lexington Books, Lexington, Mass.

Harvey, D. (1973) *Social Justice and the City,* Edward Arnold, London

Harvey, D. (1978) 'Labor, capital and class struggle around the built environment in advanced capitalist societies', in K.R. Cox, (ed.), *Urbanization and Conflict in Market Societies,* Methuen, Inc., New York, 9-37

Hooper, A. (n.d.) *Class, Coalition and Community,* unpublished ms., Department of Land Management, Reading University, Reading, England

Janelle, D. (1977) 'Structural dimensions in the geography of locational conflicts', *Canadian Geographer,* **21,** 311-28

Knox, P.L. (1983) 'Residential structure, facility location and patterns of accessibility', in K.R. Cox and R.J. Johnston, (eds.), *Conflict, Politics and the Urban Scene,* St. Martin's Press, New York, 62-87

Kolko, G. (1978) 'Working wives: their effects on the structure of the working class', *Science and Society,* **42,** 257-277

Ley, D., and J. Mercer (1980) 'Locational conflict and the politics of consumption', *Economic Geography,* **56,** 89-109

Mair, A.J. (1982) *Urbanism and Locality, Capitalism and the Form of the Welfare Function,* unpublished paper presented at the annual meeting of the Association of American Geographers, San Antonio

Marx, K. (1973) *Grundrisse,* Penguin Books, Harmondsworth, Middlesex

Marx, K. (1975) *Early Writings,* Penguin Books, Harmondsworth, Middlesex

Marx, K. (1976) *Capital, Volume 1,* Penguin Books, Harmondsworth, Middlesex

Maser, S.M., W.H. Riker, and R.N. Rosett (1977) 'The effects of zoning and externalities on the price of land: an empirical analysis of Monroe County, New York', *The Journal of Law and Economics,* **20,** 111-32

Modell, J. (1979) 'Suburbanization and change in the American family', *Journal of Interdisciplinary History,* **9,** 621-646

Molotch, H. (1972) *Managed Integration: Dilemmas of Doing Good in the City,* University of California Press, Berkeley and Los Angeles

Neenan, W.B. (1972) *Political Economy of Urban Areas,* Markham Publishing Company, Chicago

Neiman, M. (1975) 'From Plato's philosopher king to Bish's tough purchasing agent: The premature public choice paradigm', *Journal of the American Institute of Planners,* **41,** 55-73

Newton, K. (1975) 'American urban politics: social class, political structure and public goods', *Urban Affairs Quarterly,* **11,** 241-64

Orbell, J.M., and T. Uno (1972) 'A theory of neighborhood problem solving: political action vs. residential mobility', *American Political Science Review,* **61,** 471-89

Ostrom, V., C. Tiebout, and R. Warren (1961) 'The organization of government in metropolitan areas', *American Political Science Review,* **55,** 831-42

Pack, H., and J.R. Pack (1977) 'Metropolitan fragmentation and suburban homogeneity', *Urban Studies,* **14,** 191-201

Parkin, F. (1972) *Class Inequality and Political Order,* Paladin Books, St. Albans, Herts

Pinch, S. (1979) 'Territorial justice in the city: a case study of the social services for the elderly in Greater London', in D.T. Herbert and D.M. Smith, (eds.), *Social Problems and the City,* Oxford University Press, Oxford, 201-233

Rakoff, R.M. (1977) 'Ideology in everyday life: the meaning of the house', *Politics and Society,* **7,** 85-104

Robson, B.T. (1983) 'The Bodley barricade: social space and social conflict', in K.R. Cox and R.J. Johnston, (eds.), *Conflict, Politics and the Urban Scene,* St. Martin's Press, New York, 45-61

Rose, D. (1981) *Home-Ownership and Industrial Change: The Struggle for a 'Separate Sphere',* Working Paper in Urban and Regional Studies, School of Social Sciences, University of Sussex, Brighton, England

Saunders, P. (1979) *Urban Politics: A Sociological Interpretation,* Hutchinson Books, London

Smolensky, E., and J.D. Gomery (n.d.) *The Urban Problem as an Exercise in the Theory of Efficient Transfers,* Discussion Paper, 100-171, Institute for Research on Poverty, University of Wisconsin, Madison, Wisconsin

Sutcliffe, M.O. (1982) *Local Political Activism in the American City: Columbus, Ohio, 1900-1980,* unpublished paper presented at the annual meeting of the Association of American Geographers, San Antonio

Tiebout, C. (1956) 'A pure theory of local expenditures', *Journal of Political Economy,* **64,** 416-24

Walker, R.S. (1978) 'The transformation of urban structure in the nineteenth century and the beginnings of suburbanization', in K.R. Cox, (ed.), *Urbanization and Conflict in Market Societies,* Methuen, Inc., New York, 165-212

Webber, M.M. (1964) 'Culture, territoriality and the elastic mile', *Papers and Proceedings of the Regional Science Association,* **13,** 59-69

Webster, B., and J. Stewart (1974) 'The area analysis of resources', *Policy and*

Politics, 3, 5-16

Werthman, C., Mandel, and T. Dienstfrey (1965) *Planning the Purchase Decision: Why People Buy in Planned Communities,* Center for Planning and Development Research, Institute of Urban and Regional Development, University of California at Berkeley, Berkeley,California, **Preprint 10**

Williams, O.P. (1971) *Metropolitan Political Analysis,* The Free Press, New York

Williams, O.P., and K. Eklund (1978) 'Segregation in a fragmented context: 1950-1970', in K.R. Cox, (ed.), *Urbanization and Conflict in Market Societies,* Methuen, Inc., New York, 213-228

Williams, R. (1973) *The Country and the City,* Chatto and Windus, London

Wingo, L. (1973) 'The quality of life: toward a microeconomic definition', *Urban Studies,* **10,** 3-18

Wolf, E.P., and C.N. Lebeaux (1969) *Change and Renewal in an Urban Community,* Praeger, New York

Wolpert, J. (1970) 'Departures from the usual environment in locational analysis', *Annals, Association of American Geographers,* **60,** 220-229

Young, K., and J. Kramer (1978) 'Local exclusionary policies in Britain: the case of suburban defense in a metropolitan system', in K.R. Cox, (ed.), *Urbanization and Conflict in Market Societies,* Methuen, Inc., New York, 229-251

Young, M., and P. Wilmott (1957) *Family and Kinship in East London,* Penguin Books, Harmondsworth, Middlesex

Young, M., and P. Wilmott (1975) *The Symmetrical Family,* Penguin Books, Harmondsworth, Middlesex

13

Neighbourhood Participation, Political Demand Making and Local Outputs in British and North American cities

Alan Burnett

Introduction

In all societies there are channels of access and communication through which citizens attempt to influence the decisions and actions of public authorities. Such channels are the mechanisms that link the governors to the governed, the political elite to the populace as a whole. Whether the channels are institutionalised or informal, there is evidence that they exist in all political systems, even those which are considered to be closed (Oliver, 1968). This chapter focuses on non-electoral political transactions (i.e. *political demands*) and is concerned with the causes and effects of localised political involvement in British and North American cities.

In the terminology of systems analysis, the chapter is both a study of environmental inputs (i.e. demands) into local political systems and of political outputs. It includes the processes of aggregation and articulation of political demands, and the means by which they are processed and sometimes converted into official decisions. Three key concepts and their causal interrelationships will be investigated — *neighbourhood participation, political demand making* and *local outputs*. Clearly, the links between these central variables are complex. demand making will be considered as both an independent and dependent variable. An attempt will be made to explain intra-urban variations in demand making with reference to, first, the neighbourhood environmental characteristics and imposed constraints and, second, the opportunities offered by political economy and national culture. In addition, political demands are considered as one explanatory variable in the allocation of municipal resources including public services.

In terms of scope, this chapter is limited to political pressure activities which have a 'neighbourhood' referent, i.e. neighbourhood organisations and localised protest groups are considered but not individual, particularised contacting or pressure groups with a wider spatial referent. A number of explicit environmental and spatial considerations are then examined e.g. whether the question of 'neighbourhood' problems are a prerequisite for such localised political activism and, if so, the kind of issues that arise in different parts of the city and involve otherwise apolitical citizens in active involvement. The undoubted importance of non-spatial factors in explaining social and spatial patterns of political participation (notably socio-economic status) notwithstanding, the chapter explores the precise impact of residential location. Issues such as whether the concept of distance decay operates in relation to localised threats to neighbourhood amenity and the resulting patterns of participation are considered. There are also important questions to be answered in relation to the intra-authority distribution of public allocations in the form of municipal services, expenditure, regulative controls and symbolic behaviour.

This chapter does not adopt any *one* theoretical standpoint for it is evident that several well-established social science paradigms are applicable to a study of this theme — systems theory; public choice theories; organisational and managerialist theory; critical/neo-Marxist theory. Each approach asks different questions and may provide contrasted interpretations.

Key Concepts — Neighbourhood Participation, Political Demand Making and Municipal Outputs

The substantial work of Verba and Nie (1972) provides a convenient starting point for a discussion of citizen participation. They defined political participation as 'instrumental activity through which citizens attempt to influence the government to act in ways which are preferred' (p.26). Four modes of participation are distinguished — voting, campaigning, individual contacting and communal activity. These are analysed on the basis of four dimensions — type of influence, amount of initiative required, scope of outcome expected and degree of conflict involved. Their classification of participants is sixfold — totally inactive, totally active, voting specialists, campaigners, parochial activists and communalists.

Groups of citizens bring their grievances, wishes, needs and preferences to the attention of those in authority between, as well as at, elections. They form and join neighbourhood associations, protest groups, raise petitions, threaten and/or take legal action, give evidence at public inquiries, attend council and committee meetings, withhold payments, demonstrate and riot, privately contact councillors and officials, and write letters to newspapers.

There is a measure of agreement evident in identification of the routes and targets for participation between elections. It is aimed at authoritative decision-makers — elected and appointed — and is concerned with extracting benefits by way of resources and regulations. Of course, some urban residents do have other options open to them. If they are dissatisfied with their home environments or are adversely affected by public plans, proposals or policies, under certain circumstances, a change of residential location may be seen as an alternative to raising their political voice (Orbell and Uno, 1973; Cox and McCarthy, 1980).

Political participation for the purposes of this study will be defined as citizen demand making which attempts to influence public authoritative allocations. More specifically, neighbourhood participation has also been variously defined: 'Local groups organised on a geographical basis concerning themselves with ways of improving their areas' (Lamb, 1976, p, and128), and 'Mechanisms whereby residents pool resources and share costs to solve common problems and secure collective benefits' (O'Brien, 1976, p.75). Residents of urban neighbourhoods, postulates Rich (1980, p.571), 'share a number of interests; they enjoy (suffer) the same quality of municipal services, use the same public facilities, are affected by each other's actions and those of public authorities'. Neighbourhood associations are conceptualised by the same author as 'institutions used by persons who identify themselves as members of a neighbourhood to promote interests they share in a residential location' (p.562). Gifford describes such organisations as 'geographically concentrated interest groups' (1978, p.94). The adjective 'neighbourhood' for the purposes of this analysis, means intra-urban, small scale, localised and spatially concentrated. No assumptions are made about the existence or otherwise of local urban 'communities' of whatever size, shape or composition.

When using the term neighbourhood political participation, we are referring to *both* formally constituted *neighbourhood associations* and informal groupings of neighbouring residents. These latter groups will be termed *protest groups*, i.e. 'groups of citizens who under certain conditions ... organise on an informal issue-specific basis to make demands on public officials through pressure processes' (Schumaker, 1975). These are the 'extra' groups analysed by Steggart (1975) in American cities emerging in response to more specific threats and disappearing when the issues have been resolved. Neighbourhood participation, therefore, is part of what Knox (1982) has called the 'parapolitical structure' and implies localised collective political action which is concerned with issues affecting housholds in or near their place of residence.

Political demand making is clearly a complex and multifaceted process. In systems analysis, political demands were originally visualised as one form of environmental input into political systems. Since then, many elaborations have been made in definitions of the concept. Cornelius (1974, p.1126) sees political demands as 'needs whose satisfaction is felt to depend upon government action and which are asserted by groups as specific claims on government', and defines them as 'collective activities aimed at extracting certain benefits from a political system by influencing the decisions of government officials'. Here, we are not concerned with *consumer demand* in the sense of potential or actual use of public services, but with the 'wants of people that have been sufficiently pressing to be articulated and which have found their way to the authorities' (Whitney, 1969, p.12) and, in particular, with the the aggregation, articulation and response processes involved. More open forms of demand making have been termed 'public influence attempts' by Davidson (1979, p.72) while Oliver has pointed to the existence of *raw demands* ie those which are not 'sorted, combined and consolidated into general proposals for political action' (Oliver, 1968, p.967).

There have been a number of praiseworthy attempts to model the demand making *process*, i.e. the stages through which citizens formulate demands from needs and wants, and express them (Cornelius, 1974; Nelson, 1980). At this stage, though, a checklist of the major dimensions of urban demand making and an indication of possible causal links is useful (see Table 13.1).

Notable features of this descriptive model which require further elaboration include *issues* which are the subject of demands, *referents, tactics* employed, and *response/outcome*. The sort of issues which generate neighbourhood action and, indeed, the

Table 13.1: A Model of Neighbourhood Demand-Making

NEIGHBOURHOOD CHARACTERISTICS

Physical Boundedness   Social Networks
Uniformity of land use   Demographic Stability
Housing Tenure   Political Marginality
Socio-Economic Status   Political Composition

ISSUES

Salutory and Noxious Facilities
Quantity/Quality of Divisible Services
Failure of Service Delivery
Location-Specific Expenditure

BEHAVIOURAL PREREQUISITES

Problem perceived as salient and costly to a number of residents
Government agency deemed suitable for resolution of problem
Exit/resignation options rejected; sense of efficacy of a tangible result
Cost/benefit ratio favourable; free-rider position avoided

TACTICS (Singly or in combination)

Private contacts; deputations; petitions; letters to newspapers; public meetings; legal action; marches/demonstrations; riots

REFERENTS

Group of Neighbours
Street/Block
Group of localised consumers
Neighbourhood(s)

FACTORS determining response/outcome/level of attainment

Balance of support/opposition; zero-sumness of issue; extent to which bureaucratic decision rules are questioned; media coverage; controlability of service output; perceived legitimacy of group and demand(s) being made and tactics employed by officials/politicians; size, longevity, cohesion, resources of organisations for staffing and sustained lobbying; openness of municipal agency; financial cost of acceding to demands and financial, legal, political and ecological constraints

LIKELY OUTCOMES

Symbolic Response (agenda/access)
Noxious facilities diverted to low status/low resistance neighbourhoods
Failure of routine service delivery rectified
Contraction of level of provision or closure of facilities prevented

---

necessity of there being a 'problem' at all, will be discussed later but it is assumed that demands are a response to actual or threatened change whether caused by the actions of public authorities or not. It is possible to classify the types of issues and on whose behalf the demands are being made. Davidson classifies tactics employed by groups of neighbouring residents as 'exclamatory' (strident, public and broadbrush) or 'explanatory' (reasoned, detailed, calm). Other authors have used different criteria to evaluate tactics, including whether or not they are conceived as helpful and legitimate by those in authority (Dearlove, 1974).

There are theoretical and empirical problems in tackling the questions of response and output, i.e. how public agencies and their representatives process demands addressed to them. A sympathetic hearing is definitely not the same as a satisfactory outcome from the point of view of the demander(s), although it may be an ideal consequence as far as the targeted officials or councillors are concerned. As Oliver states, 'not all demands need to be given actual material satisfaction ... mere acceptance of a demand by local officials with some expression or indication of interest and concern can create support ... even though the regime persists in the policies that created the conditions that gave rise to the demand' (1974, p.475). All or part of what is being demanded may be attained but the chances of this happening are scant, bearing in mind that there are other significant criteria which govern the allocation of resources. In relation to service delivery, for example, neighbourhood demands are 'sporadically generated and difficult to fit into the route of service provision' (Jones, 1977, p.301) and municipal bureaucrats have little to fear from 'distributing resources in accordance with technical considerations or professional norms rather than in response to public demands' (Antunes and Mladenka, 1976, p.163).

The point to note, then, is that a whole range of responses/outcomes are possible 'as a result' of demands made, and there are numerous plausible factors which may account for whatever level is achieved. The outcome largely depends on the willingness and capacity of politicians and officials to make concessions, and this turns on such factors as perceptions of need on the part of decision-makers and the cost of acceding to demands and the financial and institutional constraints as well as how ably and persistently neighbourhood spokesmen can make their case and what support and opposition is generated in the process. Clearly, local pressure is only one and not necessarily the most significant of a set of factors determining the allocation of resources or service delivery (Pinch, 1980). Lowe (1977) may be correct in assuming that the relative success of locality-based environmental pressure groups is attributable to disparities in political clout between rich and poor neighbourhoods as may Dearlove (1974) who suggests that it all depends on how interest groups and their demands are perceived by councillors. However, there is evidence that these explanations are too simplistic and there are several crucial variables which ought to be examined empirically.

Municipal outputs are the policies, plans, decisions and actions of local governments and the resources and regulations implied by those transactions. Policy outputs are decisions and non-decisions concerning the allocation of public resources; these may be material (public funds and facilities), symbolic, or both. The most important are concerned with public expenditure and land-use. In Marxist analysis, municipal expenditure takes the form of 'social investment' — serving the profitability of private companies and 'social consumption' which supports the reproduction of labour (Saunders, 1980). In terms of the present paper, area policies, service delivery, the control of land-use and the location of facilities will constitute significant local municipal outputs. Local outputs should also be regarded as bestowing public attention, effort and largesse between neighbourhoods. It should also be borne in mind that public authorities make *both* beneficial and harmful allocations, and that facilities are hybrid in that positive and negative externalities are often generated.

The Study of Neighbourhood Participation

This chapter is concerned with identifying intra-urban spatial patterns in political participation but is also concerned to tease out geographical and political causes and effects. One question which has generated conflicting views is whether and in what way 'neighbourhood' problems are the basis of localised political action. Some writers are in no doubt — 'a neighbourhood must experience a number of locally-based issues to stir ... at least some of its residents' and 'demand making begins with an issue some neighbourhood residents define as a problem ... without the identification of a problem there is no stimulus to political activity' (Davidson, 1979, pp.24 and 129). The same author even asserts that some issues *force* those affected to act. On a more cautious note Munns (1976, p.654) finds that contradictory demands arise from a single environmental condition and Rich (1980, p.571) notes that some sorts of neighbourhoods do not organise despite the presence of problems. Cox and McCarthy (1980) discuss at some length whether or not neighbourhood problems are a prerequisite for political action. They conclude that the effect of such problems is of 'an emphatically contingent nature' (p.23). Households of high socio-economic status, who own their own homes and have children, are more likely to be active politically in the neighbourhood. It is suggested that in usual circumstances neighbourhood activism is attributable in some way to environmental change and perceived threats to the physical, social or financial well-being of a group of neighbouring residents.

What sort or scale of problems would we anticipate being the basis of collective mobilisation and demand making? Lowe (1978) suggests that local environmental pressure groups — residents' and tenants' associations, amenity societies, action groups and the like, are preoccupied with issues of amenity and accessibility. Lamb (1975) stresses the significance of public service issues in poor neighbourhoods. There is ample evidence from the literature on locational conflict, at least in American and Canadian cities, that issues vary in volume and type from one ecological zone in the city to another (Janelle and Millward, 1976; Ley and Mercer, 1980). Several authors have emphasised that the object of much neighbourhood action is the *exclusion* of 'noxious' facilities (Dear, Fincher and Currie, 1977; O'Hara, 1977; Massam, 1980; Smith and Hanham, 1981). However, a broader perspective is taken by many observers who suggest that groups constrain, minimise or otherwise eliminate negative externalities and create, maintain or otherwise maximise the benefits of positive externalities (Cox, 1981, 1973; Stephenson, 1979). In terms of *scale* of issues, it is likely that they will be of neighbourhood scale — a few households next door to each other, several roads or streets, or an area comprising several thousands. In terms of public services, it is those which are of *medium* divisibility (not delivered to entire cities or to individuals but to small areas such as primary school catchments and area improvement schemes) which affect the well-being/ill-being of residents and, therefore, stimulate political demands.

Dowse and Hughes (1971) have observed that causes are espoused which affect people in *spatial* or social proximity, but no study has fully investigated the exact extent of the function of distance upon patterns of political participation. Harrop (1979) has shown that where one lives (in relation to an issue) makes a difference as to whether you are active or not. Several authors have indicated that certain sorts of neighbourhoods are likely to generate specific forms of organisational mobilisation. It is evident that neighbourhood organisations appear to be more common in areas of cities which are physically bounded, socially homogeneous, integrated, and subject to environmental change (Verba and Nie, 1972; Hall, 1978; Crenson, 1979; Davidson, 1979). The few detailed studies which have documented inter-neighbourhood variations in several demand making dimensions — issues, tactics, targets and outcomes — will be outlined later. As far as explaining differential outcomes, Rich (1980) suggests that poor neighbourhoods have service needs that are so extensive as to be too costly to satisfy. Lineberry (1978, p.77) states that — 'the costs of satisfying the demands for publicly provided collective goods are likely to be lower in affluent areas than in poor areas since it is easier to secure marginal changes in service delivery than to fundamentally reallocate public resources among services or geographic areas'. So *part* of the explanation of inter- and intra-neighbourhood variations in demand making, and public responses to it, may be 'geographical' , together with social, political, and economic factors.

Assumptions

While the aims of the study are, therefore, varied and, in part, spatial, the approach is based on a number of assumptions. First, of course, that spatial location and differentiation are salient to political participation. In a broader context, though, it should be noted that to many citizens in Britain at least *any* form of participation, except perhaps voting, is relatively infrequent and seen to be only marginally relevant to their daily lives. Either the demands of daily life preclude active involvement and/or politics is perceived as remote and uninteresting. If British political culture, especially, and institutions of representative democracy are not conducive to participation, then it is not surprising that many people are apolitical or at least sporadic activists. It is assumed that for the majority, political activities *between* elections is instrumental, though social advancement and comradeship should not be entirely ruled out. In terms of localised activity, Davidson suggests — 'the motivation to engage in the political defence of one's neighbourhood frequently derives less from a sentimental attachment to one's neighbourhood than from a more pragmatic desire to maintain the quality of one's immediate residential area and in certain cases investment in property' (1979, p.18).

A second major assumption to be noted concerns the function of political demand making and the interests of those who are involved in the process. As has already been implied, it must be clearly recognised that those in authority do not necessarily share the same perspective as the member of the public who participates. To councillors and officials, political demands serve a variety of purposes including providing feedback on existing policies , revealing popular attitudes, and giving information and an opportunity to build support. As Hain (1980) has amply shown in the case of the Covent Garden Forum, it is a mechanism to neutralise dissent and mobilise support for official policies. From a Marxist perspective, much of political participation in a capitalist society serves to further the interests of the ruling class by diverting fundamental economic dissatisfactions into manageable channels and therefore conceding minor concessions to demands from the working class. Cockburn (1977) has attempted to prove that the local state will control and manage popular participation in its own interests and that of private capital. Certainly, a full understanding of demand making requires a close scrutiny of the backgrounds and behavioural characteristics of *all* participants and the organisational, and structural constraints to which they are subjected.

In a recent attempt to clarify at what *scale* political issues should be observed and analysed, Taylor (1981) suggests that the urban scale is one of *experience* (the state is 'ideology' and world economy 'reality'). Most people still lead their lives in certain cities and, indeed, within a given neighbourhood. This study does not share the assumption which is apparently held by some theorists that what happens politically at the *micro scale* is somehow trivial and mundane. Judging from recent riots in British inner cities, 'insensitive' policing is just as severe a problem to young blacks as the lack of jobs. Casual inspection of any local newspaper in Britain or the United States or analysis of urban surveys will reveal that there are amenity and public service issues which are apparently significant in local politics and salient to the lives of ordinary citizens.

Reasons for studying neighbourhood participation

The relative dearth of detailed political/geographical studies on urban localised demand making has been noted by several writers — 'the available literature supplies a rich supply of hypotheses and assumptions concerning the possible causes and effects of neighbourhood involvement but almost no data by which these claims may be assessed' (Cole, 1974, p.78); 'Despite a number of excellent case studies of neighbourhood organisations and their activities, systematic evidence is very limited' (Cox, 1976, p.3); 'Future research might explore the relationships between non-electoral modes of participation and the allocation of resources' (Mladenka, 1977, p.286). Research in this field is evidently uneven and incomplete. Too many assumptions are made about neighbourhood variations in demand making in British and American cities, particularly in relation to *how* municipal authorities respond to, and process demands, and why.

In an age of theory-building, the minutae of street problems and political action may seem to some too humdrum. Then there is the point that demand making, like citizen-initiated contacting, lacks the suspense and drama of elections. Thirdly, there are difficulties in data collection — certainly when compared to voting studies — as many potential sources are semi-confidential, fragmentary, and detailed reliable statistics are hard to come by. It is especially difficult to find out what happens to political demands and why. As Darke succinctly puts it, the policy-making process is complex, extended, elaborate and opaque (1976). Some students of the distribution of public services may shy away from studying the influence of political demands because it is felt that *needs* warrant greater attention. 'The correlation between need for public goods and the ability to articulate effective demands may be negative ... with the provision of goods being strongly biased in favour of elements in the community where needs are relatively few but whose calls for action are the loudest and most difficult to ignore' (Muir and Paddison, 1981, p.179).

While accepting the logic behind some of these points, there is no shortage of substantial reasons why neighbourhood participation in the form of demand making should be studied in depth. It is readily conceded that many citizen demands are ignored, suppressed or accorded only a teken response and, indeed, that a multiplicity of groups may be a strategy of manipulation (Fincher, 1981). Nevertheless, some demands at least are converted into authoritative outputs. From the limited scope of the geographical literature on political participation, one would assume that political activity between elections barely existed and was insignificant in resource allocation. Spatial studies of voting exist in profusion and the 'vote buying model' may offer a plausible explanation of distributional decision-making on some occasions (just before and after elections, for example). Electoral processes are not, however, necessarily the most effective method of communicating citizens' needs and preferences: 'Messages via the ballot box are easily distorted, may arrive too late to affect a specific decision' (Davidson, 1979, p.23). Furthermore, unlike elections or even referenda, *citizens* choose the content, timing and targets in demand making. 'Citizen-initiated contacts on some problems ... may be very narrow but the citizen chooses the agenda of the participatory act ... Though the outcome may have little measurable impact on the overall system it may be very important to them ... Their own activity *may* make a difference ... furthermore a set of demands may represent a major allocative mechanism in society' (Verba and Nie, 1972, p.54).

But what can citizens contribute by way of neighbourhood demands given that elected representatives in theory safeguard the interests of their constituencies, and professional officials supply the technical expertise for municipal policy-making? One major contribution that residents can make is to alert those in city halls and civic offices to the impacts of their decisions and actions on the ground. Local authorities, with very few exceptions, are functionally organised, whereas local residents as consumers in a particular area can see and feel the overall effects of official service and other outputs or the lack of them. Smith (1976) has found evidence that ordinary citizens know a great deal more about *localised* environmental hazards and problems than those in municipal offices. It has long been accepted, especially in planning circles, that those who are at least directly affected by official proposals, plans and actions, should have an opportunity to express their views before decisions are made and a special right to be consulted in their implementation.

There has been a debate during the 1970s as to the most effective mechanisms for encouraging and supporting neighbourhood level participation. In Britain neighbourhood councils (Community Councils in Scotland and Wales) have been established on a semi-statutory basis. Voluntary organisations such as amenity societies, residents', tenants' and ratepayers' associations exist in many areas of British cities. The neighbourhood movement and experiments in neighbourhood decentralisation are even more developed in North America. If our goal is to achieve a 'comprehensive and balanced representation of interests' (Rich, 1980, p.591) then more detailed research is required into existing organisational structures. Furthermore, the forms and degree of success with which people participate and try to influence the distribution of public goods can tell us a great deal about modern urban life and local political systems.

A final justification for studying neighbourhood demand making lies in its relation to public outputs. It is obvious that neighbourhood influences are only one of several key determinants of who (which neighbourhoods) get what from the public purse. The mix of forces is an empirical question and may vary temporally and geographically. But 'only in the case of political demands can one conclude that inputs from the neighbourhood can affect service levels ... in each of the other possibilities it is a function of forces which are not proximate to the neighbourhood' (Jones, 1977, p.300). Unless it is assumed that officials and councillors have a monopoly of wisdom and knowledge, and residents in different neighbourhoods of British and American cities know little (except at election time), and care even less, then neighbourhood demands should be taken seriously by policy makers and academics.

A Review of Empirical Research

The body of literature on neighbourhood mobilisation is extremely disparate in terms of disciplinary background, methods and findings. The following material is arranged partly by topic but mainly by continental location. North American research is noted first and then related to British case studies, including reference to the author's own work in Portsmouth, England.

The selection of empirical studies discussed in this section has been governed by a desire to include some work from diverse academic backgrounds, to include studies which have exmained different aspects of the relationship between neighbourhood mobilisation and public outputs, to represent a fair cross-section of published research on either side of the Atlantic, and to present work which the author himself has found stimulating.

Studies in North American Cities

Canadian Studies of locational conflict. There now exists an enormous amount of literature — mainly North American — on the theme of locational conflict. A number of detailed case studies have documented issues relating to land use and the location of facilities which are the basis of disagreements on the part of city authorities, private developers, entrepreneurs and neighbourhood groups. Such conflicts rise from 'divergent interpretations of best interest' with respect to the spatial allocation of amenity and noxious facilities, and the delimitation of jurisdictional boundaries. Locational conflicts are characterised by 'a strong spatial basis to the arguments advanced by participants' (Janelle and Millward, 1975, p.102). They involve disagreements about the use of a site — including both form and function, so that 'conflicts ranged from a conventional redevelopment proposal to a zoning (planning) controversy to lobbying for a pedestrian traffic light!' (Ley and Mercer, 1980, p.96). Two important studies have been undertaken in London (Ontario) and Vancouver (British Columbia). Both are concerned, on the basis of content analysis of the columns of local newspapers, to describe the distribution of conflicts, classify the issues by type and intensity, analyse the participants involved and their arguments, and investigate eventual outcomes. They interpret the patterns of conflict in terms of the changing geography of the city and/or the environmental values of political groups of residents.

Janelle and Millward examine the links between *conflict generating forces,* such as population growth and urban expansion, structural ageing and renewal, with different types of issues (redevelopment, preservation, transportation, housing, public services and utilities, recreational and cultural provision) and plotted their spatial distribution over different ecological zones (core, transition zone, established residential zones and peripheral areas). The patterns of conflict were identified by means of gradients from city centre to outer suburbs 10 km away. The authors demonstrate that certain types of conflicts arose in specific zones — in general most were reported in inner zones and a peak was also reached about three miles from the centre of London. Conflicts were found in areas being redeveloped or not possessing the full range of modern urban facilities *and* newly developed outer residential neighbourhoods where there was a lag in the provision of services. Little (regrettably) is said about the characteristics of conflict participants, although this deficiency is partially remedied in a later reformulation of the research (Janelle, 1977).

Ley and Mercer's study of Vancouver covered a two year period in the early 1970s. They were more interested in the role of the 'guiding ideologies' of the participants than environmental changes as explanatory variables of land use controversies. The authors also recorded details of 'participants and their expressed grounds for involvement ... and which participants were successful and which were not'. (Ley and Mercer, 1980, p.96) They found a predictably high concentration of major conflicts in the central business district and inner city surrounding it. Community groups were found to be particularly active in opposition to land use changes. Half of the conflicts involved group mobilisation, one third petitions and in one fifth a demonstration was staged.

Not surprisingly, citizens' groups, including neighbourhood associations, were more vigilant in *residential* districts. West side groups were markedly more active than those in the east — the evidence strongly supported the existence of an articulate and politicised citizenry in the higher income, white collar, west side districts who could engage issues and enlist the involvement of the city council. Pedestrian crossings seem to have been frequently demanded by community interests, and it was often conflict between residents and the city engineer's office. Safety and visual appearance were frequently cited as arguments. Finally, in relation to outcomes, citizen groups were victorious in more than 40 per cent of cases when they opposed developments, and in seven out of ten conflicts with a definite resolution, when they were proposers. Ley and Mercer conclude with some caveats. They note that arguments shift; there are compromises and postponements; the mismatch between short term and long term effects compound any notion of winners and losers; and conflicts may be suppressed.

*Noxious facilities and localised demand making.*There is a substantial body of literature on what constitutes noxious facilities, the type and extent of their perceived or actual negative impacts, and political action taken either to oppose the siting of such a facility in a neighbourhood or to try and get an existing facility removed. Several British and American studies have classified noxious facilities and investigated their 'spatial externality field' i.e. the total area affected. (Bale, 1978; Dear, M., 1977; Dear, Fincher and Currie, 1977; Hodgart, 1978; Smith and Hanham, 1981; Wolpert, Dear and Crawford, 1975).

One somewhat idosyncratic study of noxious facilities and responses to them has been provided by O'Hare (1977) in a review paper entitled 'Not on my block you don't'. The negative effects of noxious facilities, he states, are localised, and may provide benefits which may be widely distributed and are perceived as 'noisy, smelly, ugly, scary or otherwise disagreeable to their immediate neighbours'. Opposition comes from neighbouring residents who argue that such a facility is not needed in general *or* on a given particular site. Demands are made that it should not be located; or removed, and residents will employ protest marches, demonstrations, petitions and negotiations to try to rid themselves of such a facility. Unlike the diffuse supporters of a noxiou⁓ facility, the opponents will be highly motivated. O'Hare is also concerned with the *justice* of locating noxious facilities and providing compensation to those individuals and neighbourhoods that suffer; this could take the form of the provision of 'desirable' facilities, reduced rates or improved service delivery to nearby residents. Alternatively he believes the only way to make rich people live near a disamenity and keep poor people away from it is to 'perpetually chase the wealthy about with new prisons, landfills and refineries' (O'Hare, p.454). There is ample evidence that it is indeed the poor and politically weak neighbourhoods which are in the end the recipients of such facilities.

Evidence on the location of the links between neighbourhood character, political mobilisation and the location of community-based treatment centres (CBTCs) has been provided by Davidson (1981) in Newcastle County, part of the Wilmington, Delaware — New Jersey — Maryland S.M.S.A. He found that no more than half of CBTCs were located in inner city, transitional, 'low resistance' neighbourhoods where supposedly 'deviant' behaviour is tolerated, where a diversity of land uses makes such centres less intrusive, and a low income, unstable, population is poorly equipped to oppose the establishment of such facilities. However, when the distribution of different *types* of centres was analysed, Davidson found that centres housing the more 'dangerous' clients (substance abusers, juvenile offenders, mentally-ill persons and homeless adults), and centres explicitly identifying their function in their name, were generally found in the sort of inner city areas which are generally associated with low organised resistance to such intrusions. In contrast, suburban centres served 'low stigma' clients, had been established for many years, and were physically isolated by barriers such as open spaces and fences from neighbouring residents who, the author speculates, therefore perceive them as separate from their 'turfs'. As an after-thought Davidson recognises that community opposition is not the only locational criteria employed in siting such centres — ecological, legal, and professional constraints also operate.

Airports and political activism in Los Angeles. Of the many studies which have been conducted on the politics of environmental nuisances, including noxious facilities, a few have tried to assess the relative significance of socio-economic, locational and attitudinal factors. One of these is the Californian study conducted by Goodman and Clary on community attitudes and action in response to Los Angeles International Airport (Goodman and Clary, 1976). It focusses on how communities around the airport reacted politically to the noise problems. Six neighbourhoods were surveyed, varying in location, socio-economic composition and jurisdictional status.

Although 59 per cent of respondents expressed some degree of annoyance with jet noise, only 29 per cent engaged in political activity aimed at reducing the noise. The relationship between annoyance, exposure to noise and political activity was found to be complex and the distance decay model did not fit exactly. Attitudes towards the 'responsibility' of the airport were significant — the less responsible a person felt the airport authorities to be, the more concerned he or she was about the noise. It is suggested that aircraft noise or relative location has an indirect effect on political activism; there may be intervening variables such as a sense of political efficacy or degree of value attached to home or neighbourhood environment. Thus, aircraft noise, while a *necessary* cause of political activism, is not a *sufficient* one. Thus, political activists tended to reside in an area of relatively higher socio-economic status, and felt that the airport lacked a sense of responsibility to the communities which were adjacent to it.

Neighbourhood organisations in Indianapolis. Collective goods theory has developed a framework by which neighbourhood organisations can be analysed as mechanisms for mobilising communities for collective action. While Olsen was the major architect of this approach it has been elaborated amongst others by O'Brien (1975) and applied by Rich in a study of neighbourhood organisations in Indianapolis. There have of course been many studies of such organisations in American cities but Rich's is of particular interest not only because of its conceptual framework but also because it focuses on the mechanisms of forming and joining such groups and shows how the distribution of public goods is affected by their activities.

Rich obtained data of 122 of the 164 neighbourhood associations in Indianapolis/Marion County, and subjected 11 of them to more detailed scrutiny. He classified them according to their organisational structure since the formal powers of an organisation to enforce rules and insure contributions is seen as a major determinant of the variability in their collective action. There were four organisational types delimited: voluntary neighbourhood organisations (VNO), government assisted neighbourhood corporations (NC), home owners associations (HOA), and municipal corporations (MC).

He expected to find that neighbourhood organisations would be more likely to form in middle-class communities than in wealthy or poor ones, and that those that do form in poor areas will tend to be voluntary and would tend to adopt more 'coercive' powers. The analysis revealed 'a striking concentration of organisations among middle-income communities' (Rich, 1980, p.576). Furthermore, 75 per cent of all neighbourhood organisations formed in poor areas were voluntary in form. Likewise voluntary organisations tended to form in stable, racially homogeneous communities.

Rich then turns his attention to organisational performance. He found that the more formally powerful organisations mobilised more resources (income) to carry out their political and co-production activities, and this was independent of neighbourhood economic status, and they also spent more on collective projects than did voluntary organisations. The author found that some organisations were able to secure services from the city even if their income was very low.

In Indianapolis Rich found that neighbourhood organisations played a significant role in seeking to improve the level of public services in their areas — street repairs, local schools, police protection and housing code enforcement. The ability to secure these marginal benefits depended on an association's internal dynamics and the differential costs and benefits facing those in varied socio economic settings.

Public influence attempts in Ann Arbor. The university city of Ann Arbor provided the setting for Davidson's study of 'political partnership' between councillors and neighbourhood residents. The pattern of electoral turnout, 'public influence attempts' and private contacts between 1970 and 1974 were analysed with reference to ecological, social and political characteristics of the city's neighbourhoods. High voting turnout was found in fringe and inner-city locations, 'pivotal' (marginal) precincts, areas of high social status, owner-occupation, and Republican support, but was not correlated with named and physically identified neighbourhoods. Groups and individuals were permitted to address the Ann Arbor city council at the beginning and end of regular council sessions. There were public hearings on planning and land use decisions and local ordinances.

There were 1869 such public influence attempts over a period of five years — a 'barrage' of public requests for action according to the author. Some neighbourhood organisations and individuals were 'regulars' at these sessions. The total number of public influence attempts were recorded for each of some 213 units in the city. Some 'neighbourhoods' made little use of this form of participation, while others did so extensively. Some 35 'active' areas accounted for over 50 per cent of the total interventions. The distribution of speakers was even more heavily skewed and a few neighbourhoods 'found a lot to shout about' (14 accounted for 305 — 44 per cent of the total).

It was found that most of the correlation coefficients between neighbourhood characteristics and the volume of public influence measures were quite low. Population size was moderately correlated with each of the public influence variables. When size and the percentage of students was controlled, the most striking result was that the socio-economic composition of neighbourhoods did not correlate strongly with any of the public influence variables, neither did tenure or location. One positive finding was that areas which had a higher proportion of administrative employees of public agencies living in them also made a larger number of demands. Davidson postulated that these 'politicos' provided information about local issues to residents which stimulated participation. Planning disputes, road construction projects and inadequate delivery of city services were frequently issues which generated public influence attempts. Some fringe areas sent a large volume of representations to city hall and others virutally none. The reason was that in the politically active areas there were local issues and 'threats' related to urban growth which continued over a *considerable period of time*. Thus it appeared that an issue of long duration or a succession of problems stirred residents to political action.

The distribution of *'private'* contacts between residents and councillors was also studied. These were both collective and individual requests to one or more councillors for assistance in resolving problems with a city department. Service-delivery calls occurred most frequently in relation to the bus system, snow removal, rubbish collection, loose dogs, tax assessments, traffic, parking problems and most of all, the 'wretched' condition of the city's streets.

Both 'explanatory' and 'exclamatory' styles were used, the latter often accompanied by electoral threats which in Ann Arbor were somewhat hollow since there were few marginal seats. Those who used an exclamatory style seemed unsure of themselves and frequently became strident and 'turned off' their audience. Most councillors, states Davidson, were moved more by the 'pathetic' outcry of a group of people who saw themselves wronged than by threats which only put the councillors' backs up.

The author had some difficulty in obtaining precise, systematic data on the distribution of private contacts since councillors varied in their ability and willingness to divulge such information. However, he discovered that there was considerable variation *between* neighbourhoods with half having no reported contacts, and fifteen having a 'high' number. Statistical analysis revealed a strikingly similar relationship between neighbourhood characteristics and poltiical activity as in the earlier analysis of public demands. There was, for example, a weak but positive effect of home ownership and socio-economic composition. Fear of neighbourhood deterioration was a constant theme behind the contacts to Ann Arbor councillors. Threats of privately initiated land use change which required public 'zoning' permission and undesirable public facilities such as half way houses were common place. Ad hoc neighbourhood groups were often formed to fight such threats and were disbanded when the threat died down. Some of the most active areas were 'fringe' neighbourhoods which fought to control developments such as federally subsidised housing for low income people, shopping centres, schools and other non agricultural land uses.

In Ann Arbor residents sometimes form close working relationships with councillors which Davidson calls political partnerships. If they do not have such partnership they tend to organise collectively and then gather resources whether it was signatures or petitions, money to hire a lawyer, 'bodies' to stage a sit-in, or commitments from other groups to support their cause — 'a group must have something to bring to bear on decision makers to get them to respond in the desired way' (Davidson, 1979, p.186). All types of neighbourhoods were successful on some occasions, those that were in political partnership with their local councillors found it easier to win, because timely interventions were made on their behalf. The fact that they could maintain a high level of neighbourhood mobilisation, and did not have to take the issue to a higher authority which could be a prolonged, expensive and potentially risky tactic was of considerable help.

Davidson's study is of interest because of the insights it provides into the level of public and private demand making between areas differing in location, identity, social composition and tenure. The crucial role of councillors in the process of demand making was deemed to be a vital element.

Neighbourhood activism in Columbus, Ohio. One of the most recent of the many theoretical and empirical studies produced by Kevin Cox and his colleagues at Ohio State University investigates the effect of five independent variables — neighbourhood problems, residential satisfaction, socio-economic status, presence of children and attitude towards home as an investment — on neighbourhood activism. (Cox and McCarthy, 1980). The data was derived from a telephone survey of a sample of 400 respondents living in the city, who were asked about their backgrounds, perception of their neighbourhoods and political activity.

The results obtained were as follows: first, although the perception of neighbourhood problems was the most effective predictor, nonetheless some claimed not to have experienced any problems but still were active. The reasons for this surprising finding were, the authors postulate, because resident organisations often anticipate *future* threats, perform a social role and also become active (on the basis of reciprocity) on behalf of others. Second, For those with chldren and those with higher socio-economic status the 'local problem effect' is intensified. Third,

'Investment orientation' did not have the anticipated effect and, fourth, the degree to which residential satisfaction was influential depended on the background of the householder.

The authors also discuss the merits and weaknesses of their model. They conclude that the focus is too much on individual actors and neglects the *contextual* influences within which individual or group behaviours are located. In terms of locational conflict they suggest that to understand neighbourhood activism the wider process of urban development must be analysed. In their findings the expansion of the built up area gives rise to problems, and in older established residential areas 'behavioural externality problems' for example vandalism, crime and barking dogs, exist. 'New development is concentrated both spatially and temporally and this enhances the sense of impaction on the part of existing residents and lends substantial impetus to that neighbourhood activism' (Cox and McCarthy, 1980, p.36).

Citizen-initiated Contacting in American Cities. Although individual contacting as a mode of political participation is not under discussion here, nonetheless it is believed that some of the findings of this body of political science research is of relevance and may help to explain the causes and effects of localised collective demand making. Furthermore, the role of neighbourhood organisations in stimulating and channelling these particularised contacts is explored (Eisinger, 1972; Jones et al, 1977; Mladenka, 1977; Vedlitz and Veblen, 1980; Nivola, 1978; Vedlitz, Dyer and Durand, 1980).

Jones and associates found that levels of 'need' and 'awareness' helped to explain the distribution of contacting in relation to environmental enforcement. Need was assumed to decrease and awareness increase as area social well being increased. It was hypothesised that contacting would be greatest among those in the middle range of social well being. Their study found some support for this hypothesis and thus the 'socio-economic model' , implying that high status means more participation, did not pertain.

The Detroit study then proceeded to examine the response of government. They sought to test whether it was the nature of the political system, the content of citizen contact, or the characteristics of the contactor which determined the outcome. They found that while all complaints were investigated not all were deemed as severe enough to warrant action. In terms of the *quality* of response (processing time and 'no action' taken) they found that having complaints relayed by a community group did not make the processing time shorter and in the face of sustained demand in a particular geographic area the organisations resources became so taxed that the quality of response suffered, i.e. there was 'organisational overload'.

The needs/awareness model developed by the Detroit researchers was tested in Dallas-Houston by Vedlitz and colleagues (1980). They used different indicators to measure an area's social wellbeing — rejecting distance from the CBD and age of housing in favour of average value of rent and median family income. They sought to explain the distribution of contacts in nine issue areas including street maintenance, animal control, refuse disposal, public utilities, planning permissions and police. What emerged from their aggregate study was that those areas with greatest need had the higher proportion of contacts. They suggest that in 'needy' areas there will be some aware individuals who know how and where to complain. Other explanations suggested were that the broader range of complaints studied affected the pattern and the centralised and 'visible' contacting system which was in operation in the two cities (but not in Detroit) and may have reduced the effect of awareness to the point at which the volume of contacts are substantially a function of variation in *need* for services.

The question of the role and effectiveness of neighbourhood organisations in channelling individual contacts has been explored in greater depth by Jones in Detroit (1981) Mladenka (1980 and 1981) in Chicago and Houston. In the former study it was found that, although community organisations acting as intermediary groups between individual citizens and the urban bureacracy were involved in complaining on behalf of individuals (unlike local party structures), they did not to any significant degree stimulate 'extra' contacts, nor were they accorded any special consideration by officials. They were unable to use or alter bureacratic rules to their area's advantage and did not co-produce services on any major scale.

In Chicago, Mladenka discovered that, despite their assertions to the contrary, ward politicians were unable to exert influence to ensure preferential treatment of citizen demands but black protests and demands had improved the distribution of parks in favour of inner city areas. Otherwise responsiveness was evidently a function of the perceived severity of the problem, the level of resources required to resolve the citizen grievance, and the rules employed by the various bureaucracies to deal with service complaints. In

Houston responsiveness to service demands depended *not* on the characteristics of the citizen initiating the contact (and presumably also whether or not it was articulated by a neighbourhood organisation) but variation depended on the *type of demand*. Minor service grievances were effectively resolved while more intractible problems remained.

The lower *overall* level of contacting in Houston is attributed by Mladenka to the positive role played by ward politicians in Chicago in the service grievance process and is nothing apparently to do with the presence and effectiveness of geographically based community organisations.

Neighbourhood groups and local governments. The degree to which neighbourhood organisations are represented in city governments and bureacracies (if at all) and indeed how they and their demands are perceived by key decision makers, is undoubtedly a crucial element in explaining differential outcomes. Explanations of *why* some groups are more successful than others at obtaining representation are varied, as are interpretations of to what extent demand making is affected. What empirical evidence can be found to clarify this crucial relationship and substantiate different perspectives?

Schumaker and Billeaux (1978) present a model which explains group representation by demographic, organisational and behavioural characteristics of the group seeking access and influence. In a survey of senior administrators in 55 American cities questions were asked concerning how responsive an agency had been to the demands of different types and why. The perceived significance of organisational stability, group cohesion, 'community-regardingness' of demands, leadership effectiveness, and unconventionality of style was elicited. Neighbourhood groups were amongst those deemed as 'least represented' in local bureaucracies. Structural characteristics of organisations — stability, cohesion and size were found *not* to be fundamental determinants of representation. On the other hand the shape of their demands and tactics were more powerful explanations. 'All that can be maintained is that some demands *are perceived* (original italics) by officials as more community-regarding than others and the demands of groups of lower status citizens are often perceived as *not* being community-regarding' (Schumaker and Billeaux, 1978, p.307).

American Studies of the distribution of local government services.
The major contours and contrasts of the Anglo-American urban
services literature has been reviewed elsewhere (Burnett, 1981). A
great deal of inter authority/inter neighbourhood research has been
and is being undertaken and varied explanations for the patterns
identified (variations in expenditure and the quantity and quality of
services delivered) have been sought. Ecological correlations with
the social/ racial characteristics of neighbourhoods, porkbarrel
processes (the vote buying model), and bureaucratic processes
including the rules and professional standards which govern routine
service allocations represent the most popular modes of analysis
and explanations. (Levy, Meltsner and Wildavsky, 1974; Lineberry,
1977; Mladenka, 1978 and 1980; Nivola, 1978).

One of the major conclusions of this research appears to be that,
unlike individual citizen initiated contacts, neighbourhood
organisations and protest groups play a minor not to say
insignificant role in distributional decision making. Neighbourhood
demands were *either* not directed at the bureaucrats who make
allocations over such services as housing inspections and
improvements, parks, refuse collection, education, fire and police,
libraries and road maintenance *or else* they were processed in such a
way that they had a minimal effect on outputs. For example, as
noted earlier, Mladenka (1980) found that only in the case of parks
allocation were black demands and protests important
determinants, and then along with other factors. Nivola's
conclusion in Boston was that it made little or no difference if
complaints were channelled through neighbourhood organisations,
the quality of response was determined at the discretion of street
level inspectors. Levy *et al.*found in Oakland that road engineers
were unsympathetic to citizen demands, although they would
occasionally stop a project or change the route of a road if
considerable public opposition was expressed. They believed that
they possessed a 'wider' view of the costs and benefits of road
schemes so that even if immediate residents might suffer, many
other people would benefit (p.129).

Oakland City Council was amenable to demands which
employed arguments designed to show that money could be saved,
and some 24 per cent of road projects were influenced by 'political'
factors. In the same Californian City the closure of small branch
libraries was prevented as a result of vocal protests but the
expenditure on books *per capita* was not influenced by such

'political' intervention.

It seems that a small proportion of service allocations are made in direct response to demands made by neighbourhood based groups, at least for the services and in the cities studied.

British Studies

Local environmental pressure groups. Lowe has described the role of local environmental pressure groups in the United Kingdom (Lowe, 1977). These include locality-based groups such as amenity, preservation and civic societies, residents' and tenants' associations and community action groups, all of which are concerned with preserving or enhancing the amenity and accessibilty of their areas. He suggests that spatial variations in access and allocation of services and facilities will combine to yield spatial inequalities between 'favoured' and 'degraded' neighbourhoods and thereby buttress variations in life-chances and real income. On the one hand amenity societies, which the author studied in detail, representing well-off, well-educated, and well-connected areas successfully defended the 'purity' of their patches, but, in contrast, tenants' associations, were less able to deal with the wide variety of problems facing them. He notes that groups representing working class areas tend to make specific and short-term demands, while all neighbourhood organisations are concerned with issues *inside* the locality unless they directly affect the pattern of peoples' lives, for example, the inconvenience of public transport. The author provides an excellent summary of the range of non-statutory local groups, their *raison d'etre,* strategies, demands and the environmental and distributional consequences of their activities. He concludes that political participation may well exacerbate inequalities between neighbourhoods, because people who are dependent on public services are least able to influence political decisions which affect them.

The major defect in the paper is that although reference is made to several empirical sudies, Lowe provides few detailed findings to substantiate his assertions.

Neighbourhood groups in England: a national survey. At the height of the debate over the advisability or otherwise of having statutory neighbourhood councils in urban areas in England, the Department of the Environment commissioned a research project on existing neighbourhood associations which was undertaken by the Institute of Local Government Studies at the University of Birmingham

(Talbot and Humble, 1976). 224 associations replied to a questionnaire of which 22 were formally constituted neighbourhood councils. Not surpringly these organisations had a variety of titles — residents' associations (57 per cent), community associations (19 per cent), neighbourhood association/societies (8 per cent), tenants' associations (8 per cent), action groups (4 per cent), and ratepayers' associations (3 per cent).

Whatever their names, these organisations had several stated aims. Making representations on behalf of the local community to public bodies, i.e., political demand making, was mentioned by 22 per cent. The goals of others included holding *ad hoc* public meetings on specific issues, scrutinising plans for areas, improving local amenities, developing social activities and community spirit; 86 per cent of groups had clearly defined boundaries in which to pursue these activities. Under 'activities' all 22 neighbourhood councils said they made representations to public bodies, 90 per cent claimed to campaign to improve local amenities and facilities, and 77 per cent to protect the local environment.

Some clear distinctions emerged between the neighbourhood councils and the other groups studied. The former made representations, were politically active, covered a defined area, considered all residents within the area to be members with full voting rights, covered an area between 3,000-15,000 population and had a committee elected by residents. In contrast, other neighbourhood organisations usually enrolled members and gave voting rights only to those enrolled, collected membership subscriptions, and generally had been in existence for longer. Apart from these differences all the organisations were remarkably similar in terms of aims, activities, democratic base, and areas.

In terms of the issues giving rise to demand making the neighbourhood councils protected their local environments by — pressing for traffic management schemes, for improved street cleaning, for tidying up neglected and derelict areas, and for the provision of open spaces. As far as campaigning for improvement of local amenities, this took the form of pressing for improved bus services, new bus shelters, waste skips, telephone boxes, improved street lighting, improvement in repair services for local authority housing and more facilities for tenants. The findings did *not* show that councils in inner city locations were significantly different from those in suburban locations in respect of aims and activities. The authors had anticipated that inner city groups would, for example, be more likely to fill in gaps in service provision and that suburban groups would be more concerned to protect the environment.

Community Councils in Liverpool. Boaden (1973) undertook an SSRC-sponsored survey of some twenty community-based organisations during the early 1970s in the city of Liverpool. He was concerned with taking 'a snapshot view' of organisations in terms of scale, organisation and activities. There were seventeen councils at the start of the research and some twenty five when it was concluded. Community councils in the city appeared mostly in working class areas (inner city and fringe estates), though not always run by working class residents. None of the areas were entirely homogeneous but, where they were, they tended to have a more obvious focus of concern. The earliest council was set up in Toxteth in 1963 (later the scene of rioting in 1981). The author suggests this community council and others in the city underwent a characteristic *life cycle* - one of increasing involvement of local residents, concentration on particular areas of the overall territory, and the choice of a narrow range of issues around which to focus activity.

Issues *and* key leaders were significant in the 'initiatory process' and they also profoundly affected internal organisation and style adopted. Their roles varied and success depended primarily on establishing legitimacy with the local authority and the local population. Community Councils in Liverpool claimed to speak for whole communities. 'The success of this claim reflected the absence of clear evidence, the equally poor performance of alternative agencies, and the need for the local authority to find community groups through which to implement statutory and local goals of participation within a consensus framework' (p.12). Plotting the distribution of topics discussed by community councils the authors found that most organisations were concerned with 'involvement', the young and old people, roads, traffic, and local amenities. Some were also preoccupied with housing and public transport. Amongst the full range of items 68 per cent involved decisions to take some sort of action (votes were rarely taken) usually to try to persuade the local authority to take remedial action or merely inform an outside body about the issue (34 per cent). Many issues were raised at well attended public meetings when residents presented complaints about the area, and clearly wanted to see something tangible done quickly. In a survey of attitudes towards community councils it was found that most people did not feel that they had any major impact. The researchers clearly felt that the public's low awareness of them was misplaced since they conclude that they *did* have an effect.

Tenants and Action Groups in Sheffield. Lowe (1978) showed that tenants' and action groups in Sheffield employed three main tactics to raise issues: writing to their local councillors (23 per cent), writing to public officials (41 per cent) and holding public meetings (24 per cent). Tenants associations monitored welfare problems and environmental complaints (including street lighting, rents, police patrolling and dog wardens). Action groups, in contrast, were concerned with redevelopment plans and similar issues affecting their areas. Both groups were active in exclusionary tactics against 'noxious' intrusions — be they factories, university and hospital extensions or road developments — but also engaged in co-production (self-help) such as play groups, playgrounds, luncheon clubs for old people, garbage removal, community transport and community centres.

Housing Protests in the East End of London. In a case study of unsuccessful protest over rehousing in high rise blocks in Newham, London, Dunleavy suggests that the policy of housing working class people in high rise blocks reflects the influence of capitalism — the interests of construction companies and the powerlessness of tenants. New housing offered an improvement in basic amenities but a decline in overall standards of provision — loss of garden, reduction of space standards, transition from familiar streets to impersonal estates located in decaying neighbourhoods and equipped with inadequate facilities. The social impacts were 'disastrous' and the transition was unpopular with those involved yet residents failed to influence policy, protest effectively or exercise the 'voice' option. Residents were clearly unhappy with their impending move to high rise accommodation but they were coerced and manipulated by the council. Dunleavy notes the massive imbalance in resources between the residents and the local authority in the conflict.

A protest committee was formed; they collected a petition with 700 signatures but plans were too far ahead to be altered. The residents' demands were rebuffed; a public meeting was held to 'explain' the situation, local Labour Party councillors refused to espouse their cause; non-committal letters were sent, and some minor concessions were made over compensation terms. The local newspaper gave some coverage to the issues and published a letter from the protest leader. 'Approaching the problem in an orderly and gentlemanly way is getting us nowhere ... if you cannot get anywhere peacefully and with common sense what is left?' (Newham Recorder, 13th February, 1969, p.13 quoted in Dunleavy, p.210). An escalating series of demonstrations and meetings were doomed to failure since all the decisions had been taken and were to be implemented regardless of protests. Protest groups' pronouncements became increasingly strident and they soon lost what little support they had from a few councillors. Their support declined and two leaders accepted offers of houses from the council — the committee fell apart and press coverage ceased.

Dunleavy explains their total defeat in terms of lack of resources, organisational base and support. The Council suppressed the conflict despite press coverage and they 'persistently refused to acknowledge the legitimacy or even the existence of the Beckton protest movement'. The Labour controlled Council in Newham were not willing to be influenced and their relative power was such that there was never any question as to the outcome of the issue.

Neighbourhood Associations in London. Cousins has investigated the extent of involvement in decision making by voluntary groups in three south London boroughs (Bromley, Lambeth and Lewisham). Residents' and tenants' associations were included in the study and classified as either 'environmental' groups or tenants' associations. Cousins found that, while residents' associations had generally good relations with officials and members they would occasionally resort to petitioning the council or holding a demonstration, tenants' associations frequently found themselves in conflict with the council but confined themselves to using 'orthodox' means of influence (Cousins, 1976, p.68). Tactics employed depended on the issue at stake and the initial response to demands made. Belligerent public tactics were often combined with 'behind the scenes' negotiations. Contacts with *officials* were deemed as being more valuable than with councillors, and it was Chief Officers who set the style of relations which any department enjoyed with voluntary organisations. There were many occasions when organisations gained more or less what they had demanded, especially where local authorities had to deal closely with groups.

Dearlove's research on the politics of the London Borough of Kensington and Chelsea has been recognised as a major contribution to the study of British local politics. It is not concerned solely with *neighbourhood* groups but nevertheless its findings are relevant because of what is shown about the links between councillors and local pressure groups. *Access,* he states, is the crucial intervening variable linking group demands to policy outputs. While recognising that the size, prestige, cohesion, leadership and distribution of members, as well as the ability to rally support and resources are all significant in affecting the capacity of any group to influence policy, above all it is how the group and its demands are perceived by councillors that is important. The 'rules' of access are set and implemented by the council decisionmakers and the predispositions of these councillors are crucial. Their ideology and policy preferences act as a screen which affects their response to demand making. 'The assumption is that councillors will be likely to allow effective access to a demand that does not run counter to their own policy preferences but they will probably deal unsympathetically with demands which run counter to their own views about what should be the scope of council activity' (Dearlove, 1975, p.160). In his study, 44 conservative councillors gave their views about 20 named groups. They were able to differentiate 'good' and 'bad' groups and proper and improper channels. Helpful groups were those whose demands reinforced or conformed to existing council policies and who worked with the council rather than just making demands of it. Working through local ward councillors was seen as the most proper channel and contacting chairmen of committees was also deemed to be acceptable. On the other hand, demonstrations, and contacts with the local press were less 'acceptable' channels. Dearlove conceives of interest groups as falling into one of two categories: helpful groups making acceptable demands in a proper way; and unhelpful groups making unacceptable demands in a style regarded as improper. He admits that this is a static scenario but argues that alternative combinations of different characteristics of groups, demands and methods are unlikely and that there is a tendency for groups, particularly those that are regarded as unhelpful, to pass through a series of stages in terms of demands and tactics. The likely links between groups, demands and tactics are discussed in a series of clearly argued propositions (Dearlove, 1974, 149-152).

Given the dynamic process Dearlove states that the end product is one of unhelpful groups turning to acceptable demands or other activities to survive, and helpful ones pursuing limited demand making to maintain their legitimacy.

Participation in Portsmouth. A major study of individual and collective political participation and municipal resource allocation in the City of Portsmouth and its suburbs is being undertaken (Burnett, 1978; Burnett and Hill, 1981; Burnett, Cole and Moon, 1981). Key features of the pattern of participation in the city are outlined and the findings of an investigation into demand making by protest groups over public service issues in 1977 are summarised.

The City of Portsmouth, located on the south coast of England, has, following Second World War bomb damage and subsequent decentralisation and overspill, a population of 180,000. Together with the adjoining suburban boroughs of Gosport, Fareham and Havant it comprises a metropolitan region in south-east Hampshire of over half a million population. Portsmouth's spatial and social structure is by no means typical of a British city. It is a peninsula city, centred on a south western CBD including the Guildhall and new civic offices. The city was, until recently, still heavily reliant for employment on HM Naval base and dockyard. The residential environment of its inner city is predominately one of Victorian redbrick terraced housing, together with inter-war and postwar municipal blocks of flats. Areas with the highest rateable value are to be found adjoining the seafront in Southsea, and in semi-detached suburbs in the north east.

Following the introduction of a two-tiered system of local government in England in 1974, the City has constituted a district within the 'shire' County of Hampshire, and decisions about important services, such as education, social services and roads are made at Winchester, albeit on the basis of local decentralisation and agency agreements. The City has its own environmental health, housing, leisure services, transportation and planning committees.

The city may look like a northern English town, but it does not vote like one. It has been estimated that the 'left' vote in the city is 10 per cent less than might be expected given its occupational structure. Many of its 130,000 electors are elderly, employed in defence industries and active or retired service personnel, and unsurprisingly are predominantly conservative. As a result, although one of the city's two Parliamentary constituencies was Labour for thirteen years until 1979, and there are, or have been, Independent Labour and Liberal councillors, it is the Conservative Party which has dominated the local political scene since the war. 'Safe' Labour wards are limited to predominantly local authority housing areas on the western side of the city.

More important for the purposes of this paper are the major dimensions of non-electoral politics in the city. It is evident that the authorities have actively encouraged citizen participation. For example, in all the 22 general improvement areas in the city, environmental changes have been planned and carried out in conjunction with residents committees elected on a street basis. Furthermore, representatives of tenants' and residents' associations for council estates, both within and outside city boundaries, sit on a *joint consultative body* with housing department officials and committee members.

On specific issues, the City Council was, until recently, one of the few in England to permit *deputations* to plead their cases before both committees and at full council meetings. As far as *individual contacting* is concerned, the City Council published in 1977, 1979 and 1981 an 'ABC of Portsmouth' to assist direct contact with City Council Departments. The leaflet offered guidance as to who to contact in relation to the whole range of public services and was distributed (with rate demands) to all householders.

The local newspaper reports on Council meetings and official plans and proposals, and gives publicity to some local issues, including locational conflicts, particularly when interpreted as injustices to readers caused by local 'bureaucrats'.

To obtain an impression of the level and type of participation from the viewpoint of citizens in Portsmouth a survey was conducted during 1981 in Southsea — the southern part of the city. A total of 174 respondents completed the questionnaire. The overall impression was one of a higher level of political participation than reported in other British studies. Half of the respondents had signed a petition and a large minority 'joined together with neighbours in protesting about a public plan or proposal or lack of action by municipal authorities'.

In Southsea the activists tended to have professional white collar occupations, to be relatively well informed, to be elderly, to live in high status conservation areas, and to be medium-term residents. Predictably, housewives, short-term residents, renters and young people were less active. Respondents then gave details of the grievances issues and problems which had concerned them and what it was about these issues which had annoyed or upset them sufficiently for them to act politically. Traffic problems and land use changes were frequently mentioned and specific issues clearly affected particular streets where amenity was threatened. The possibility of moving (the exit option) was explored and it was apparent that to many the positive aspects of living where they did offset any local problems. Local problems that did not give rise to political activism were also reported. Demands were communicated by a variety of means with family, friends, and occasionally neighbours being involved in the process. Questions as to the response to and outcome of reported political activity is indicated. A majority felt that they had been given a fair hearing and a sizeable minority considered that they had achieved some tangible and beneficial public action.

As far as the question as to whose demands were successful and which issues (if any) were more conducive to a positive outcome, findings were some,what inconclusive. For example, planners in the city appear to give demands concerning noxious facilities a sympathetic hearing but went ahead and allowed the perceived intrusion to take place.

This notwithstanding, the ambiguities of the questionnaire and the evident tendency of some citizens to exaggerate the scale of their involvement, householders in Southsea actively participate in local affairs (although 28 per cent were inactive apart from voting). Some sorts of people participate more than others and while not all those upset, angered or perplexed by local problems make political demands (for a variety of reasons) in a sense issues are a prerequisite for action. Moving house is apparently rarely considered as an alternative course of action. In most cases Southsea respondents were not displeased by the initial reception they got from councillors and officials even if at the end of the day their demands were not always successful.

Protest Groups and Public Services in the City. This study was specifically concerned with the allocation of resources in the form of public facilities and service delivery by central, local and other public authorities. Demands for, or in response to, public regulation such as traffic, parking, land use and licenses have been excluded, apart from where they involve the location of public facilities.

Data was obtained from the local evening paper in Portsmouth. As indicated earlier, this newspaper gives extensive coverage to local affairs including council deliberations and decisions. Citizen grievances and demands are reported in feature articles, reports, photographs and occasionally editorials. A total of 28 protest issues were identified during 1977.

The information contained in the newspaper was varied but usually included (1) a description and photograph of the problem together with details of the protesters, (2) quotes from the protest 'leaders', (3) an immediate response/explanation from councillors (often committee chairmen) or a senior official and (4) some indication of the outcome, particularly if it was positive. The degree of space devoted to each issue also varied depending on the intensity and longevity of the case. Limited additional data was derived from City Council minutes or those of its Planning and Transportation Committees, and informal talks with some of the participants.

The location of the 28 issues can be seen on Figure 13.1.

There is no guarantee, of course, that all protests over public services which did take place during 1977 were reported, but there is some evidence to suggest that protest groups which were formed during the year were given publicity even if the scope and tone of the coverage varied considerably.

Dramatic events were occasionally given front page headlines while, in a few cases, editorials gave qualified support for campaigns where either personal tragedies were involved or those affected were deemed to have suffered from civic incompetence. Outcomes were rarely reported in any detail, and occasionally not at all.

An uneven pattern of protest is evident and as such it resembles, in some degree, the distribution of locational conflicts found elsewhere. In Portsmouth working class neighbourhoods are 'demanding' zones. A total of 19 out of the 28 protest groups arose in the officially delimited inner city. In contrast, more affluent peripheral private estates in the north east of the city make few if any public demands. The spatial incidence of protest does *not* appear to have been influenced by the existence or otherwise of neighbourhood associations or GIA residents' committees since it occurs in both areas covered by such organisations and those where they do not exist. Nor are the well delineated community areas found by Hall more often the locale for protest groups. On the other hand dependence on public services and political representation by minority Labour Party councillors seems to be spatially correlated with the pattern of such protest activity.

The issues at stake were equally divided between those involving the quality and quantity of service delivery and the location or use of public facilities. In the latter case neighbouring residents were clearly upset by the actual or proposed location of facilities deemed to be noxious. Perhaps more surprising was the fact that while 16 of the 28 protest groups were 'reacting' to officials proposals or actions, a sizeable minority were objecting to unacceptable conditions resulting from a *lack* of public attention and resources allocation.

Given that the externality fields of local facilities are often spatially concentrated, it is not surprising to find that most

Figure 13.1: Protest Groups in Portsmouth

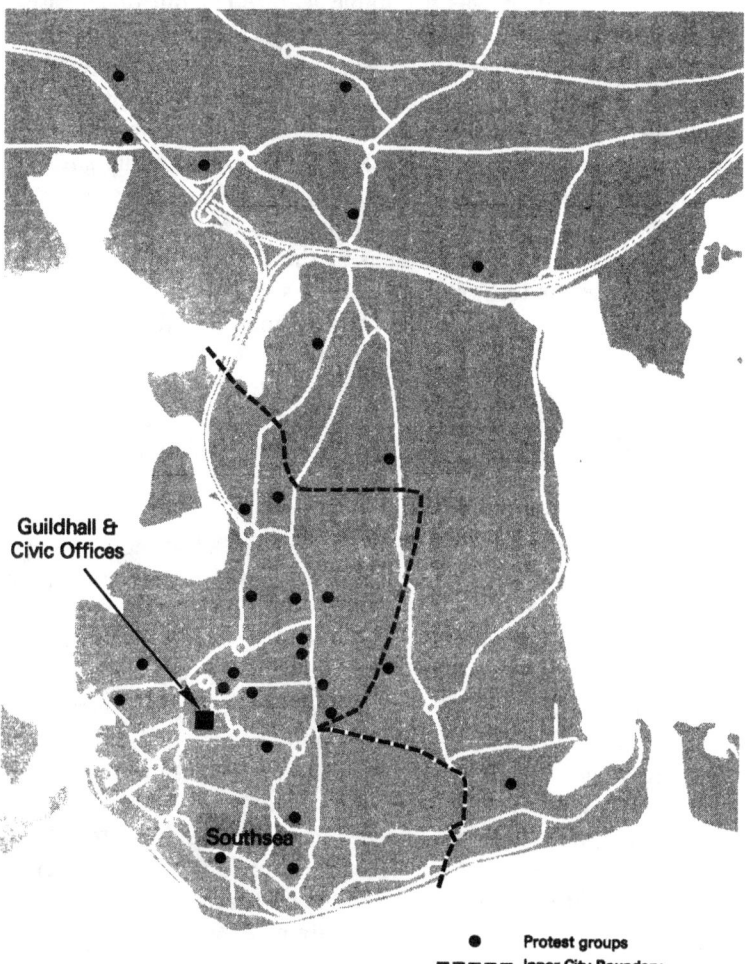

Guildhall &
Civic Offices

Southsea

●   Protest groups

– – – – –   Inner City Boundary

demands were made on behalf of either a single street or block of flats. A dozen campaigns were backed by a hundred or fewer residents, while only two petitions gained more than 1000 signatures. Supporters evidently resided in close proximity or by virtue of their needs were similarly affected (single parents using a day nursery; non car owners in a peripheral council estate relying on a bus service).

In terms of tactics employed by protest groups to bring their grievances to the notice of the authorities and/or exert pressure on them, it is clear that a variety of strategies was tried. The raising of *petitions* in campaigns was a notable feature (17 out of 28 cases), and *deputations*, as has already been noted, are 'welcomed' by the City Council and its committees. Why was petitioning so prevalent? Probably because in Portsmouth, as elsewhere, they 'prove' that people are behind the protest (at least so far as to write their name and address on the petition). Signatures are usually easily gathered and provide tangible evidence of strength of feeling, and as such are acceptable to politicians and officials. Local councillors were frequently contacted and the help of the then Labour party MP, Frank Judd, seems to have been readily solicited and given.

More 'militant' tactics in the form of marches, demonstrations and public meetings were employed in few cases. Demands were frequently initially addressed to officials by letter, but subsequently, when protestors felt that they were achieving little, they resorted to more visible forms of pressure on more senior officials and committees.

City council committees and departments deemed to be the appropriate targets for most protests although in at least one case the statutory responsibility for the service in question lay elsewhere. On the evidence of this small sample, non-metropolitan districts like Portsmouth may have lost some of their major functions, but the ones that they retained — housing, roads (via agency agreements), environmental health, planning control — are those which generate this type of political involvement.

It is apparent that policy makers in Portsmouth always give a symbolic response to protest groups. 'Access' was granted in all cases, with their complaints and demands being subject to official investigation and deliberation. There was only one instance where a deputation was turned away without being heard. In half the cases the goals of protest groups were wholly or substantially achieved, while in eight others they were totally unsuccessful. In a number of cases some sort of compromise was reached, while other outcomes were unknown or inconclusive. Facilities were located, relocated or not located in the sites originally proposed in accordance with the wishes of local residents; yet other facilities were moved or used regardless of pressure exerted by the public. The provision of services was on occasions altered in line with expressed preferences.

The results are somewhat inconclusive in explaining why some protests succeeded while others failed. With the exception of those issues clearly threatening or actually having caused death or serious injury to members of the public, no particular type of problem was consistently solved to the satisfaction of residents. If the type of issue was not crucial to the outcome, neither were the tactics employed nor the size or scale of community *support* forthcoming. Neither was intervention by an MP or councillors — even senior Conservative politicians of the controlling party in the city — important in affecting outcomes. Demanding the *status quo* may have improved the chances of success but it did not guarantee a victory any more than if protesters enjoyed the approbation of the editor of the local newspaper.

Demands which did not require large amounts of public expenditure, or saved money were acceded to, but so were some which entailed considerable financial commitment. It seems that if money 'had' to be found then funds were somehow raised to meet the demands of protestors.

Some valuable, albeit fragmentary clues are to be found in the reports of the individual issues. Officials clearly evaluated demands made upon them in the light of their own professional standards — perception of 'real' need, practicability and consistency. Councillors also responded to pressure on occasions presumably because they were convinced as to (1) the merits of the case, (2) the 'genuine' concern of those involved in protesting, or (3) the 'sensible' way they presented their case. They clearly gave priority to 'city wide' considerations on some occasions at the expense of the demands of even their own constituents. In one case at least conflict between individual officers and councillors as to the best course of action was apparent.

It has been shown, nonetheless that in this city people do protest when they are dissatisfied with what public authorities are providing, or planning, by way of services, facilities or other service outputs. Pluralists will be gratified to observe that people in Portsmouth from a variety of backgrounds and areas are involved, even if only sporadically. What is more, they are encouraged to participate. They make the most of several channels of communication — not least the local newspaper and open council committee meetings — to make their views known to those who govern the city. Such demands are not only articulated and placed on the agenda, but on occasions at least, are acceded to by those in authority. Combined with the alternate modes of participation noted earlier there is evidence that local people do have a say in matters which are salient to them.

Those favouring a more neo-elitist interpretation would note that even if *public* protesting over public services is merely the tip of the iceberg of group participation in the city — nonetheless the total number of cases is relatively few over the space of a year. There is surely a case to be made for consulting those to be affected by proposals (as is the case in most planning issues) earlier in the decision making process. Marxists would not doubt point to the localised, fragmented nature of these protests over consumption issues which in no way radically alter the overall social allocation of public resources or private wealth. In at least two of the cases in Portsmouth where demands from working class neighbourhoods conflicted with the interests of private capital accumulation the results went in favour of the latter. Furthermore, the reduction in public expenditure which is a feature of central government policy is at least one of the causes of muncipal cutbacks and threats of facility closure. Pressure from such international institutions as the IMF may well have played a crucial role in forcing or fostering a climate of retrenchment in public spending (Taylor, 1980).

In Portsmouth then, groups of neighbours do protest about public services. Many protest groups do 'spring up' apparently spontaneously, but some protest campaigns were aided and abetted, if not instigated, by organisations both locally-based and from outside. For example, neighbourhood associations were 'behind' several campaigns during 1977 and city-wide or national bodies supported others. Likewise local politicians — the M.P. and parliamentary candidate in Portsmouth North (a marginal constituency) and councillors — played more than a passive role in framing several protests.

Nonetheless apolitical residents seem to have been crucially involved in these protests. They have found petitions, deputations and the local newspaper convenient vehicles to voice their demands to officials and councillors. No doubt the fact that some of these channels seem to be successful elsewhere in the city is one reason why they are used — i.e., there is a 'spillover' effect in operation. This was especially evident in the threat and use of legal action by groups of Council tenants against the City Council under the 1938 Public Health Act over dampness in their properties.

More problematic is the question of why some demands succeed and others fail and still others partially succeed. Size and solidarity of support seem to be important (as evidenced for example by a petition), gaining powerful allies may be vital, but so also is — to officeholders at least — what is involved in acceding to a demand however effectively expressed and amply supported.

A symbolic output costs nothing, and this may well explain the ubiquity of this type of response. But more tangible responses may depend on such factors as how well the case is argued; whether it can be seen as 'special' or might set a precedent; if it is likely to win or lose votes in a marginal seat and, finally, if it will enhance or reduce departmental domains. The process whereby demands are evaluated is a complex and crucial one and involves both the willingness and ability of officeholders to make concessions and thereby satisfy the public demands.

Clearly political demands are not the only, or even the most important criteria in the allocation of urban public resources or service provision. However, some evidence has been presented here which suggests that officials and councillors in one British city do respond to the squeaky wheel of citizen pressure. How and why they do is a subject for more empirical research — whether they should do so is another question altogether.

Anglo-American Comparisons

Key concepts associated with localised political demand making have been discussed and a varied (not to say, diffuse) body of empirical work has been described. Some comparative conclusions can now be drawn out not withstanding the fact that only a small sample of the relevant research has been noted (additional studies are cited in the bibliography).

There are certainly constrasts in the causes, characteristics and consequences of neighbourhood mobilisation between individual cities. Given that bureaucratic rules govern the allocation of services; that budgets are determined incrementally; and that conservative governments are cutting back on public expenditure on both sides of the Atlantic, some degree of uniformity should be anticipated. On the other hand no one would dispute the fact that British and American cities demonstrate marked constrasts in political structure and culture; the role of political parties; as well as their built environment and residential structure. Thus some diversity in neighbourhood activism should be expected.

There is, or has been, a 'neighbourhood movement' on both sides of the North Atlantic but it is apparent that the British one is a pale shadow of its American counterpart. For all its problems and ambiguities (Goering, 1981) the movement has flourished in the 1960s and 1970s in the United States. Thousands of neighbourhood associations have been established (with only a few being systematically investigated — mainly in university cities and districts!) There is also a range of federally inspired experiments in operation. Meanwhile in Britain there has been very limited debate on the neighbourhood dimension of urban politics and precious few neighbourhood initiatives funded by central or local authorities.

There are, of course, limits to the effectiveness of such localised political interventions. The conclusion reached by Cole that 'citizen participation clearly will not solve all the problems facing America's cities ... however it does appear capable of solving a few problems and of providing a few people with opportunities to participate in politics which they would otherwise not experience' (1974, p.137) seems valid. It is widely accepted that localised participation does not always achieve tangible benefits — organisations and groups are sometimes manipulated, co-opted and suppressed and accorded only a symbolic response. Urban bureaucrats and politicians are in control even if they themselves are subject to economic, organisational and ecological constraints. No evidence has been produced which shows that major inequities in service provision have been redressed, budgets systematically altered, or bureaucratic decision rules affected as a result of neighbourhood action. In contrast however, some findings indicate specific distributional decisions are influenced, service provision is marginally affected, and victories recorded in some political locational conflicts. It would appear that in both British and American contexts while broad patterns of resource allocation are not materially affected, some specific service outputs are altered as a result of neighbourhood demands.

It has been suggested that the degree of neighbourhood based political influence in the service delivery process can be explained by three factors — the nature of the government system in which the agency operates, the penetratability or openness of the agency to political influence, and, the nature of the agency's service product (Jones, 1981). British municipal authorities are more 'closed' and evidently less willing than their American counterparts to accede to disparate and often raw demands from neighbourhood groups. As indicated in Table 13.1, there are a host of factors which determine the response to and outcomes from neighbourhood demand making. It is difficult to isolate any of these explanatory variables which are consistently more important in either American or British cities.

The structure of urban political processes in America contrasts markedly to that in Britain. Neighbourhood activity is also less apparent in Britain. On those occasions when it does emerge the issues are quite different and issues of public safety and local schools are notable for their absence. Much more common are concerns over traffic resulting from road widening ... implementation of one way street systems, obnoxious land uses and the distribution of historically meritorious physical fabric. The evidence from the previous section of the paper thus seems to confirm Cox's characterisation (1978, p.97). The overall level of neighbourhood activity is greater in American cities and is more sporadic and ephemeral in Britain. A recent study by Henig into neighbourhood mobilisation in response to redevelopment plans in Chicago and Minneapolis would seem to confirm this finding. Nonetheless, in Portsmouth, and no doubt elsewhere in the United Kingdom, neighbourhood associations do exist and protest groups arise when issues upset, anger or worry urban residents. These demands reach the political agenda and are sometimes resolved to the satisfaction of these affected by public actions or proposals or neglect. As far as issues are concerned they would seem to differ in degree than kind. Groups everywhere are concerned with various categories of locational conflict, and maintaining/improving the quantity and quality of public services of medium divisibility. They also channel particularised complaints though not, it seems, necessarily stimulate the volume of such individual contacts. British citizens who are politically active may be more concerned with amenity issues than American urban residents. On the other hand a degree of 'convergence' is apparent in the sort and spatial pattern of demands being made in cities of comparable size and social composition. For example, policing and public safety are 'burning' issues in London and Liverpool as well as Miami and Detroit. Recently with financial retrenchment and falling school rolls, school reorganisation and closures are significant issues in many British cities.

Neighbourhood organisations and groups in Anglo American cities employ the whole range of 'conventional' and 'militant' strategies to bring issues to the attention of those in authority and to try to pressurize them into making beneficial concessions. Even 'respectable' middle-class residents and amenity societies in Britain use strident tactics when it suits them. Groups representing working-class areas have less choice. A notable feature of British local politics is the active role played in the process of ward based local councillors and the influence of local party caucuses on authoritative decision making. This is hardly the case in American 'reformed' cities, although it obviously is in Ann Arbor.

It is likely that more valid comparisons can be made between individual cities and services. What is needed is more direct, cross national, theoretically-eclectic research into the various aspects of the demand making process.

References

Agnew, J.A. (1978) 'Market Relations and Locational Conflict in Cross-National Perspective', in K.R. Cox, (ed.), *Urbanisation and Conflict in Market Societies*, Maaroufa Press, Chicago, 128-144

Agnew, J.A. (1981) 'Home Ownership and the Capitalist Social Order', in M. Dear and A.J. Scott, (eds.), *Urbanisation and Urban Planning in Capitalist Society*, Methuen, London, 458-480

Antunes, G., and K. Mladenka (1976) 'The politics of local services and service distribution', in L.H. Massotti and R.L. Lineberry, (eds.), *The New Urban Politics*, Ballinger, Cambridge, Mass.

Arnstein, S.R. (1969) 'A Ladder of Citizen Participation', *Journal of American Institute of Planners*, **35**, 216-224

Baer, M.A. (1980) 'Political Participation in New Towns', *British Journal of Political Science*, **8**, 237-255

Boaden, N. (1973) *Community Councils in Liverpool*, unpublished SSRC Report

Brier, A.P., and R.E. Dowse (1969) 'The Politics of the A-political, *Political Studies*, **17**, 334-339

Buell, E.H., Jr. (1980) 'Busing and the defended neighbourhood. South Boston 1974-1977', *Urban Affairs Quarterly*, **16**, 161-188

Buller, H. (1981) *Pressure Groups and the Pluralist Model of Society: the example of local amenity societies*, Kings College, Geography Dept., University of London, Occasional Paper No. 14

Burnett, A.D. (1976) 'Legislating for Neighbourhood Councils', *Local Government Studies*, **2**, 31-38

Burnett, A.D. (1978) 'Political Demands and Public Services in Portsmouth', *Department of Geography, Portsmouth Polytechnic, Discussion Paper*

Burnett, A.D., K. Cole and G. Moon (1982) 'Political Participation and Resource Allocation', in M.A. Busteed, (ed.), *Developments in Political Geography*, Academic Press, London

Burnett, A.D. (1981) 'The Distribution of Local Political Outputs and Outcomes in British and American Cities: A Review and Research Agenda', in A.D. Burnett and P.J. Taylor, (eds.), *Political Studies from Spatial Perspectives*, Wiley, Chichester

Burnett, A.D., and D.M. Hill (1981) 'Neighbourhood Organisations and Local Political Outputs in British Cities', in R.C. Rich, (ed.), *The Politics of Urban Public Services*, Lexington Books, Lexington, Mass.

Button, J.A. (1981) 'Political Strategies and Public Service Patterns', in R.C. Rich, (ed.), *The Politics of Urban Public Services*, Lexington Books, Lexington, Mass.

Cole, R.L. (1974) *Citizen Participation and the Urban Policy Process*, Lexington Books, Lexington, Mass.

Cornelius, W.A. (1974) 'Urbanisation and Political demand making: Political Participation among the Migrant Poor in Latin American Cities', *American Political Science Review*, **68**, 1125-1146

Cousins, P.F. (1976) 'Voluntary Associations and Local Government in Three South London Boroughs', *Public Administration*, **54**, 53-81

Cox, K.R. (1978a) *Urbanisation and Conflict in Market Societies*, Maaroufa Press, Chicago

Cox, K.R. (1979) *Location and Public Problems*, Blackwell, Oxford

Cox, K.R., and J.L. McCarthy (1980) 'Neighbourhood Activism in the American City: Behavioural Relationships and Evaluation', *Urban Geography*, **1**, 22-38

Cox, K.R. (1981) 'Capitalism and Conflict Around the Communal Living Space', in M.J. Dear and A.J. Scott, (eds.), *Urbanisation and Urban Planning in Capitalist Society*, Methuen

Crenson, M.A. (1978) 'Social Networks and Political Process in Urban Neighbourhoods', *American Journal of Political Science*, **22**, 578-594

Cullen, J.D., and P.L. Knox (1981) 'The triumph of the eunuch: planners, urban managers and the suppression of political opposition', *Urban Affairs Quarterly*, **17**, 149-172

Darke, R. (1979) 'Public Participation and State Power', *Policy and Politics*, **7**, 337-355, Leonard Hill, London

Davidson, J.L. (1979) *Political Partnerships: Neighbourhood Residents and Their Council Members*, Sage, Beverly Hills

Davidson, J.L. (1981) 'Location of community-based treatment centres', *Social Science Review*, 221-241

Dear, M.J., R. Fincher and L. Currie (1977) 'Measuring the External Effects of Public Programmes', *Environment and Planning A.*, **9**, 137-147

Dear, M.J., and J. Long (1978) 'Community Strategies in Locational Conflict', in K.R. Cox, (ed.), *Urbanisation and Conflict in Market Societies*, Chapter 5, 113-128

Dearlove, J. (1974) 'Councillors and Interest Groups in Kensington and Chelsea', *British Journal of Political Science*, **1**, 129-153

Dowse, R.E., and J.A. Hughes (1971) 'Sporadic Interventionists', *Political Studies*, **25**, 84-92

Dunleavy, P. (1977) 'Protest and Quiescence in Urban Politics: A Critique of Some Pluralist and Structuralist Myths', *International Journal of Urban and Regional Research*, **1**, 193-218

Eisinger, P.K. (1972) 'The Pattern of Citizen Contacts with Urban Officials', in H. Hann, (ed.), *People and Politics in Urban Sociey*, Sage, Beverly Hills

Elkin, S.L. (1974) 'Comparative Urban Politics and Intergovernmental Behaviour', *Policy and Politics*, **2**, 289-308

Fincher, R. (1981) 'Local Implementation strategies in the urban built environment', *Environment and Planning A*, **13**, 1233-1240

Fitzgerald, R.M., and R.F. Durant (1980) 'Citizen Evaluation and Urban Management: semi delivery in an era of protest', *Public Administration Review*, **6**, 585-595

Getter, R.W., and P.D. Schumaker (1978) 'Contextual Bases of Responsiveness to Citizen Preferences and Group Demands', *Policy and Politics*, **6**, 249-279

Gittell, M. (1980) *Limits to Citizen Participation: The Decline of Community Organisations*, Sage, Beverly Hills

Goldsmith, M. (1980) 'Structuring Community Participation', Unpublished paper SCRC Seminar in Urban Politics, Edinburgh

Golaskiewicz J. (1981) 'Interest group politics from a comparative perspective', *Urban Affairs Quarterly*, **16**, 259-280

Goering, J.M. (1979) 'The National Neighbourhood Movement: a preliminary analysis and critique', *American Planners Association Journal*, **45**, 506-514

Goodman, R.F., and B.B. Clary (1976) 'Community Attitudes and Action in Response to Airport Noise', *Environment and Behaviour*, **4**, 441-470

Goodwin, R.E. (1977) 'Symbolic Rewards: Being Bought Off Cheaply', *Political Studies*, **25**, 382-396

Hain, P. (1980) *Neighbourhood Participation*, Temple Smith, London

Hall, D.R. (1977) 'Applied Social Area Analysis: Defining and Evaluating Areas for Urban Neighbourhood Councils', *Geoforum*, **8**, 277-309

Harrop, K.J. (1979) 'Nuisances and Their Externality Field', unpublished PhD thesis, University of Newcastle upon Tyne

Henig, J.R. (1982) *Neighbourhood Mobilisation*, Rutgers University Press, New Brunswick, New Jersey

Hill, D.M. (1978) *Participating in Local Affairs*, Penguin, Harmondsworth

Honey, D.R., and D.R. Reynolds (1978) 'Conflict in the Location of Salutary Facilities', in K.R. Cox, (ed.), *op cit.*, 144-162

Humble, S., and J. Talbot (1976) 'Investigation into Neighbourhood councils', Inlogov, University of Birmingham

Janelle, D.G., and H.A. Millward (1982) 'Locational Conflict Patterns and Urban Ecological Structure', *Tijdschrift von Economische en Social Geografie*, **67**, 102-114

Janelle, D.G. (1977) 'Structural Dimensions in the Geography of Locational Conflicts', *Canadian Geographer*, **21**, 311-328

Johnston, R.J. (1982) (forthcoming) 'The Courts as a Focus for Neighbourhood Conflict', in R.J. Johnston and K.R. Cox, (eds.), *Conflict, Politics and the Urban Scene*, Longman, London

Jones, B.D., S.R. Greenberg, C. Kaufman, and J. Drew (1977) 'Service Delivery Rules and the Distribution of Local Services: Three District Bureaucracies', *Journal of Politics*, **40**, 332-368

Jones, B.D. (1980) *Service Delivery in the City*, Longman, New York

Jones, B.D. (1981) 'Party and Bureaucracy: the influence of intermediary groups on urban public service delivery', *American Political Science Review*, **75**, 688-700

Jones, K., and A. Kirby (19820 'Provision and Wellbeing: an agenda for public resources research', *Environment and Planning A*, **14**, 297-310

Knox, P.L. (1982) *Urban Social Geography*, Longman, London

Lamb, C. (1975) *Political Power in Poor Neighbourhoods*, Schenkman, Chicago

Lambert, J., B. Blackaby, and C. Paris (1975) 'Neighbourhood Poltics and Housing

Opportunities', *Community Development Journal*, **10**, 95-112

Levy, F.S., A.J. Meltsner, and A. Wildavsky (1974) *Urban outcomes: Schools, Streets and Libraries*, University of California Press, Berkeley

Ley, D., and J. Mercer (1980) 'Locational Conflict and the Politics of Consumption', *Economic Geography*, **56**, 89-109

Lineberry, R.L. (1977) 'The Politics and Economics of Urban Services', *Urban Affairs Quarterly*, 267-271

Lowe, P.D. (1977) 'Amenity and Equity: A Review of Local Environmental Pressure Groups in Britain', *Environment and Planning*, **9A**, 35-58

Mladenka, K.R. (1980) 'The Urban Bureaucracy and the Chicago Political Machine: Who gets What and the Limits of Political Control', *American Political Science Review*, **74**, 991-998

Mollenkopf, J. (1981) 'Neighbourhood Political Development and the Politics of Urban Growth: Boston and San Francisco, 1958-78', *International Journal of Urban and Regional Research*, **5**, 15-39

Molotch, H. (1979) 'Capital and Neighbourhood in the United States: Some Conceptual Links', *Urban Affairs Quarterly*, **4**, 289-312

Munns, J.M. (1975) 'The Environment, Politics and Policy Literature: A Critique and Reformulation', *Western Political Quartersly*, **28**, 646-667

Nelson, B.J. (1980) 'Help Seeking From Public Authorities: Who Arrives at the Agency Door?', *Policy Sciences*, **12**, 175-192

Newton, K. (1969) 'City Politics in Britain and America', *Political Studies*, **17**, 208-218

Newton, K. (1973) 'Community decision makers and community decision making in England and the United States', in T.N. Clarke, (ed.), *Comparative Community Politics*, Wiley, New York

Newton, K. (1978) 'Conflict avoidance and conflict suppression: the case of urban politics in the United States', in K. Cox, (ed.), *Urbanisation and Conflict in Market Societies*, Methuen, London

Nivola, P.S. (1978) 'Distributing a Muncipal Service: a case Study of Housing Inspection', *Journal of Politics*, **40**, 59-81

O'Brien, D.J. (1975) *Neighbourhood Organisation and Interest Group Processes*, Princeton University Press, Princeton

O'Hare, M. (1977) 'Not on my block you don't: Facility siting and the strategic importance of compensation', *Public Policy*, **25**, 407-458

Oliver, J.H. (1968) 'Citizen Demands and the Soviet Political System', *American Political Science Review*, **63**, 465-475

Orbell, J.M., and T. Uno (1973) 'A Theory of Neighbourhood Problem Solving: Political Action Versus Residential Mobility', *American Political Science Review*, **66**, 471-489

Peterson, P.E., and P. Kantor (1977) 'Political Parties and Citizen Participation in English City Politics', *Comparative Politics*, **9**, 197-217

Pickvance, C. (1980) 'Analysing Urban Protest', unpublished paper given at SSRC Seminar on Urban Politics, Edinburgh

Pinch, S.P. (1980) 'Local Authority provision for the Elderly: An Overview and Case Study of London', in D.T. Herbert and R.J. Johnston, (eds.), *Geography and the Urban Environment*, 3, Wiley

Prottas, J.M. (1978) 'The Power of the Street Level Bureaucrat in Public Service Bureaucracies', *Urban Affairs Quarterly*, **13**, 285-312

Prottas, J.M. (1981) 'The cost of free services: organisational impediments to access to public services', *Public Admin Rev.*, **5**, 526-534

Rich, R.C. (1977) 'Equity and Institutional Design in Urban Service Delivery', *Urban Affairs Quarterly*, **12**, 383-410

Rich, R.C. (1979) 'Neglected Issues in the Study of Urban Service Distributions',

Urban Studies, **16**, 143-156

Rich, R.C. (1979) 'The Roles of Neighbourhood Organisations in Urban Service Delivery', *Urban Affairs Papers*, **1**, 81-93

Rich, R.C. (1980) 'The Political Economy Approach to the Study of Neighbourhood Organisations', *American Journal of Political Science*, **24**, 558-592

Rich, R.C. (1980) 'The Dynamics of Leadership in Neighbourhood Organisations', *Social Science Quarterly*, **60**, 570-587

Rich, R.C. (1982) 'Urban Development and the political economy of public production of services', unpublished paper presented to the Institute of British Geographers, University of Southampton, January 6

Richardson, A. (1979) 'Thinking About Participation', *Policy and Politics*, **7**, 227-245

Rose, G. (1971) *Local Councils in Metropolitan Areas*, Fabian Research Series No 296

Rumley, D. (1980) 'Some Aspects of the Geography of Political Participation in Western Australia', *Environment and Planning A*, **12**, 671-684

Saunders, P. (1979) *Urban Politics: A Sociological Interpretation*, Hutchinson

Schumaker, P.D. (1975) 'Policy Responsiveness to Protest Group Demands', *Journal of Politics*, **34**, 489-521

Schumaker, P.D., and D.M. Billeaux (1978) 'Group Representation in Local Bureaucracies', *Administration and Society*, **10**, 285-316

Sharpe, L.T. (1979) 'Instrumental Participation and Urban Government', in J.A.G. Griffiths, (ed.), *From Policy to Administration*, Allen and Unwin, London

Sharp, E.B. (1980) 'Citizen Perceptions of Channels for Urban Service Advocacy', *Public Opinion Quarterly*, , 362-375

Smith, G.C. (1976) 'The Response of Policy Makers to Urban Environmental Hazards', *Area*, **8**, 279-283

Steggart, F.X. (1975) *Community Action Groups and City Governents: Perspectives From 10 American Cities*, Ballinger, Cambridge, Mass.

Stephenson, L.K. (1979) 'Towards a Spatial Understanding of Environmentally Based Voluntary Groups, *Geoforum*, **10**, 195-201

Taylor, P.J. (1980) *A Materialist Framework for Political Geography*, Department of Geography, University of Newcastle-upon-Tyne, Seminar Paper No. 37

Vedlitz, A., J.A. Dyer, and R. Durand (1980) 'Citizen Contacts with Local Governments: A Comparative View', *American Journal of Political Science*, **24**, 50-67

Webster, B.A. (1980) 'Policy Making and Response to Local Government',unpublished paper delivered to American/ European Conference on Neighbourhood Level Government, Florence, Italy

Whitaker, G.P. (1980) 'Co-Production: Citizen Participation in Service Delivery', *Public Administration Review*, **3**, 240-246

White, L.G. (1976) 'Rational Theories of Participation: An Exercise in Definitions', *Journal of Conflict Resolution*, **20**, 225-278

Williams, P. (1982) 'Restructuring Urban Managerialism: Towards a Political Economy of Urban Allocation', *Environment and Planning*, **14A**, 95-105

Wolpert, J.A., A. Mumphrey, and J. Seley (1972) *Metropolitan Neighbourhoods: Participation and Conflict Over Change*, Association of American Geographers, Resource Paper 16, Washington D.C.

Yin, R., and D. Yates (1975) *Street-Level Governments: Assessing Decentralisation and Urban Services*, Lexington Press, Lexington, Mass.

14

Political Decision-making and the Distribution of Public Benefits: A Political Science Perspective

Bryan D. Jones

Deeply embedded in the traditions of analysis in political science is a concern with the distribution of social values in societies. Political scientists are not concerned with all distributions of values, although more than one political scientist has indicated that such a broad orientation is desirable. Most noted in this tradition is Harold Lasswell's definition of politics as 'who gets what, when, and how' (Laswell, 1936). Far more common among political scientists, however, is a preoccupation with value distributions that result from the operation of certain kinds of social decision-making structures — those structures that produce public policies.

Indeed, the distribution of social values is intimately connected with policy-making processes in society. As David Easton (1959, p.129-30) has put it:

> The essence of a policy lies in the fact that through it certain things are denied to some people and made accessible to others. A policy, in other words, whether for a society, for a narrow association, or for any other group, consists of a web of decisions and actions that allocates values.

Policies which are authoritative are the basic subject-matter of political science. Easton (1959, p.132) notes that a policy is authoritative 'when the people to whom it is intended to apply or who are affected by it consider that they must or ought to obey it'. The tendency of people to view some policies as authoritatively binding and others as not depends on the source of the command, and is connected to the legitimacy of a society's government. This is a general enough social phenomenon to define politics, with Easton, as the authoritative allocation of values in society.

There is nothing modern about the idea that public policy can be defined in terms of the acceptance of the promulgating institutions by the governed. Glaucon, probably the earliest advocate of the social contract theory of government, describes the theory to Socrates thus:

> (T)hose who have not the power to seize the advantage and escape the harm decide that they would be better off if they make a compact neither to do wrong nor to suffer it. Hence they begin to make laws and covenants with one another; and *whatever the law prescribed they called lawful and right*. (Plato, 1945, p.43-44, emphasis added).

A public policy is authoritative action that affects the distribution of values in society. One of the key concerns in political science is linking the decision-making structures of a society with the distribution of values in that society. In this chapter I shall review some attempts by political scientists to link social decision-making structures with value distributions. In particular, I hope to add a dose of theoretical rigour to a literature that has primarily consisted of empirical tests of relatively low-range theory.

Public Goods

Although in my opinion distributional considerations are at the forefront of political analysis, there is very definitely an opposed tradition. That tradition emphasises the use of government in the common good, the public interest, or, in the language of modern public choice theorists, to produce 'collective goods'. Government itself, according to Thomas Hobbes, is a collective good; we are all better off with the social order enforced by government than without it. While it is undeniably true that many public policies have strong collective effects, it is just as true that all collective goods have distributional aspects. When the Hobbesian state of nature was replaced by the Sovereign, the weak clearly benefitted more than the strong. So it is with all collective goods (see Goldwin, 1977, for further thoughts on the distributional aspects of collective goods).

A collective good is one which is characterised by nonexclusion (no citizen can be excluded from the benefits of the good) and jointness of consumption (two or more citizens can take advantage of the benefits provided by the good or service without using it up). Samuelson's (1954) original forumulation of the problem suggested that goods are either public or private. However, later formulations have conceived of a continuum of public goods, from the pure public good, through a series of more or less divisible goods, termed 'impure public goods' by Buchanan (1968) to pure private goods (see Hanson, 1978). If impure public goods are provided by government, they will affect the distribution of social values because they cannot affect all citizens equally.

Were all goods and services able to be categorised according to the pure Samuelson dichotomy, life would be simple. In this utopia, private entrepreneurs would provide private goods, and reach a Pareto optimum social allocation for these goods. Governments would produce collective goods. If there are many governmental producers of public goods, as occurs in many North American metropolitan areas, there will occur an optimum social allocation of public goods and services analogous to that provided by the private sector (Tiebout, 1956).

The real problem with this economic utopia is that there are no social mechanisms to stop governments from producing private goods and services. Governments produce all sorts of goods and services that do not come close to satisfying the criteria of nonexclusion and jointness of consumption. This problem is conceptually distinct from the problem of defining collective goods. It would occur even if there were a perfect dichotomy between collective and private goods.

Collective goods will be undersupplied by the market, because there is no way to package them (exclude non-users from the benefits). Because they cannot be packaged, the price mechanism is ineffective. The more collective (or less impure) the public good, the greater the extent of such market failure.

A second class of goods are primarily private goods, yet they are supplied by government. The economist Richard Musgrave has termed such goods *merit* goods. He says that merit wants

are satisfied by the market within the limits of effective ddemand. They become public wants if considered so meritorious that their satisfaction is provided for through the public budget, over and above what is provided for through the market and paid for by private buyers (Musgrave, 1951, p.13).

Such a theory can explain the provision of public transportation systems, social services, public airports, and public colleges and universities. But the problem with the theory of merit goods is that society has no decision-making mechanisms that are capable of deciding objectively which goods are meritorious and which are not. Indeed, so long as citizens view policies that are issued by government as legitimate and worthy of obedience, the supply of goods and services in democratic societies will be determined by the actions of the supremely political institutions of society — political parties, interest groups, and transient political movements — not by an objective evaluation of philospher-kings. These institutions forge policy-making coalitions that affect the adoption and implementation of public policies in society. Such an arrangement would seem to be inherently incapable of distinguishing between collective and private goods, or between merit wants and 'selfish' wants. Because the existing social decision-making structures are incapable of making such distinctions, it becomes the job of the analyst to examine the linkages between distributional patterns and the policy-making process. Formal theorising about the nature of goods and services will not take one very far.[1]

Allocation and Distribution

The determination of 'who gets what' through the authoritative decision-making structures of society occurs by way of two processes, allocation and distribution. *Allocation* involves the selection of a mix of public outputs that will be provided, and is best represented by the governmental budget. Budgets give us scant clues as to how government selected the goals that it did; nevertheless, they do show, quantitatively, just what public expenditures are being made, and for what general purposes. *Distribution* involves how the outputs of government affect population groupings, whether spatially, culturally, ethnically, or economically distinguished.

The selection of certain governmental policies, and the associated allocation of effort to achieve the ends implied by those policies, often-times automatically distributes values. The largest domestic programmes in the United States, and I presume most industrial democracies, are not in the form of collective goods, but are direct income transfers from one class of citizens (usually taxpayers) to another class (retired workers, the elderly, the poor). The policies, if straightforwardly implemented, have straightforward distributional effects.

Other policies, in particular, urban public services, are not automatically distributed by the allocation process. The distribution of outputs can be influenced by a number of factors, only one of which is the allocation process. In particular, the manner in which the policy is implemented can affect the output distribution.

There exist, then, both authoritative allocations and authoritative distributions of values in society. At times they are connected by the very nature of the policy adopted by public decision-making structures. At others, the process of distribution and the process of allocation proceed quite independently. Knowing just how a municipality allocates its resources among its various functions does not automatically indicate what citizens receive what levels of service. Knowing, however, that the national government has altered the eligibility requirements for receiving an in-kind transfer payment such as food stamps allow one to calculate in a reasonably straightforward manner what the distributional implications are.

Political Economy, Political Ecology, and Political Distribution

Public policies are invariably goal-oriented. Moreover, in most cases they are designed to influence a very limited number of social conditions. Indeed, it is only a slight simplification to suggest that most domestic public policies pursued by liberal democracies are designed to do two things: promote the capitalist economic system, or to limit the harms generated by unfettered capitalism. Richard Rich (1982) has pointed out that we cannot understand the distributional impact of urban public services unless we recognise the role of local governments in fostering capital accumulation. Following the work of James O'Connor (1973), he sees the 'local state' as providing the 'social capital' in the form of social investment projects (the urban public infrastructure) and social consumption projects (policies and services that lower the cost of labour for private entrepreneurs — education, public health, etc.). The state also maintains social control both by providing police protection and by initiating welfare programmes designed to keep the poor quiescent.

Modern Marxists view the state and the capitalistic economy holistically, and see the state as an instrument of the ruling classes, a perpetuator of the existing social structure, and an integral part of the capitalistic political economy (see Clark and Dear, 1981 for a review). The potential for change is carried in the inherent contradictions of the political economy. In particular, the need to use public expenditures to foster capital accumulation and to ensure social peace provides grist for the dialectic.

The structuralists are quite correct in pointing to a *political economy of distribution,* a distribution of governmental outputs that occur because of the particular manner in which governments and the policies they create interact with the capitalist economic system. The economic structure channels public sector activities in a manner that limits the universe of possible value distributions.

There is, however, a competing perspective. Institutions, and particularly public institutions not subject to the vissicitudes of market competition, invariably take a life of their own. Hence even the most subtle of analyses cannot always predict just what shape a policy will take even a few years after its origin. The agencies created to implement policies interact in strange and complex ways with their policy environments. Regulatory agencies, it was once thought, followed a life cycle from agressive regulators to submissive captives of the industries they were supposed to regulate (Bernstein, 1955). Recent regulatory history, however, indicates that the situation is far more complex. The Environmental Protection Agency, the champion of consumers and the bane of the powerful automobile companies in the administration of President Jimmy Carter, became the darling of the automobile manufacturers within weeks of the transition to a Republican administration. Such sudden change in the role of a political organization suggests that political processes are occurring that have important ramifications for the distribution of social values, but which cannot easily be fitted into a political economy perspective.

The point here is that there exists a *political ecology of distribution* that proceeds somewhat independently of the institutional interaction between government and the private sector. Political ecology concerns the interaction of policy-making institutions with their environments. This environment primarily consists of other organisations: poltical parties, interest groups, bureaucracies, other policy-making institutions at all levels of government, and mass publics. The necessity of paying attention to the ecology of distribution is well-illustrated by the recent history of the Environmental Protection Agency or, for that matter, the recent history of certain price-regulating agencies such as the Federal Aviation Agency (FAA). These are not just minor eddies in the main flow of public policy. They are important changes in the way in which the public and private sectors relate to one another.

What we have here is a level of analysis problem, with no easy bridges from one level to the other. At the level of the public economy it is undeniable that governmental institutions and the policies they create interact with the private sector to produce a distribution of values. At the ecological level, public outputs are influenced by the interaction between government agencies and their policy environments — clients, other bureaucracies, and policy-makers. These interactions also produce value distributions.

While this proposition is unlikely to be controversial to this point, I would take the argument one step further. There is no *a priori* way to determine which process is a more important determinant of social value distributions. Indeed, the two levels are very definitely connected causally in ways not well-understood at present. At least we can note that the realities of the currect structure of the public economy effectively channel the behaviour of political organisations, and that the ecological interactions among citizens, groups, and public organisations cause changes in the structure of the public economy.[2]

Figure 14.1 depicts the two basic levels of analysis, political economy and political ecology, along with a third level of analysis, micropolitics, which will not serve as a focus of this chapter. The diagram indicates relationships between each element in each level of analyis, and it indicates causal relationships between the levels of analysis.

Building Codes: An Example of the Interaction of Political Ecology and Political Economy

Some insight into the respective roles of the on-going interactions of public organisations and their publics and the broader public economy can be gained by a relatively detailed examination of the regulation of building and housing in cities.

There have been laws regulating constuction in American cities since 1647, when New Amsterdam (later New York) passed an ordinance regulating the construction of chimneys, in an attempt to minimise the occurence of fires. Although many ordinances were passed by cities attempting to control fires through construction techniques, it was not until 1849 that New York passed the first comprehensive building code, a law which is the basis of all subsequent building laws (Veiller, 1900, p.11).

Shortly thereafter, housing reformers in the United Kingdom (see Deswnup, 1907 and Stewart, 1900) and in the United States (Veiller, 1900; Lubove, 1962) began to see housing regulation as a potential policy instrument in social reform. Until the middle of the nineteenth century building laws had been written primarily to control the external effects of unregulated construction — particularly the occurrence of fire. After that period, reformers became interested in housing regulation as a way of upgrading the condition of the poor urban labourer by requiring landlords to construct and maintain quality housing regardless of the market demand for housing. The efforts of these social reformers led to the enactment and diffusion of tenement housing laws and, later, housing codes applicable to all types of dwelling-units: multiple family, single family, rental, owner-occupied.

Today building and housing regulation remains a function accomplished primarily by local governments. There is a great deal of similarity in regulations among cities, due to the impulse of technological innovations in construction and the diffusion of these innovations, primarily through professional associations of bulding code officials and their regularly updated model codes. Yet there is much room for diversity in the substance of regulations and in enforcement procedures, a fact of life that disturbs builders who operate in more than one jurisdiction.

Political Economy

Any public policy invariably raises issues of both political economy and micropolitics, and building regulation is no exception. Three issues of political economy are involved.

The first issue involved the degree to which the housing question is linked to broader social problems. The social reformers who advocated regulatory housing policy saw the urban environment, and in particular the housing that immigrants to industrialising cities occupied, as the root of urban social problems. New York housing reformer Jacob Riis wrote in 1890 that the poor 'are shiftless, destructive, and stupid; in a word, they are what the tenements have made them' (Riis, 1957, p.207). Improve housing, and, according to the reformers, you would ameliorate the social problems plaguing cities.

Today's social reformers (and most social scientists) see deteriorated housing as only one manifestation of the broader condition known as poverty. Unemployment, poor health, lack of education, drug and alcohol abuse, broken families and poor housing conditions are linked in a syndrome that cannot be broken by segmenting problems and treating symptoms. A final possibility is that the housing question is but one particular manifestation of the exploitation of the working class by capitalists (see Engels, n.d.).

A second issue in political economy concerns whether housing regulation in a capitalist economy can be effective in improving the conditions of the poor. In a competitive economy, any costs associated with upgrading the housing stock will be passed on to tenants, or will reduce a landlord's rate of return on his investment. This will, according to some analysts, either raise the price of housing, or cause less housing to be built (because of the lower rate of return), or both. If existing housing is closely regulated, abandonment can result as regulations cause previously profitable housing to be unprofitable because of the inability of tenants to afford rent increases (see Ackerman, 1971; Hartman, Kesler and Le Gates, 1974). On the other hand, it is not clear that housing rregulations are a major cost of doing business, nor is it clear that the costs imposed are sufficient enough to cause abandonment or withdrawal of investment from the housing market (see Komesar, 1973; Markovits, 1976).

A final issue of political economy involved the degree to which housing regulation can be viewed as state action designed to lower the reproductive cost of labour. Clearly safe, clean housing can improve the health and general well-being of labour, thereby presumably improving labour's productivity. This presumes, of course, that housing regulation is successful. Moreover, for this interpretation to hold, it must be the case that the cost of housing improvements made at the insistence of government not simply be passed along to tenants. If such costs are passed along, then the general costs of subsisting in society will be pushed up, and so will labour costs — at least in a society governed by the laws of Ricardo where wages tend to fall to the subsistence level.

More problematic for the exploitation thesis is that housing regulation imposes the most direct costs on the owners of tenements. If regulation serves the manufacturing capitalists, it harms the housing capitalists. Everywhere housing regulations have been adopted, they have been fought by builders, owners, and manager of buildings, primarily on the ground that such regulations interfere with the free enterprise system. Nineteenth-century social reformer Jacob Riis put the issue directly:

> It is to be remembered that the health officers, in dealing with this subject of dangerous houses, are constantly treading upon what each landlord considers his private rights, for which he is ready to fight to the last. Nothing short of the strongest pressure will avail to convince him that these individual rights are to be surrendered for the clear benefit of the whole (Riis, 1957, p.205).

Frederich Engels noted the same phenomenon in England in 1872: 'In the town councils, the owners of unsound and dilapidated dwellings are almost everywhere strongly represented either directly or indirectly', resulting in applications of laws allowing authorities to close down dilapidated houses 'only in the most scandalous cases', (Engels, n.d., 69).

It is worth noting that Engels himself believed in the potential efficacy of housing regulation: 'in the hands of a government which would at last really administer [the housing laws], *it would be a powerful weapon for making a breach in the existing social state of things*' (Engels, n.d., 70; emphasis added).

Political ecology

Below the level of analysis I have termed political economy there exist complex, on-going interchanges between legislatures, bureaucracies, interest groups, interested individuals, and political parties. These interchanges occur within a set of legal, organisational, and cultural expectations influenced by the political economy. But in turn these interactions define and subtly alter the public economy. That is what I mean by interaction between the two levels of analysis.

In the United States, building regulation has been left to the states and localities. Hence one must look to the localities for the micropolitical interactions that define the on-going policy-making

Figure 14.1: Levels of Political Analysis

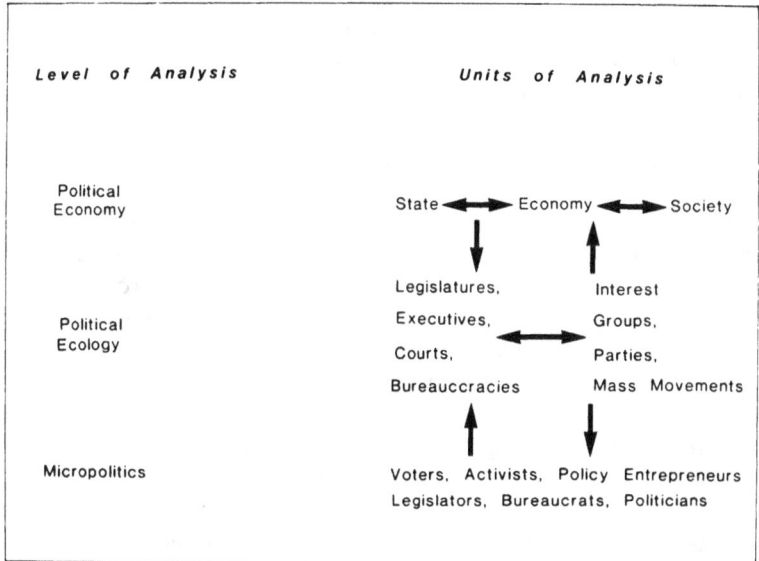

Interactions of course occur among elements at a single level (between institutions at the ecological level, for example). But the levels themselves are also causally related. Institutional interactions at the ecological level are governed by the broader political economy, and these interactions, in turn, affect how individuals behave (at the micropolitical level). There also exists a reverse causal flow, with individual behaviours causing institutional change and interactions among institutions causing evolution in the political economy.

process.

There are three central issues of political ecology involved here. They are, first, how is formal policy made? Second, how does implementation and administration influence operative policy? Third, how are the outputs of this process, determined as they are by both formal policy-making and administration, distributed among groups of citizens?

Studies of building code policy-making are few. However, in a study of the process of building code amendment in the city of Chicago, I found a very closed policy system in operation. A committee, appointed by the mayor, was responsible for code modifications; the mayor and city council invariably accepted the recommendations of the committee. The committee, titled the Mayor's Advisory Commission for Amending the Building Code, consisted of many affected interests: architects, engineers, officials from building trade unions, insurance underwriters, building managers, and building code enforcement officials from the fire and building departments of city government. Not serving on the committee, and therefore effectively shut out of the policy-making process, were tenants and neighbourhood organisations.

Building department officials maintained ties to national organisations of code officials. They thus had a great deal of knowledge about practices and proposed changes in other jurisdictions. Because of this superior knowledge, and because of their day-to-day experiences in the code enforcement process, these officials had disproportionate influence in the policy-making process. Indeed, the Commissioner of the Department of Buildings chaired the Advisory Commission, and he was responsible for many code innovations. Nevertheless, he always had to deal with the interests structured into the policy process, so that the code amending process often involved a great deal of negotiation and compromise. Those closed out of the process, of course, had little opportunity to air their views, much less become more involved.

Three aspects of this formal policy-making process are relevant to the interaction between political ecology and political economy. First, code officials, the public bureaucrats, have disproportionate power in the policy process. They are not simply tools of the affected interests; indeed, they often take a stand in favour of very rigorous code provisions, especially those involving 'life safety'. This often antagonises the private sector interests, particularly the architects and builders. Moreover, code officials in Chicago have tended to side with trade unionists on the issue of new, cheaper construction technologies that would cause loss of construction jobs. In the second place, there is a great deal of diffusion of innovations in policy changes among jurisdictions, due to the influence of national trade associations. Finally, the various interests structured into the policy process often do not agree among themselves, and these disagreements must be compromised. This policy system, then, has a political life of its own. As it acts on itself, ththe role of the local state in the public economy changes, albeit glacially.

A second ecological issue involves the extent to which formal policies are modified as they are administered. In the tradition of Max Weber, most political scientists view bureaucratic organisations as pursuing their own power interests that are not always reflective of the political system nor of broader society. This certainly seems to be the case for many urban services. Virtually all studies of urban public services by political scientists have concluded that outputs are bureaucratically determined (Levy *et al.*, 1974; Jones *et al.*, 1980; Mladenka, 1978, 1980; Antunes and Plumlee, 1977). In the case of building code enforcement in Boston Nivola (1979, p.154) concludes that the process 'was primarily a *bureaucratic process* — in the sense of an operation determined more by the dynamics of the local political system as a whole'. Because of this, Nivola (1979, p.156) quite properly notes that 'a city government's *outputs* (the character of key services, for instance) cannot always be traced to its *decisions*'. By modifying and not infrequently replacing formal policy decisions, policy administrators not only alter the character of the policy-making process, they also subtly alter the manner in which the state influences the political economy.

A final ecological issue in housing regulation is the distribution of outputs. One cannot determine the distributional pattern by a reading of the relevant statutes and ordinances, nor by a study of budgetary allocations. Distributional patterns are primarily determined by the operation of the bureaucracies responsible for administering policy. To some extent, the manner in which these bureaucracies operate vary according to political culture. In Detroit, long-known for its entrenched public bureaucracies, we found that spatial distributional patterns could be linked to organisational procedures. Indeed, distribution of building regulations outputs, as well as other services, were an unintended side consequence of operating according to standard bureaucratic decision rules (Jones *et al.*, 1980). Nivola, however, found that the immediate task environment of street-level bureaucrats was important in understanding distributional patterns in Boston (Nivola, 1979). Finally, in a study in Chicago, I found that distribution of building regulation outputs to neighbourhoods was a function both of bureaucratic procedures and the political strength of Democratic Party Ward Organisations (Jones, 1981). Each of these situations imply different decision-making structures for the distribution of social values, and different modes of operation of the local state in the local political economy as well.

I have detailed the operation of this particular policy system to try to indicate in a concrete manner the complexities of what is known as the local state in Marxist literature, and to suggest that the role of government in local society is not predetermined by underlying economic imperatives. Although those economic imperatives exert strong influence on the operation of local policy systems such as this one, the relationship is not determinative. Moreover, what occurs within the policy system exerts an independent influence on the political economy, and on the distribution of social values as well.

The Political Ecology of Policy Distribution

The distribution of publicly-produced benefits at the ecological level occurs through a number of institutional arrangements that interact with one another in quite complex ways. At this level of analysis, the Marxist unitary view of the state is of little utility. So is the equally unitary view of government often used in conventional analyses of public service delivery. In this unitary model, 'the 'government' aggregates consumer preferences, procures and organises means of service production, and delivers services as a monopoly supplier to constituents. Decisions about output and expenditure levels are assumed to be made by simple referenda or by omniscient and benevolent administrators' (Parks and Ostrom, 1981, p.171). Yet, as Parks and Ostrom (1981) indicate, the processes producing public outputs are far more complex, and the linkages between these processes and the distribution of benefits is more complex still.

In this section, I will try to tie explicitly existing social decision-making mechanisms to the distribution of governmentally-produced benefits. I do not pretend that this classification is exhaustive; only that it is a beginning at organising existing research on distribution. Three mechanisms of policy distribution are particularly important: the bias of institutional arrangements, policies that deliberately affect the distribution of social values, and administrative arrangements that are inadvertently distributive.

Institutional Arrangements

The first, and perhaps the most important, influence on the distribution of public sector outputs is the set of political institutions in society. No political arrangement is neutral in its effects. This is the case even though many institutional arrangements provide far more in collective benefits than in distributional ones. The American constitutional structure, for example, provides a method for aggregating preferences, reconciling conflict, and producing public policies, and that method is widely accepted in American society today. Nevertheless, political scientists never tire of instructing their students in the distributional effects of a system constructed explicitly to limit the influence of the mass public.

In conceiving of institutional bias and distributional patterns, one might think of both collective and private goods being produced. The collective goods could be conceived as the provision of an accepted method of making social decisions, less the decision costs of the method. The private goods are produced because of the distributional bias of the institution. The institution ought to be evaluated in terms of both effects.

Figure 14.2 illustrates this situation. Those benefits of an institutional arrangement are plotted against a distributional variable (such as class membership). All classes benefit to some extent from the arrangement; but because the institutins tend to produce policies that favour one class over another, part of the benefits produced are distributive in nature. (I would speculate that the ratio of collective to private goods produced is bound up with the legitimacy of the arrangement as perceived by citizens.)

In the United States, one of the most troublesome institutional arrangements is that of local control of policy-making powers. The constitutional institution of federalism and the tradition of local autonomy has meant that local governments have significant policy-producing powers. Because local governments have different resources, citizens will have access to different mixes and levels of public services. The tendency of classes, races, and ethnic groups to be sorted out on the landscape of a metropolis means that the overlay of territorial political jurisdictions will correspond, to some extent, with other social divisions.

Traditional lore has it that the wealthy will insulate themselves from the poor, often locked in central cities, and will provide themselves with services that are not available to less fortunate citizens because of resource disparities. While this analysis contains more than a grain of truth, it is not the crux of the problem. Often the wealthy suburbs actually provide *less* in the way of services for their citizens, as Gary Miller (1981) has so admirably documented. The residents of these communities do not want services and they do not want taxes. Through the mechanism of suburban incorporation, they insulate their wealth from the taxing power of jurisdictions where the poor concentrate. Hence the governmentally-fragmented metropolis is a political institution with strong distributive implications.

The existence of small policy-producing jurisdictions affects the distribution of social values in other ways. Most importantly, it allows private corporations to have more influence in the policy process than would be the case in a more centralised system. A corporation may be able to gain special tax exemptions or other benefits by getting a municipality wishing the corporation to locate facilities there to bid with other municipalities. As the competition for industry increases, so do the public incentives offered by municipalities.

Tax exemptions for new businesses push the costs of public services on to residents and older businesses. Moreover, an asymmetry of information exists between a municipality and a corporation that is considering relocation. The corporation knows what public incentives are necessary to influence its locational decisions, but the municipality does not. (Indeed, most studies indicate that the effect of tax incentives is minimal in the corporate location decision. See Vaughan, 1979, for example). This allows a corporation to extract more from a municipality than is minimally necessary to attract it to a particular location, a condition we have termed the *corporate surplus* (Jones, Bachelor, and Wang, 1981).

This system of small jurisdictions and a scarce 'supply' of

Figure 14.2: Benefits Produced by Institutional Arrangements

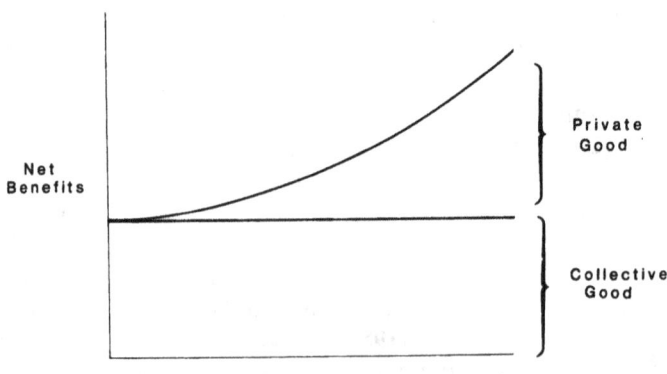

Distributional Variable (e.g., Class)

profitable economic enterprises had led Paul Peterson (1981) to argue that city governments can effectively pursue only policies that enhance the economic position of the city. While this analysis probably stretches the case too far, it is nevertheless true that the fragmented urban governmental system prevailing in the United states today does contain significant institutional bias. The system results in less service for the poor and more corporate influence in local decision-making than would be the case in a more centralised system.

A strong countervailing argument has, of course, been made by the public choice theorists (see Bish and Ostrom, 1973). They argue that fragmentation best approximates the collective good by providing a socially efficient allocation of goods and services. This is accomplished by a metropolitan public economy that approximates the market, having as it does many producers (in the form of local governments) and many citizen-consumers. A citizen will move to the locality providing the tax/service mix that best approximates his or her desired level. The collective result is a match between effective (economic) demand and supply. Thus the efficiency benefits derived from this arrangement must be compared to the distributional effects they produce.

The major problem with the above discussion is that the metropolitan public economy described in this literature does not exist. The extreme inequality that results from the operation of the purely competitive public economy has been limited by the intervention by higher levels of government. Intergovernmental revenue transfers from the federal government to the states, from the states to municipalities, school districts, and other local units of government, and from the federal government directly to local governments has ameliorated some of the most severe inequalities within metropolises. This has been accomplished by allocating increasing amounts for functions that disproportionately aid the poor. In 1960, for example, most federal grants went for highway construction, and, to a slightly lesser extent, income security. By 1980, federal grants were going to community development, health, income security, education, social services, and employment services, all programmes that have substantial benefits for the poor. Transportation was no longer a major priority.

The amelioration of interjurisdictional disparities has also been accomplished by formulas that distribute funds disproportionately to poorer juridictions. Community development block grants, for example, are provided according to population, poverty, and housing decay.

The current Reagan administration clearly understands the distributional bias inherent in the decision concerning what level of government is proper for performing a function. The administration has sharply curtailed many domestic programmes, and has proposed transferring many others to the states. This will withdraw the influence of the redistributive influence of the federal government from the scene, leaving poorer stats with fewer resources. It will also subject states to the logic of competition among small districts, discussed above.

Direct distributional policies.

Although the United States government is involved in literally thousands of programmes, there are but two really 'big ticket' items: national defence and income security. In the 1981 fiscal year, total budget outlays were $657.2 billion. Of that, $135.9 billion went for defence and $316.6 billion in payments to individuals, most of which came in the form of income security payments — social security retirement benefits, unemployment compensation, food stamps, etc.. Straightforward transfer payments to individuals dominate the transactions of the federal government in the national income accounts ($279.7 billion); substantially less goes to the purchase of goods and services ($218.3 billion). Additionally, some of the $90.1 billion in grants to state and local government goes for direct transfer payments — particularly for welfare, which is a joint function of the states and the federal government. (See the *Budget of the US Government, Fiscal 1983*, 9-59 and 9-61).

Between 1962 and 1981, defence spending in current dollars tripled, but payments to individuals increased elevenfold. Payments to individuals increased from 29.9 per cent of outlays to 48.2 per cent. As late as 1972, purchases of goods and sevices consumed 43.2 per cent of national government expenditures, but by 1981 this category of expenditures had declined to 32.7 per cent.

These figures indicate a dramatic change of function of the federal government in society, from provider of primarily collective goods (defence, highways, and hospitals) to redistributor of income. Most of these payments went not to the very poor but involved intergenerational transfer payments — over $163 billion was expended in fiscal 1981 from the social security retirement and disability fund, the railroad retirement fund, and for federal employee retirement and disability. These figures are far more compatible with an interpretation of government growth as a response to constituency pressures in a democratic society, coupled with changes in the age structure of society than as payments on behalf of capitalism to purchase social peace. Several seemingly incremental changes, and, in particular, the increases in benefit levels for social security reciptients and the tying of benefits to one measure of inflation (the Consumer Price Index) has resulted in a dramatic change in the role of the national government in society. Here is a very clear example of just how several disjointed actions at the ecological level can cause changes in the structure of the public economy.

Spillovers from Policy Implementation Arrangements.

Much of the distribution of policy benefits occurs in the course of trying to do something else. Distribution is accomplished inadvertently as a government agency attempts to achieve a goal or perform a task that is assigned to it. This normally happens as agencies grapple with administering policies adopted by the formal policy-making branches of government.

Inadvertent distributional effects can occur in two different situations, distinguishable on the basis of the nature of the immediate environment of the policy-implementing organisation. In one situation, the environment of the implementing agency is relatively quiescent, leaving the implementing organisation pretty much to itself in establishing the procedures according to which policy will be implemented. In the second situation, the environment is politically active, making demands on the implementing organisation and otherwise making difficult the straightforward implementation of the policy.

Most studies of local public service delivery have been studies of organisations in the former type of environment. Antunes and Mladenka note that most local services are provided in a political vacuum within which delivering organisations are isolated from political pressures and from overhead control by elected governmental officials:

The level of demand for services is low. Citizens are relatively content with existing services and programs; and, although service provision is not devoid of interest group politics, the diverse and localistic nature of local services inhibits most interest group activity. In addition, at-large elections and the absence of local [political] parties tend to isolate the government from the citizenry, while civil service reforms isolate the bureaucracy from local control. (Antunes and Mladenka, 1976, p.163)

Within this quiet political environment, service distribution is an unintended by-product of the service organisation's task-oriented behaviour. Relatively low-level decision rules dominate organisational behaviour, and the level of services received by groups in the city can be linked to the operation of these rules (see Levy *et al.* 1980). The rules tend to be procedurally fair, in the sense of not being discriminatory toward individuals. Because different people have different levels of political knowledge and inclinations to demand service, however, the decision rules that drive the organisation may be used to gain services that would not otherwise be available. If, for example, an agency will deliver service on demand, then high-demand groups will benefit disproportionately. If, however, capacity to deliver service is equal across a jurisdiction, then these high-demand groups will suffer a decline in service per demand.

Service distribution, then, is influenced primarily by administrative considerations in quiescent environments. Such a situation gives a great deal of autonomy to the administering organisation, and it can often deflect pressures for change both from clients and from overhead elected officials.

In a politicised environment, distribution proceeds in a radically different matter. Political forces and administrative forces struggle for ascendency in the establishment of value patterns. Not infrequently an administrator will find him or herself extremely cross-pressured between the demands of politicians for a responsive policy distribution and the administrative imperative to provide neutral administration. The conflict between politics and administration is played out in the offices of policy administrators confronted with such an environment.

While it is true that most urban services are delivered into quiescent environments, it is most assuredly *not* true that such environments have disappeared. Such environments certainly exist where local political parties remain strong, and they may well exist elsewhere.

The existence of turbulent political environments does not relieve the service delivery organisation from the repetitive tasks that must be performed in order to deliver services to citizens. Hence the organisation's behaviour is stil rule-driven. In such a situation the organisation seems to operate according to parallel service delivery rule structures. One set of rules are the normal, procedurally-neutral rules known in the literature as *bureaucratic decision rules*. The second set of rules have been termed *attention rules* by Crecine (1969). Organisational behaviour is conditional on the source of demands for action, with some groups (politically powerful neighbourhoods) receiving preferential treatment. Other groups must rely on bureaucratic decision rules for action; they do not generally go without service (see Jones, 1981).

The existence of a politicised environment, even one where a political machine thrives, does *not* imply that the political party structure has established hierarchical control over the service organisation. Although urban political machines in the United states have a reputation for being able to centralise power, machines are inherently decentralised operations. Only in limited situations have political 'bosses' been able to centralise meaningfully, generally by centralising the distribution of patronage. Even in such situations, significant decentralisation remains, because the party structure is based on a geography of decentralisation. Wards, the building-blocks of local machines in partisan cities, are distinct political entities with their own organisational lives and access to resources in the form of votes that ward leaders can control.

Table 14.1 presents evidence of both the operation of attention rules and the failure of hierarchical control of service delivery organisations in a machine city. The data are from a study of building regulations in the City of Chicago, the classic American machine city. Measures of outputs delivered to wards have been controlled for the operation of bureaucratic decision rules, which exerted a strong, independent influence on the distribution of outputs. This allows us to examine the influence of politics on the distribution of outputs disentangled from the influence of purely administrative factors.

The table classifies wards according to recognised electoral blocs. It also tabulates the average strength of the ward organisations according to the ability of wards to produce votes for a minor candidate (county sheriff) in a general election. This particular

Table 14.1: Building Regulation Outputs, Controlled for Bureaucratic Decision Rules, By Electoral Blocs

Electoral Bloc[a]	Average Ward Strength[b]	Average Residualised Output[c]
Machine Core (5 wards)	159.22	0.88
South Side Ethnic (9 wards)	122.65	0.44
North Side Ethnic (3 wards)	103.95	0.34
Black (15 wards)	119.79	0.19
Electorally Strongest (8 wards)	137.12	0.81
Electorally Weakest (7 wards)	99.86	-0.52
Northeast 'Polish' (10 wards)	62.28	-0.16
Reform (8 wards)	47.25	-1.34

Notes:
a. Based on Zikmund (1982, p.47). I have classified the 5th Ward as Reform and the 40th as Northwest; otherwise I have retained Zikmund's classification.
b. $(D-R)/\%21$, where D = number of votes for the Democratic Candidate for Sheriff, November, 1978 general election; R = votes for Republican opponent; $\%21$ = percentage of residents over 21 (1970). See Jones (1981) for justification.
c. Outputs are measured as the logarithm of the frequency of severe enforcement actions taken, where severity involved filing a court case or an action before a building department hearing officer. Actions taken because of decision rules are controlled by using residuals from a regression modelling the decision rules. The model regressed agency outputs on the number of citizen complaints, logged, and the age of the buildings.

office is important because of the substantial patronage associated with it. As can be seen, the electoral blocs differ systematically on the ward strength measure.

More importantly, the ward organisations are able to obtain building regulation outputs for their constituents in direct proportion to their electoral strength. The ward organisations take advantage of attention rules built into the city building department to gain preference for their constituents' demands for building-regulatory actions. Moreover, this political influence transcends racial divisions. The eight black wards that are electorally strongest receive outputs at almost the same level as do the core machine wards, but the black wards that do not produce for machine candidates are severely deprived in terms of such outputs.

This division also indicates a second point. Factional divisions in mayoral contests, upon which the bloc classification is based, are less important than is the ability of the ward organisation to deliver votes for minor elected officials. This power is translated into influence within service delivery organisations. It is not so much that the mayor, a creature of the party structure, controls the urban service bureaucracies and uses that control to deliver outputs to supporters. Rather, each ward organisation makes its separate claims on the service organisation, and the organisation responds according to its programmed attention rules. Hence the political machine has a very decentralised structure at the level at which service delivery actually takes place.

In both quiescent and active environments, policy distribution is not under the explicit control of the formal policy-making organs of government. Rather, distribution is accomplished through the activities of administering agencies and the organisations that have motive to influence those agencies. There is nothing deliberate or intentional about the resulting distributional patterns.

Conclusions

In this chapter I have argued that the study of the allocation and distribution of social values through the authoritative decision-making structures are at the heart of political analysis. Because there are no mechanisms to limit government to the provision of collective goods alone, many of the policies and services produced by government will be distributive.

Distribution occurs at two separate levels. *Political ecology* concerns the interaction of policy-making institutions with their environments. The environments of these organisations consists most importantly of other organisations: political parties, interest groups, bureaucracies, other policy-making organisations at various levels of government, and mass publics. The interaction among these organisations results in authoritative allocations and distributions of social values. *Political economy* concerns the manner in which the state (government) interacts with the economic structure and with broader society. The term has been primarily used in recent writings by Marxists, many of whom see the state as a reflection of the capitalist economic structure and the chief protector of that order. But one does not have to adopt the entire structuralist perspective to see that the relationship between the state, the economy, and the broader society are fit topics for analysis, topics that have been bypassed by both behaviouralists and institutionalists in political science (see Rich, 1980, for a comparison of approaches with reference to urban politics).

Two other points raised by structuralist analyses seem well-taken. The first is that the structure of the political economy distributes social values in society. The second is that the relationship between the state and the economy affects interactions at the level of what I have called political ecology, although I would not accept the determinism implied by the approach.

I have argued here that the political ecology of a society's policy-making institutions can influence the society's broader political economy. By examining one policy system, that of building regulation, I have tried to indicate how issues of both political economy and political ecology are raised, and that the workings of political ecology exerts an independent influence on the political economy. Finally, I have described the manner in which social decision-making mechanisms generate benefit distributions using an ecological perspective. The major ways in which distribution occurs are (i) through the bias of institutional arrangements; (ii) through intentionally distributional policies; and (iii) through administrative arrangements that are inadvertently distributional.

Social change, and, in particular, changes in value distributions, can occur because of the manner in which the state and the economy interact. It may be the case that the key contradiction of the role of the state in capitalist society, that of fostering capital accumulation and ensuring social peace through social expenditures, causes social change because of a dialectical logic. On the other hand, social change may be more evolutionary and less fraught with contradictory tendencies. Political economies may evolve due to cultural changes, or changes in technology, or pressures from other national poltical economies.

My argument that the on-going relationships between policy-making institutions and their oganisational environment can cause change in the broader political economy probably at root implies an evolutionary model of change. While I can conceive of fairly rapid change in the role of government in society due to organisational interactions, I cannot fit such a model within a dialectical framework — although such a possibility ought to be explored.

Notes

1. One might try to salvage the connection between collective goods provision and government by arguing that political demands will emerge for collective and merit goods but not private goods. Such an argument runs counter to much of what we know about the policy-making process. Especially problematic for such a theory are such phenomena as compromise, legislative log-rolling and 'side payments', the role of interest groups as interest articulators, and the role of political parties in the interest aggregation process. All of these political activities involve reconciliation of diverse interests and policy proposals, most of which are desired by some citizens but not by others (and are hence neither pure public nor meritorous private goods). Politics has more to do with the resolution of diverse demands for the public provision of private goods than with the straightforward provision of public goods.

2. The level of analysis problem has long been recognised by social scientists. Usually it is thought of as a technical problem of data analysis, on the one hand, or a philosophical problem of the 'proper' level of analysis on the other. The possibility that the two levels are casually interrelated has not been explored; indeed, I owe the idea itself to evolutionary biology. It is possible to conceive of both species adaptation and individual adaptation to environment. The phenomenon of 'overspecialisation', in which individual advantage restricts the ability of the species to adapt, is a case in point. Gould (1982, p.385) writes of 'the negative interaction of species-level disadvantage and individual-level advantage', linking casually individual and species survival. 'The general phenomenon must also regulate much of human sociey, with much higher-level institutions comprised or destroyed by the legitimate demands of individuals' (Gould, 1982, p.385).

References

Ackerman, A. (1971) 'Regulating Slum Housing Markets on Behalf of the Poor: Of Housing Codes, Housing Subsidies, and Income Distribution Policy', *Yale Law Journal*, **80**, 1093

Antunes, G., and K. Mladenka (1976) 'The Politics of Local Services and Service Distribution', in L.H. Masotti and R.L. Lineberry, (eds.), *The New Urban Politics*, Ballinger, Cambridge, Massachusetts

Antunes, G., and J. Plumlee (1977) 'The Distribution of an Urban Service: Ethnicity, Socioeconomic Status, and Bureaucracy as Determinants of Neighborhood Streets', *Urban Affairs Quarterly*, **13**, 73-94

Bernstein, M. (1955) *Regulating Business by Independent Commission*, Princeton University Press, Princeton

Bish, R., and V. Ostrom (1973) *Understanding Urban Government*, American Enterprize Institute, Washington, D.C.

Buchanan, J. (1968) *The Demand and Supply of Public Goods*, Rand McNally, Chicago

Clark, G., and M. Dear (1981) 'The State in Capitalism and the Capitalist State', in M. Dear and A.J. Scott, (eds.), *Urbanization and Urban Planning in Capitalist Society*, Methuen, London

Crecine, J.P. (1969) *Government Problem- Solving*, Rand McNally, Chicago

Dewsnup, E.R. (1907) *The Housing Problem in England*, The University of Manchester Press, Manchester

Easton, D. (1959) *The Political System*, Knopf, New York

Engels, F. (n.d.) *The Housing Question*, International Publications, New York

Goldwin, K.D. (1977) 'Equal Access vs. Selective Access: A Critique of Public Goods Theory', *Public Choice*, **2**, 52-71

Gould, S.J. (1982) 'Darwinism and the Expansion of Evolutionary Theory', *Science*, **216**, 380-87

Hanson, R.A. (1978) 'Towards an Understanding of Politics Through Public Goods Theory: A Review Essay', in W. Loehr and T. Sandler, (eds.), *Public Goods and Public Policy*, Sage, Beverley Hills, California

Hartman, C., R. Kessler, and R. LeGates (1974) 'Municipal Housing Code Enforcement and Low-Income Tenants', *American Institute of Planners Journal*, **40**, 90 = 104

Jones, B.D. (1981) 'Party and Bureaucracy: The Influence of Intermediary Groups on Urban Public Service Delivery', *American Political Science Review*, **75**, 688-700

Jones, B., L. Bachelor, and R. Wang (1981) 'Rebuilding the Urban Tax Base: Local Policy Discretion and the Corporate Surplus', Paper presented at the Annual Meeting of the Midwest Political Science Association, Cincinnati, Ohio, April 16-18

Jones, B.D., with S. Greenberg, and J. Drew (1980) *Service Delivery in the City*, Longman, New York

Komesar (1973) 'Return to Slumville: A Critique of the Ackerman Analysis of Housing Code Enforcement and the Poor', *Yale Law Journal*, **83**, 1175

Lasswell, H. (1936) *Politics: Who Gets What, When and How*, McGraw-Hill, New York

Levy, F., A.J. Meltsner, and A. Wildavsky (1974) *Urban Outcomes*, University of California Press, Berkeley, California

Lubove, R. (1962) *The Progressives and the Slums*, Univesity of Pittsburgh Press, Pittsburgh

Markovits, R. (1976) 'The Distributive Impact, Allocative Efficiency, and Overall Desirability of Ideal Housing Codes: Some Theoretical Clarifications', *Harvard Law Review*, **89**, 1915-46

Mlandenka, K. (1978) 'Rules,Service Equity, and Distributional Decisions', *Social Science Quarterly*, **59**, 192-202

Mlandenka, K. (1980) 'The Urban Bureaucracy and the Chicago Political Machine: Who Gets What and the Limits to Political Control', *American Political Science Review*, **74**, 991-98

Miller, G.J. (1981) *Cities by Contract: The Politics of Municipal Incorporation*, MIT Press, Cambridge, Massachusetts

Musgrave, R.A. (1959) *The Theory of Public Finance*, McGraw-Hill, New York

Nivola, P. (1979) *The Urban Service Problem*, Lexington Books, Lexington, Massachusetts

O'Connor, J. (1973) *The Fiscal Crisis of the State*, St. Martins, New York

Office of Management and Budget (1982) *Budget of the United States Government Fiscal Year 1983*, US Government Printing Office, Washington, D.C.

Parks, R., and E. Ostrom (1981) 'Complex Models of Urban Service Systems', in T.N. Clark, (ed.), *Urban Policy Analysis*, Sage Publications, Beverly Hills, California

Peterson, P. (1981) *City Limits*, University of Chicago Press, Chicago

Plato (1945) *The Republic of Plato*, translated with Introduction and Notes by F.M. Cornfield, Oxford University Press, New York

Rich,R.C. (1980) 'The Complex Web of Urban Governance: Gossamer or Iron', *American Behavioral Scientist*, November

Rich, R.C. (1982) 'Urban Development and the Political Economy of Public Production of Services', paper presented at the Annual Meeting of the Southwestern Political Science Association, March

Riis, J. (1957) *How the Other Half Lives*, Hill and Wang, New York

Samuelson, P.A. (1954) 'The Pure Theory of Local Expenditure', *The Review of Economics and Statistics*, **36**, 387-89

Stewart, C.W. (1900) *The Housing Question in London, 1855-1900*, Jas. Truscott and Son, London

Tiebout, C.M. (1956) 'A Pure Theory of Local Expenditure', *Journal of Political Economy*, **44**, 416-24

Vaughan, R.J. (1979) *State Taxation and Economic Development*, Council of State Planning Agencies, Washington, D.C.

Veiller, L. (1900) *Tenement House Legislation in New York 1852-1900*, Brandow Printing Co., Albany, New York

Zikmund, J., II (1982) 'Mayoral Voting and Ethnic Politics in the Daley-Bilandic-Byrne Era', in S.K. Gove and L.H. Masotti, (eds.), *After Daley: Chicago Politics in Transition*, University of Illinois Press, Urbana, Illinois

15

Public Choice and Private Power:
A Theory of Fiscal Crisis

Frances Fox Piven
and
Roger Friedland

The fiscal history of a people is above all an essential part of its general history ... In some historical periods the immediate formative influence of the fiscal needs and policy of the state on the development of the economy and with it on all forms of life and all aspects of culture explains practically all the major features of events; in most periods it explains a great deal and there are but a few periods when it explains nothing. Schumpeter (1954)

The public budget is an historical repository of the effects of economic change and political conflict. New modes of production transform the location and forms of wealth and thereby also transform the state's capacity to finance its expenditures. New groups thrust up by economic developments reach for state power and turn that power into state expenditures in their own interests. The history of struggles for empowerment and enrichment, and against domination and impoverishment, is imprinted in patterns of public expenditures and taxation.

Nor is this politics of state budgets always smoothly incremental and adaptive. Instabilities in public finance have historically been associated with severe ruptures in the organisation of political and economic power, ruptures which in turn presaged large scale changes, even revolutionary changes, in the organisation of the state. Thus the fiscal crises that erupt when expenditures outstrip revenues have often been harbingers of new modes of governance, as when fiscally bankrupt absolutist states in France in the eighteenth century, or in Russia in the twentieth century, collapsed in the face of insurrection; or when municipal fiscal crises in industrialising American cities of the late nineteenth and early twentieth century ushered in reform governments; or when the fiscal collapse of municipalities in the Great Depression precipitated the rise of a Federal welfare state.

Now, once again, in the United States and elsewhere, and at local and national levels, intense political conflicts accompany the making of public budgets, expenditures outstrip revenues, and cries of fiscal crisis are raised. The intensity of political conflict over the public purse, and the fact that these conflicts accompany the appearance of limits to economic growth in capitalist economies, confirms what history suggests — that fiscal strains have deep roots in the political and economic organisation of a society, and that the resolution of these strains may require comparably large scale changes in the organisation of the state. Yet the prevalent theories of state finance are not adequate to explain these events, in part because they each restrict their purview to one or another aspect of the complex and interactive developments that produce fiscal crisis. In this chapter we first review a number of such theories as they have been developed to explain the urban fiscal crisis, then suggest the beginnings of a more comprehensive perspective which incorporates but also transcends these theories, and finally apply our perspective to an interpretation of the fiscal crisis of American cities.

Public Choice

Perhaps the most widely used theory of state finance, and the most parsimonious, is the theory of public choice, which employs the model of a market place to analyse patterns of municipal expenditure and taxation. Elected officials, anxious to remain in office, provide a package of public goods which approximates the preferences of the median voter. Citizens, in turn, use their information about public services and tax liability either to vote for officials that deliver their preferred bundle of public services and taxes, or to move to a location that does. The resulting pattern of voting and migration produces an equilibrium solution in which the marginal tax price and the marginal expenditure benefit are equal (Borcherding and Deacon, 1972; Bish, 1979; Peterson, 1975; Deacon and Shapiro, 1975).

Viewed from the perspective of the public choice model, urban fiscal strains reflect imperfections in the market mechanisms which control the provision of public services. These imperfections result from the fact that public services are not explicitly priced. Taxation certainly provides an implicit price system in the metropolitan market place, but this price system is deeply flawed. One way that it is flawed is that most public services are universally available; if police services are provided, they are provided for all, no matter what taxes they pay. Moreover, because explicit prices are not used to allocate resources — i.e. tolls do not rise at rush hour — there tends to be great slippage between demands for such services and their supply (Thompson, 1976).

Institutional barriers to entry are a related source of inefficiency in the public market place. In the private market, if a firm is not producing a good at the cost or quality customers desire, other firms are likely to enter to capture this potentially lucrative market. Public choice theorists view the proliferation of local governments as analogous to such inter-firm competition. In other words, the fragmentation of municipal governments in the United States, combined with the large measure of authority each jurisdiction has to set its own spending and taxing policies, increases the power of voters vis-à-vis the local state. Governmental fragmentation thus converts the entire metropolis into a marketplace, one analysed as such by public finance economists. It follows that local governmental consolidation is undesirable, in a way analagous to concentration in the economic marketplace. But, since government officials often view fragmentation as irrational or inimical to existing city interests, they have erected obstacles to the creation of new jurisdictions, or even have attempted to consolidate old jurisdictions. A public choice perspective argues that the impact of such market restrictions is to increase *per capita* local government costs (Martin, 1976).

Public choice analysts also argue that the fiscal strains of the central cities result from the very success of the public market place. In the postwar period, the central cities experienced a massive influx of poor residents. Because these residents consume large amounts of public services and provide little in public revenues, it is rational for homeowners to move out of the central cities. Suburbanisation provided the homeowner with preferred public services at less cost. Consequently, in metropolitan areas where suburban service levels are high and tax levels low relative to their central cities, city to surburban movement has been more intense (Frey, 1979). Among those who remain in such cities, the median voter has considerably less tax liability than the average tax payer

— whether resident homeowner or private firm — with the result that there is a growing disjuncture between the demands for public services and the willingness of local taxpayers to finance them. Fiscal strains thus signal that the city's residents cannot obtain everything they want; they can only get what their taxpayers are willing to pay for.

There are a number of striking inadequacies in the public choice model. In positing that the provision of public goods is controlled by votes and 'invisible feet', the theory presumes a rough equality among voters, and does not really confront the inequalities among voters that result from their unequal tax generating capacities. Moreover, not only are taxable resources distributed unequally, but it is those who control local investment who control the generation of these taxable resources. This suggests that the policies necessary to generate electoral majorities are determined by the many, while those necessary to generate taxable resources are determined by the few. As Rokkan once remarked, 'votes count, but resources decide' (1966, p.105). Studies consistently indicate that the impact of economic growth on public expenditure and tax structure is overwhelming, while that of party competition or partisan control is much smaller or insignificant (Dye, 1972; Fried, 1975; Alford and Friedland, 1975). But public choice economists cope with this difficulty by transmuting the fiscal insignificance of electoral politics into its opposite. They do this by treating economic growth as if it subsumed the preferences of the resident population. Thus the significant effect of median income on local public expenditures is interpreted simultaneously as an effect of fiscal capacity and the preferences (or income elasticities of demand) of the median voter. That the electoral process through which such voters are supposed to exert influence often has little fiscal impact has not deterred the analysis.[1]

Why should electoral politics matter so little in the determination of public expenditure, while patterns of economic growth matter so much? First, policies which support private investment are widely thought to be at least self-financing, if not fiscally profitable (although as we will shortly note this may not always be the case). Borrowing for local capital spending, in particular, is determined by the anticipated ability of such spending to stimulate a sufficient flow of taxable private investment to pay off the loan. Policies which maintain electoral majorities are not self-financing, but a drain on the revenues available to local government. Most residential units provide less in taxable revenues than they consume in public expenditures. Moreover private investment often provides local employment as well as a net fiscal surplus, so that local governments are particularly attuned to the expenditure demands of investors.

Second, dominant investors have considerably more locational discretion than do voters. In the Western economies, the great bulk of all commodity and capital flows are generated by a relatively small number of multilocational firms. Smaller single-location firms either provide inputs for the multilocational firms, or service the households whose members they employ (Pred, 1977). The multilocational structure of investment allows such firms to make marginal adjustments in their investments in response to inadequate local public policies with low risk and low costs.

A city's residents are far more locationally constrained than its multilocational investors. A household's decision to migrate involves a total transformation in life conditions. The costs of search are high, the available information about alternatives quite low, and the risks of failure great. Relocation often involves the destruction of irreplaceable networks of family, friendship and neighbourhood. These networks are a sort of sunken cultural capital which, unlike buildings, tend to appreciate with time.[2]

Because a city's population is less mobile than its capital, it is less powerful vis-à-vis city government. A city's voters and their personal properties are captives, while its biggest investors are freer to shift their capital elsewhere. The relative immobility of population restricts residents to votes as a source of political power, while capital is better able to exert influence through disinvestment or the threat of disinvestment. Perhaps that is part of the reason that large business concerns are able to withdraw from local politics, while remaining influential. It may also help explain the ferocity of the state and local tax revolt which swept through areas of the United States in the late 1970s. Voters were not sufficiently able or willing to vote with their feet. It was through the ballot, particularly the referendum, that they were forced to operate. That such tax expenditure revolts should occur, often capturing three-quarters of the vote, is inexplicable from a public choice perspective which posits an efficient, democratic market for public goods.

In sum, the public choice model largely ignores investors, their preferences, and their impact on local public expenditure and revenue patterns (Deacon, 1977). But other theoretical perspectives which purport to explain the urban fiscal crisis have taken this realm of politics as their own.

Private Government

The public choice approach assumes that elected officials control municipal government and that the agencies of government are neutral respondents to a marketplace in which votes and movement are the main currencies. An alternative approach argues that public agencies are not controlled by elected officials, still less by the electorate. Rather, municipal agencies tend to be autonomous. In its simplest variant, this approach treats agency autonomy as a consequence of bureaucratic vested interests and the complex procedures they generate on the one hand, and the decline of urban partisan organisations able to control the bureaucraticised agencies on the other hand.

In this model, the interests of citizen-consumers and the public generally are simply excluded from the bureaucratic political system (Sharpe, 1973; Offe, 1972). Voters, even wealthy voters, do not significantly influence public budgets, as in Lineberry's investigations showing that neither race nor class nor the political power of residents affected the inter-neighbourhood distribution of park and fire services (1977). Instead of responding to the preferences of the general citizenry or elected officials, public agencies use their autonomous power to continue to garner resources from the public purse, impervious to changes in urban social composition or electoral organisation. Indeed, popular discontent over public services may ironically only increase the power and purse of the public agencies as the bureaucracies use the occasion of such discontent to make new claims for bureaucratic expansion, which may have little effect on the quality or distribution of agency services (Alford, 1975; Piven, 1977; Friedland, Piven and Alford, 1977). In partial confirmation of this model, a considerable body of empirical research has found that previous expenditure for a given programme is the strongest predictor of current expenditure for that programme (Fried, 1975; Meltsner, 1971; Sharkansky, 1970; Cowart, 1969; Davis, Dempster and Wildavsky, 1966). These findings are sometimes interpreted as the result of a stable structure of inter-bureaucratic power, and sometimes as reflecting the inability of elected officials to politically control and evaluate all agency budgets, with the consequence that they rely on simplifying, nonpolitical rules to allocate scarce funds (Dye, 1972; Domhoff, 1967; Wildavsky, 1964; Lindblom, 1961).[3]

While the image of powerful and autonomous bureaucracies is familiar and compelling, the actual sources of bureaucratic power remain somewhat opaque in much of this work. Another and more satisfactory variant of the bureaucratic approach is less mysterious about the ultimate sources of bureaucratic power. In this variant, the significance of bureaucratic autonomy is not that insulation from the political world itself yields power, but that insulation from the realm of electoral politics yields opportunities for the formation of alliances with powerful clientele interest groups. Thus bureaucratic power results not only from the autonomy yielded the agencies by their own bureaucratic vested interests and complex procedures, and the declining capacities of electoral politicians, but from the strategic manoeuvering of economic interest groups who want to protect the agency policies they rely upon from political challenge.

Where public choice theory populates the political world with consumer-citizens and largely ignores the investor, it is investors who are central to the determination of public expenditure in this alternative model. Investors — because of their intense interest, their control over many of the parameters that public agencies wish to influence, and their organisational concentration — tend to dominate public agencies and become their chief source of political support (Alford and Friedland, 1975). Thus public agencies tend to be controlled by those groups who have production interests in their services. Local banks dominate finance boards, developers the zoning boards, downtown corporations the urban renewal agencies, doctors the local health systems, and so on (Alford 1975; McConnell, 1966; Marmor *et al.*, 1975; Piven, 1977).

In the political world posited by the theorists of private government, fiscal strain results in part simply from the ability of bureaucratic-investor alliances to manipulate the public budget. As a consequence, programme piles upon programme, the budget of each determined by how long it has been in existence and the power of its clientele. Furthermore, the fragmentation of public authority — both within the city and between cities — provides no locus for coordination and no incentives for a public agency to be accountable for the social and fiscal costs of its actions. Thus, urban renewal agencies may displace light industry and local retail trade without having to account for the local unemployment and rising welfare expenditures that displacement has caused. Or highway agencies increase the flow of private automobiles, and, with it, local pollution, congestion, and auto accidents. The skein of bureaucracies approximates the mercantile world, each agency using its political power to protect and expand its boundaries and access to resources.

Fiscal strains are also likely to emerge with changes in the economic structure of the city or the entry of new claimants into the contest for public services. Existing public expenditures may contribute little to, or perhaps even undermine, the economic performance and thus the fiscal capacity of the city; or they may provide few meaningful benefits to new constituencies. But bureaucratic power is such that these expenditures are not cutback or reoriented. Instead, the political destabilisation that new claims threaten to engender merely provides an opportunity for the expansion of established agencies (Alford, 1973). From this private government perspective, the tax revolts of homeowners can be viewed as evidence of the inability of residents to control urban budgets through their elected representatives.

There is no question but that the private government perspective explains much about public policy that public choice (and other variants of democratic theory) cannot explain. Nevertheless, not all public policies can reasonably be construed as responses to investor interests. To be sure, the question of who exerts a determining influence on policies, and who benefits from them, is complicated. The considerable scepticism with which official explanations of policy are now treated reflects an awareness of these complexities. It is indeed true that programmes to provide housing or medical care for the poor, for example, have often been bent in other directions by private sector groups who saw opportunities for profit in these programmes. But this sort of explanation cannot be extended to account for all or even most government expenditures, particularly when a good many public expenditures are in fact vigorously opposed by investor interests. Not least, such a perspective cannot make sense of the current concerted effort by American investor interests to strip down regulatory programmes and slash expenditures on income maintenance and social service programmes, not only on the federal level, but on the state and local level as well. On these issues, investors speak with virtually one voice, and that voice is hostile. A perspective that attributes public expenditures to a private government dominated by investor interests cannot make sense of the public budget taken as a whole, or of the formidable opposition that has arisen to large portions of that budget among investors.

Local Capitalist State

Public choice theory assumes electoral control of public budgets and a politically neutral state. Theories of private government assume investor control and a bureaucratically fragmented state. Theories of the local capitalist state assume that public finance is subordinated to the requirements of capitalism (O'Connor, 1973; Castells, 1977; Lojkine, 1976).

According to this perspective the expansion of public expenditures is driven by the dual, and contradictory, requirements of maintaining capital accumulation and political legitimacy. In O'Connor's (1973) influential formulation, the state must, on the one hand, counteract the inherent crisis tendencies of capitalism — insufficient demand and inadequate profits — by increasingly absorbing the private costs of production (social capital) and lowering the costs of labour power (social consumption). On the other hand, to pacify the increasingly large surplus population which either cannot find sufficient work or wages to survive, the state must increasingly absorb the social costs of production (social expenses) as well.

Other analysts in this group have argued that the steady growth of urban expenditures derives from the problematic nature of consumption under advanced capitalism (Castells, 1977). On the one hand, the monopolisation of capitalist enterprise combined with greatly increased productivity make the scope of effective demand increasingly problematic. On the other hand, the increasing spatial and functional complexity of production and consumption render the private market for consumption goods inadequate to the reproduction of labour power. Industries can produce more than the populace can buy and people frequently cannot buy what is necessary for them to produce. Both the need to expand private consumption and to adapt individual capacities to produce and consume to a more complex economic organisation come to depend increasingly on public provision of consumption goods. Thus, for example, post World War II US highway construction, dismantlement of streetcar lines, and homeowner tax subsidies are analysed as public interventions to stimulate individual commodity consumption. The provision of public housing in French cities after World War II is analysed as a government attempt to increase labour mobility at a time of rapid urbanisation of investment combined with inadequate private production of housing (Castells, 1977, pp. 386-92, 161-3).[4]

From these capitalist state perspectives, fiscal strains are a transposition into the public realm of the crisis of corporate profitability. Both capital and labour push vigorously for greater state support for production and consumption: surplus capital seeks profitable outlets, workers strive to maintain their conditions of life, and surplus labour seeks to survive. Expenditures escalate, yet the private surplus remains out of public reach. The result is fiscal crisis. Consequently the tax revolts of homeowners represent a popular response to the inability of the public sector to finance the public expenditures required by advanced capitalism without also cutting deeply into popular incomes.

The usefulness of the capitalist state perspective is in the insistence that events occurring in the city can only be understood if the scope of analysis is broadened to a systemic or societal level. This enlarged focus is illuminating, but serious flaws remain. One such flaw is the tendency to assert the effects of public expenditures on the basis of *a priori* categories, rather than subjecting these effects to empirical scrutiny. Concepts like social consumption, for example, are used to categorise public expenditures without an effort to ascertain whether such expenditures actually do lower the costs of reproducing labour power. But whether or not expenditures on public housing or public education, for example, lower the labour costs of capital is contingent at the very least on the incidence of tax costs and expenditure benefits, as well as on the opportunity costs of providing the services through the private as opposed to the public sector. Similarly, public subsidies for private suburban housing construction cannot be assumed by *a priori* definition to stimulate a style of life conducive to commodity consumption and therefore to capitalist growth; the actual effects of such public subsidies on capitalist growth need to be estimated empirically.

A related and less easily remediable flaw has to do with the tendency to treat such assumed effects of public expenditures as causes of these expenditures. An awesome and systemic rationality is imputed to some segment of the state, whether it is the Federal executive or urban planners, and the problematic character of the link between the uses of public authority and the systemic requirements of capitalist growth disappears. A smooth and circular functionalism thus replaces the conflict and contradiction which is central to the Marxist theory of accumulation of private capital. But surely political experience suggests that state expenditures are also the focus of conflict, between poor and rich, consumers and producers, workers and caitalists. And just as capital uses its political power to bolster its economic power, so do the victims of capitalist growth use politics to reshape the distribution of income or the quality of consumption generated by the private market. Considerable data now exist to indicate that class-based partisan politics do affect national and local expenditure patterns (Stephens, 1980; Aiken and Martinotti, 1979). That such a conflictual politics should result in a public budget which is optimal for capitalist growth and political stability would be miraculous. In sum, both the effects of particular patterns of public expenditure in restraining or furthering capitalist growth, and the effects of political conflict in hindering or sustaining particular patterns of public expenditure, have yet to be specified theoretically and estimated empirically by theorists of the local capitalist state.

Each of these perspectives on urban fiscal crises sketches a political landscape with different actors and different political processes, and hence offers different explanations of state fiscal crises. The public choice model recognises voters and taxpayers, who register preferences through an electoral system that works like a market place where political officials strive to offer packages of goods to match the preferences of political consumers. Consistently, fiscal crisis is attributed not to the essential workings of this market, but to the imperfections in the public market that result largely from inadequate price-indexing of public goods or barriers to movement. The private government model recognises bureaucracies and investors as the key actors in the political world, and it is the distinctive structural features of bureaucracies which make possible the collusive special interest politics of bureaucratic-investor alliances. Consistently, fiscal crisis is attributed to the plunder of the public budget made possible by private government. The capitalist state model recognises not voters or bureaucracies but capitalism and the state. The politics of voters and special interest groups recede into the background, and the fiscal crisis is understood as the eruption within the state budget of the systemic crisis of the capitalist economy itself. Broadly conceived, none of these arguments is wrong, yet none is adequate by itself to account for the specific character of contemporary public fiscal crisis in relation to its historic precedents. We will argue that the origin and intensity of the urban fiscal crisis is rooted in the changing relationship between citizens, investors and governments in urban areas. But that relationship in turn is structured by historically specific institutional arrangements which regulate the interaction between voters, investors and government.

Institutional Structure and the Resource Requirements of Governance

In its sparest form, the institutional structure of Western systems can be described by the relationship between capitalism, democracy and the state. In capitalist societies, the state, including the local state, is legally constrained to guarantee public political rights to speak freely, to organise politically, to participate electorally. So, too, state authority is circumscribed by the guarantee of private property ownership rights — to possess and dispossess, to buy and sell, to borrow and lend, to invest and disinvest, to hire and fire. Taken together, these rights pattern the basic relations between the state, democracy and capitalism.

The institutional arrangements in which these rights are embedded specify the main vulnerabilities of the state to the larger society. Because state leaders require voting majorities, they depend on the mass publics who supply those majorities. Furthermore, because state leaders require revenues, they depend on private investors who ultimately are the source of state revenues.

In other words, the institutional arrangements which guarantee political rights and property rights generate institutionalised sources of power vis-à-vis the state. The power of mass publics includes not only their right to vote, but their right not to vote and their ability on some occasions to express their demands through non-institutionalised protest which may ultimately threaten electoral majorities. The power of private investors derives from the dependence of all incomes, and thus taxable revenues, upon profitable investment. Mass publics attempt to convert their voting power into policies which improve their living standards, particularly their consumption levels. Private investors attempt to convert their revenue-producing powers into public policies that improve the profitability of their investments.

But the state does not merely register and respond to the demands of voters and investors. It also acts to protect these external resources upon which it depends. On the one hand, the state strives to ensure that mass political participation is channeled through electoral institutions, and that electoral majorities are secured. Since political rights define the necessity of voting majorities as a resource for governance, the state will use its authority and expenditures to try to secure those voting majorities. On the other hand, the state must ensure that property owners continue to invest and that some portion of the private revenues which such investment produces are secured by the state through taxation. Since property rights make the state dependent on economic investments which it does not control, the state will use its authority and expenditures to try to promote investment that is subject to taxation. Failure to command both votes and revenues leads to a crisis of state power, whether political crisis or fiscal crisis, or both political and fiscal crisis. Public policies, and the public purse in particular, are thus the currency of exchange between the state on the one hand, and mass publics and private investors on the other. Public policies must be capable of simultaneously securing voting majorities and adequate public revenues.

This schematic model is intended to describe institutional arrangements created not by some mystical functional processes, but rather by an actual historical politics, a politics that was conflict-ridden and uneven. The specific inistitutional arrangements which pattern the state's vulnerability to mass publics and investors in democratic capitalist societies did not emerge automatically through the unfolding of some sort of evolutionary process, but were forged by the actual efforts of specific groups and classes to enhance their power and advantage by means of their relationship to the state, and by the actual efforts of the state to enhance its power and advantage by means of its relation to specific groups and classes. The property rights which ensure the state's ultimate revenue dependence on private investment did not merely evolve; they were won by an emerging bourgeoisie in the course of a centuries-long challenge to the power of the feudal and then the

absolutist state. The unique forms of capitalist property rights —
the unfettered right to buy and sell land, possessions and labour,
the right to trade for a profit, to make and enforce contracts, to
lend money at interest — were secured only slowly, unevenly, and
through conflict. Similarly, political rights did not evolve
automatically, but were won, sometmes only as a consequence of
revolutionary challenges to state power by insurgent populations.

Moreover, the relation between property rights and political
rights is historically complex, for these rights were perceived as
both complementary and contradictory; the struggle for capitalist
and democratic rights was not only a struggle between state and
society, but also a struggle between capitalist and democratic
rights, and therefore a struggle within society. Thus although a
rising capitalist class fought for the political rights that would
secure its property rights, and sometimes raised the banner of
political rights high as a means of securing popular support, when
its own battles were won it perceived the extension of political
rights to unpropertied groups as a threat to these property rights.
And the unpropertied themselves perceived the struggle for political
rights as a means of securing economic rights, as when insurgent
French workers in the revolutions of the nineteenth century called
for the 'Democratic and Social Republic' (Rude, 1979). This
conflict has been regulated, but it has never been resolved. Indeed,
the underlying and recurrent tension between property rights and
political rights has been a force in the periodic reorganisation of the
elaborate state structures which reflect and embody property rights
and political rights in capitalist and democratic societies, including,
as we shall argue, the elaborate institutional structures of urban
government in the United States.

Historically as well as schematically, the state was also an actor
in the process through which rights were institution- alised; it did
not merely register and react to external demands, but acted in its
own interests in a political environment characterised by competing
economic and political demands, and by military challenge. In
particular, the state was more likely to cede legal rights to property
or to political participation when it was itself internally weakened,
or militarily threatened. The struggles of the bourgeoisie for
property rights were often won through an alliance between crown
and merchants against feudal authorities, an alliance in which the
crown ceded laws favourable to trade in exchange for taxes and
custom duties (Tigar and Levy, 1977, p.47). The expansion of

property and political rights was thus not only the consequence of mobilisations against the state, but also a means used by the state to extract the revenues and manpower it needed.

This was most particularly so when the state was engaged in war, for military conflict intensified the state's dependence on the larger society. Warfare escalated the needs of the state for resources — for money, food and men — which had to be extracted from the society over which the state claimed sovereignty. At the same time, external war strained the capacity of the state to secure compliance and crush endemic resistance within by means of military force (Braun, 1975). And the ever more sophisticated and complex means of warfare, and the increasing scale of warfare, required ever more intensive and extensive state resource extraction (Finer, 1975). A large part of the history of fiscal reform can be understood as the history of states struggling to increase their resources while manoeuvering to avoid either popular tax revolts or opposition from their banker and businessman financiers when they are strained by the demands of war. As Rudolph Goldscheid, a fiscal sociologist, remarked, 'warfare is the moving motor of the whole development of public finance' (cited in Braun, 1975, p.311).[5]

But warfare was not the only motor. Evolving patterns of production, exchange and consumption generated new forms and new distributions of wealth, and correlatively new forms and distributions of taxable resources. The gradual elaboration and extension of property rights and democratic rights can be explained in part as a series of strategic concessions made by the state to social groups who had resources the state required — to mercantile groups who controlled trade with its bountiful yield of excise and customs duties, to capitalists who provided the state with low interest loans which severed state debt from solvency, to the working class who provided tax revenues and who also provided the manpower for standing armies mobilised through mass conscription. The extension of formal rights to property and political participation facilitated the extraction of resources from these groups by the state. In other words, we propose our model sketching the relationship of formal rights to state finance not as a replacement for an historical analysis, but as a model of contemporary institutional arrangements that are the summation of a complex historical politics.

Votes, Revenues and Local State Structures

We noted earlier that public choice, private government, and capitalist state perspectives each contruct a distinctive politics, with distinctive actors and distinctive processes. Since these actors and processes can all be found in urban politics, each perspective is at least partly right. Thus public choice begins by asserting the centrality of voters and voting in determining public expenditures, and there is evidence that votes do matter in fiscal politics. It is because local governments are compelled to try to manage voter participation that they provide social services. Moreover, the quantity and quality and costs of these services have become increasingly important, both as components of the real income of urban residents and the quality of urban life, and as focal issues in urban political conflict. These developments argue that public choice theorists have grasped something important in urban politics. But what they have grasped is only one aspect of a more complicated process. By itself, a concentration on voters and voting falls far short of explaining the unfolding of the urban fiscal crisis. Moreover, the role of voters and voting in patterning urban expenditures is not an historical constant, but changes dramatically over time, and that too needs to be explained.

Our model also acknowledges the importance of votes. More than that, it offers an explanation of this aspect of urban fiscal politics by rooting voter politics in specific institutional arrangements which themselves derive from a concrete history of conflict. Muncipal governments attempt to absorb popular political participation as a consequence of those institutional arrangements which make them vulnerable to popular discontents. Most important and long-lasting is the institutionally-specified dependence on electoral support of those who occupy positions of authority in the local state. However, by arguing that these electoral arrangements are only a part of the structure of interdependencies that pattern the relationship between the local state and urban society, our model moves toward remedying the partial character of public choice explanations. Finally, as we shall soon argue, by positing this more complicated structure of interdependencies, we are able to account for historical changes in the relative influence of voters on urban public expenditures.

Just as the public choice theorists can point to evidence of voter influence, so can theorists of private government point to evidence of bureaucratic/investor alliances and their impact in shaping urban public policies. The bulk of private investment takes place in cities. This private investment requires public investment, and much of it is provided by municipalities. In 1974-75, for example, US city government expenditures accounted for fully half of all government capital outlays for construction (Sbragia, 1979). Like the theorists of private government, we also argue that municipal governments will attempt to support private investment. We propose, however, that the politics of bureaucratic/investor alliances that underly these policies to support capitalist profitability is generated and sustained by specific institutional arrangements. Most important and enduring is the institutionally-specified dependence of the local state on the taxable revenues generated by private investment. However, since this revenue dependence defines only one aspect of the interdependence between the local state and the city, investor politics is only one aspect of the politics of public expenditure. Finally, because we posit a more complex structure of interdependencies, we are able to account for historical changes in the relative influence of investors on urban fiscal policy.

Theorists of the capitalist state assert that all capitalist governments, including local governments, must facilitate both economic growth and mass political participation. But they fail to specify the political processes through which these systemic imperatives are translated into govermental policies, or the structural arrangements which generate and sustain such political processes. Instead, they rely mainly on their own generally untested assessments of the consequences of urban policies to derive arguments about the political process which generated these policies.

Our model expands and elaborates on theories of the capitalist state by proposing that policies which promote profitability, and policies which promote political legitimacy, arise from an actual politics of investors and investment, and an actual politics of voters and voting. The politics of investment and the politics of voting, in turn, originate in the institutional arrangements which pattern the relations between capitalist democratic governments and the larger society. This specification permits empirical investigation of the groups and processes which generate public policy responses. By thus specifying the causes of public policy, and separating them from their consequences, it escapes from the circular quandary of assuming that explanations of the consequences of public policies are necessarily also explanations of their causes.

Our argument that institutionally-defined voting and revenue arrangements mediate the interdependence of state and society, and account for the periodic eruption of fiscal crises, needs to be specified and elaborated, which we will do through a discussion of the current fiscal crisis of American cities.

Votes, Revenues and Local Government

We assert two realms of public expenditure. One is governed by the institutionally-patterned logic of vote generation. This is the politics of the median voter to which public choice theorists direct their attention, and it is largely oriented to policies which improve the conditions of mass consumption. Another is governed by the institutionally-patterned logic of revenue generation. This is the politics of the dominant investor with which the theorists of private government are preoccupied, and it is oriented to policies which improve the profitability of production. At the local level, the first is denoted by labour-intensive services and financed by current expenditures, while the second is denoted by capital intensive services, and financed by long-term debt.

If historically the relationship between property rights and political rights was both complementary and contradictory, this is no less so in the contemporary world of local government. Most students of local governments, and almost all public finance analysts, emphasise the complementary relationships between property rights and political rights. Public expenditures and tax policies which stimulate local economic growth are not only self-financing, but, as the argument goes, they tend to be self-legitimating as well (Peterson, 1979). The bottom line is that fiscal carrots, if you can get local investors to nibble, are also good politics, simply because local private investments that increase local incomes also generate votes. Locally employed workers whose incomes are going up are likely to support such business boosterism. Moreover, local profitable investments generate local income flows which are the ultimate source of revenues for all policies. When cities lack such fiscal capacity, they are unable to finance potentially redistributive public services. If votes have a weaker hold over urban expenditures than do private investors, their interests nevertheless do not appear to be conflictual.

But this happy coincidence of interest is conditional upon a steady rate of growth, a relatively stable economic structure, and the ability of local residents to capture the income flows which private investments set in motion. Under such conditions the logic of securing electoral majorities and adequate revenues is not conflictual. The policies which sustain the one also sustain the other. But such conditions often do not hold, and, when they do not, political rights are likely to conflict with property rights.

Under conditions of economic slowdown, the local population makes intense demands for public employment and public services to compensate for the hardships imposed by the private market. Simultaneously private investors make vociferous demands for public expenditures and tax subsidies to restore the profitability of investment. But economic slowdown also means the fiscal capacity of urban governments is seriously impaired. When the pie is shrinking and both popular and investor demands are rising, the potential for intense political conflict is high.

Conditions of rapid structural change in the local economy may have similar effects. Private investors make demands for new public expenditures to facilitate new types of investment. The local resident labour force may be maladapted to the new employment oportunities and in any case must compete for employment generated by local private investment with workers from other jurisdictions. Those who did not benefit from the new growth, and may even be its victims through residential or employment displacement, also make new demands on the public weal. At the same time, the taxation system may not tap the new economic wealth as effectively as it tapped old economic wealth. When limited fiscal capacity is combined with double jumps in demands for production and citizen-oriented policies, local budgets are strained and investors and voters are likely to be pitted against one another.

Finally, even when the local economy is growing, local residents may be unable to capture many of the income benefits of local private investment. This has a number of causes. Local residents may have little hometown advantage, as is indicated by the absence of any relationship between local economic growth and unemployment (Molotch, 1975). Moreover, when multilocational firms make local investments, the multipliers of such investments — both backward and forward linkages — are located all over the map (Pred, 1977). This means that the benefits of economic growth

— both income and profits — may be exported outside the municipality to suburbs or firms in other towns. In such circumstances, the city government is something like a banana republic which must not only pacify the local natives, but get them to vote for local subsidies for United Fruit.

Under any of these conditions the policy requisites of electoral support and revenue collection are likely to diverge. At such times, the interest of the median voter and median investor may not be the same. This can be shown graphically (Figure 15.1). The entire area in Figure 15.1 is the total level of urban expenditure. The area A consists of those public expenditures necessary to sustain electoral majorities. The area B consists of those public expenditures necessary to generate sufficient profitable investment to sustain adequate public revenue.[6]

Figure 15.1: The Policy Requirements of Vote and Revenue Generation

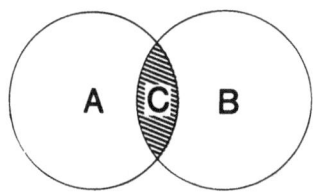

A public expenditures which sustain electoral support

B public expenditures which sustain public revenues

C public expenditures which sustain both electoral support and public revenues

The area C, the intersection of A and B, consists of those public expenditures which simultaneously generate votes and revenues. This area is the philosopher's stone of public finance. The share of the public budget which both generates electoral support and new private investment depends primarily on the extent to which public spending that stimulates local private investment also generates local income and employment and taxable resources. Under these conditions, the potential for conflict is low. But under any of the circumstances where local investments do not generate local income and employment, and may not even generate tax revenues sufficient to offset the public investments they require, the area of coincidence of A and B shrinks, and the potential for conflict between voters and investors is high.

Under these circumstances, we would expect voters to use their distinctive and institutionally-based form of power, the vote, to undercut policies demanded by local investors by making intense demands for government expenditures which do not contribute to local profitability and cut into the revenues that might otherwise be used to support investment. And, under these circumstances, we would expect investors to make intense demands of their own for government expenditures which do not generate local voter support and usurp the revenues that might otherwise be available to finance the programmes that could generate voter allegiance. Similarly, at such times, we would expect voters to struggle to minimise the incidence of taxation on their incomes, while investors fight to reduce taxes on their profits. In other words, the enduring tension between property rights and political rights underlies contemporary urban politics as well, and is reflected in the potential incompatibility between the politics of the vote and the politics of public revenues.

The Structure of Vote and Revenue Generation

Nevertheless, these tensions do not often erupt in political conflict between urban voters and local investors, because the politics of vote- and revenue-generation diverge. They diverge because they are acted out in different parts of the local state, with the result that voter politics and investor politics tend each to be insulated from the other.[7] They diverge in another sense as well, for each is shaped by the very different organisational arrangements that characterise these different parts of the state.

Perhaps part of the reason for the contrasting organisational forms of state agencies charged with voter-oriented policies and agencies charged with investment-oriented policies are the distinctive organisational environments created by voters and investors as constituencies. When governments attempt to generate electoral majorities, they deal with fragmented and relatively disorganised mass publics. When governments attempt to generate revenues, they deal with concentrated, highly rationalised firms. The nature of the external constituencies of public policies oriented to electoral stabilisation as opposed to those oriented to stimulating private investment would suggest such policies would be housed in different structural forms. A multiplicity of volatile constituencies encourages a sprawling, divided structure with which to serve them. Organisations which confront a more certain environment, dominated by a few large, predictable clients, tend to be more centralised.

But there is another and perhaps more basic source of the tendency toward the structural segregation and differentiation of agencies. The state's interest in maintaining the dualistic resources on which it depends leads it to push toward such differentiation. Thus the state's use of some public policies to maintain electoral majorities requires that these policies be accessible to the electorate and highly visible, if they are to be electorally effective. The state's use of public policies to sustain private investment must satisfy not mass publics, but economic elites. Such policies need not be politically adjusted through electoral mechanisms to be effective at revenue generation, nor need they be highly visible. Indeed, the competitive nature of private markets and the profits to be made through advance information or protected access to public agencies means that policies oriented to investors are often only effective if they are executed in almost secretive fashion. More than that, the state's interest in avoiding conflict between property rights and political rights encourages the segregation and insulation of the agencies which implement investor-oriented policies, simply because visibility and easy access would facilitate the assertion of political rights that challenge property rights.

Thus the convergent impact of organisational and constituency dynamics, and the interests of the state in optimising its access to potentially conflictual electoral majorities and revenue generating investors, tends toward the segregation and differentiation of state structures. The evidence of such structural segregation and differentiation is striking. Policies aimed at absorbing mass political participation through the provision of public services and employment are located in agencies which are relatively accessible to voting publics, as schools and social service agencies, for example, tend to be. Policies aimed at sustaining investment and fiscal capacity are located in agencies to which popular access is difficult while access by private investors is unhampered, as is true of highway or sewerage agencies, for example. These latter agencies aptly fit the characterisation of the theorists of private government. They are indeed insulated from elected officials or popular influence. Instead, they are controlled by officials who are not elected, and financed by revenues which do not depend upon electoral approval.

Because such investment-oriented agencies are freed from

electoral oversight and partisan political constraints, they develop strong clientele relationships with those private investors that have the most intense interests in their policies. Their success comes to depend upon their ability to serve investor interests efficiently, a dependency which is intensified by the insulation of the agency from electoral control. Because of the greater predictability of private investment behaviour, the apparent rationality of profitable activities, and the tight bonds which tie the agency to the market, a technical ideology pervades the operation of the agency. The agency clientele for its part understands the complex criteria of agency decision-making, given that such agencies themselves approximate the logic of a business. This technocratic lexicon in turn legitimates the insulation of the agency, and dissuades those popular groups who would try to intervene, for it argues that what is being done is not political.

As patterns of urban development become more potentially conflictual, the number of such insulated agencies multiplies. Thus there has been a steady proliferation of special districts and public authorities to finance infrastructure critical to private investment, such as ports, highways, water, sewerage, and industrial parks. These agencies have sources of financing independent of the local electorate, such as bonds (special districts account for a growing share of all borrowing (Boast, 1977)) and Federal grants. Because municipal borrowing occurs in a highly concentrated market for private capital, the private investment community is able to assure that such investments are oriented to stimulating profitable local economic activity. In addition, since the resultant profitable investments often generate a long-term flow of public revenues — whether in user charges or tax increments — necessary to finance such borrowing, these agencies have the greatest potential to ensure their own revenue sources through current surpluses (Boast, 1977). Such surpluses provide these agencies with better credit ratings in the capital market, minimise their revenue dependence on other jurisdictions, and assure that a large share of the public revenues skimmed from the profits yielded by public expenditures are used to re-finance other public expenditures which will provide still more profits. The public financing of production is thus severed from the financing of public services.

By contrast, agencies which absorb mass political participation are far more visible and politicised. Services such as schools, fire, police, parks, transit, health care and a variety of social services tend to be controlled by municipalities or districts whose officials are elected, and their budgets derive from general revenues which must face electoral approval. Capital spending for such agencies is more likely to be raised through general obligation bonds and thus face public scrutiny at the polls. Operating budgets tend to be financed out of current tax revenues, with the consequence that the financing of these agencies is subject to intense political review. Moreover it is in the nature of such services not to be self-financing, and this undercuts their ability to borrow funds and increases their vulnerability to electoral influence.[8]

The structural segregation and differentiation of the policies oriented to revenue generation and those oriented to vote generation allow governments to moderate the tension between property rights and political rights, to jocky the policies and politics necessary to sustain public revenue and electoral majorities.[9] But under some conditions such arrangements also tend to produce fiscal strain.

Structural Segregation and Fiscal Strains

When the local economy declines or changes precipitously in ways that increase the potential for conflict, the pattern of structural segregation of electoral and investment policies which moderates political conflict may have disastrous fiscal consequences.

Structural segregation means that those agencies which have some authority over the generation of local income and employment are separate from those agencies which must absorb the political participation of those who are unemployed or whose real income falls as a result of economic change. It also means that these investor-oriented agencies are insulated from popular political influence. Structural arrangements thus separate the public agencies with some leverage over the causes of poverty from the public agencies which must somehow absorb the consequences of impoverishment, and also insulate these agencies from the politics of the impoverished. When unemployment becomes severe, for example, the unemployed direct their protests at welfare agencies, and not at economic development agencies, and they do so because the welfare agencies are exposed and accessible, while the economic development agencies are not. But since these politically accessible parts of the state lack authority to deal with the causes of impoverishment, potential demands for social change are converted by this interaction into demands for public services and greater participation (Friedland, Piven and Alford, 1977). As a consequence, an aroused electoral constituency generates an expansion of the paraphernalia, patronage and services of agencies that are helpless to intervene in economic development patterns.

Conversely, the insulation of public agencies oriented to private investment from electoral pressures or partisan scrutiny can also have negative fiscal consequences. Bureaucratic insulation makes them susceptible to cannibalisation by investor groups who can often secure public largesse that contributes to the profitability of investments that would have occurred anyway, or even use public benefits to underwrite a process of local disinvestment. In a study of muncipal industrial aid bonds, for example, it was found that while corporations used their locational freedom to bargain for public aid, the majority of projects and seven-tenths of all of the investment would have occurred in the same location without public aid (Apilado, 1971). Similarly, analyses of the impact of central city urban renewal suggest it had no net impact on the aggregate level of industrial or high-rise residential investment (Friedland, 1982). Further, the administrative nature of public investment subsidy programmes, particularly routine allocative rules, depoliticises these programmes and reduces the necessity of investor political participation to secure a continuous flow of public benefits. When local market conditions or land-use patterns change, however, such institutionalised routines are adapted to these changes only with great difficulty. As a result, public investments are not well callibrated to the local requirements of economic growth (see Feshbach, 1979; Mollenkopf, 1979). Finally, because such agencies are insulated from popular opposition, consideration of their policy impact on the local population is not central. As a result, these public agencies have no incentive to consider the external social costs of the local private investment they are so desperately trying to woo.

This segregation of electoral and investment policies thus reinforces the impotence of the electorate over local production, and ensures the indifference of private investors to their impact on local populations. In this way, conflict is minimised. But it is minimised by structural arrangements which provide each segment of the state with the incentives and opportunities for budgetary expansion. The inability of the state to generate both electoral and fiscal support thus comes to be expressed in fiscal strains, a budgetary alternative to destabilising political conflict. For the city, like a banana republic, enormous deficits are sometimes an alternative to civil strife.

Fiscal crisis is thus a symptom of a deep underlying disjuncture in the institutionally-specified relationships between the state, democracy and capitalism. It signals that arrangements developed to cope with the electoral and revenue requirements of governance, while moderating the recurrent tension between them, are strained, and in fundamental ways. Historically such strains have often led to efforts to alter or even transform the specific institutional arrangements which shape the expression of the recurrent tension between political rights and property rights. And there is evidence that, once again, fiscal crisis is prompting comparable efforts. In some cases, there are moves to change the relationship between the state and democracy so as to attenuate the state's need for voting majorities, and thereby weaken the political power of mass publics. In other cases, there are efforts to alter the relationship between the state and capitalism so as to attenuate the state's need for privately generated revenues, and thus the power of private investors. The former solution undercuts democratic institutions, as occurred in New York City where the business-initiated and controlled Municipal Assistance Corporation and Emergency Financial Control Board were empowered in the mid-1970s to reorganise the municipal budget. The city's elected officials, and by implication its voters, were thereby rendered politically less effective. The latter solution, to intrude upon capitalist institutions, occurred in Sweden in the postwar period. In his comparison of Denmark and Sweden, Esping-Anderson has shown how, in contrast to Denmark, the governing Swedish Social democratic party politicised the private investment process through selective investment of public pensions in particular industries and regions (1979). The party thereby gained greater control over the economic conditions which generated electoral demands for public consumption supports, as well as greater capacity to finance these programmes. The Swedish Social Democratic party was thus able to avoid the extreme erosion of popular support suffered by their Danish counterpart.

Conclusions

Many theorists have argued that the ability of a locality, or indeed a nation, to foster economic growth sets the limits within which partisan politics must operate. It follows that, at a time of economic slowdown and restructuration, we must assure that government provides private investors with what they require to profitably compete at home and abroad. Only then, the argument goes, can politics make a difference. But the ability of private investment to dictate the terms of exchange of public resources is not external to politics. That ability is itself political, rooted in the institutionally-framed dependencies of the state created by an historical politics. And the specific character of those institutional arrangements in American cities have rendered resident voters relatively helpless in affecting the allocation of public resources necessary to private investment. It is not that economic growth determines the margin of operation for politics. Rather it is that the state's role in economic growth is itself the consequence of politics; but it is a politics which is obscured because it is deeply embedded in the very structure of the state.

Notes

1. Peterson (1979) makes this subordination of politics explicit in the course of elaborating an essentially public choice perspective into what he calls a 'unitary' model of local government taxation and expenditure policies. In brief, the unitary model characterises local governments as firms in a competitive economy. Lacking control over its economic environment, local government of necessity pursues policies which will maximise local prosperity in the context of these factors. Peterson intends this model to supplant older and more familiar models of local government policy-making which posit bargaining and conflict among local interests as the determinants of policy. The Peterson model not only supplants bargaining and conflict models, but supplants political models entirely, for in his argument the politics and policies of local communities are determined by external economic variables, and therefore can be derived from these variables. Moreover, in the translation of economic imperatives into public policy, the local community is indeed characterised as 'unitary', for the policies shaped by calculations of economic prosperity presumably rebound to the benefit of all urban groups. This presumption is clearly contradicted both by the intense conflicts that actually accompany a good many urban political decisions, and by our actual knowledge of the very unequal distribution of the costs and benefits attached to such policies as urban renewal, for example. Finally, the relatively smooth translation of calculations of economic advantage into politics and policy posited by Peterson leaves us unable to explain such developments as municipal fiscal crises except as the effect of overall economic contraction. In fact, however, municipal fiscal strains have occurred under

conditions of economic growth as well as contraction.

2. The relatively greater locational discretion of investors shows up clearly in their greater willingness to migrate to new economic opportunities. There is a hierarchy of spatial elasticities: portfolio investments move longest and quickest in response to locational differences in return; plant investment moves shorter distances and more slowly; and labour moves the shortest distance and more sluggishly (Holland, 1976, Chapter 4). In both the southern United States and Italy, two areas of relative poverty, the level of postwar migration has not exceeded the natural rate of population increases. In the United States, five-sixths of all migration between 1947 and 1967 was intra-state (Holland, 1976, p. 104).

3. This literature very likely overstated the incrementalist finding due to the probable correlation of residual variation across time, which is attributed to the incrementalist relation (Hibbs, 1974).

4. Other analysts, notably Lojkine, have argued that not only must the state intervene increasingly in the consumption process, but that the consumption process itself has become increasingly collective (Lojkine, 1976; 1977).

5. Given the need for immediate access to revenues, wartime saw the introduction of more visible and politically problematic direct taxes which provided quicker returns than did indirect taxes (Braun, 1975, p.312). Thus the first income tax was introduced during the Napoleonic War as an emergency financial measure (Braun, 1975, p.311). In the United States, decline of Federal reliance on indirect, largely tariff-based, tax revenues in favour of more direct forms of income taxation between 1900 and 1920 can similarly be explained by the need for more dependable and more expansive forms of revenue during World War I (Brownlee, 1977). Later, the revenue requirements of World War II saw an extension of the Federal income tax, probably further decreasing its aggregate progressivity, and an introduction of withholding procedures which diminished the political visibility of this form of taxation.

Thus the state's extraordinary need for revenues during war has frequently provided the stimulus for fiscal reforms. However the state's need for mass popular legitimation has also provided the leverage for progressive political movements to shape those fiscal reforms in redistributive directions. Brownlee makes this point about the fiscal reforms of the World War I period:

> The war crisis, with its large demands for revenue and the fiscal leverage it gave to radical critics of the war effort, had produced an income tax system that imposed strikingly high progressive-rates and sought, through a net of excess-profits taxation, to redistribute income away from large corporations. The revenue act of October 1917 increased income tax rates, which had previously extended from 1 to 13 per cent, to a graduate scale reaching from 4 to 63 per cent on individual incomes and from 20 to 60 per cent on business profits that exceeded 1911-1913 levels (Brownlee, 1977, p.14).

Once the war was over, the progressive features of the income tax were dismantled, although the tax remained the dominant Federal revenue instrument. And in general, such 'emergency' innovations are frequently institutionalised as means of state resource extraction. Moreover, although new mechanisms of finance may be reorganised, and expenditure structures changed, public taxation levels remain well above their prewar level (Peacock and Wiseman, 1961).

6. This is theoretically more problematic than is usually assumed because the conversion of private investment into public revenues involves a political conflict over level and incidence of taxation. This analysis assumes that the most important constraint on public revenues is the level of private capital formation.

7. See Friedland, Piven and Alford (1977) for an earlier formulation of this part of our argument.

8. This structural difference between the policies of investment and consumption is also apparent at the Federal level. The Federal tax structure is filled with invisible 'implicit subsidies' which are overwhelmingly directed to property owners and unearned income. Subsidies to consumers and to their earned incomes tend to be explicit and therefore more politically visible (Pechman and Okner, 1972).

9. The impact we impute to these structural differences is supported by the fact that redistributive consumption policies tend to be susceptible to electoral influence, while infrastructural spending only responds to patterns of economic growth (Dawson and Robinson, 1963).

References

Aiken, M. and G. Martinotti (1979) 'Left politics, the urban system and public policy: an analysis of municipal expenditures among the 325 largest cities in Italy' , unpublished manuscript

Alford, R. (1973) 'Social Needs, Political Demands and Administrative Responses', unpublished paper, University of California, Santa Cruz

Alford, R. (1975) *Health Care Politics,* University of Chicago Press, Chicago

Alford, R. and R. Friedland (1975) 'Political Participation and Public Policy', *Annual Review of Sociology,* **1**, 429-497

Apilado, V. (1971) 'Corporate-Government Interplay: The Era of Industrial Aid Finance', *Urban Affairs Quarterly,* **7**, 219-241

Bish, R.L. (1979) 'Public Choice Theory for Comparative Research on Urban Service Delivery', *Comparative Urban Research,* **1**, 18-26

Boast, T. (1977) 'Federal Programs, Urban Resources and the American Capital Market', paper presented at the Conference on Urban Choice and State Power, Center for International Studies, Cornell University

Borcherding, T.E. and R.T. Deacon (1972) 'The Demand for the Services of Non-Federal Governments', *American Economic Review,* **62**, 891-901

Braun, R. (1975) 'Taxation, Sociopolitical Structure, and State Building: Great Britain and Brandenburg-Prussia', in C. Tilly(ed.) *The Formation of National States in Western Europe,* Princeton University Press, Princeton, N.J., 243-327

Brownlee, W.E. (1977) 'The American Tax System: An Historical Overview', paper delivered at the Conference on Taxes and Community Services: The Ethical Choices, November 18, 1977, The Center for the Study of Democratic Institutions

Castells, M. (1977) *The Urban Question,* Edward Arnold, London

Cowart, A.T. (1977) 'Anti-Poverty Expenditures in the American States: A Comparative Analysis', *Midwest Journal of Political Science,* **13**, 219-236

Davis, A., M.A.H. Dempster, and A. Wildavsky (1966) 'A Theory of the Budgetary Process', *American Political Science Review,* **60**, 529-547

Dawson, R. and J.A. Robinson (1977)'Interparty Competition, Economic Variables and Welfare Policies in the American States', *Journal of Politics,* **25**, 265-239

Deacon, R.T. (1978) 'A Demand Model for the Local Public Sector', *Review of Economics and Statistics,* **50**, 184-192

Deacon, R.T., and P. Shapiro (1975) 'Private Preference for Collective Goods Revealed Through Voting on Referenda', *American Economic Review,* **65**

Domhoff, W. (1970) *Who Rules America?* Random House, New York

Dye, T.R. (1972) *Understanding Public Policy,* Prentice Hall, Englewood Cliffs, N.J.

Esping-Anderson, G. (1979) 'Comparative Social Policy and Political Conflict in

Advanced Welfare States: Denmark and Sweden', *International Journal of Health Services*, **9**, 269-293

Feshbach, D. (1979) 'What's Inside the Black Box: A Case Study of Allocative Politics in the Hill-Burton Program', *International Journal of Health Services*, **9**, 313-339

Finer, S.E. (1975) 'State- and Nation-Building in Europe: The Role of the Military', in C. Tilly (ed.) *The Formation of National States in Western Europe*, Princeton University Press, Princeton, N.J.

Frey, W.H. (1979) 'Central City White Flight: Racial and Nonracial Causes', *American Sociological Review*, **44**, 425-448

Fried, R. (1975) 'Comparative Urban Performance', in F.I. Greenstein and N.W. Polsby (eds.) *Handbook of Political Science*, **6**, Addison-Wesley, Reading, Mass.

Friedland, R. (1982) *Power and Crisis in the City*, Macmillan, London

Friedland, R., F.F. Piven and R.R. Alford (1977) 'Political Conflict, Urban Structure and the Fiscal Crisis', in D. Ashford (ed.), *Comparing Public Policies*, Sage, Beverly Hills, 197-225

Hibbs, D. Jr. (1974) 'Problems of Statistical Estimation and Causal Inference in Time-Series Regression Models', in H.L. Costner (ed.) *Sociological Methodology 1973-74*, Jossey- Bass, San Francisco, 252-308

Holland, S. (1976) *Capital Versus the Regions*, St. Martin's Press, New York

Lindblom, C.E. (1961) 'Decision-Making in Taxation and Expenditure', *Public Finances, Needs, Sources and Utilization*, National Bureau of Economic Research, Princton, N.J., 295-336

Lineberry, R.L. (1979)'Equality, Public Policy and Public Services: The Underclass Hypothesis and the Limits to Equality', *Policy and Politics*

Lojkine, J. (1976) 'Contribution to a Marxist Theory of Capitalist Urbanisation', in C. Pickvance, (ed.), *Urban Sociology*, Tavistock Publications, London

Lojkine, J. (1977) *Le marxisme, l'état et la question urbaine*, Presses Universitares de France, Paris

McConnell, G. (1966) *Private Power and American Democracy*, Knopf, New York

Marmor, T.R., D.A. Wittman and T.C. Heagy 'The Politics of Medical Inflation', *The Journal of Health Politics, Policy and Law*, **I**, 69-84

Martin, D.T. (1979) *The Institutional Framework of Community Formation: The Law and Economics of Municipal Incorporation in California*, Ph.D dissertation, Department of Economics, Virginia Polytechnic Institute and State University, cited in Bish, 1979

Meltsner, A.J. (1971) *The Politics of City Revenue*, University of California Press, Berkeley

Mollenkopf, J. (1979) 'Untangling the Logics of Urban Service Bureaucracies: The Strange Case of the San Francisco Municipal Railway', *International Journal of Health Services*, **9**, 255-268

Molotch, H. (1975) 'The City as a Growth Machine: Toward a Political Economy of Place', *American Journal of Sociology*, **82**, 309-331

O'Connor, J. (1973) *Fiscal Crisis of the State*, St. Martin's Press, New York

Offe, C. (1972) 'Political Authority and Class Structures — An Analysis of Late Capitalist Societies', *International Journal of Sociology*, **3**, 73-108

Ostrom, V. and F.P. Bish, (eds.), (1977) *Comparing Urban Service Delivery Systems*, Sage, Beverley Hills

Peacock, A. and J. Wiseman (1961) *The Growth of Public Expenditures in the United Kingdom*, National Bureau of Economic Research, Princton, N.J.

Pechman, J.S. and B.A. Okner (1972) 'Individual Income Tax Erosion by Income Classes', in U.S. Congress, Joint Economic Committee, *The Economics of Federal Subsidy Programs*, Part I — General Study Papers, GPO, 92nd Congress, 2nd Session, Washington, 13-40

Peterson, G. (1975) 'Vote Demand for Public School Expenditures', in J. E. Jackson, (ed.), *Public Needs and Private Behavior in Metropolitan Areas*, Cambridge, 99-115

Piven, F.F. (1977) 'The Urban Crisis: Who Got What, and Why?' in R. Alcaly and D. Mermelstein, (eds.) *The Fiscal Crisis of American Cities*, Vintage, New York, 132-144

Pred, A. (1977) *City-Systems in Advanced Economies*, John Wiley and Sons, New York

Rokkan, S. (1966) 'Norway: Numerical Democracy and Corporate Pluralism', in R. Dahl, (ed.), *Political Oppositions in Western Democracies*, Yale University Press, New Haven, 70-115

Rudé, G. (1980) *Ideology and Popular Protest*, Lawrence and Wishart, London

Sbragia, A. (1979) 'Borrowing to Build: Private Money and Public Welfare', *International Journal of Health Services*, **9**, 207-226

Schumpeter, J. (1954) 'The Crisis of the Tax State', in W.F. Stolper and R.A. Musgrave, *International Economic Papers*, **4**, MacMillan, New York, 5-38

Sharkansky, I. (1979) *The Routines of Politics*, Van Nostrand Reinhold, New York

Sharpe, L.J. (1973) 'American Democracy Reconsidered', *British Journal of Political Science* **3**, 13-20

Stephens, J. (1980) *The Transition from Capitalism to Socialism*, London

Thompson, W. (1976) 'The City as a Distorted Price System', in H.M. Hochman, (ed.), *The Urban Economy*, W.W. Norton, New York, 57-73

Tigar, M. and M.R. Levy (1977) *Law and the Rise of Capitalism*, Monthly Review Press, New York

Wildavsky, A. (1964) *The Politics of the Budgetary Process*, Little, Brown, Boston

For Product Safety Concerns and Information please contact our EU
representative GPSR@taylorandfrancis.com
Taylor & Francis Verlag GmbH, Kaufingerstraße 24, 80331 München, Germany

www.ingramcontent.com/pod-product-compliance
Lightning Source LLC
Chambersburg PA
CBHW050558270326
41926CB00012B/2102